THE LUCKY ROAD

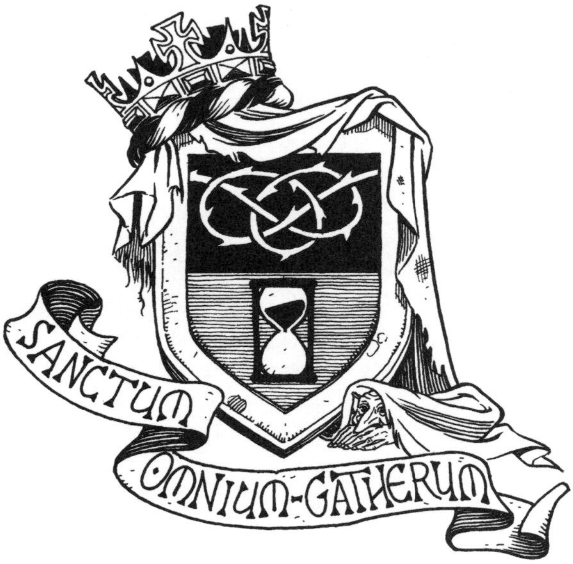
SANCTUM
OMNIUM-GATHERUM

For
Michael Kaluta

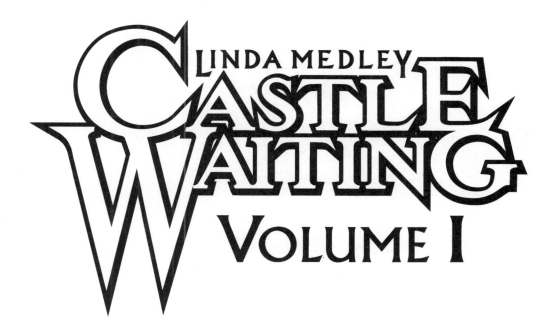

LINDA MEDLEY
CASTLE WAITING
VOLUME I

THE LUCKY ROAD

LETTERING BY
TODD KLEIN

COVER COLOR BY
DAVE STEWART

CARTOON BOOKS
COLUMBUS, OHIO

For information write:
Cartoon Books
P.O. Box 16973
Columbus, OH 43216
www.boneville.com

ISBN: 1-888963-07-7

10 9 8 7 6 5 4 3 2 1

Printed in Canada

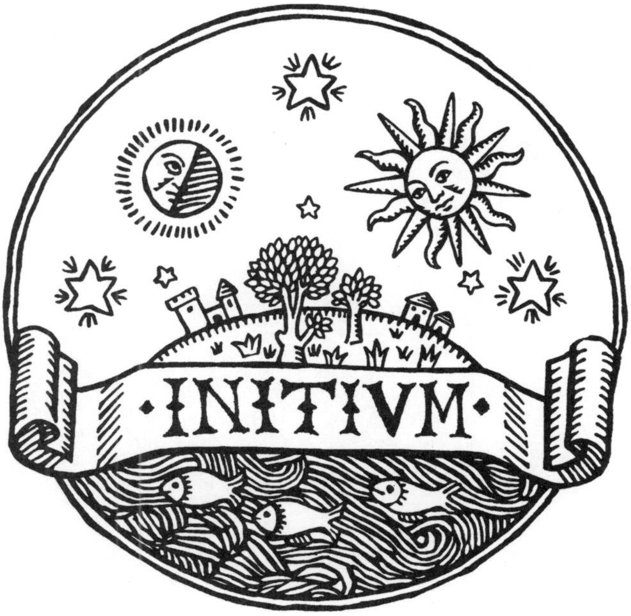
·INITIVM·

The rule of the road is a paradox quite,
Though custom has prov'd it so long;
If you go to the left, you go right,
If you go to the right, you go wrong.

–Mother Goose

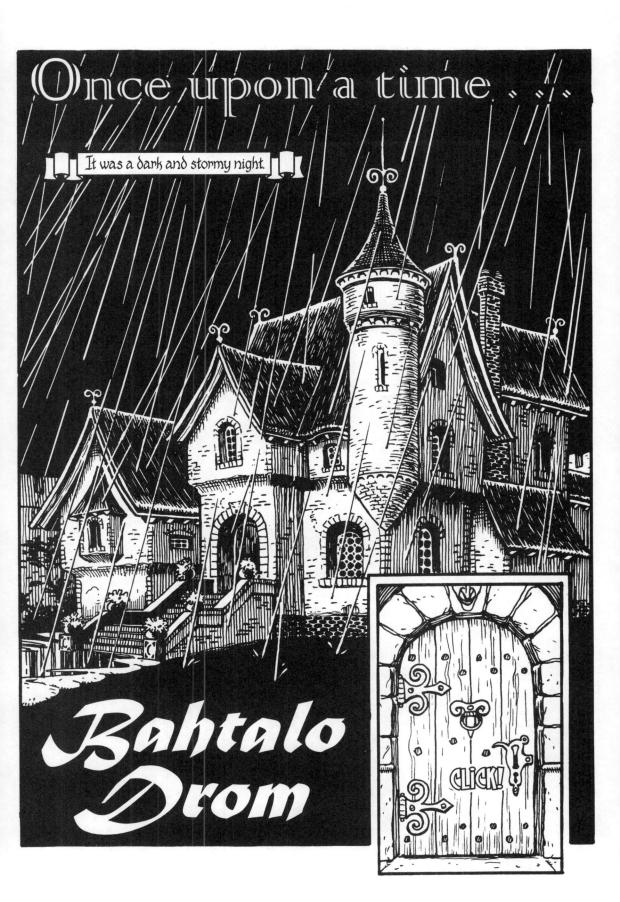

Once upon a time . . .

It was a dark and stormy night.

Bahtalo Drom

CLICK!

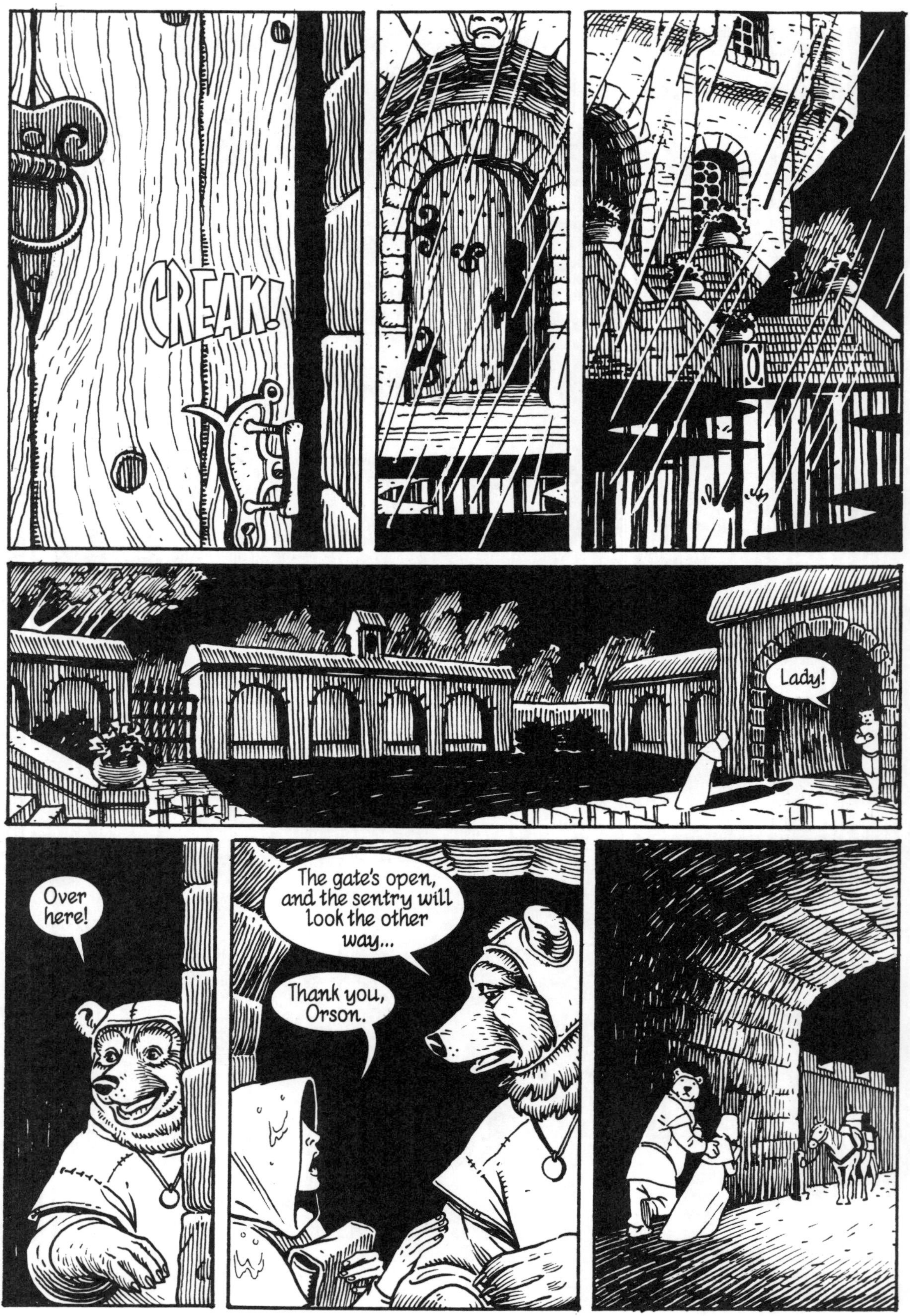
CREAK!
Lady!
Over here!
The gate's open, and the sentry will look the other way...
Thank you, Orson.

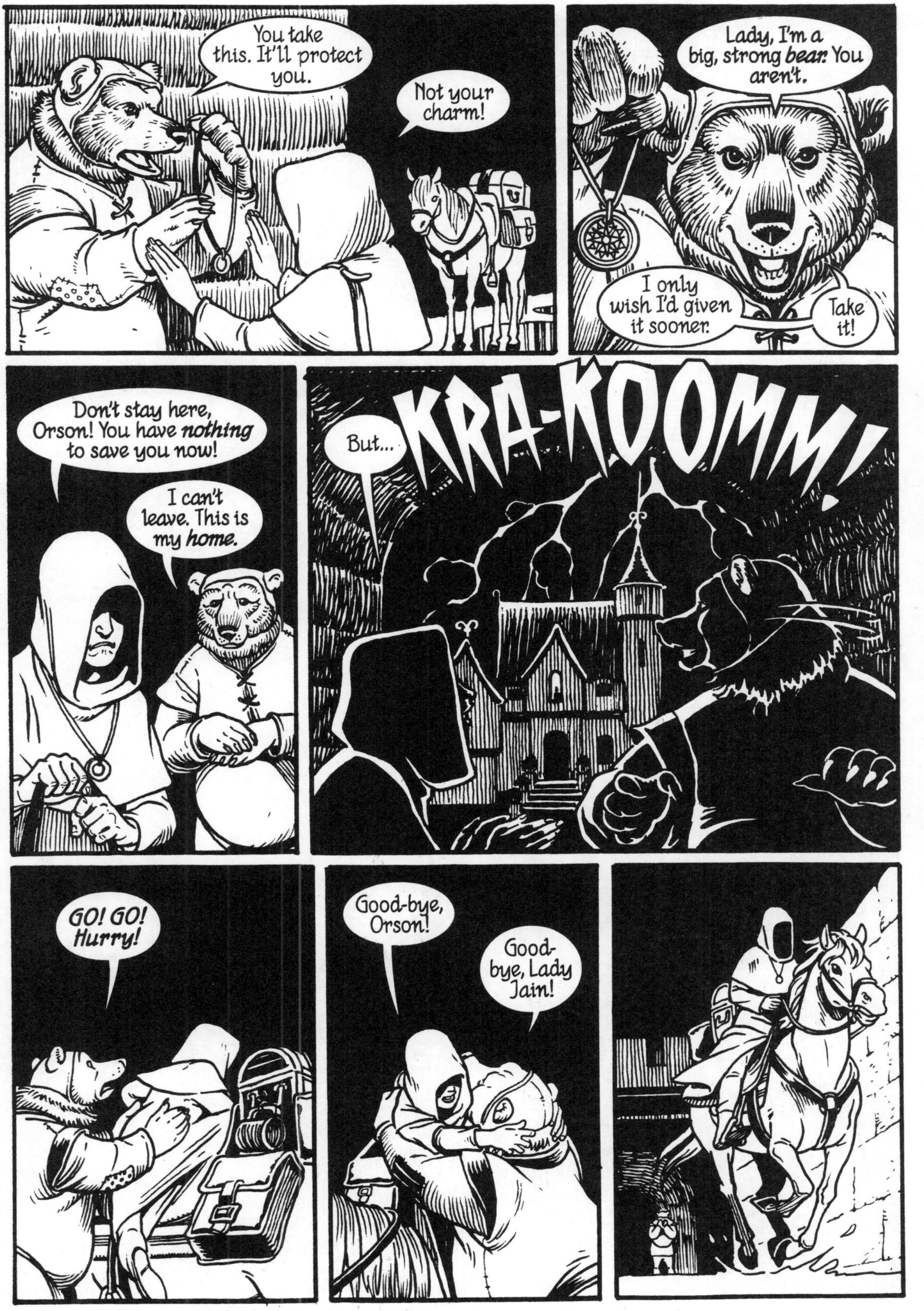
You take this. It'll protect you.
Not your charm!
Lady, I'm a big, strong bear. You aren't.
I only wish I'd given it sooner.
Take it!
Don't stay here, Orson! You have nothing to save you now!
I can't leave. This is my home.
But...
KRA-KOOMM!
GO! GO! Hurry!
Good-bye, Orson!
Good-bye, Lady Jain!

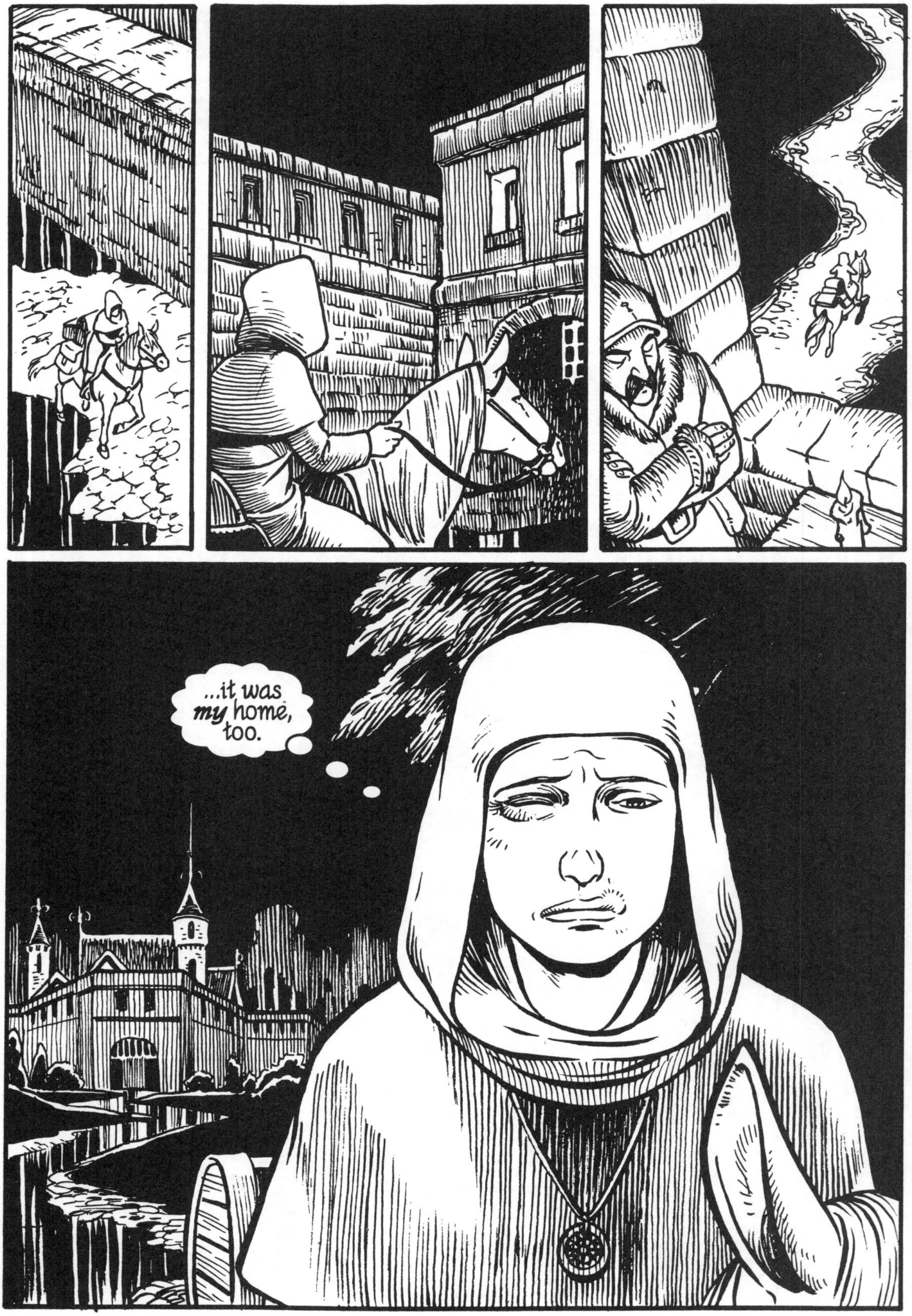
...it was
my home,
too.

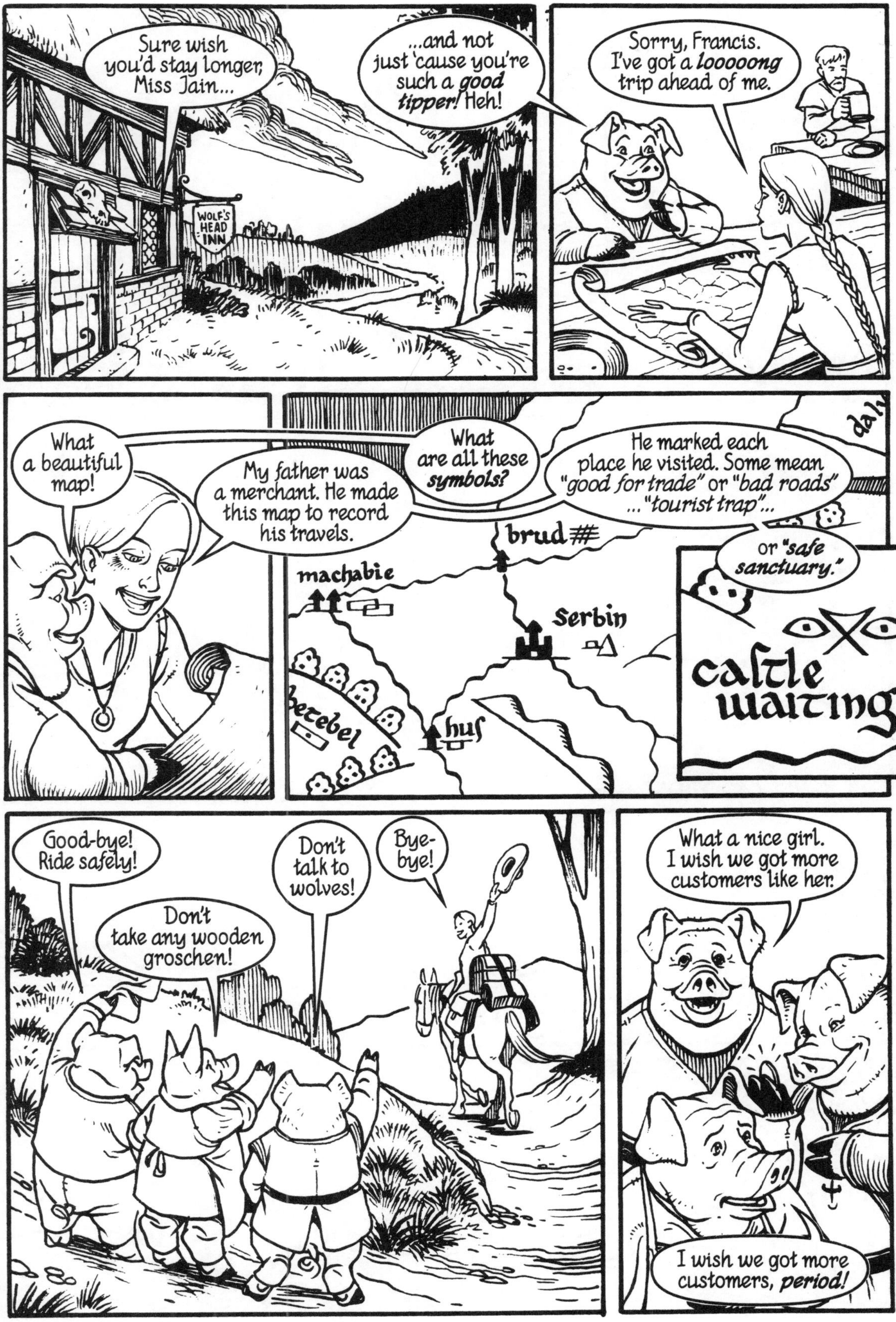

Sure wish you'd stay longer, Miss Jain...
WOLF'S HEAD INN
...and not just 'cause you're such a **good tipper!** Heh!
Sorry, Francis. I've got a **looooong** trip ahead of me.
What a beautiful map!
My father was a merchant. He made this map to record his travels.
What are all these **symbols?**
He marked each place he visited. Some mean *"good for trade"* or *"bad roads"* ...*"tourist trap"*...
or ***"safe sanctuary."***
machabie
brud
Serbin
hus
Castle Waiting
Good-bye! Ride safely!
Don't take any wooden groschen!
Don't talk to wolves!
Bye-bye!
What a nice girl. I wish we got more customers like her.
I wish we got more customers, ***period!***

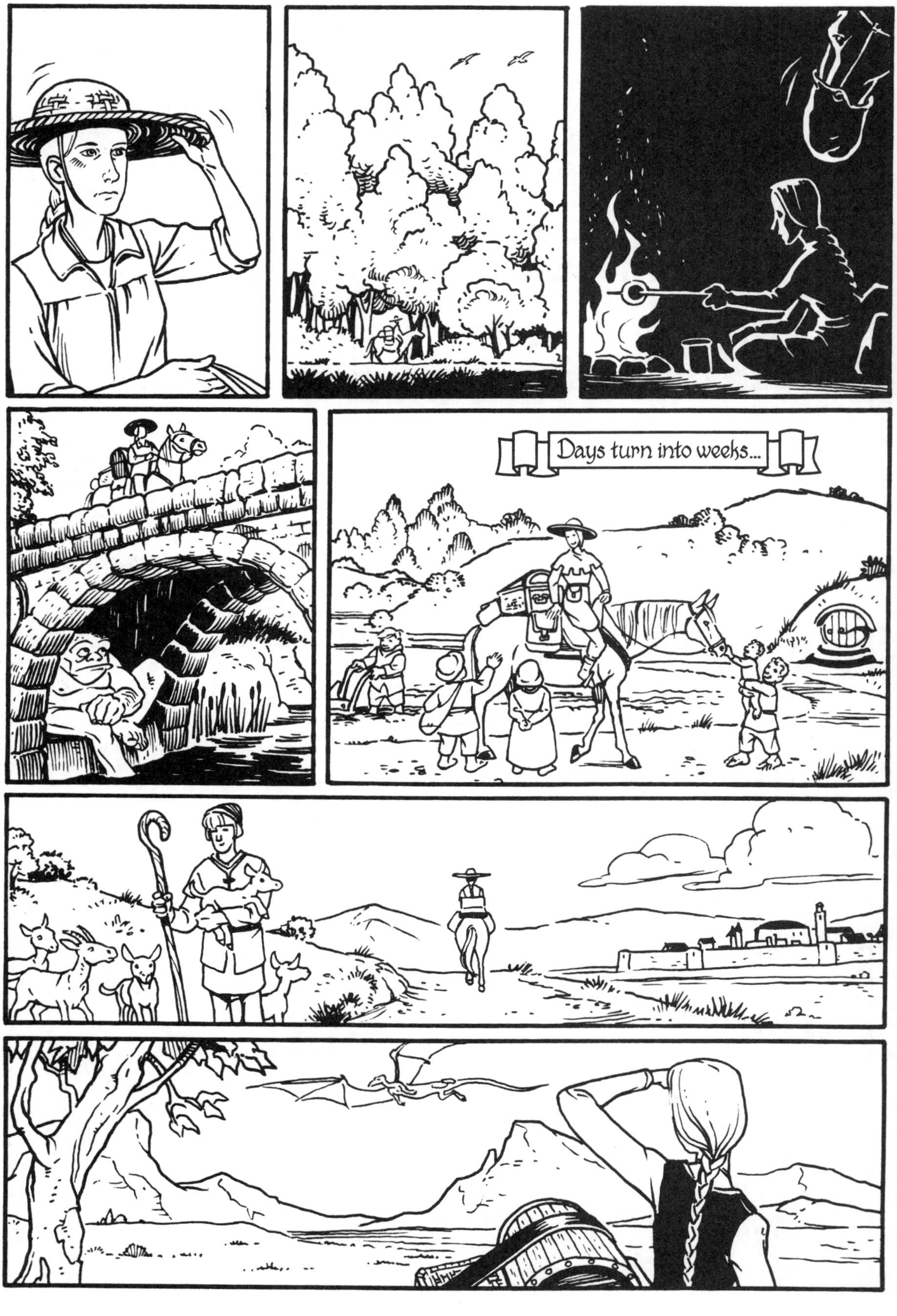
Days turn into weeks...

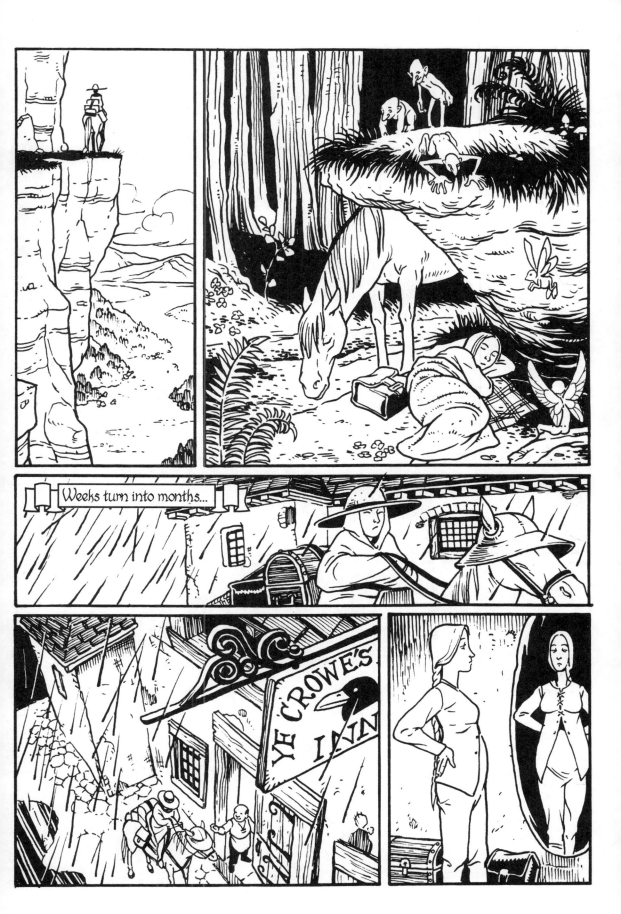

Weeks turn into months...

YE CROWE'S INN

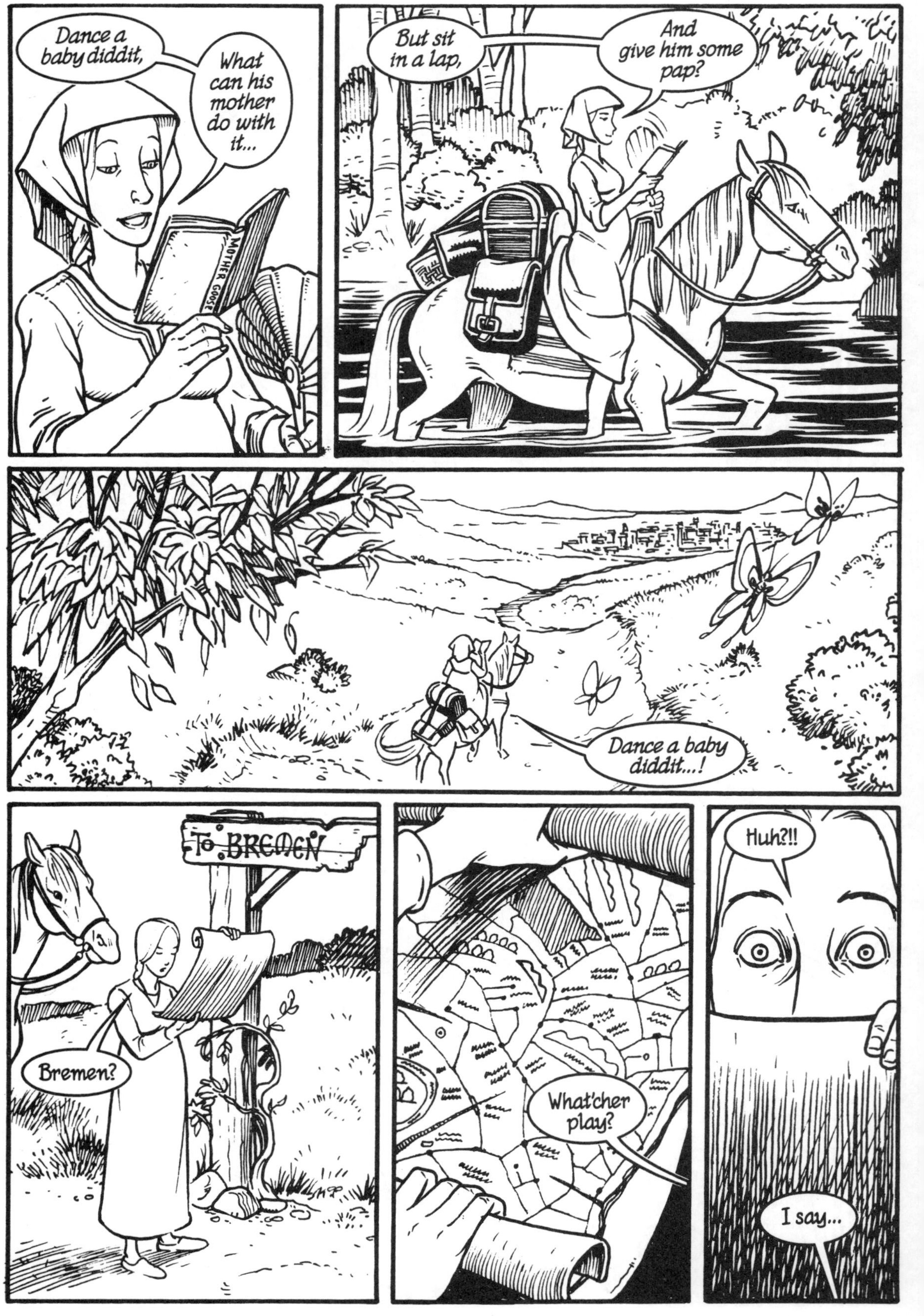

Dance a baby diddit,
What can his mother do with it...
MOTHER GOOSE
But sit in a lap,
And give him some pap?
Dance a baby diddit...!
TO BREMEN
Bremen?
What'cher play?
Huh?!!
I say...

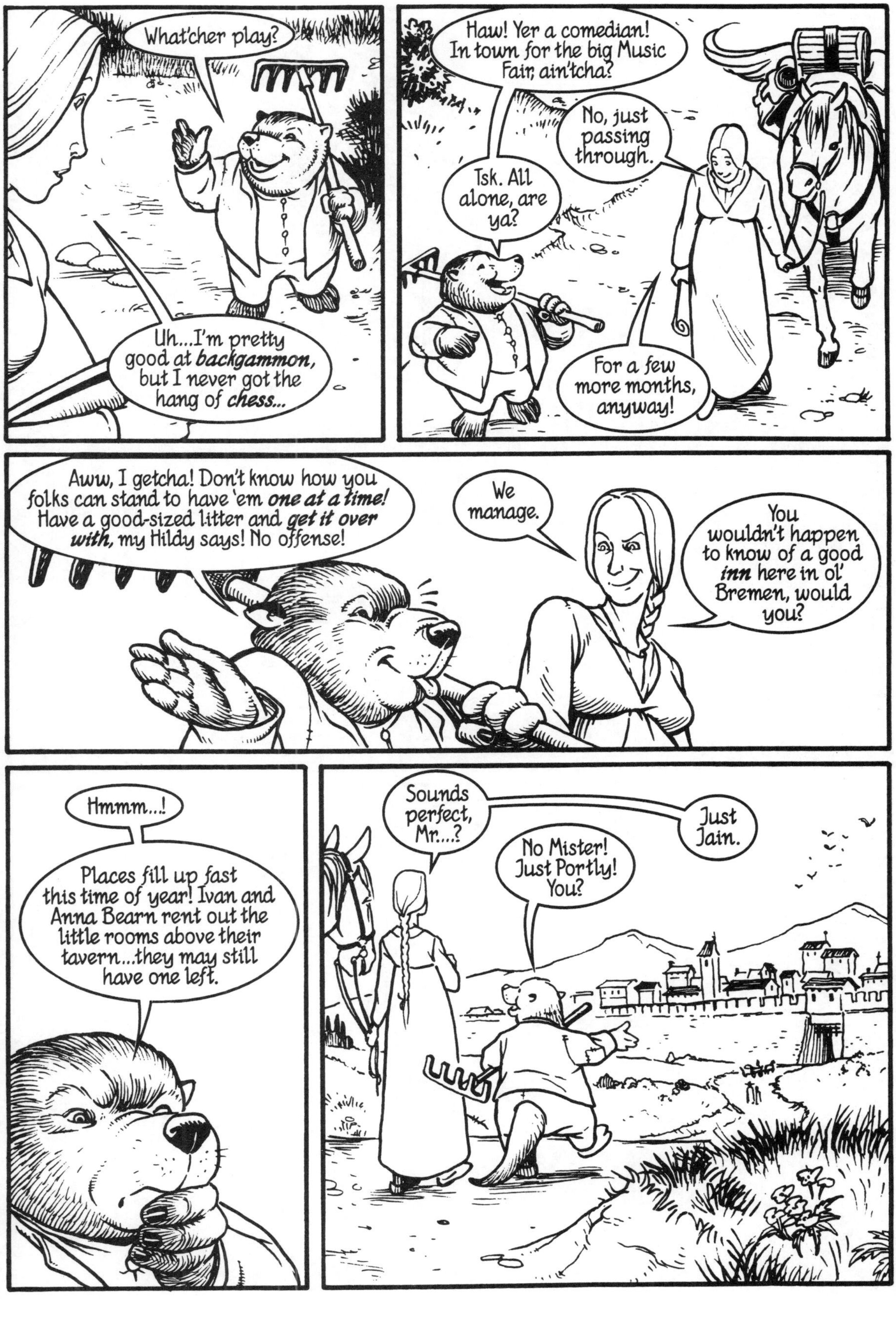
What'cher play?
Uh...I'm pretty good at ***backgammon,*** but I never got the hang of ***chess...***
Haw! Yer a comedian! In town for the big Music Fair, ain'tcha?
No, just passing through.
Tsk. All alone, are ya?
For a few more months, anyway!
Aww, I getcha! Don't know how you folks can stand to have 'em ***one at a time!*** Have a good-sized litter and ***get it over with,*** my Hildy says! No offense!
We manage.
You wouldn't happen to know of a good ***inn*** here in ol' Bremen, would you?
Hmmm...!
Places fill up fast this time of year! Ivan and Anna Bearn rent out the little rooms above their tavern...they may still have one left.
Sounds perfect, Mr....?
No Mister! Just Portly! You?
Just Jain.

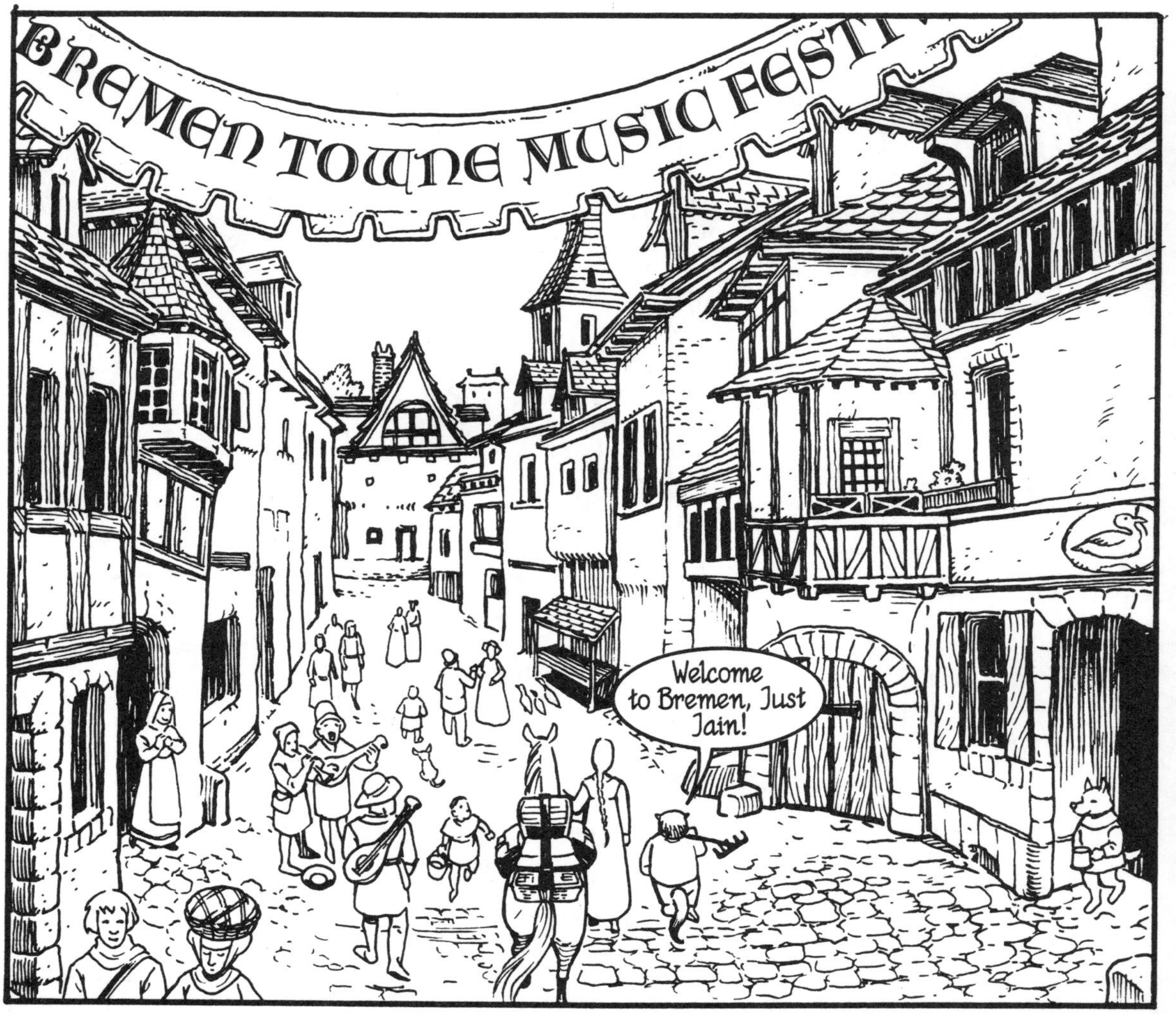
BREMEN TOWNE MUSIC FESTI
Welcome to Bremen, Just Jain!

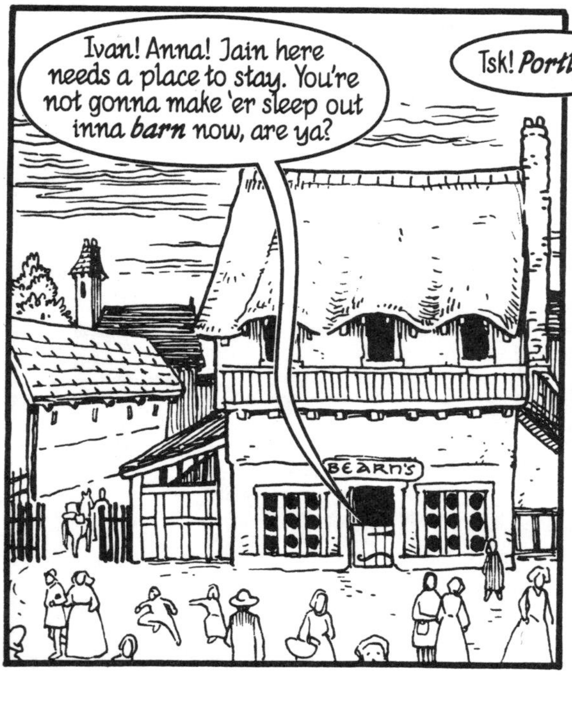
Ivan! Anna! Jain here needs a place to stay. You're not gonna make 'er sleep out inna *barn* now, are ya?
BEARN'S

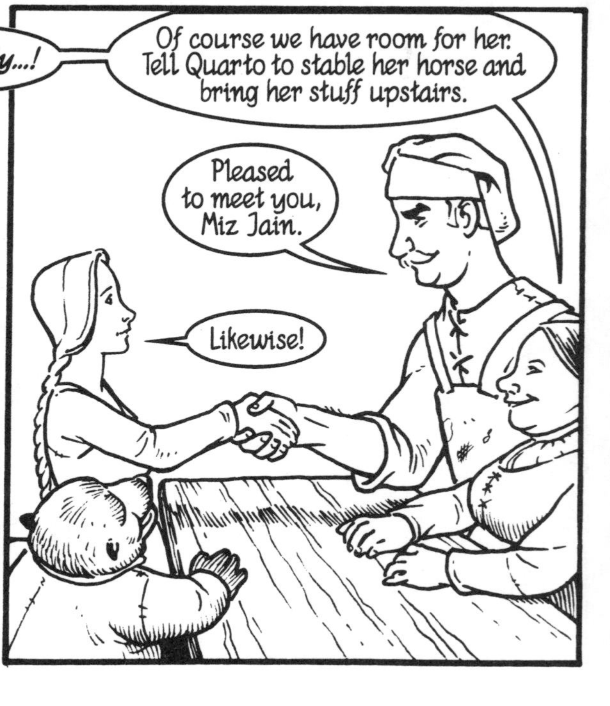
Tsk! ***Portly...!***
Of course we have room for her. Tell Quarto to stable her horse and bring her stuff upstairs.
Pleased to meet you, Miz Jain.
Likewise!

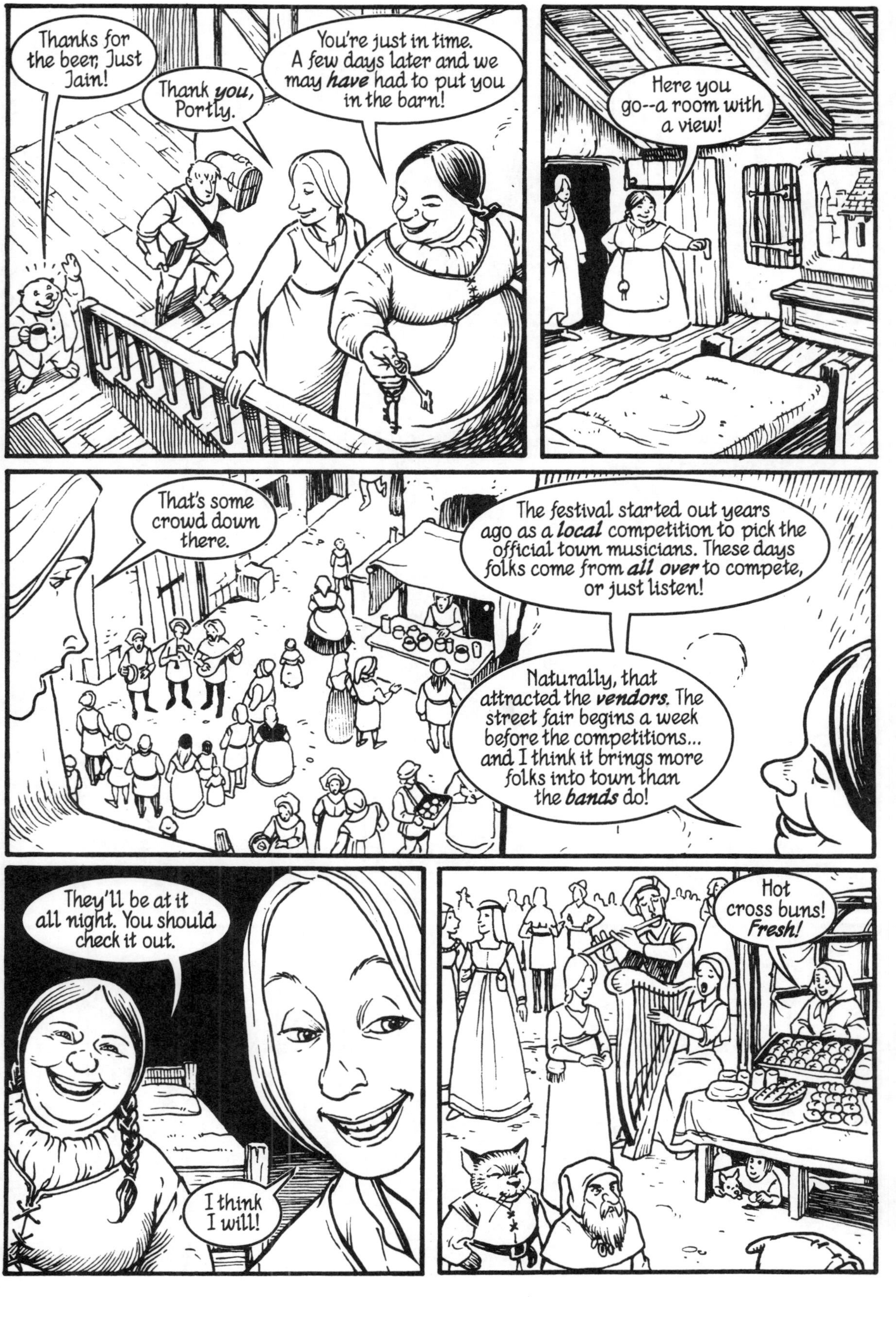
Thanks for the beer, Just Jain!
Thank *you*, Portly.
You're just in time. A few days later and we may *have* had to put you in the barn!
Here you go--a room with a view!
That's some crowd down there.
The festival started out years ago as a *local* competition to pick the official town musicians. These days folks come from *all over* to compete, or just listen!
Naturally, that attracted the *vendors*. The street fair begins a week before the competitions... and I think it brings more folks into town than the *bands* do!
They'll be at it all night. You should check it out.
I think I will!
Hot cross buns! *Fresh!*

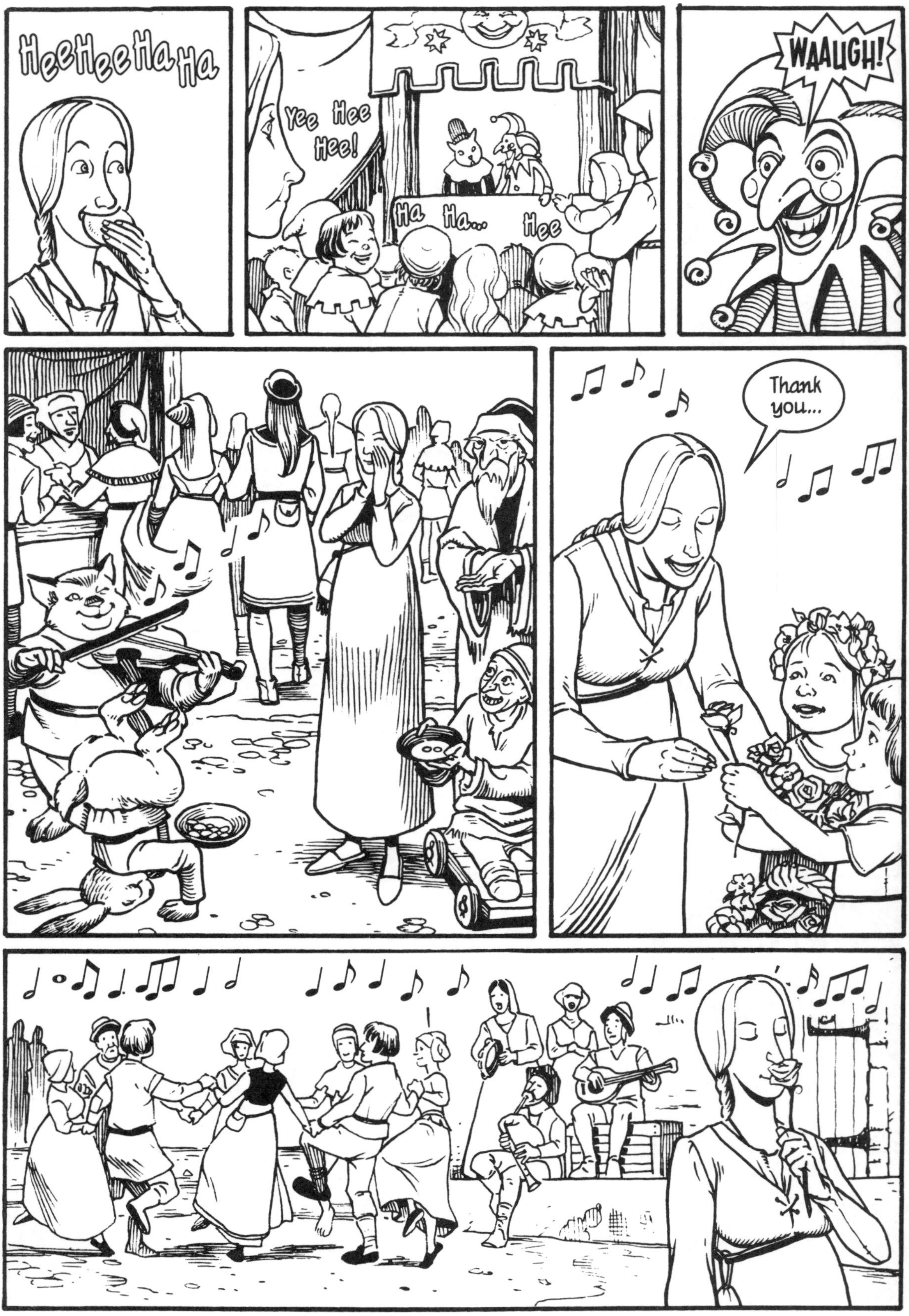
HeeHeeHaHa Ha
Yee Hee Hee!
Ha Ha... Hee
WAAUGH!
Thank you...

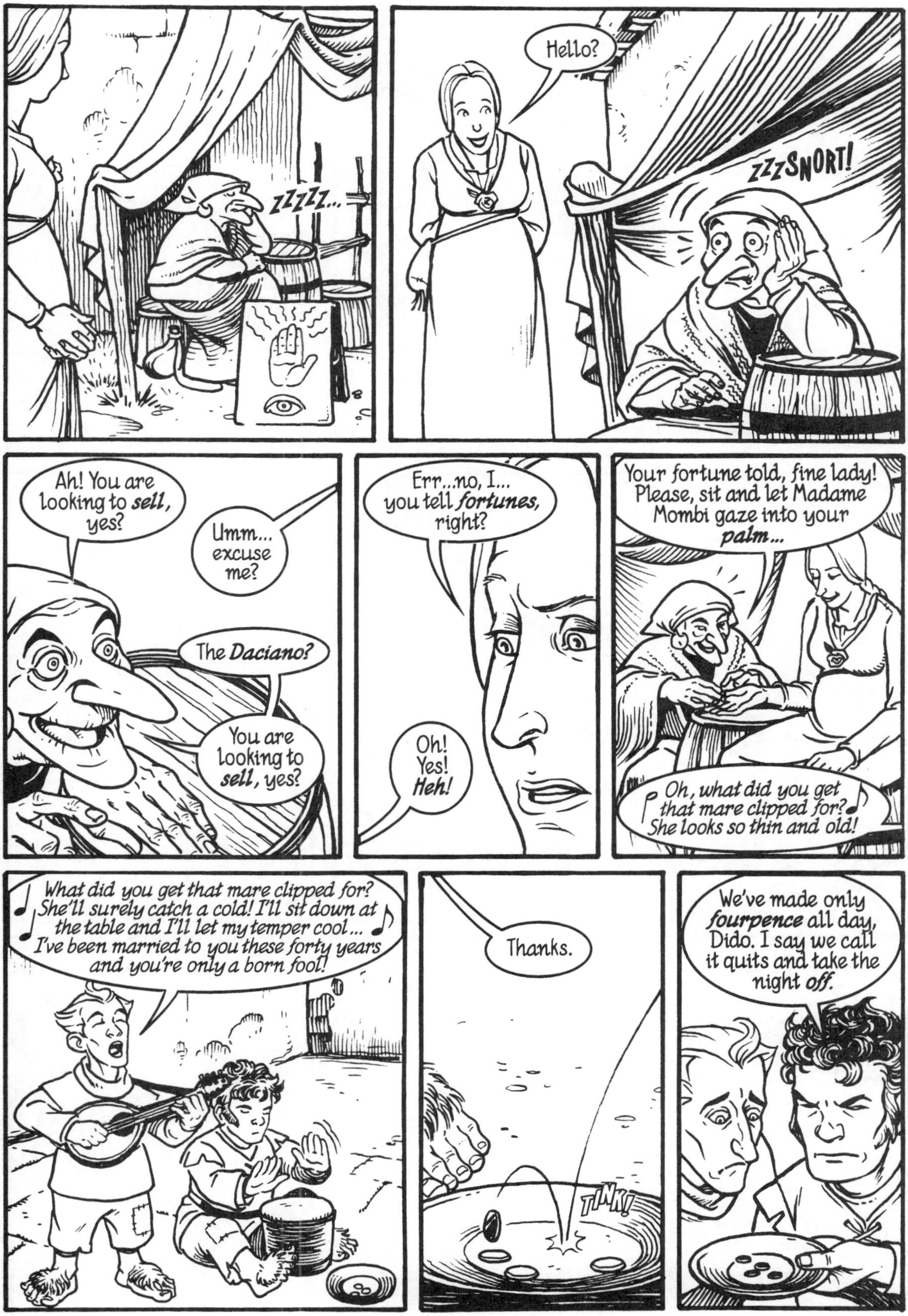
ZZZZZ...
Hello?
ZZZSNORT!
Ah! You are looking to *sell*, yes?
Umm... excuse me?
The *Daciano?*
You are looking to *sell*, yes?
Err...no, I... you tell *fortunes*, right?
Oh! Yes! *Heh!*
Your fortune told, fine lady! Please, sit and let Madame Mombi gaze into your *palm*...
Oh, what did you get that mare clipped for? She looks so thin and old!
What did you get that mare clipped for? She'll surely catch a cold! I'll sit down at the table and I'll let my temper cool... I've been married to you these forty years and you're only a born fool!
Thanks.
TINK!
We've made only *fourpence* all day, Dido. I say we call it quits and take the night *off*.

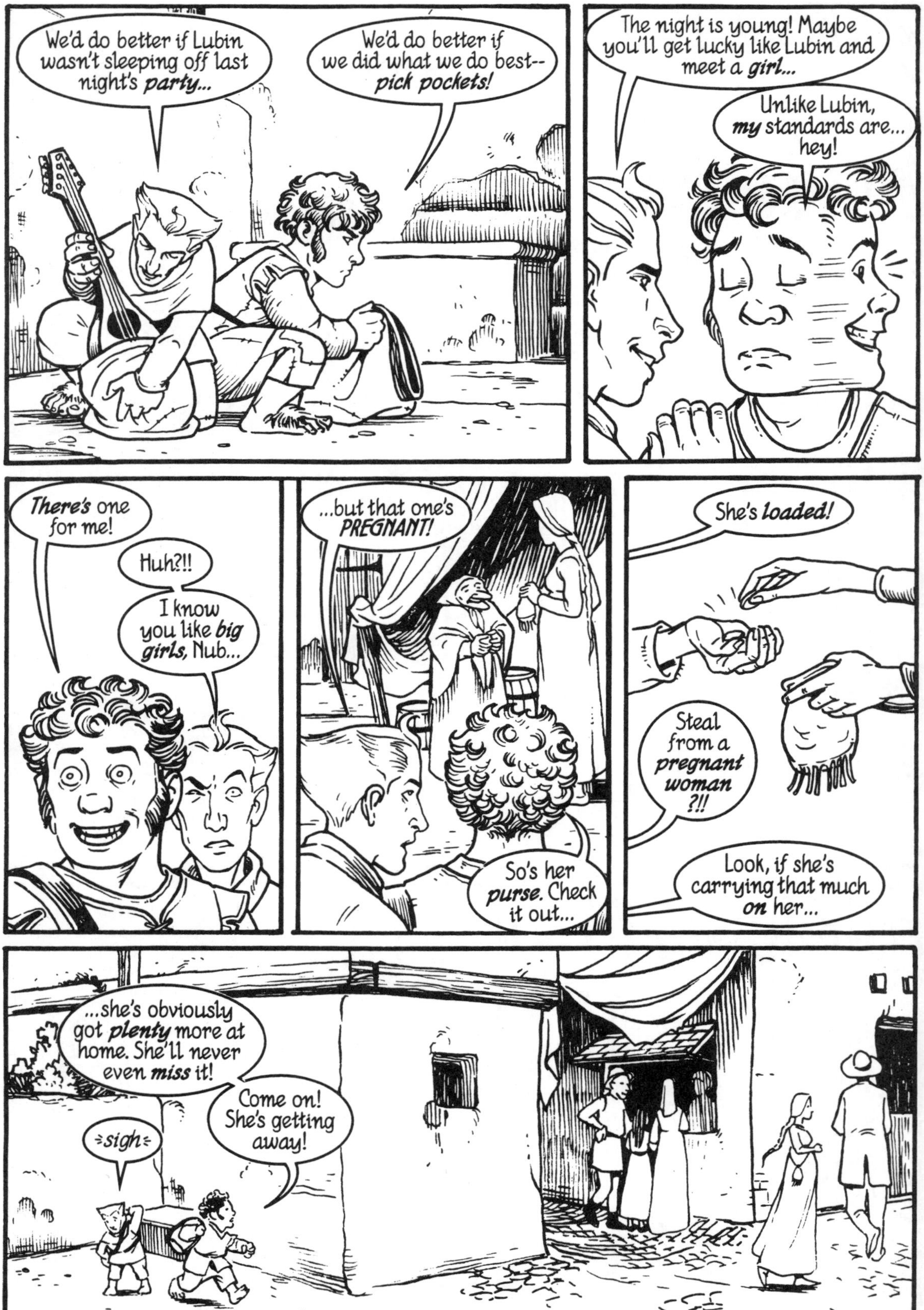
We'd do better if Lubin wasn't sleeping off last night's *party...*
We'd do better if we did what we do best-- *pick pockets!*
The night is young! Maybe you'll get lucky like Lubin and meet a *girl...*
Unlike Lubin, *my* standards are... hey!
There's one for me!
Huh?!!
I know you like *big girls,* Nub...
...but that one's *PREGNANT!*
So's her *purse.* Check it out...
She's *loaded!*
Steal from a *pregnant woman* ?!!
Look, if she's carrying that much *on* her...
...she's obviously got *plenty* more at home. She'll never even *miss* it!
Come on! She's getting away!
sigh

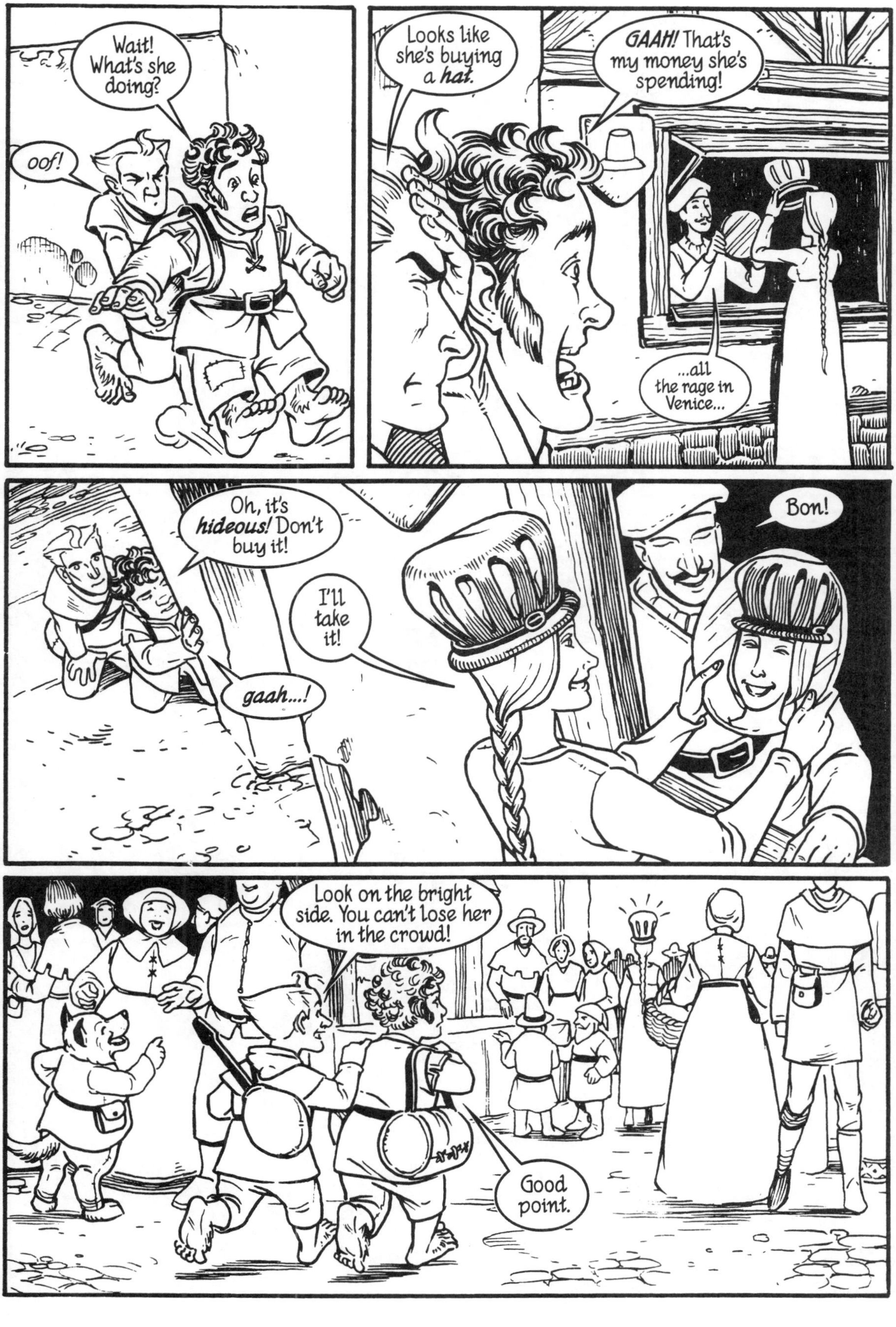

Wait! What's she doing?
oof!
Looks like she's buying a ***hat.***
GAAH! That's my money she's spending!
...all the rage in Venice...
Oh, it's ***hideous!*** Don't buy it!
I'll take it!
gaah...!
Bon!
Look on the bright side. You can't lose her in the crowd!
Good point.

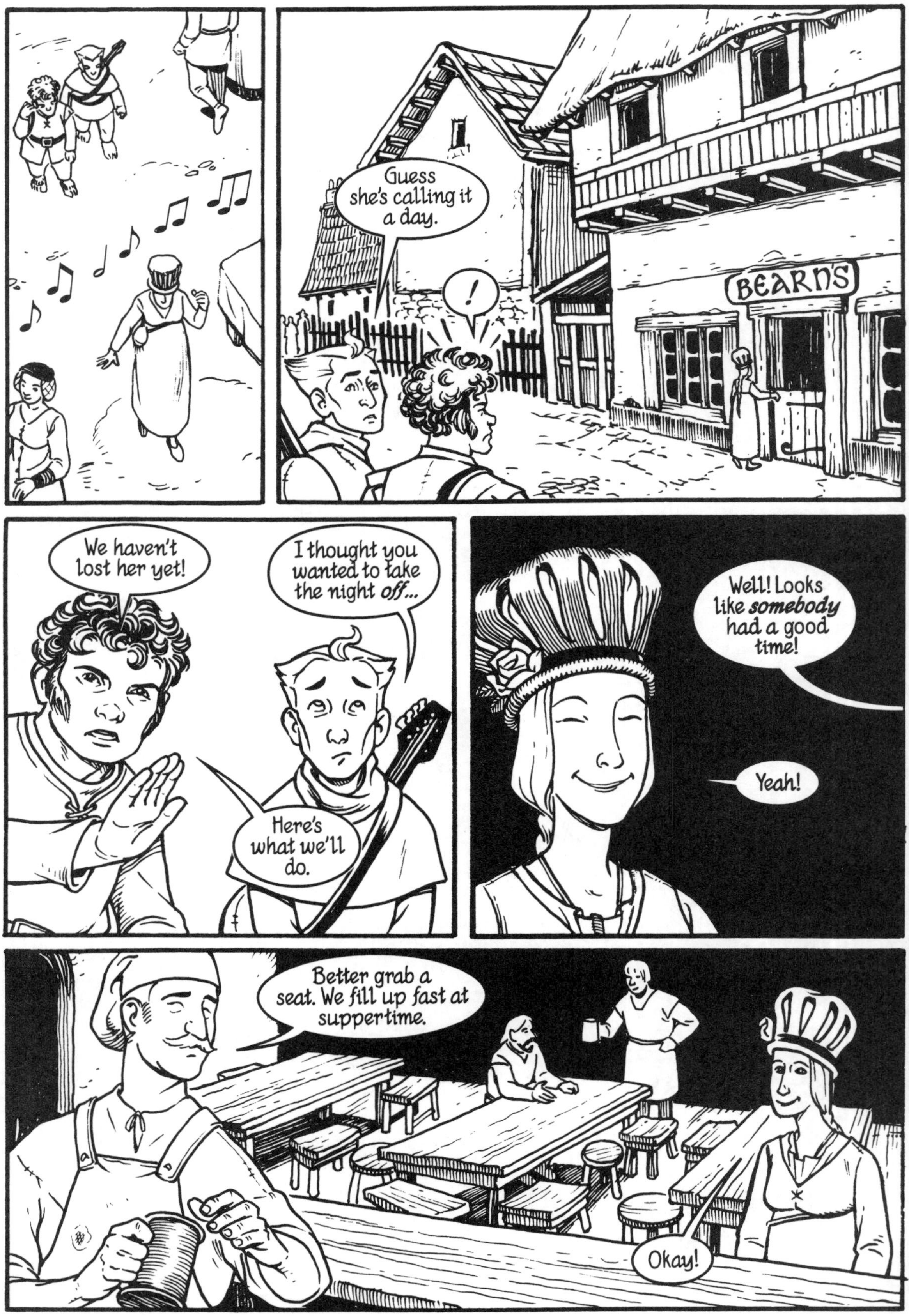
Guess she's calling it a day.
!
BEARN'S
We haven't lost her yet!
I thought you wanted to take the night *off*...
Here's what we'll do.
Well! Looks like ***somebody*** had a good time!
Yeah!
Better grab a seat. We fill up fast at suppertime.
Okay!

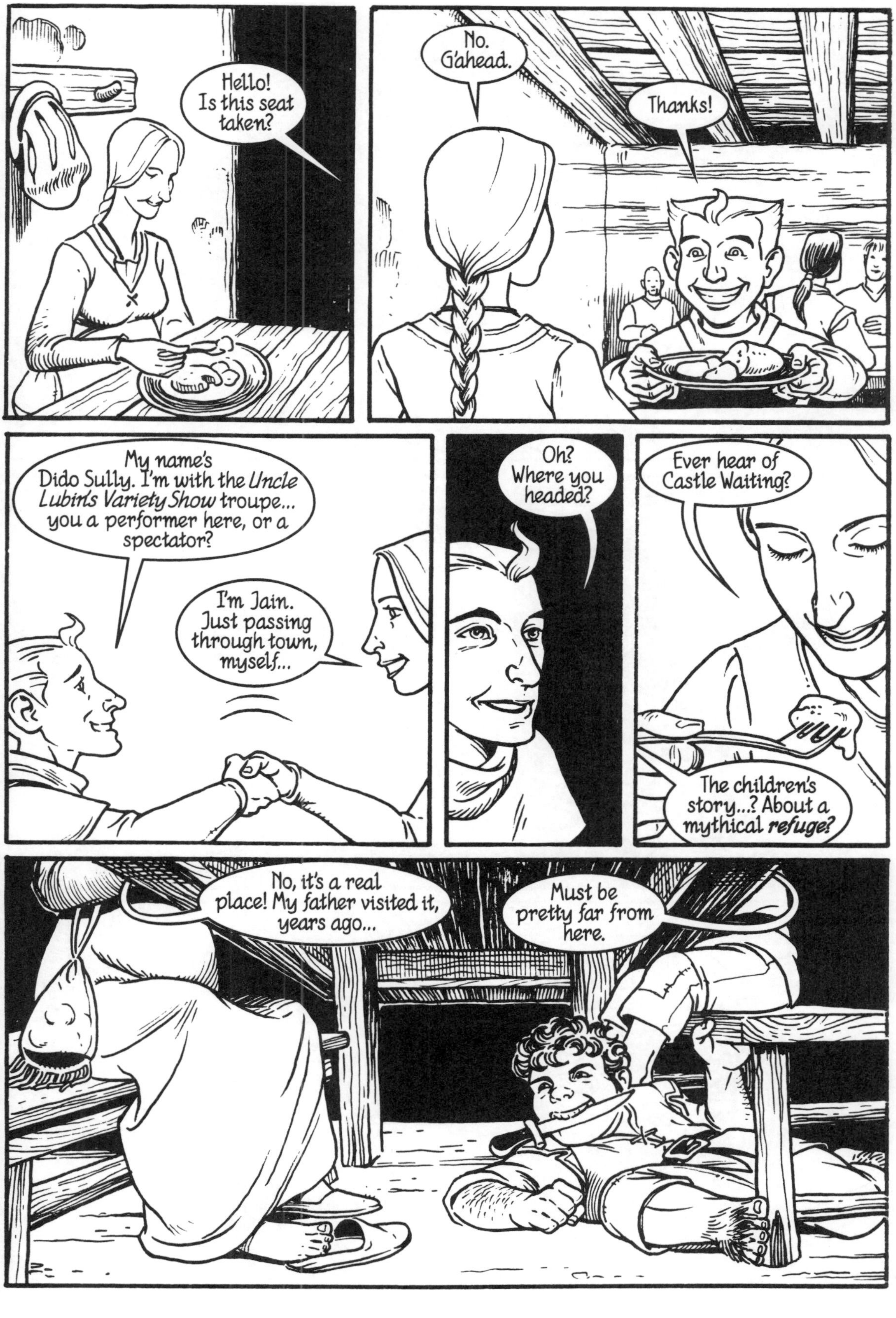
Hello! Is this seat taken?
No. G'ahead.
Thanks!
My name's Dido Sully. I'm with the *Uncle Lubin's Variety Show* troupe... you a performer here, or a spectator?
I'm Jain. Just passing through town, myself...
Oh? Where you headed?
Ever hear of Castle Waiting?
The children's story...? About a mythical ***refuge?***
No, it's a real place! My father visited it, years ago...
Must be pretty far from here.

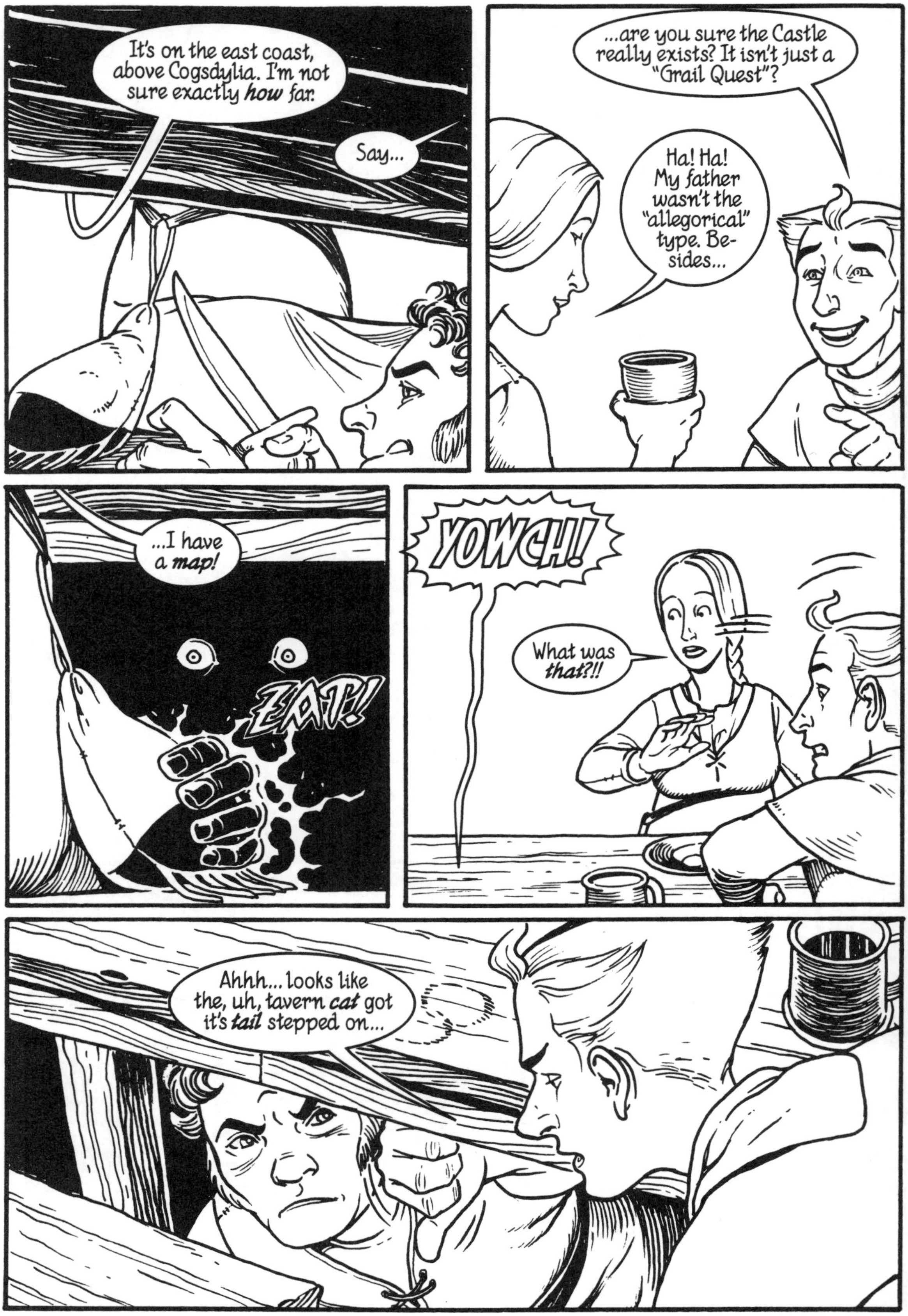
It's on the east coast, above Cogsdylia. I'm not sure exactly *how* far.
Say...
...are you sure the Castle really exists? It isn't just a "Grail Quest"?
Ha! Ha! My father wasn't the "allegorical" type. Besides...
...I have a *map!*
ZAT!
YOWCH!
What was *that?!!*
Ahhh... looks like the, uh, tavern *cat* got it's *tail* stepped on...

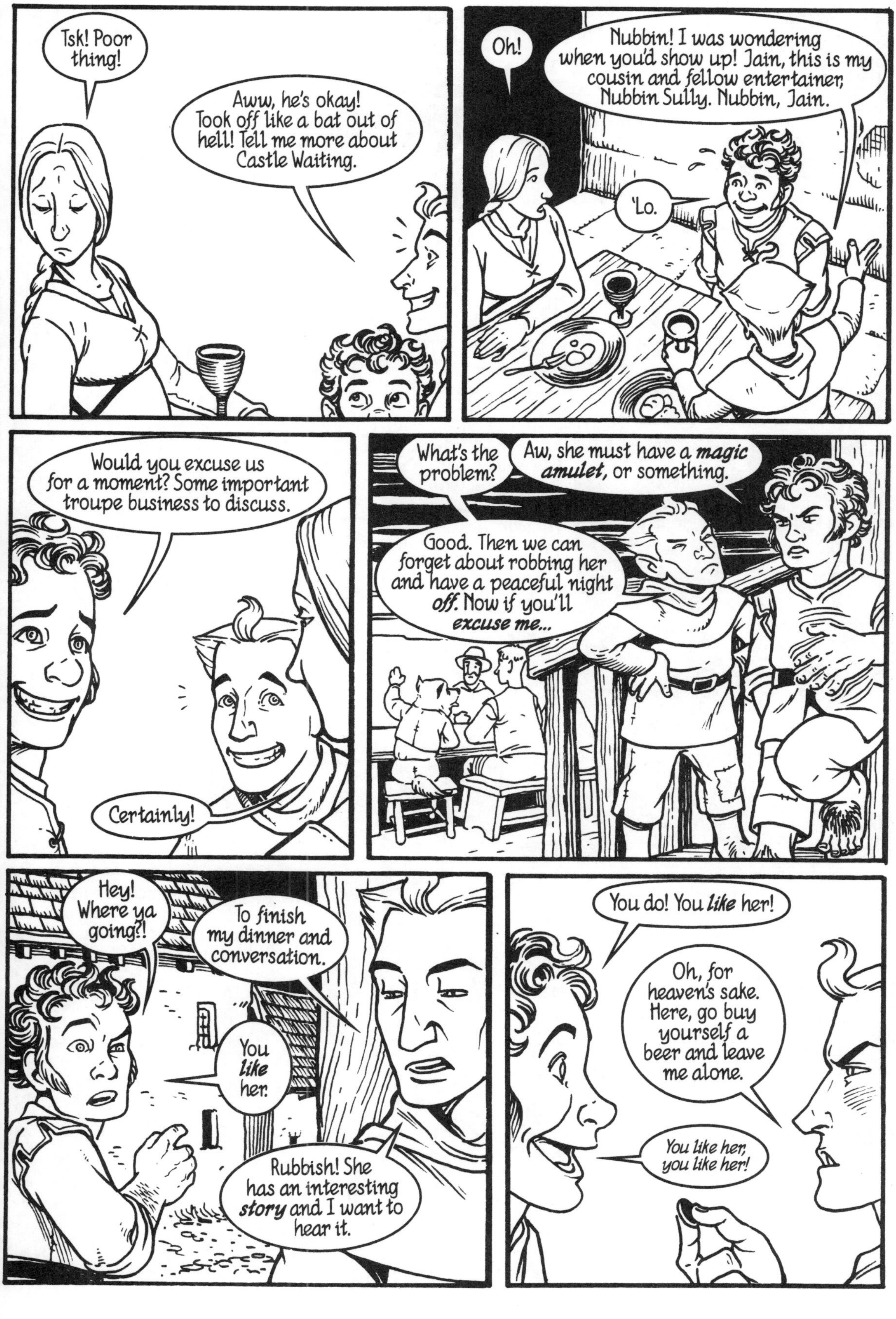
Tsk! Poor thing!
Aww, he's okay! Took off like a bat out of hell! Tell me more about Castle Waiting.
Oh!
Nubbin! I was wondering when you'd show up! Jain, this is my cousin and fellow entertainer, Nubbin Sully. Nubbin, Jain.
'Lo.
Would you excuse us for a moment? Some important troupe business to discuss.
Certainly!
What's the problem?
Aw, she must have a ***magic amulet***, or something.
Good. Then we can forget about robbing her and have a peaceful night ***off.*** Now if you'll ***excuse me...***
Hey! Where ya going?!
To finish my dinner and conversation.
You ***like*** her.
Rubbish! She has an interesting ***story*** and I want to hear it.
You do! You ***like*** her!
Oh, for heaven's sake. Here, go buy yourself a beer and leave me alone.
You like her, you like her!

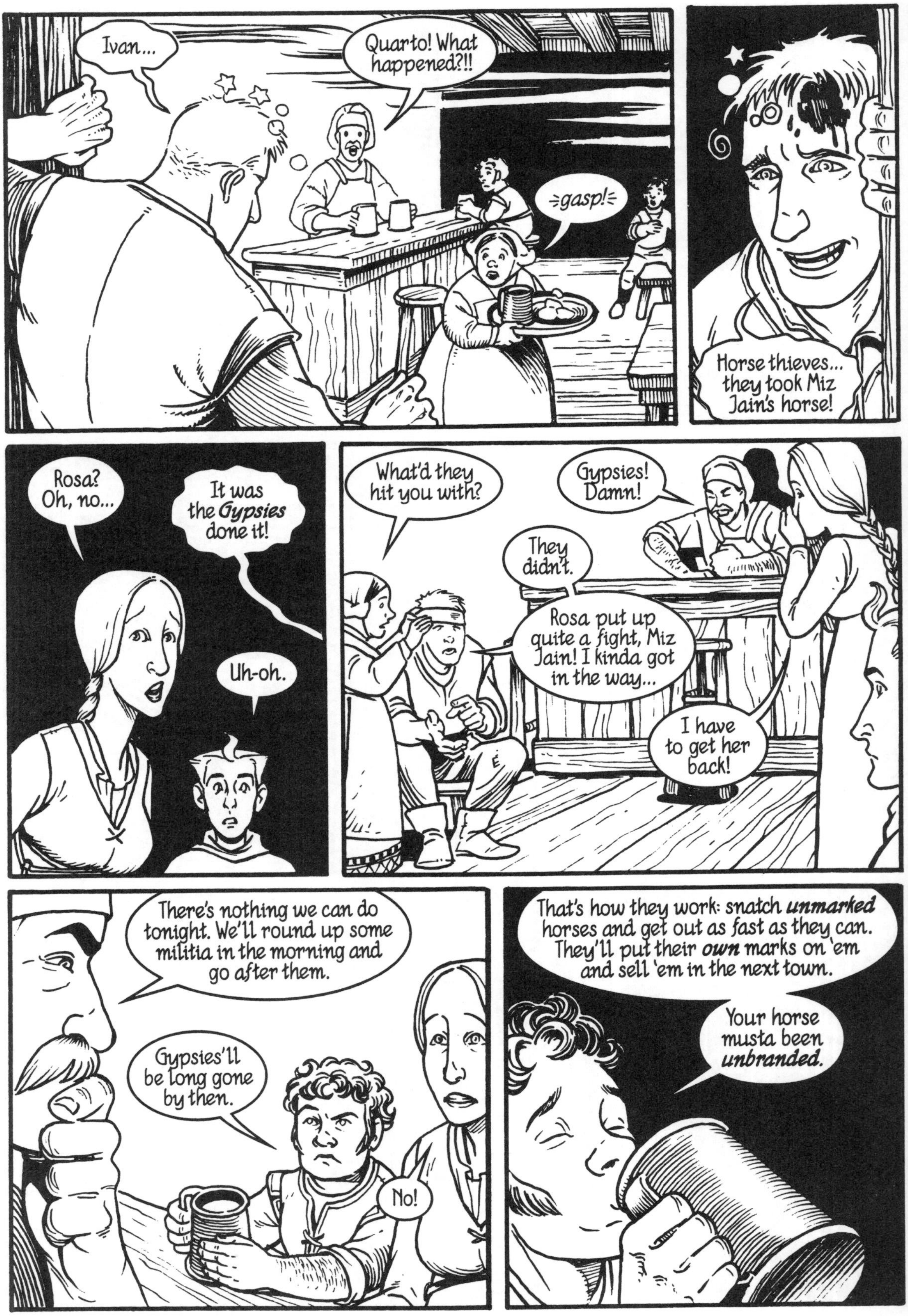
Ivan...
Quarto! What happened?!!
=gasp!=
Horse thieves... they took Miz Jain's horse!
Rosa? Oh, no...
It was the **Gypsies** done it!
Uh-oh.
What'd they hit you with?
Gypsies! Damn!
They didn't.
Rosa put up quite a fight, Miz Jain! I kinda got in the way...
I have to get her back!
There's nothing we can do tonight. We'll round up some militia in the morning and go after them.
Gypsies'll be long gone by then.
No!
That's how they work: snatch **unmarked** horses and get out as fast as they can. They'll put their **own** marks on 'em and sell 'em in the next town.
Your horse musta been **unbranded**.

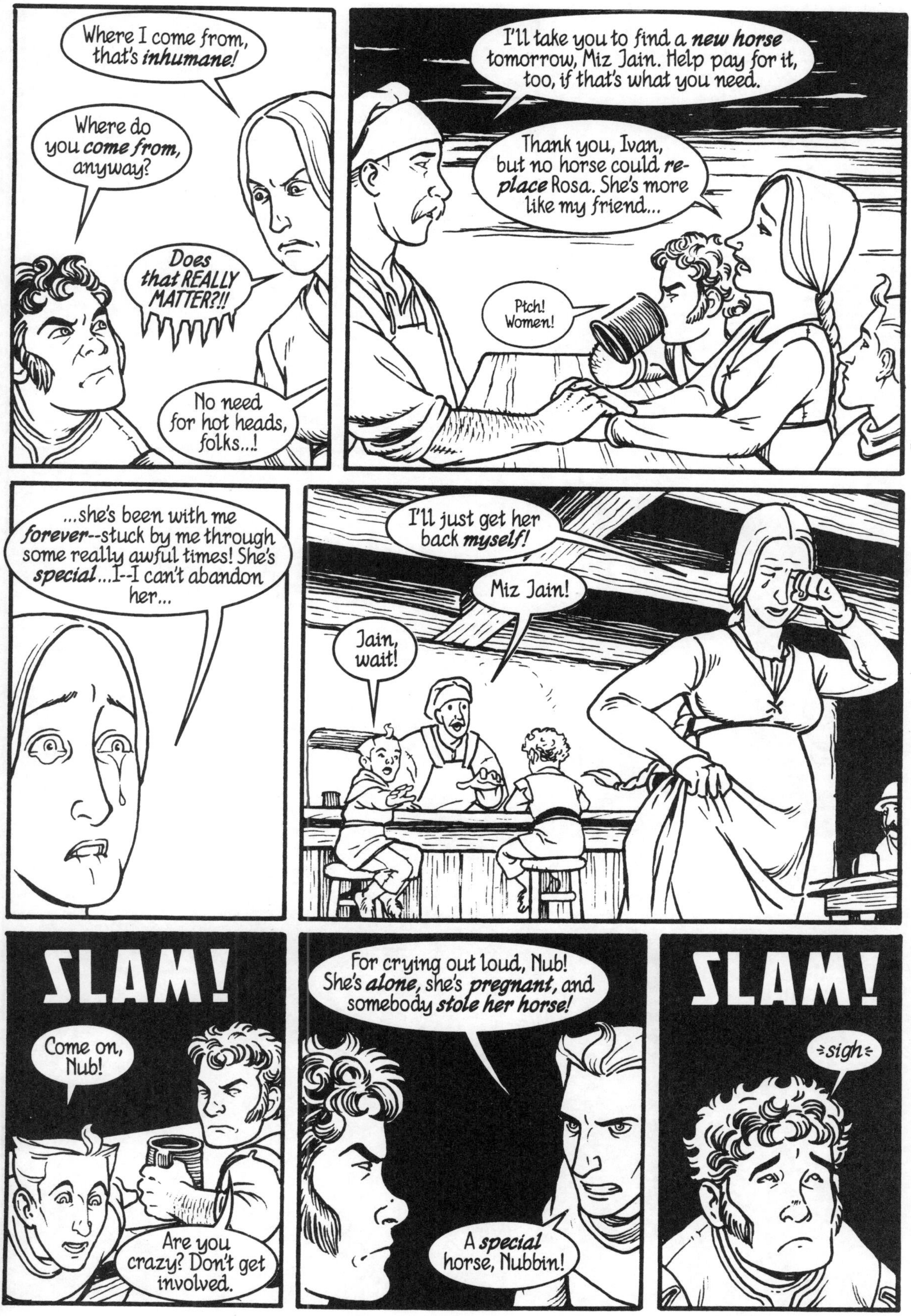
Where I come from, that's *inhumane!*
Where do you *come from,* anyway?
Does that REALLY MATTER?!!
No need for hot heads, folks...!
I'll take you to find a ***new horse*** tomorrow, Miz Jain. Help pay for it, too, if that's what you need.
Thank you, Ivan, but no horse could ***re-place*** Rosa. She's more like my friend...
Ptch! Women!
...she's been with me ***forever***--stuck by me through some really awful times! She's ***special***...I--I can't abandon her...
I'll just get her back ***myself!***
Miz Jain!
Jain, wait!
SLAM!
Come on, Nub!
Are you crazy? Don't get involved.
For crying out loud, Nub! She's ***alone***, she's ***pregnant***, and somebody ***stole her horse!***
A ***special*** horse, Nubbin!
SLAM!
sigh

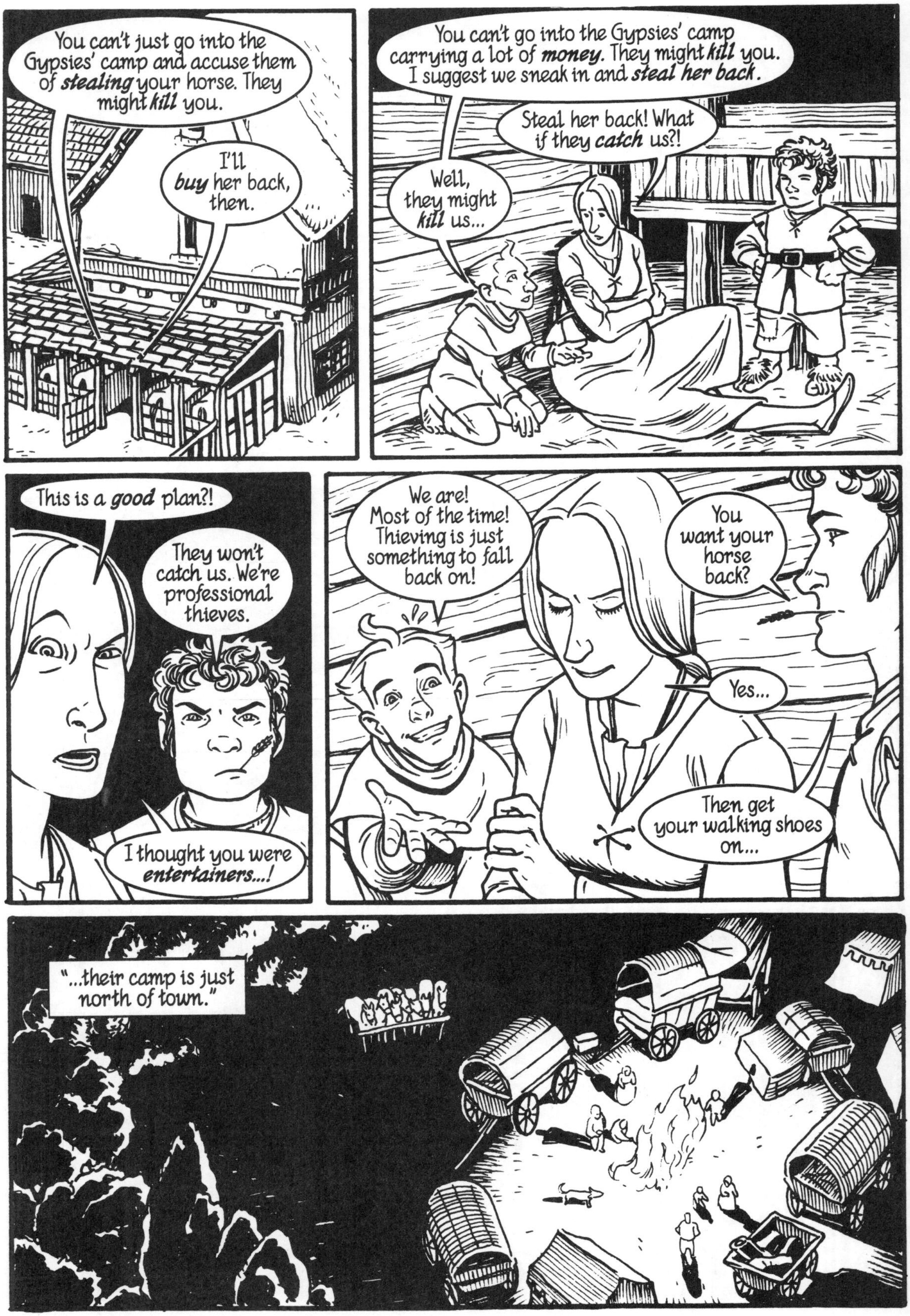

You can't just go into the Gypsies' camp and accuse them of *stealing* your horse. They might *kill* you.
I'll *buy* her back, then.
You can't go into the Gypsies' camp carrying a lot of *money*. They might *kill* you. I suggest we sneak in and *steal her back*.
Steal her back! What if they *catch* us?!
Well, they might *kill* us...
This is a *good* plan?!
They won't catch us. We're professional thieves.
I thought you were *entertainers*...!
We are! Most of the time! Thieving is just something to fall back on!
You want your horse back?
Yes...
Then get your walking shoes on...
"...their camp is just north of town."

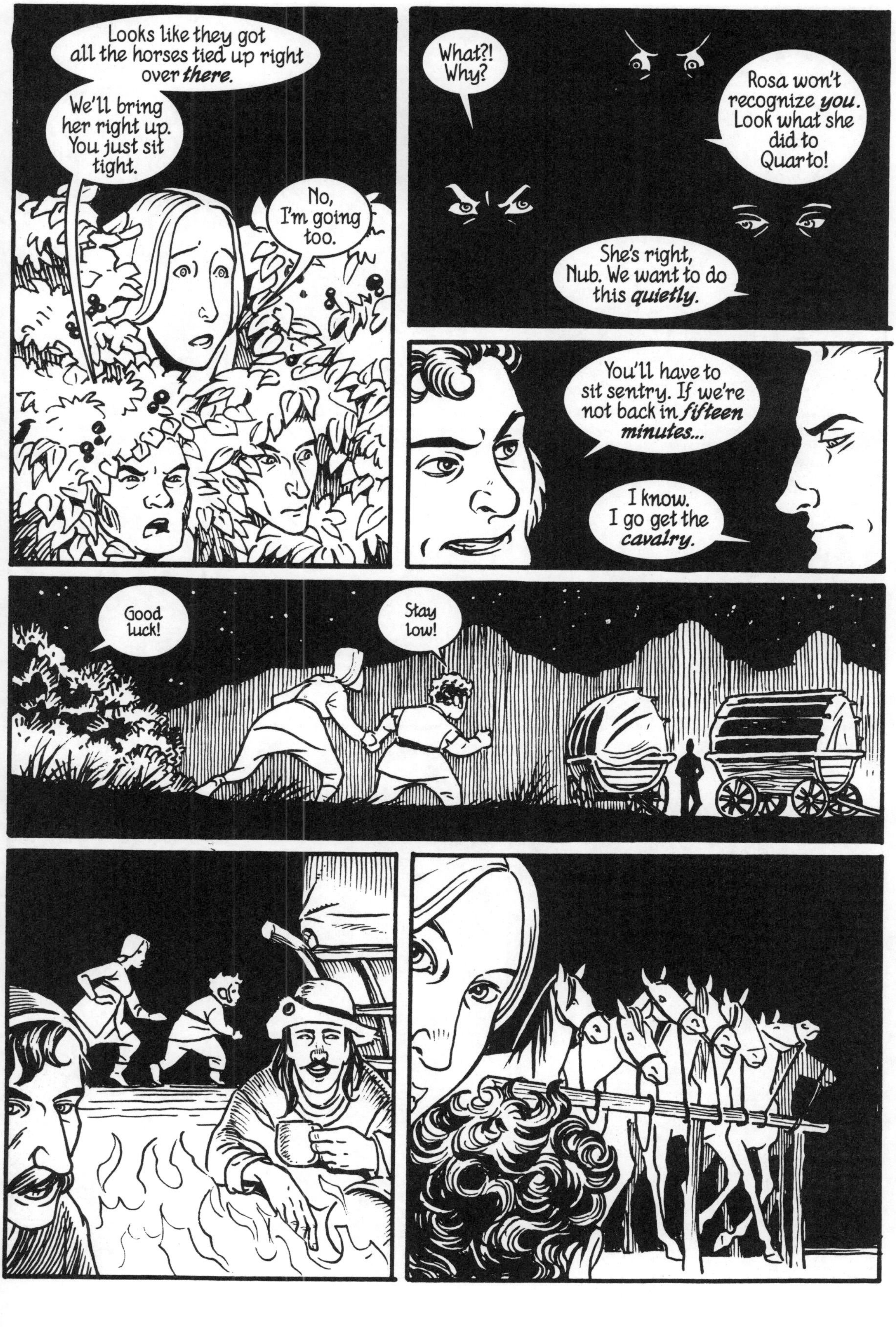
Looks like they got all the horses tied up right over *there*.
We'll bring her right up. You just sit tight.
No, I'm going too.
What?! Why?
Rosa won't recognize *you*. Look what she did to Quarto!
She's right, Nub. We want to do this *quietly*.
You'll have to sit sentry. If we're not back in *fifteen minutes...*
I know. I go get the *cavalry*.
Good luck!
Stay low!

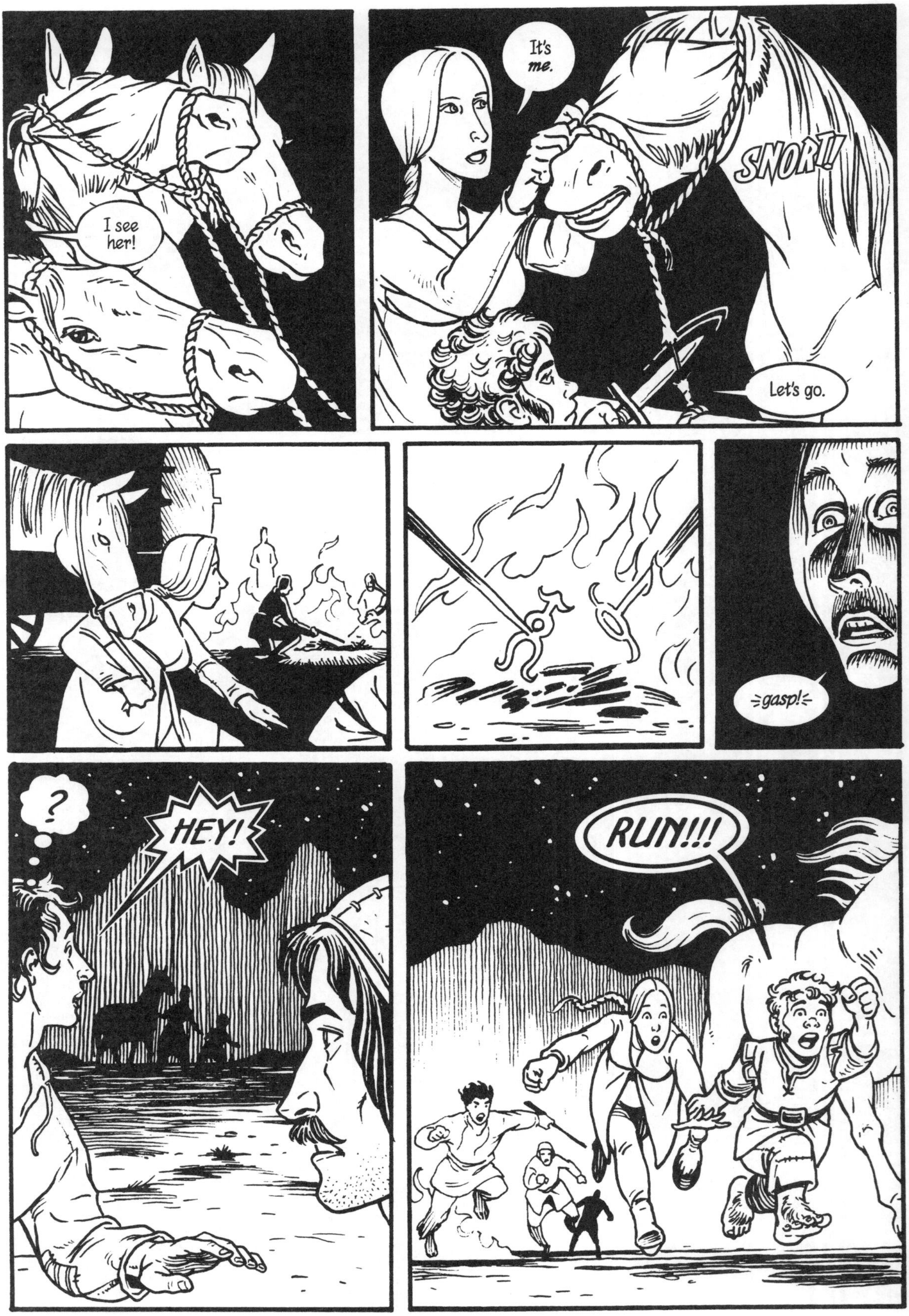
I see her!
It's *me.*
SNORT!
Let's go.
gasp!
?
HEY!
RUN!!!

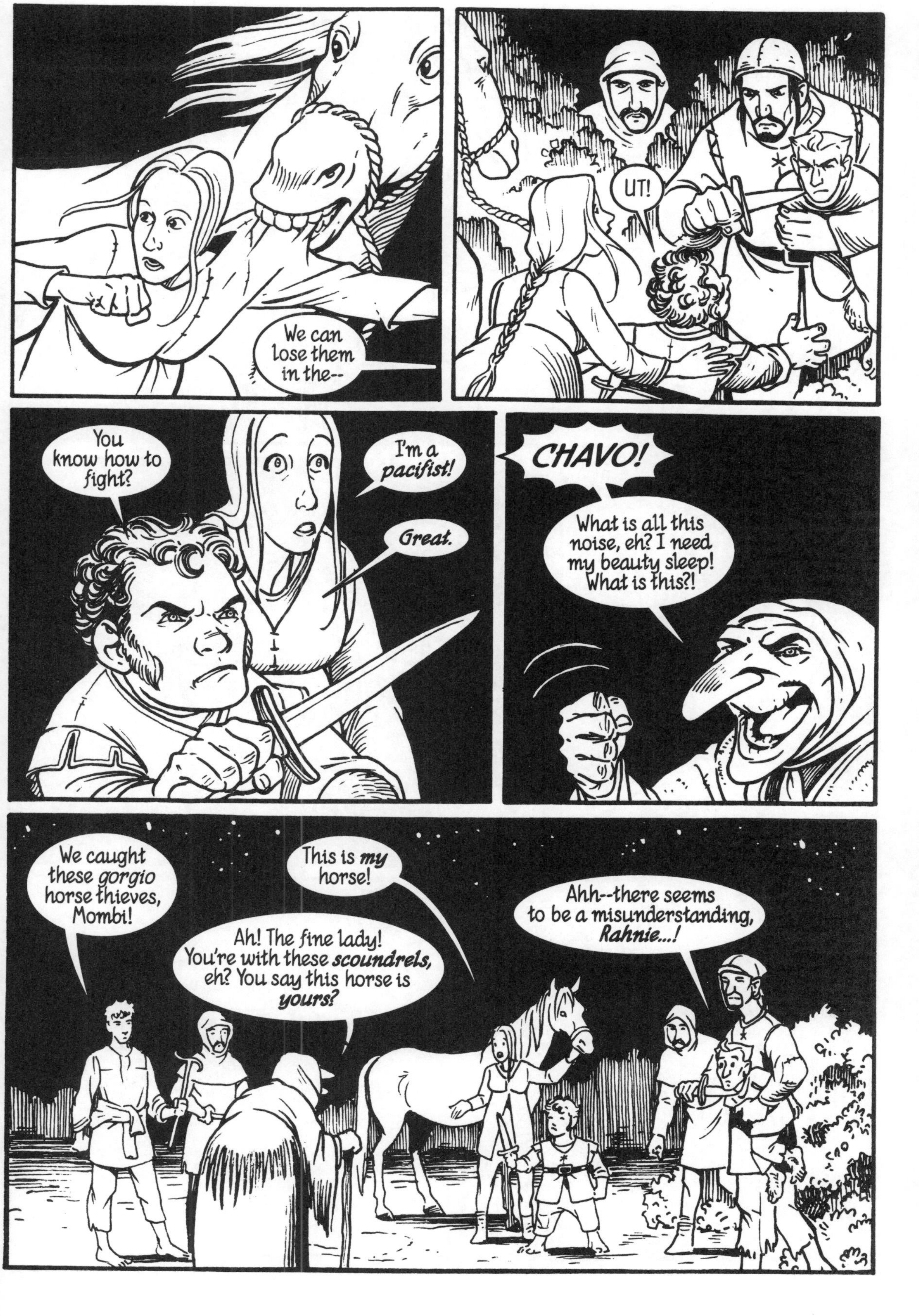
We can lose them in the--
UT!
You know how to fight?
I'm a *pacifist!*
Great.
CHAVO!
What is all this noise, eh? I need my beauty sleep! What is this?!
We caught these *gorgio* horse thieves, Mombi!
This is *my* horse!
Ah! The fine lady! You're with these ***scoundrels,*** eh? You say this horse is ***yours?***
Ahh--there seems to be a misunderstanding, ***Rahnie...!***

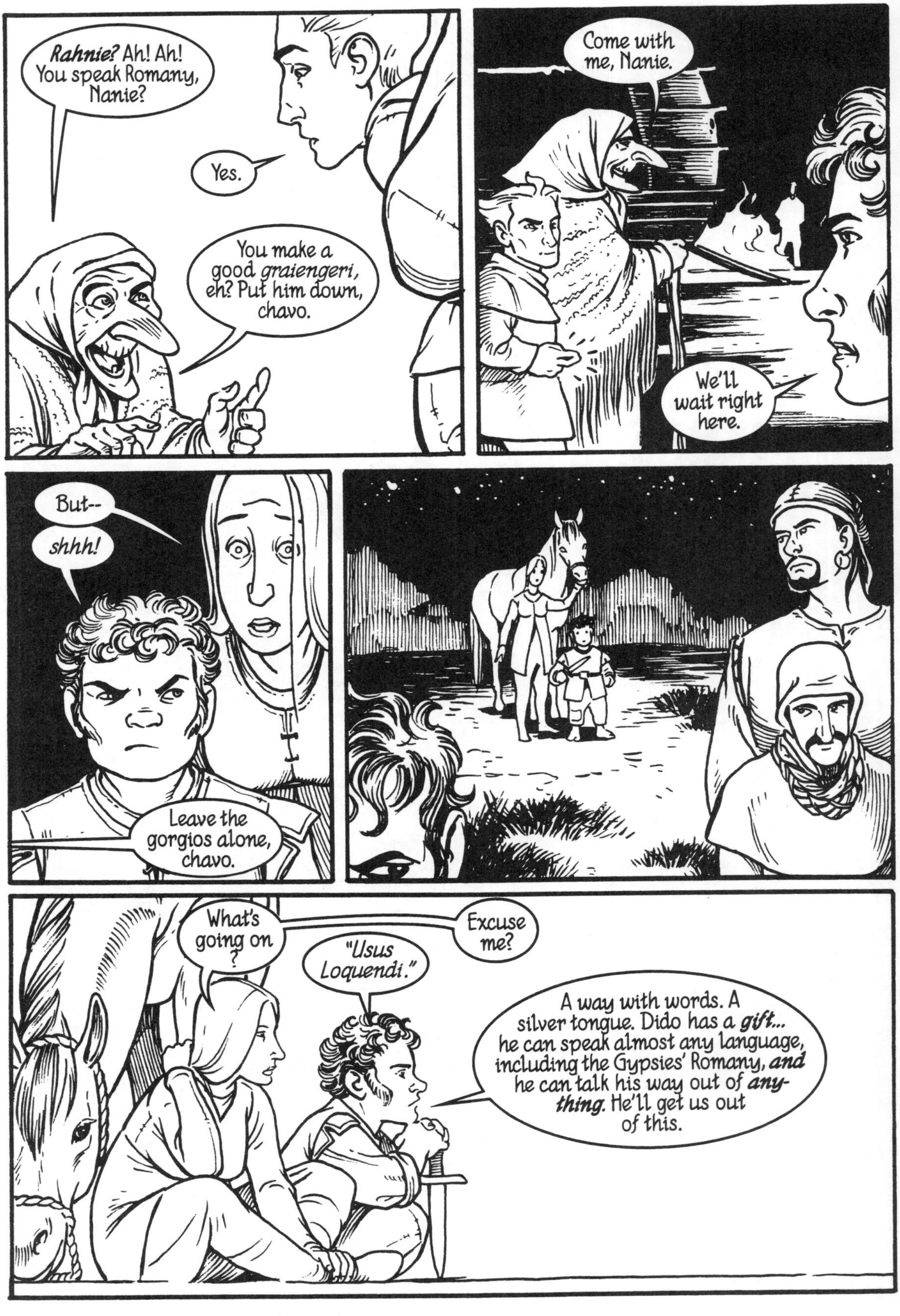

Rahnie? Ah! Ah! You speak Romany, Nanie?
Yes.
You make a good *graiengeri*, eh? Put him down, chavo.
Come with me, Nanie.
We'll wait right here.
But--
shhh!
Leave the gorgios alone, chavo.
What's going on ?
Excuse me?
"Usus Loquendi."
A way with words. A silver tongue. Dido has a ***gift...*** he can speak almost any language, including the Gypsies' Romany, ***and*** he can talk his way out of ***anything***. He'll get us out of this.

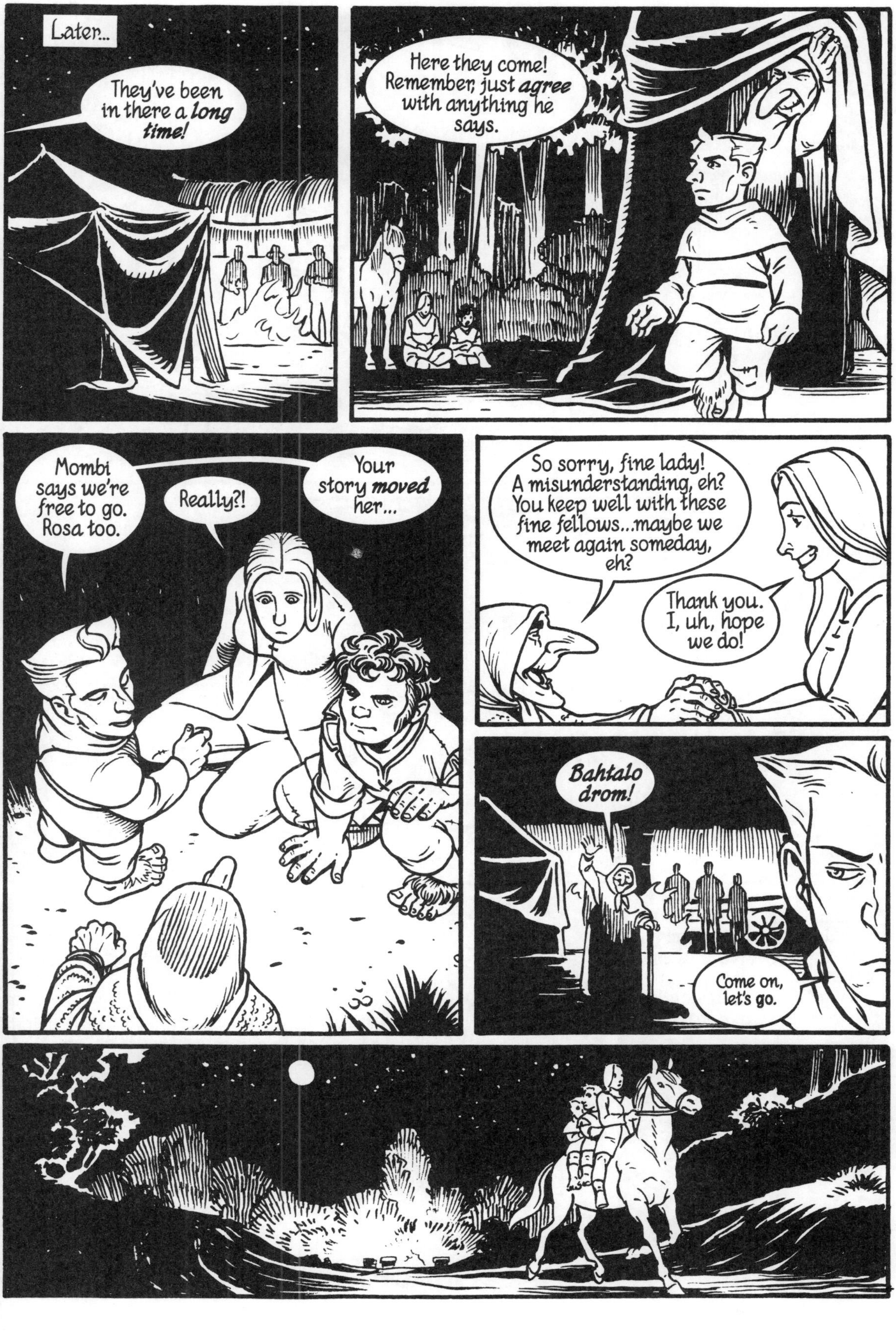
Later...
They've been in there a *long time!*
Here they come! Remember, just *agree* with anything he says.
Mombi says we're free to go. Rosa too.
Really?!
Your story *moved* her...
So sorry, fine lady! A misunderstanding, eh? You keep well with these fine fellows...maybe we meet again someday, eh?
Thank you. I, uh, hope we do!
Bahtalo drom!
Come on, let's go.

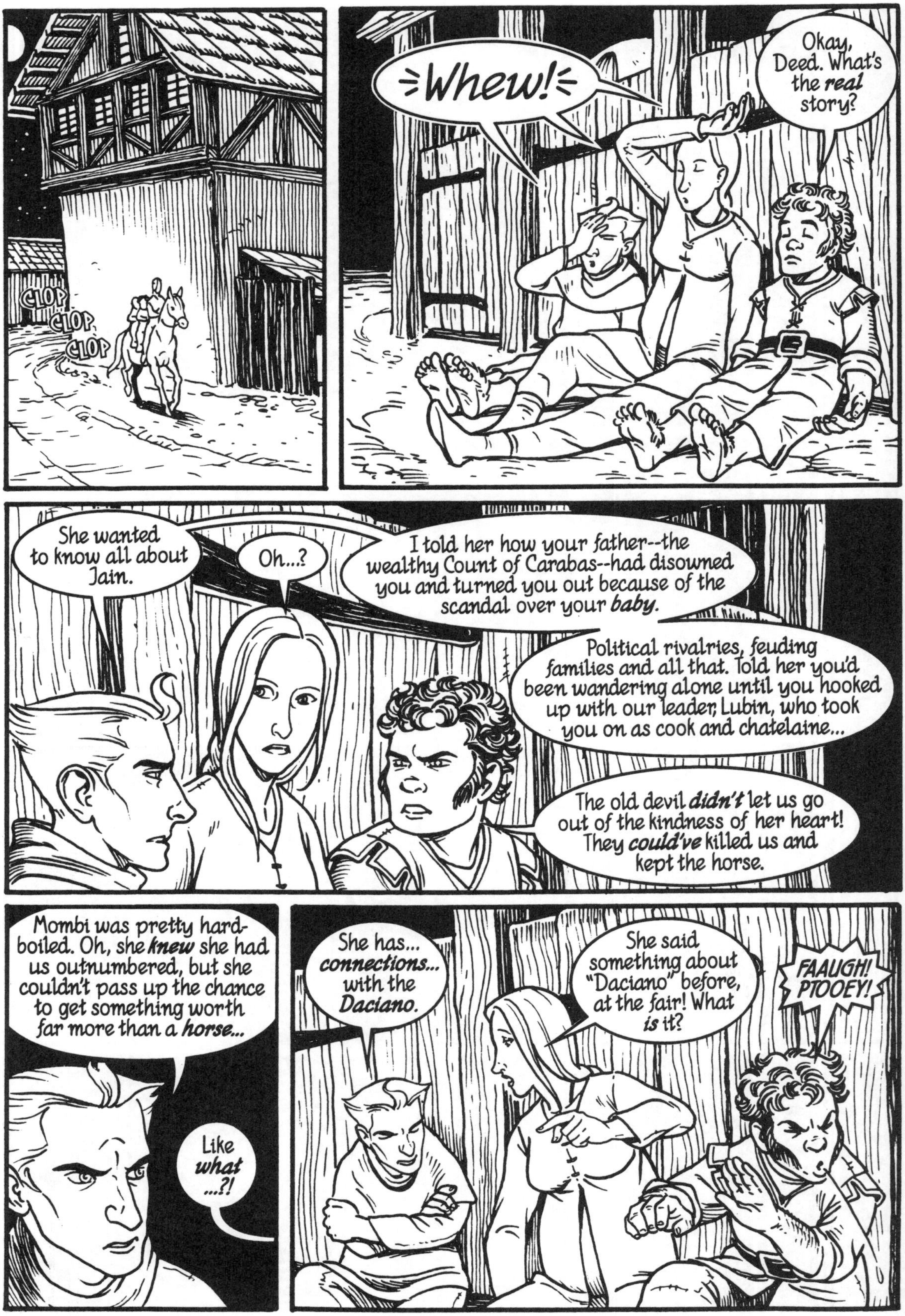
CLOP
CLOP
CLOP
Whew!
Okay, Deed. What's the **real** story?
She wanted to know all about Jain.
Oh...?
I told her how your father--the wealthy Count of Carabas--had disowned you and turned you out because of the scandal over your **baby**.
Political rivalries, feuding families and all that. Told her you'd been wandering alone until you hooked up with our leader, Lubin, who took you on as cook and chatelaine...
The old devil **didn't** let us go out of the kindness of her heart! They **could've** killed us and kept the horse.
Mombi was pretty hard-boiled. Oh, she **knew** she had us outnumbered, but she couldn't pass up the chance to get something worth far more than a **horse...**
Like **what** ...?!
She has... **connections...** with the **Daciano**.
She said something about "Daciano" before, at the fair! What **is** it?
FAAUGH! PTOOEY!

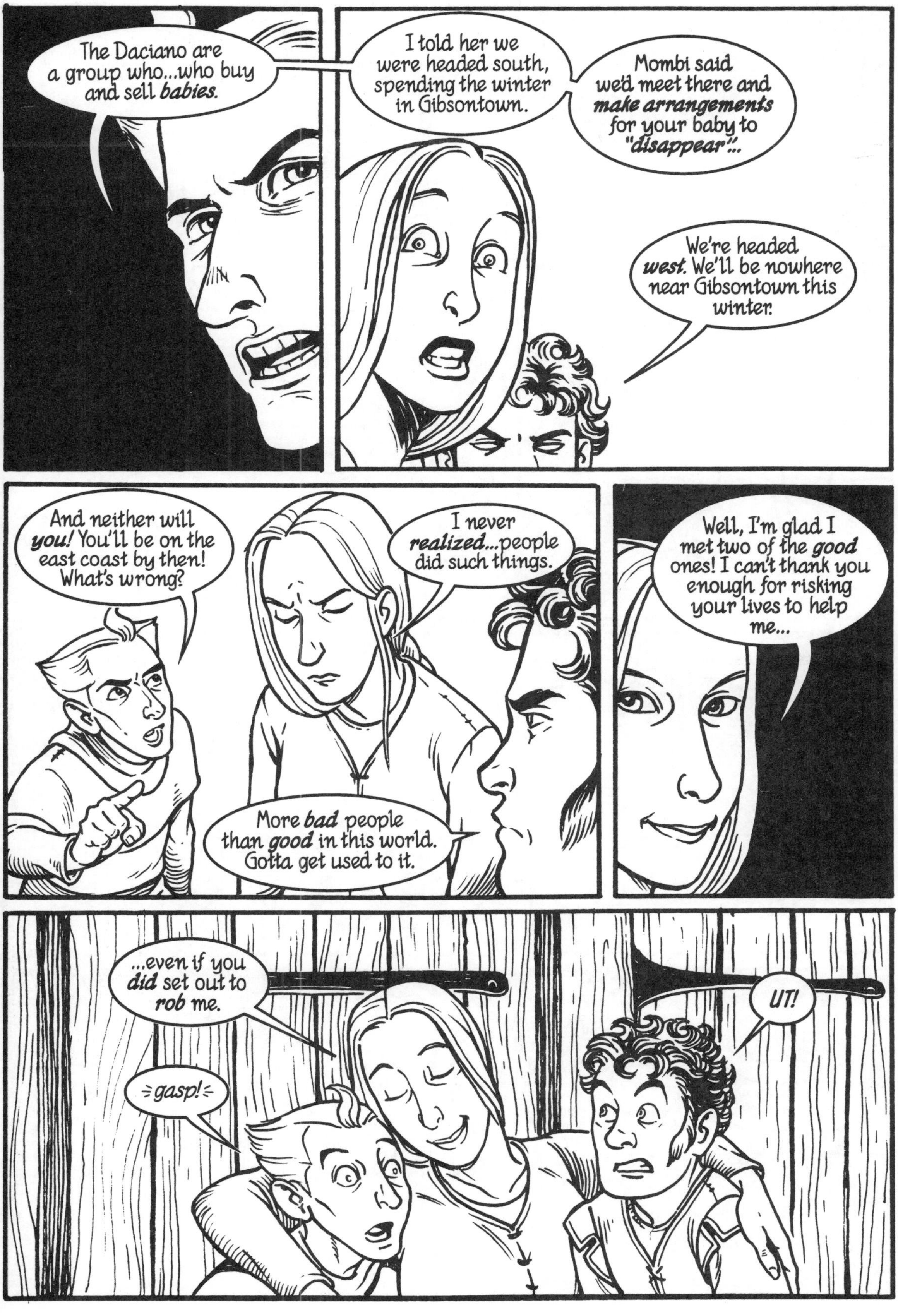

The Daciano are a group who...who buy and sell *babies.*
I told her we were headed south, spending the winter in Gibsontown.
Mombi said we'd meet there and ***make arrangements*** for your baby to "***disappear***"...
We're headed ***west.*** We'll be nowhere near Gibsontown this winter.
And neither will ***you!*** You'll be on the east coast by then! What's wrong?
I never ***realized...*** people did such things.
More ***bad*** people than ***good*** in this world. Gotta get used to it.
Well, I'm glad I met two of the ***good*** ones! I can't thank you enough for risking your lives to help me...
...even if you ***did*** set out to ***rob*** me.
UT!
gasp!

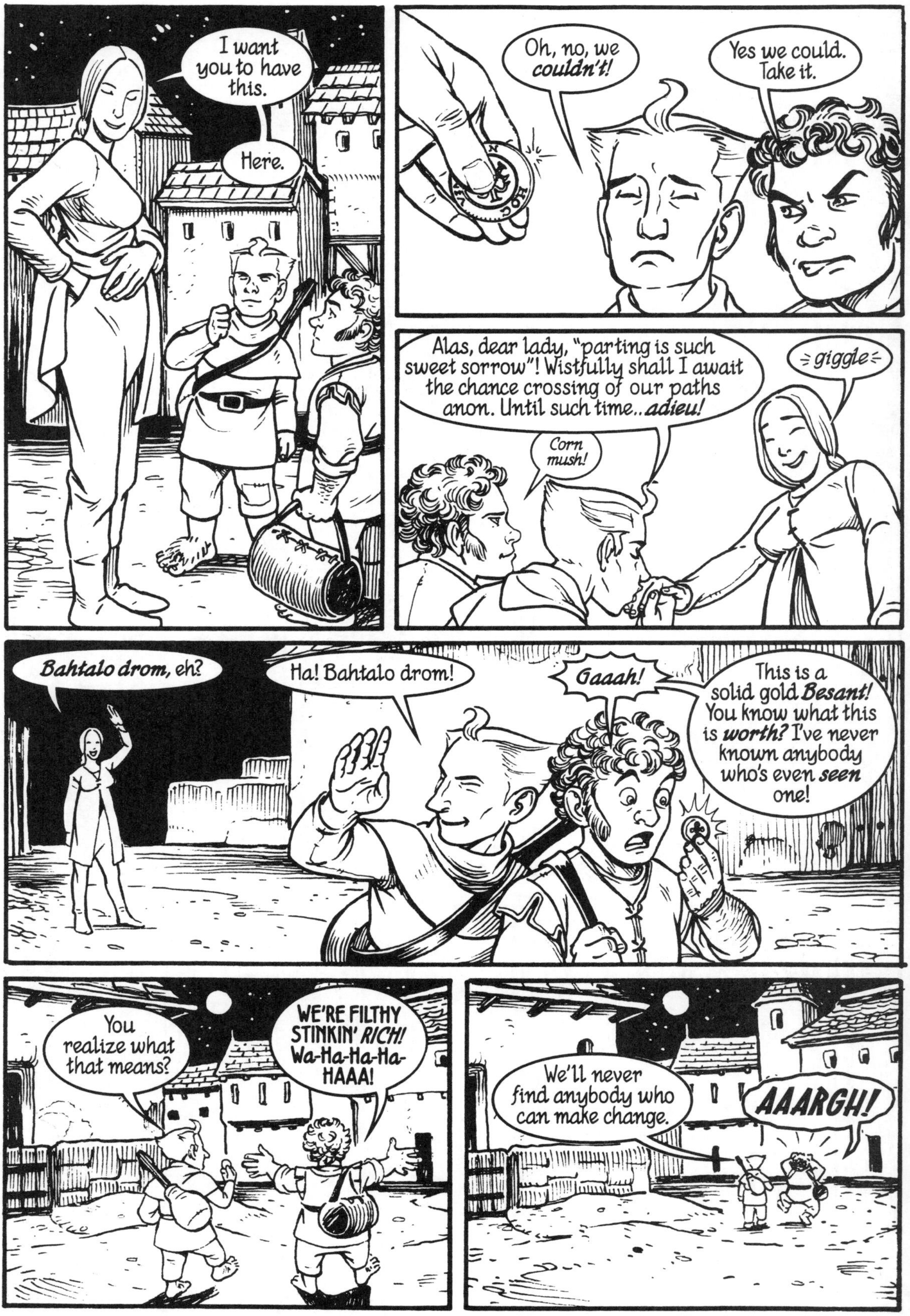
I want you to have this.
Here.
Oh, no, we couldn't!
Yes we could. Take it.
Alas, dear lady, "parting is such sweet sorrow"! Wistfully shall I await the chance crossing of our paths anon. Until such time.. adieu!
giggle
Corn mush!
Bahtalo drom, eh?
Ha! Bahtalo drom!
Gaaah!
This is a solid gold Besant! You know what this is worth? I've never known anybody who's even seen one!
You realize what that means?
WE'RE FILTHY STINKIN' RICH! Wa-Ha-Ha-Ha-HAAA!
We'll never find anybody who can make change.
AAARGH!

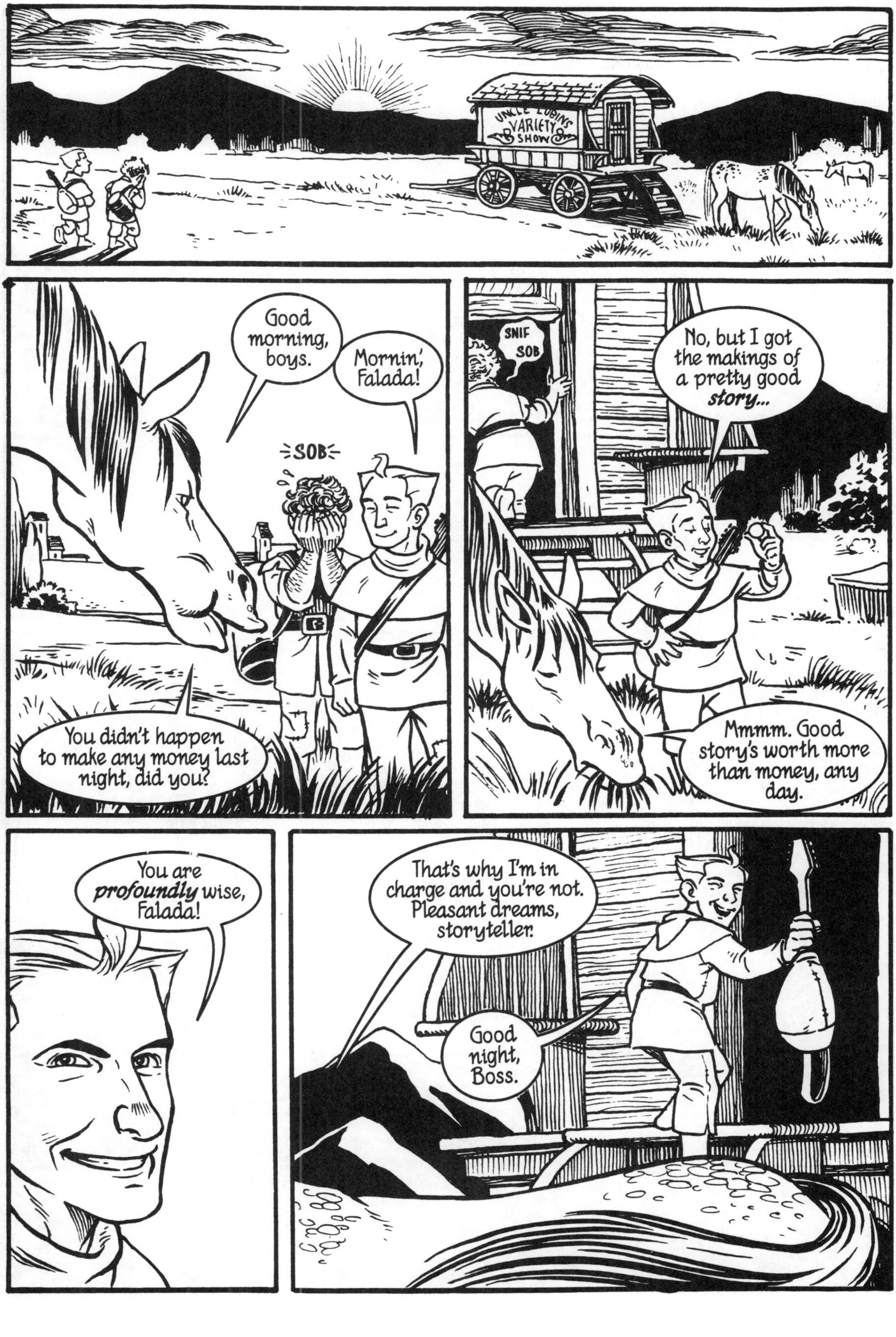
UNCLE LUBIN'S VARIETY SHOW
Good morning, boys.
Mornin', Falada!
SOB
You didn't happen to make any money last night, did you?
SNIF SOB
No, but I got the makings of a pretty good ***story...***
Mmmm. Good story's worth more than money, any day.
You are ***profoundly*** wise, Falada!
That's why I'm in charge and you're not. Pleasant dreams, storyteller.
Good night, Boss.

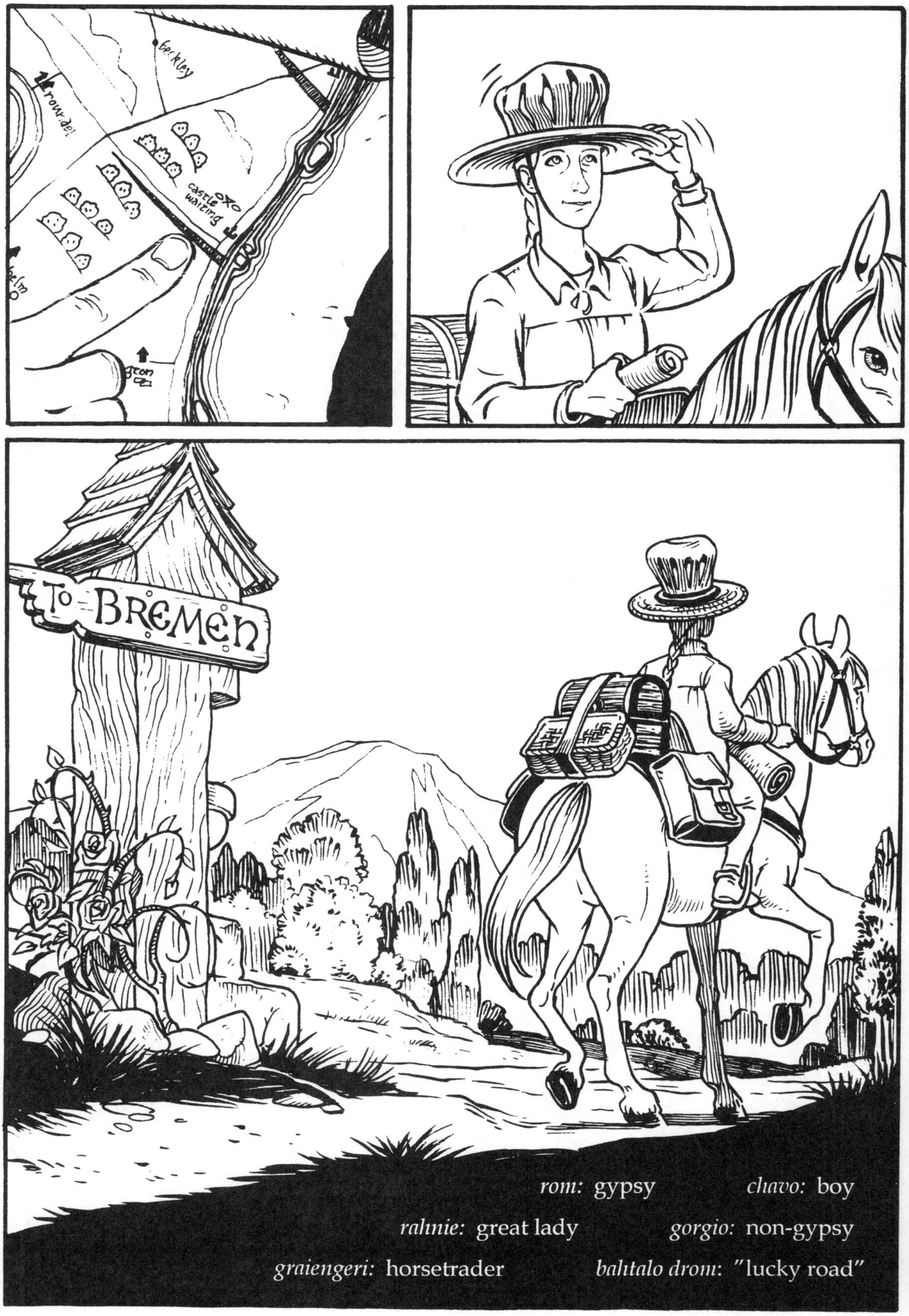
beckley
castle waizing
To BREMEN
rom: gypsy
chavo: boy
rahnie: great lady
gorgio: non-gypsy
graiengeri: horsetrader
bahtalo drom: "lucky road"

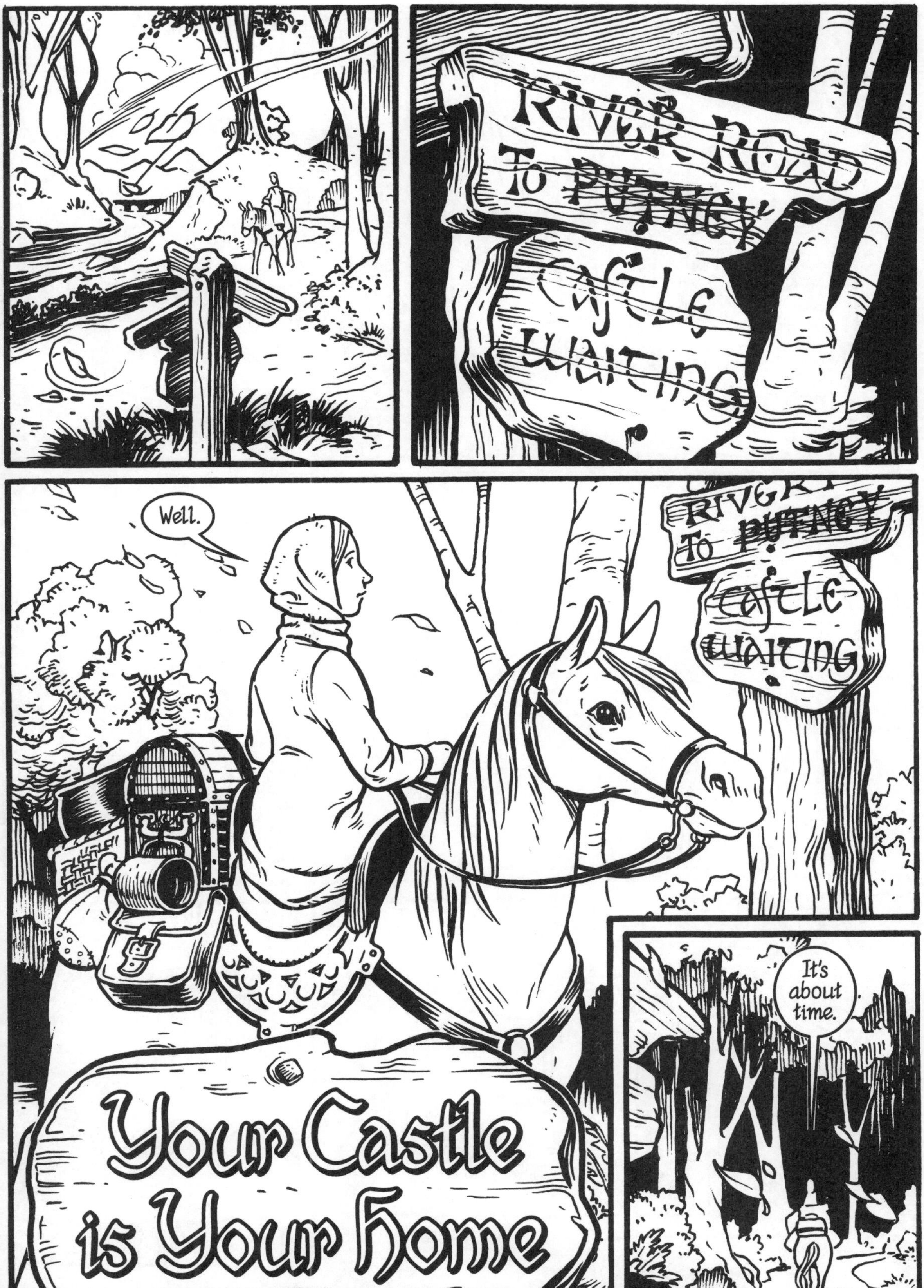

RIVER ROAD
TO PUTNEY
CASTLE WAITING
Well.
RIVER
TO PUTNEY
CASTLE WAITING
Your Castle is Your Home
It's about time.

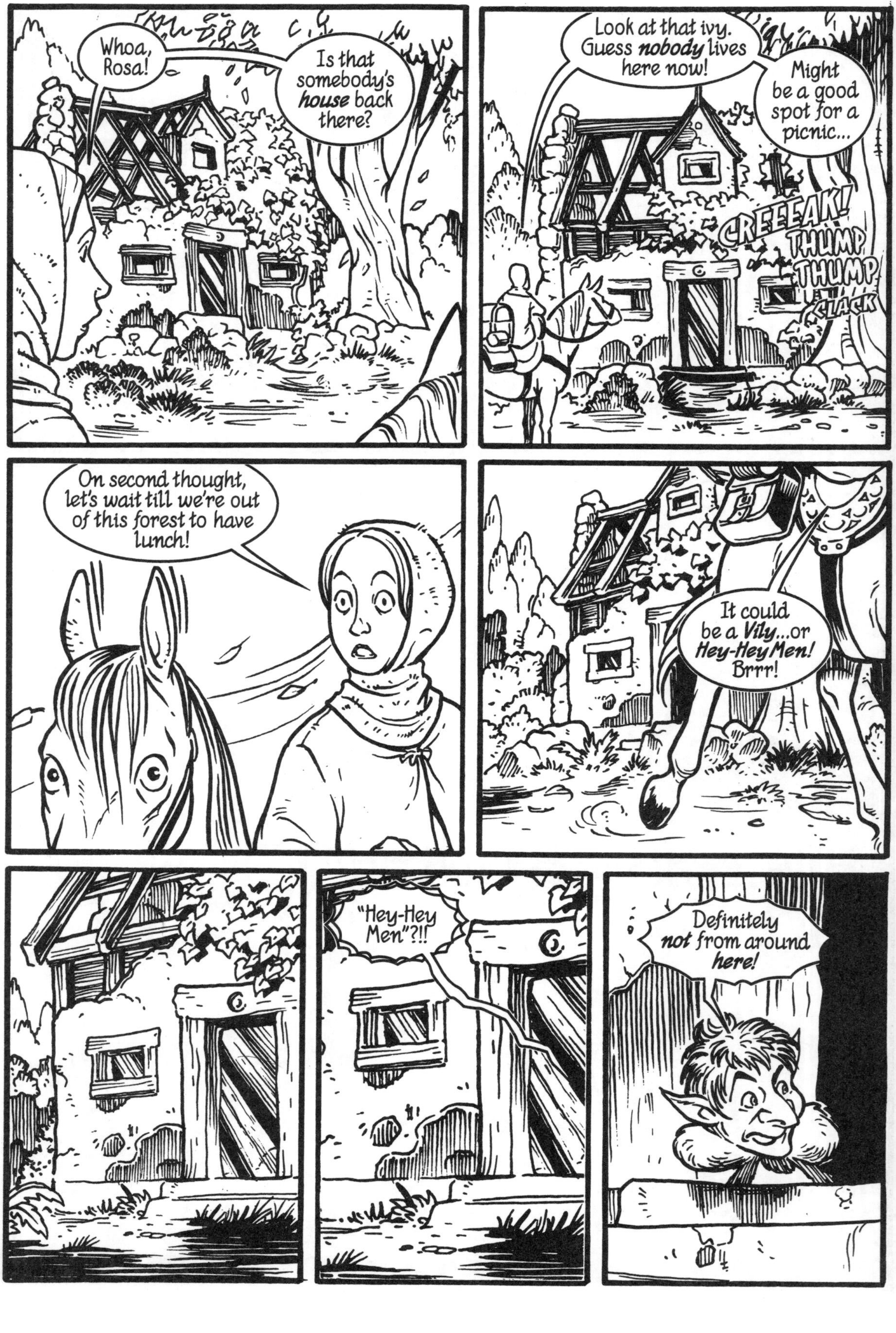

Whoa, Rosa!
Is that somebody's *house* back there?
Look at that ivy. Guess *nobody* lives here now!
Might be a good spot for a picnic...
CREEEAK! THUMP THUMP CLACK
On second thought, let's wait till we're out of this forest to have lunch!
It could be a *Vily*...or *Hey-Hey Men!* Brrr!
"Hey-Hey Men"?!!
Definitely *not* from around *here!*

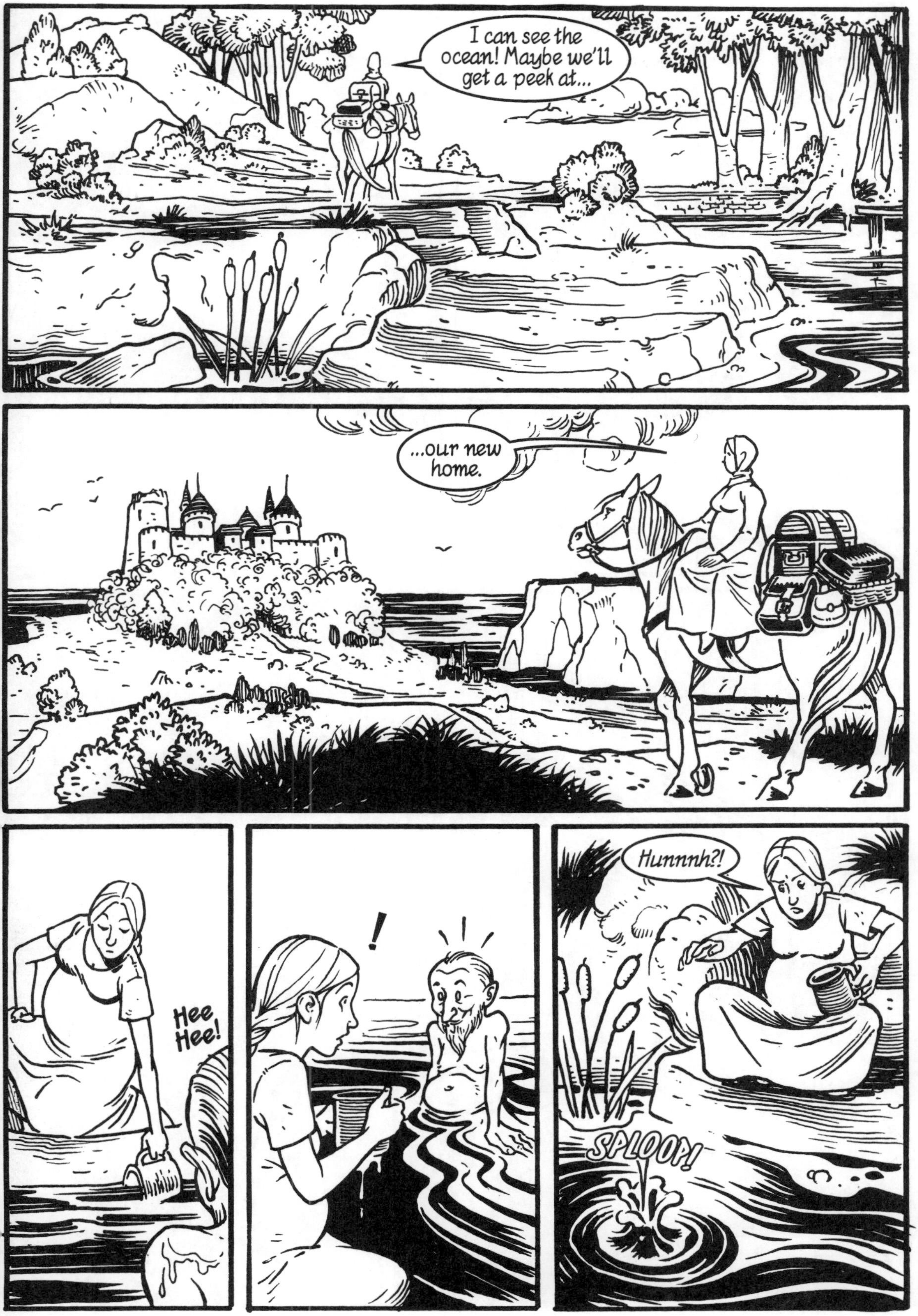
I can see the ocean! Maybe we'll get a peek at...
...our new home.
Hee Hee!
!
Hunnnh?!
SPLOOP!

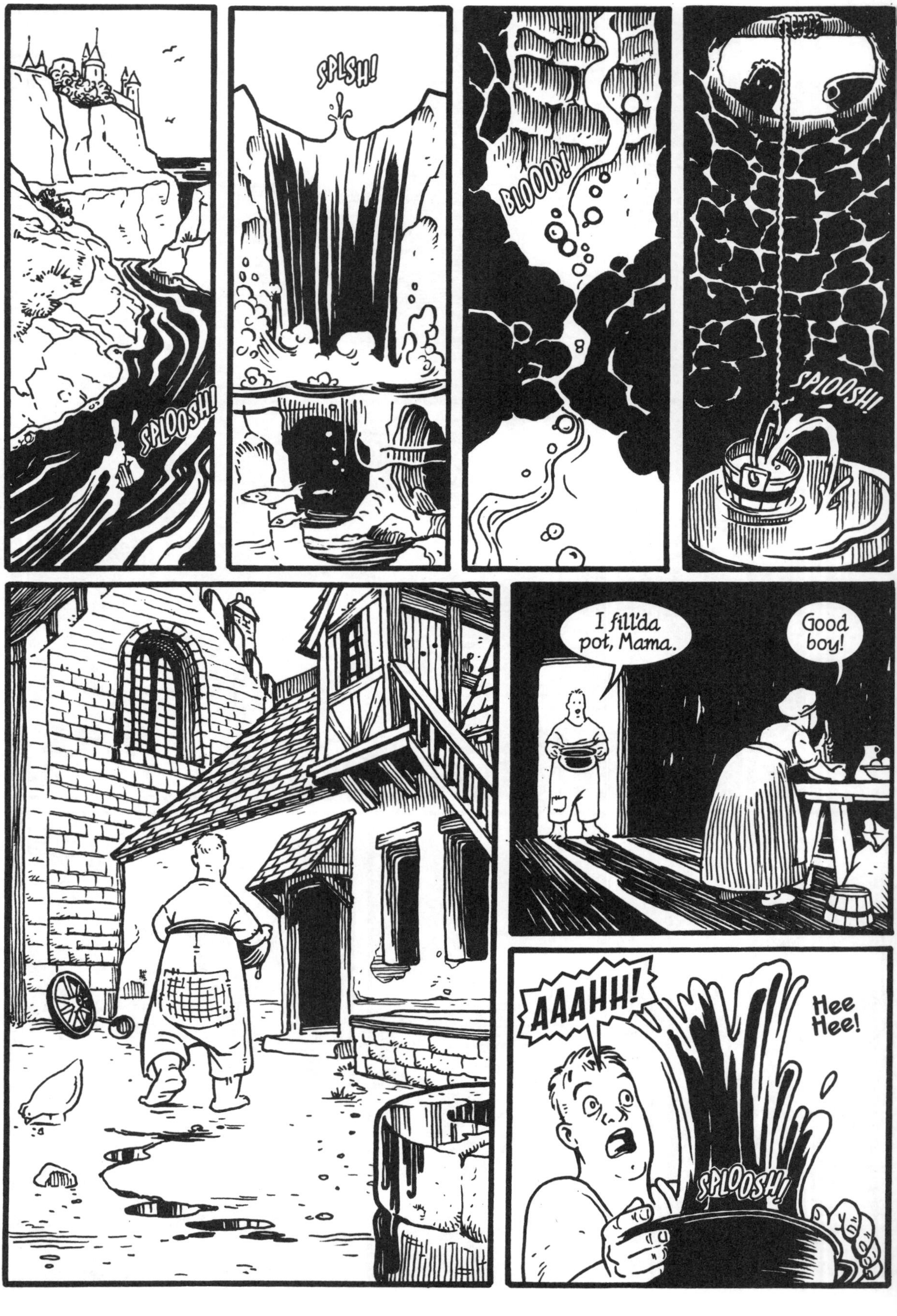
SPLOOSH!
SPLSH!
BLOOOP!
SPLOOSH!
I fill'da pot, Mama.
Good boy!
AAAHH!
Hee Hee!
SPLOOSH!

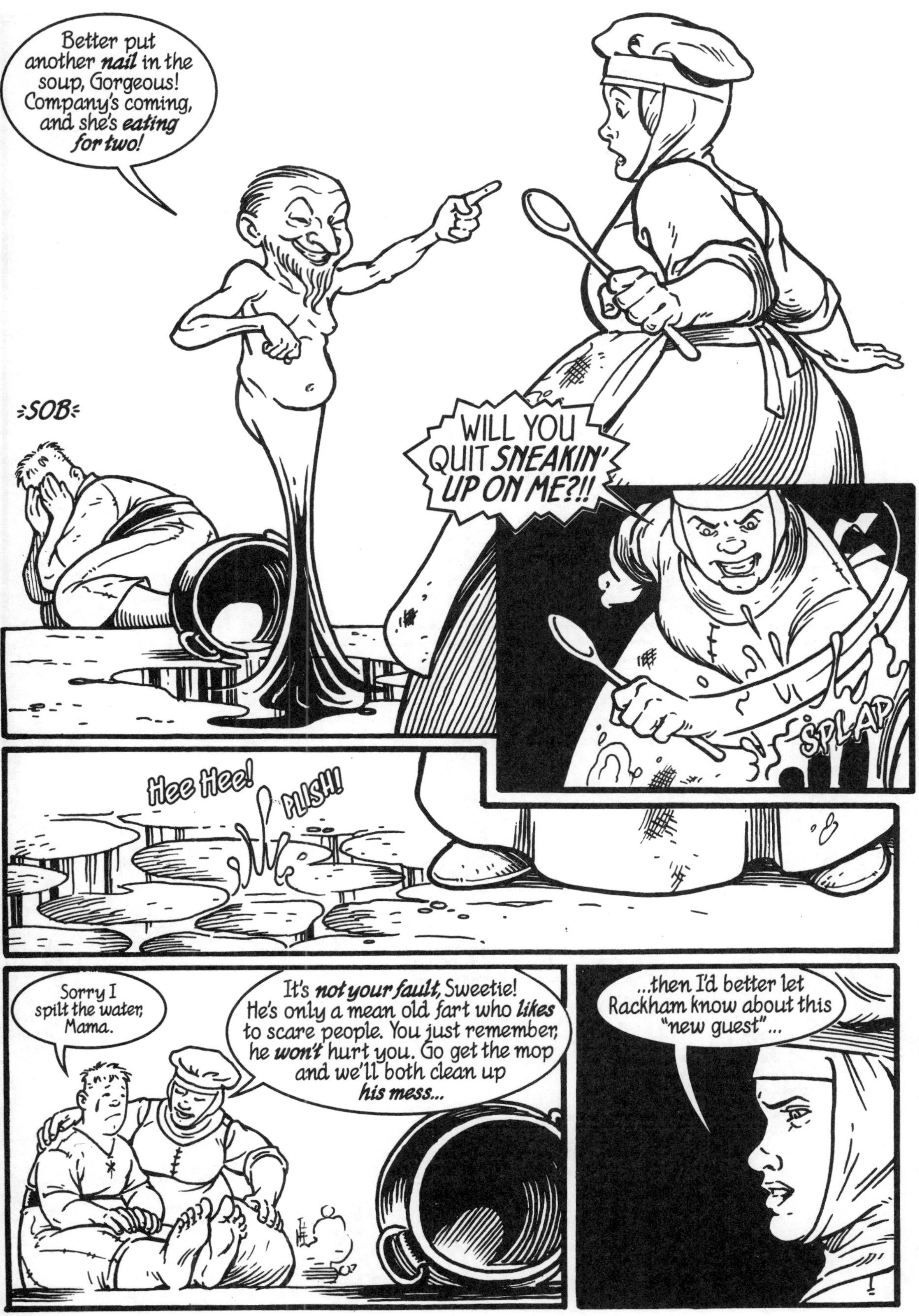

Better put another nail in the soup, Gorgeous! Company's coming, and she's eating for two!
SOB
WILL YOU QUIT SNEAKIN' UP ON ME?!!
SPLAP
Hee Hee!
PLISH!
Sorry I spilt the water, Mama.
It's not your fault, Sweetie! He's only a mean old fart who likes to scare people. You just remember, he won't hurt you. Go get the mop and we'll both clean up his mess...
...then I'd better let Rackham know about this "new guest"...

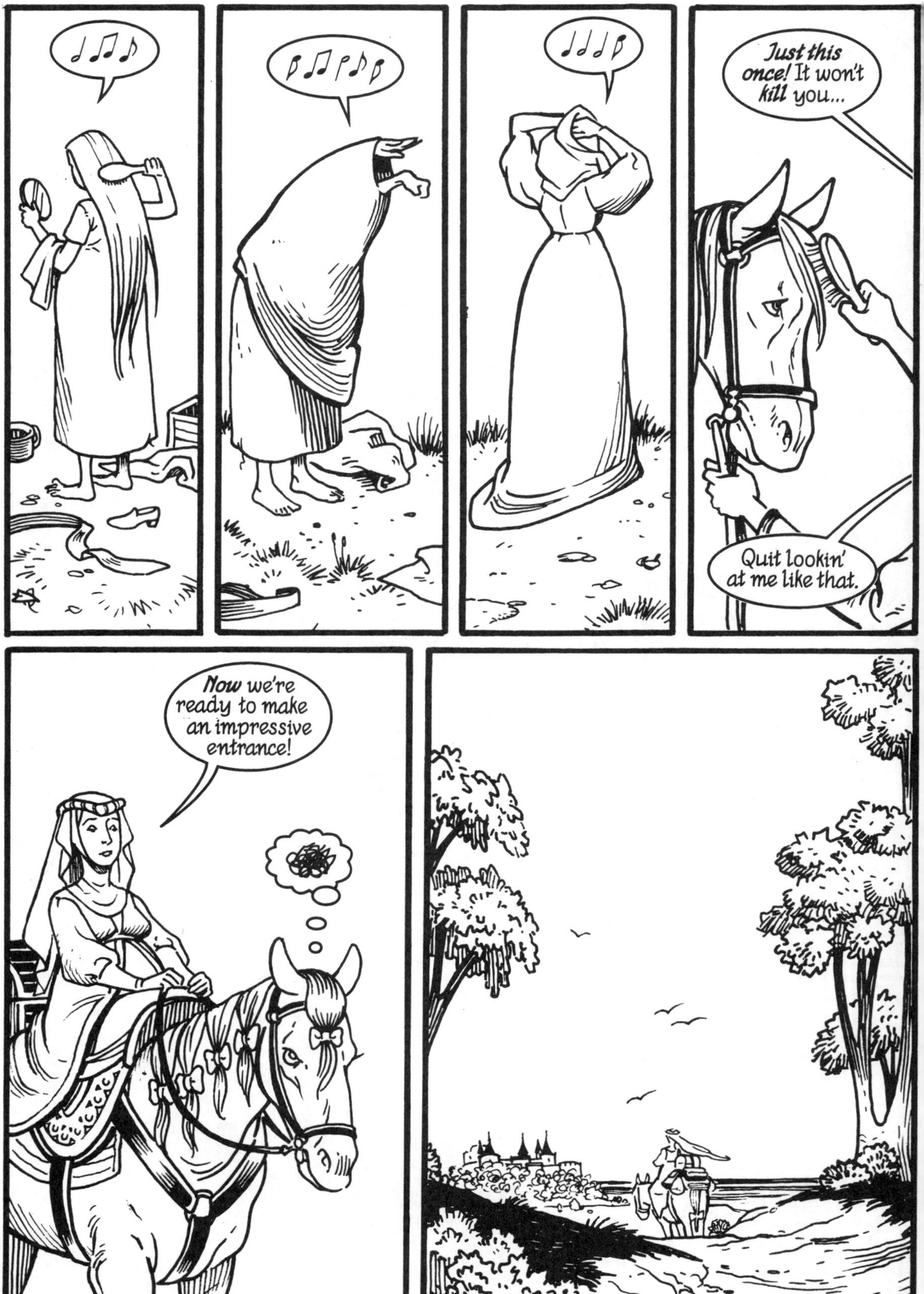
♩♫♪
♪♫♪♪♪
♩♩♩♪
Just this once! It won't kill you...
Quit lookin' at me like that.
Now we're ready to make an impressive entrance!

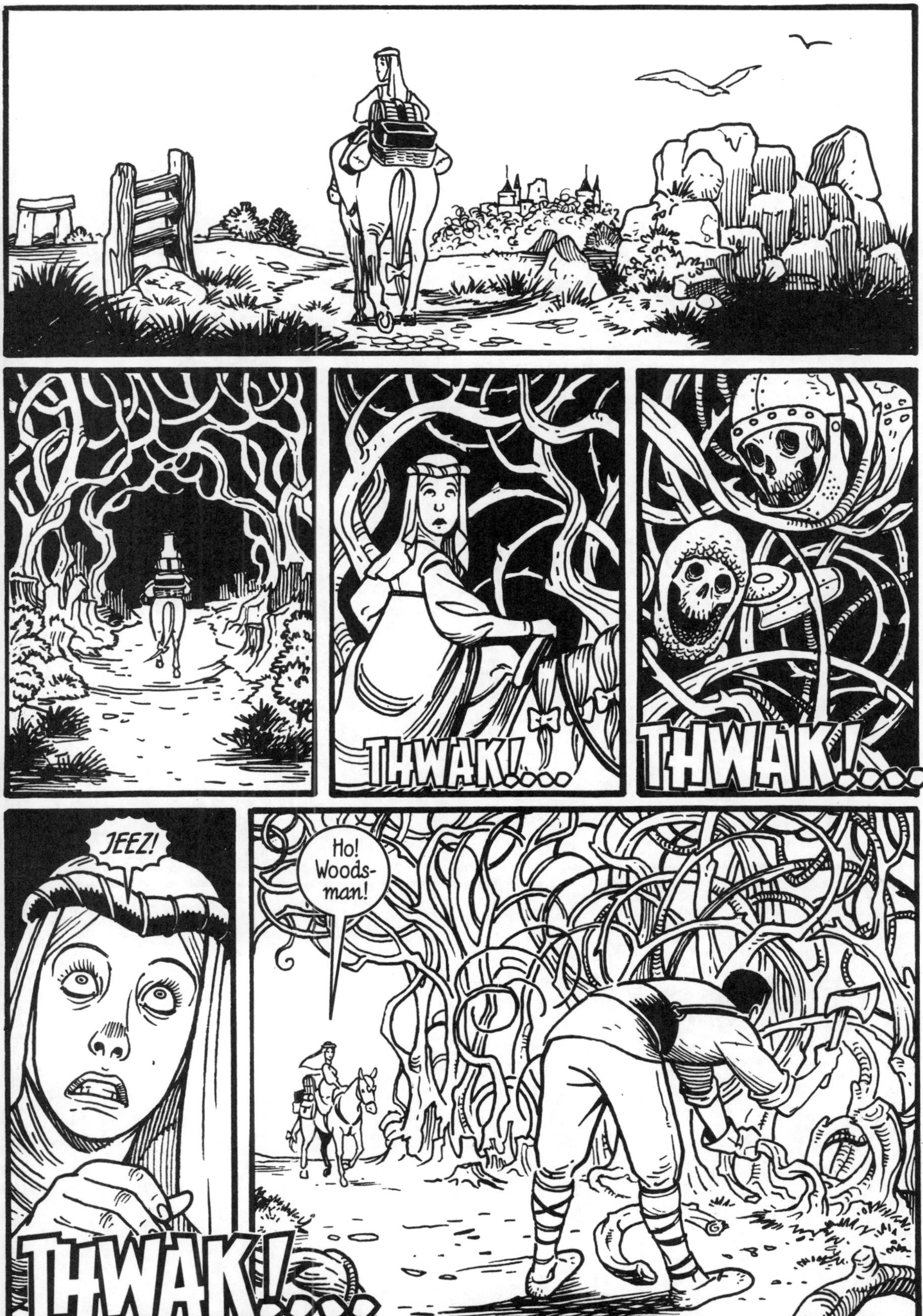
THWAK!....
THWAK!....
JEEZ!
THWAK!....
Ho! Woods-man!

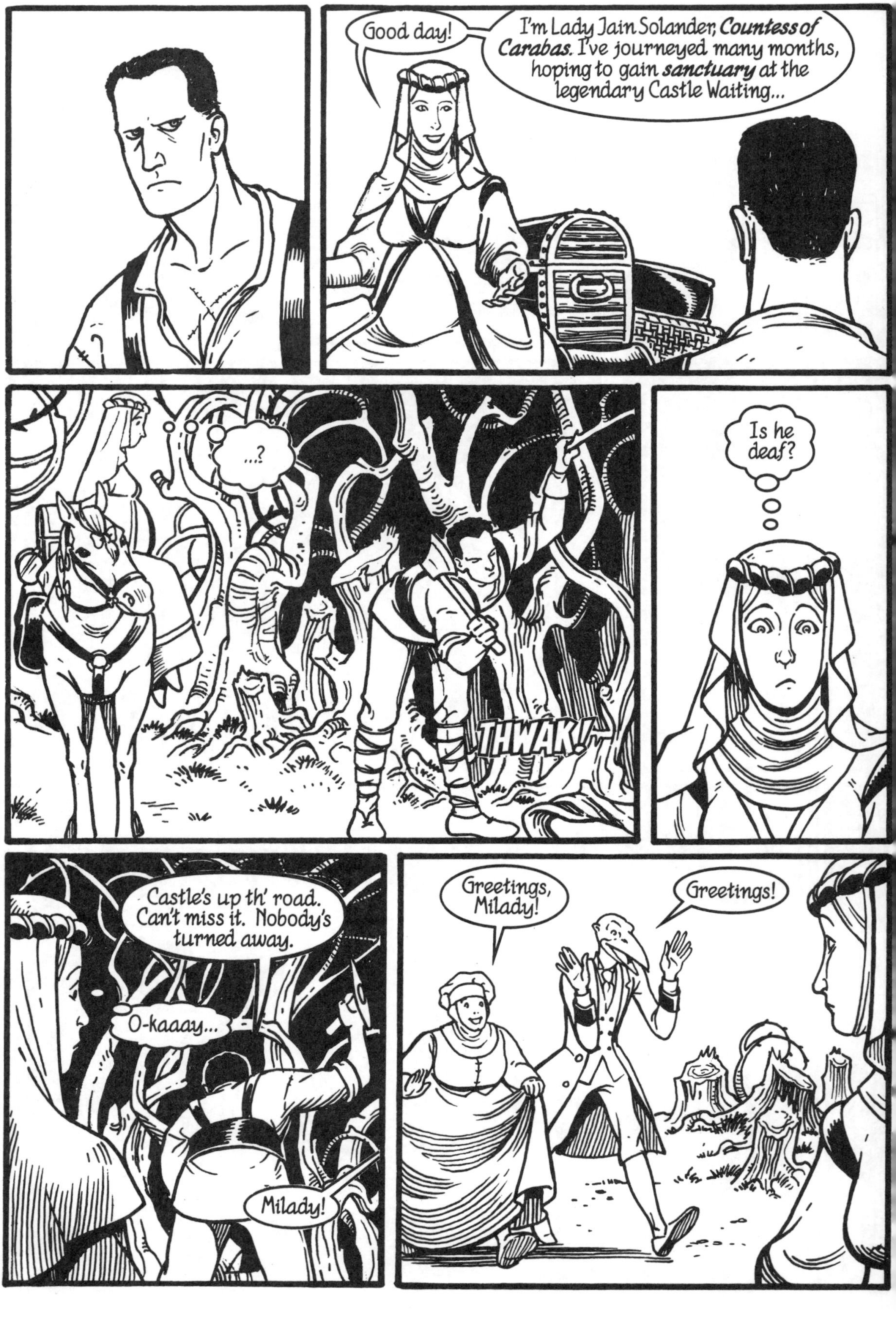
Good day!
I'm Lady Jain Solander, Countess of Carabas. I've journeyed many months, hoping to gain sanctuary at the legendary Castle Waiting...
...?
THWAK!
Is he deaf?
Castle's up th' road. Can't miss it. Nobody's turned away.
O-kaaay...
Milady!
Greetings, Milady!
Greetings!

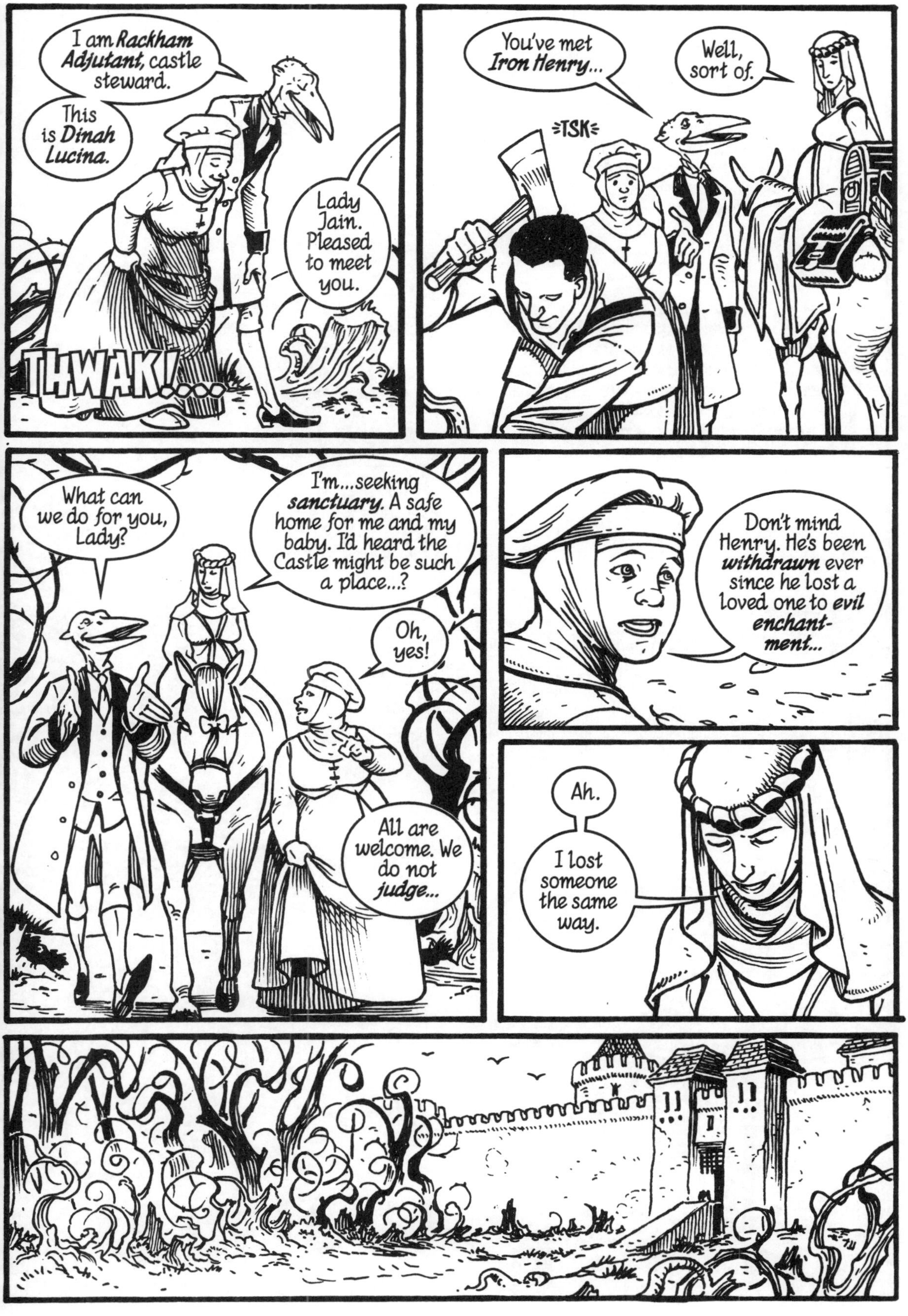
I am Rackham Adjutant, castle steward.
This is Dinah Lucina.
Lady Jain. Pleased to meet you.
THWAK!
You've met Iron Henry...
Well, sort of.
TSK
What can we do for you, Lady?
I'm...seeking sanctuary. A safe home for me and my baby. I'd heard the Castle might be such a place...?
Oh, yes!
All are welcome. We do not judge...
Don't mind Henry. He's been withdrawn ever since he lost a loved one to evil enchantment...
Ah.
I lost someone the same way.

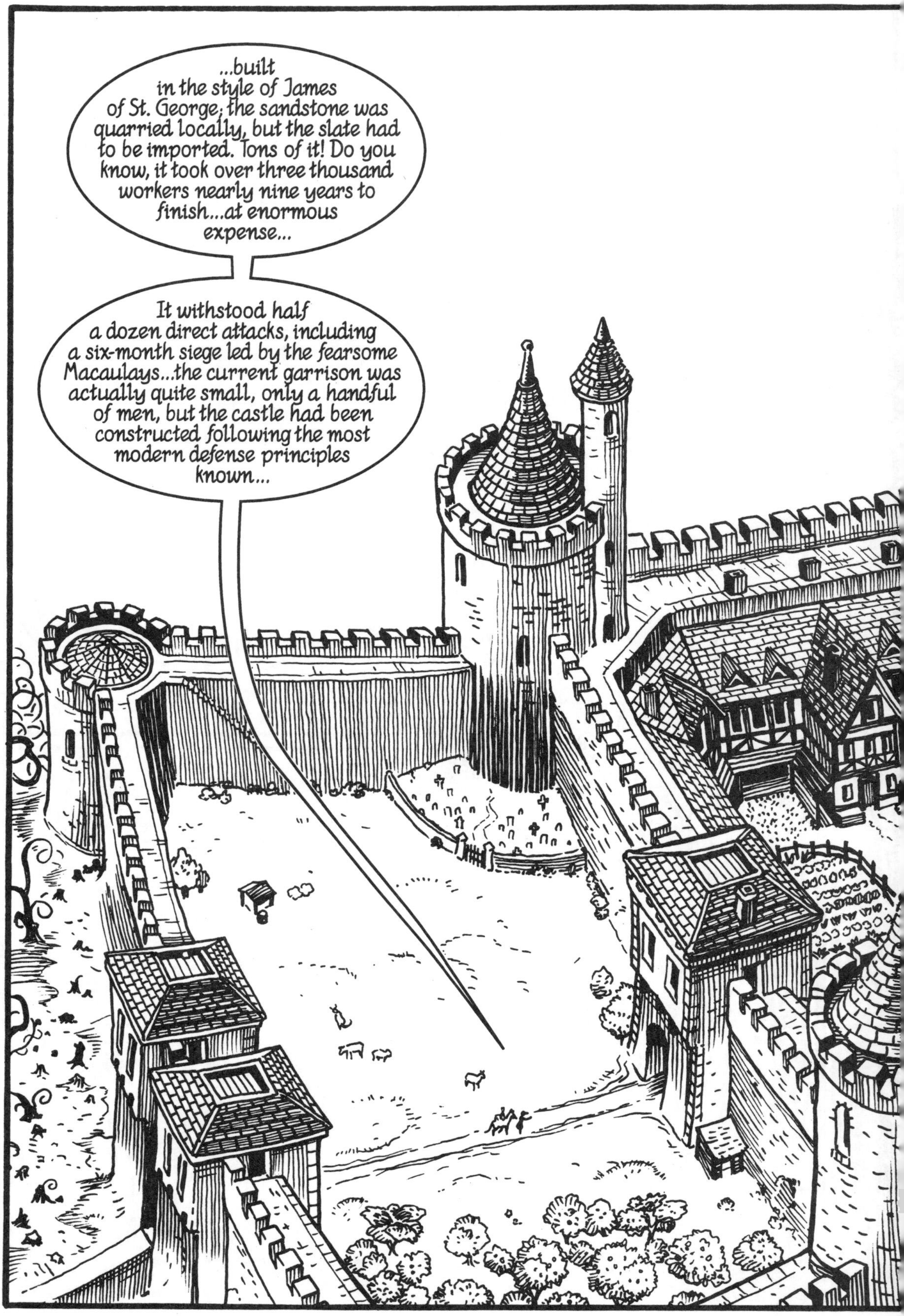
...built in the style of James of St. George; the sandstone was quarried locally, but the slate had to be imported. Tons of it! Do you know, it took over three thousand workers nearly nine years to finish...at enormous expense...
It withstood half a dozen direct attacks, including a six-month siege led by the fearsome Macaulays...the current garrison was actually quite small, only a handful of men, but the castle had been constructed following the most modern defense principles known...

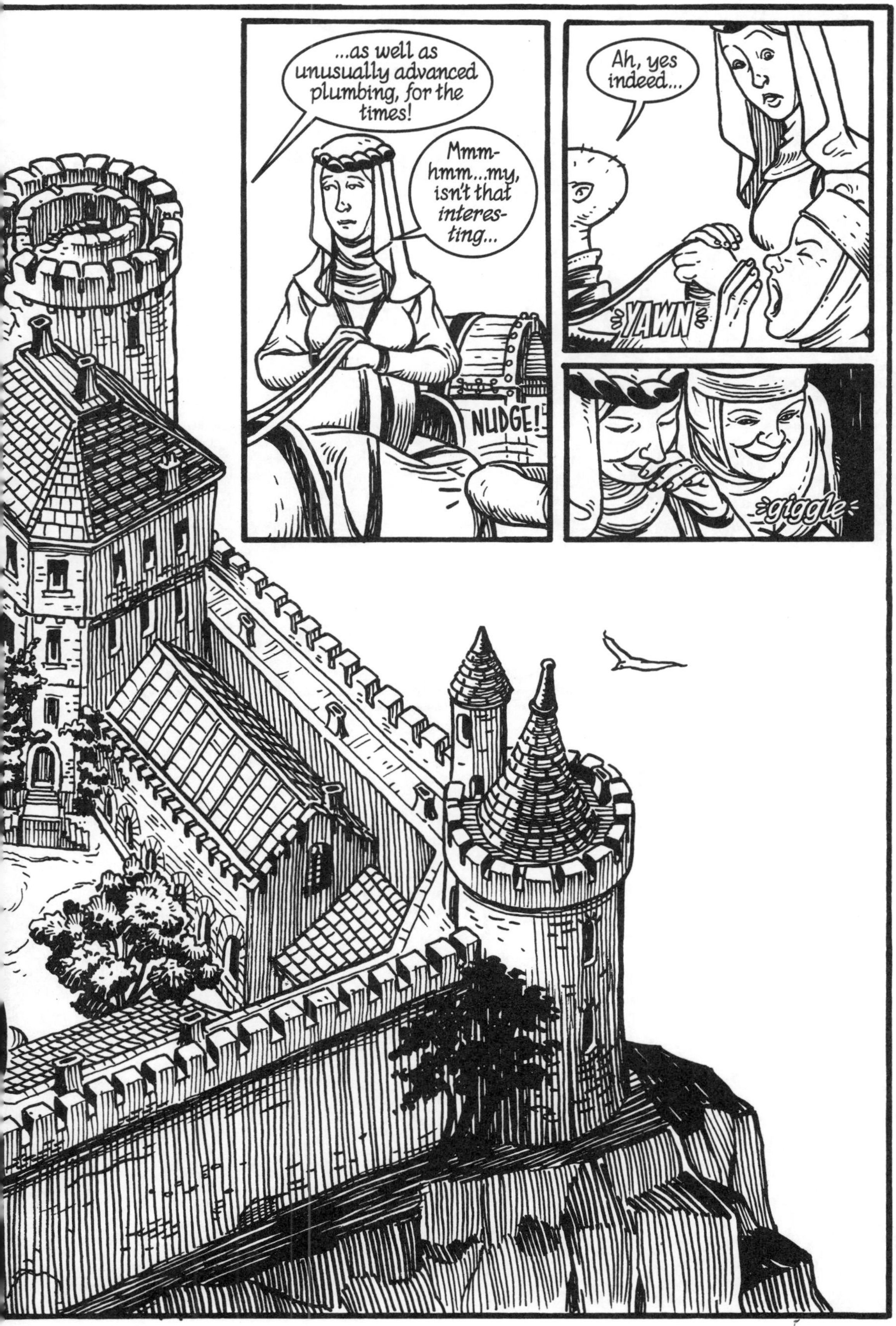
...as well as unusually advanced plumbing, for the times!
Mmm-hmm...my, isn't that interes-ting...
NUDGE!
Ah, yes indeed...
YAWN
giggle

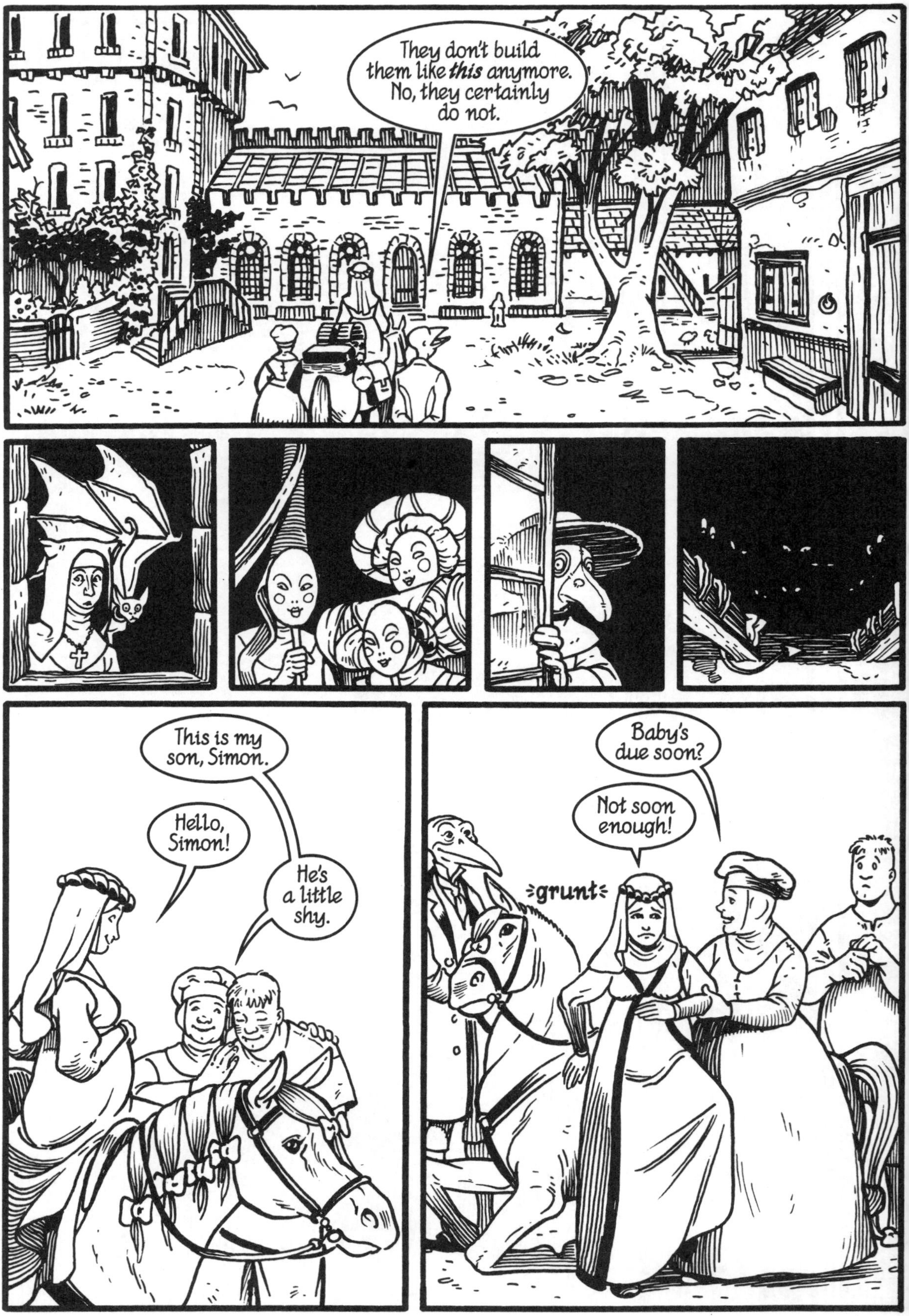
They don't build them like *this* anymore. No, they certainly do not.
This is my son, Simon.
Hello, Simon!
He's a little shy.
Baby's due soon?
Not soon enough!
grunt

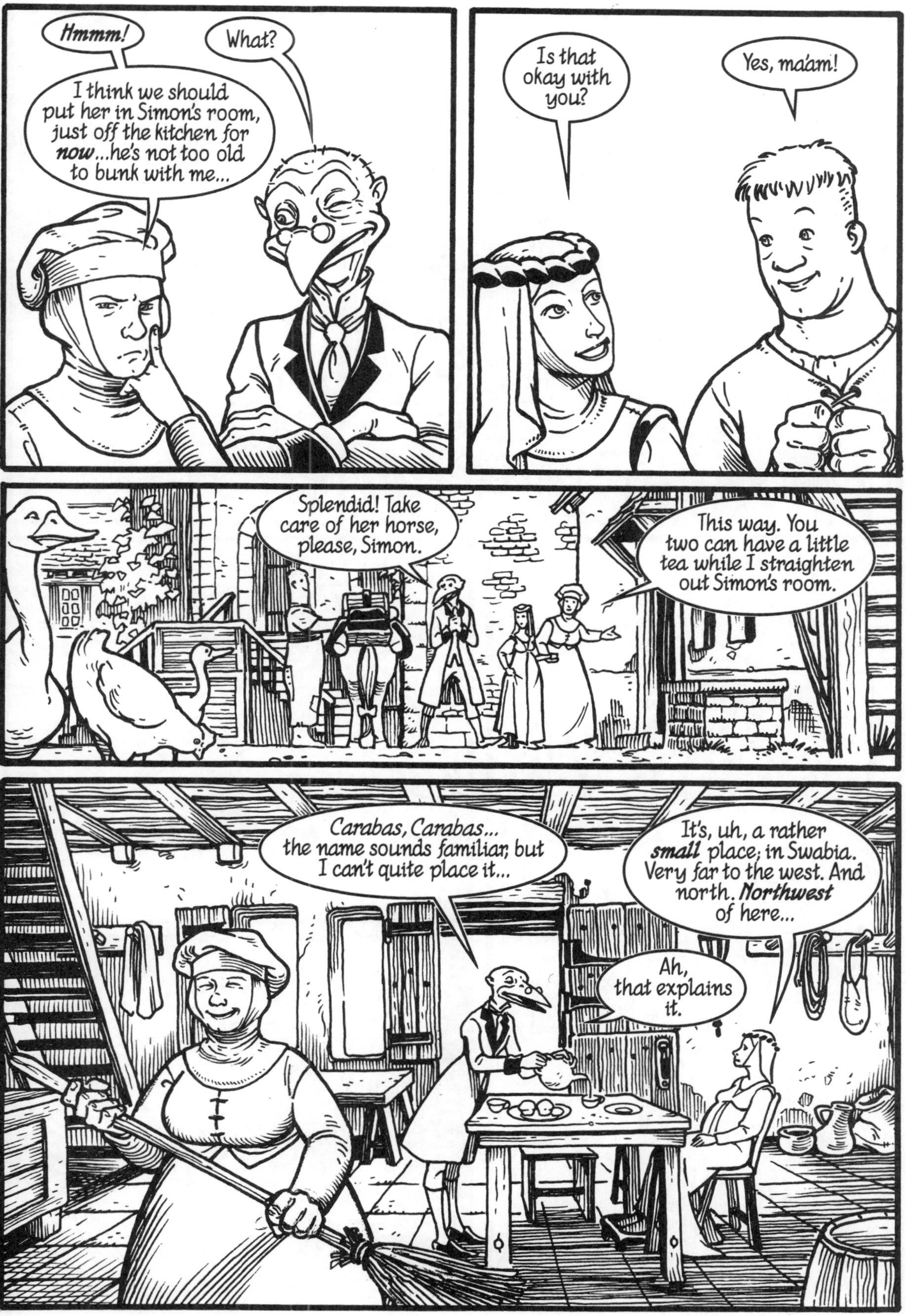
Hmmm!
I think we should put her in Simon's room, just off the kitchen for *now*...he's not too old to bunk with me...
What?
Is that okay with you?
Yes, ma'am!
Splendid! Take care of her horse, please, Simon.
This way. You two can have a little tea while I straighten out Simon's room.
Carabas, Carabas... the name sounds familiar, but I can't quite place it...
It's, uh, a rather *small* place; in Swabia. Very far to the west. And north. *Northwest* of here...
Ah, that explains it.

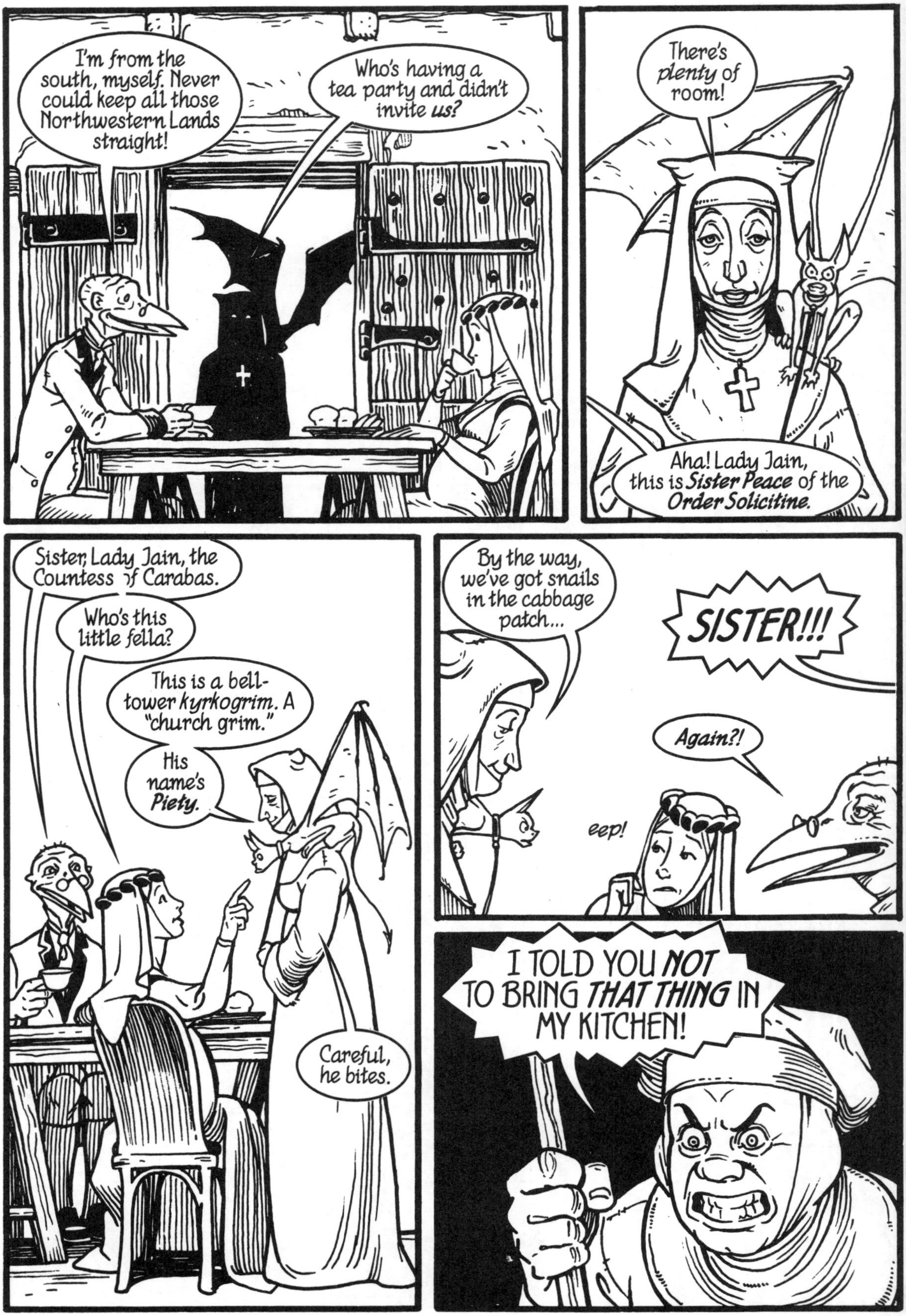
I'm from the south, myself. Never could keep all those Northwestern Lands straight!
Who's having a tea party and didn't invite *us?*
There's *plenty* of room!
Aha! Lady Jain, this is ***Sister Peace*** of the ***Order Solicitine.***
Sister, Lady Jain, the Countess of Carabas.
Who's this little fella?
This is a bell-tower *kyrkogrim*. A "church grim."
His name's ***Piety.***
Careful, he bites.
By the way, we've got snails in the cabbage patch...
SISTER!!!
Again?!
eep!
I TOLD YOU *NOT* TO BRING *THAT THING* IN MY KITCHEN!

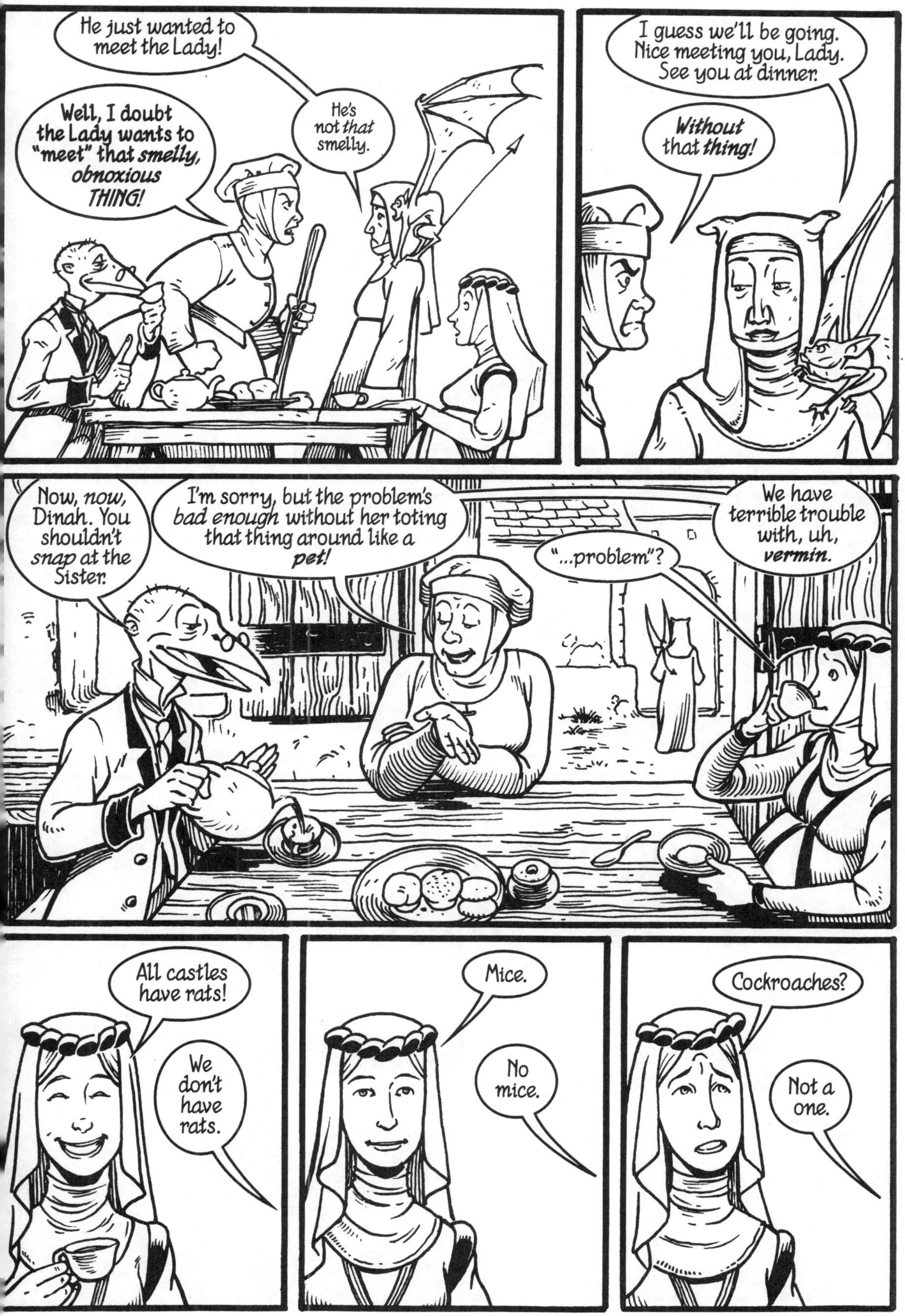
He just wanted to meet the Lady!
Well, I doubt the Lady wants to "meet" that smelly, obnoxious THING!
He's not that smelly.
I guess we'll be going. Nice meeting you, Lady. See you at dinner.
Without that thing!
Now, now, Dinah. You shouldn't snap at the Sister.
I'm sorry, but the problem's bad enough without her toting that thing around like a pet!
We have terrible trouble with, uh, vermin.
"...problem"?
All castles have rats!
We don't have rats.
Mice.
No mice.
Cockroaches?
Not a one.

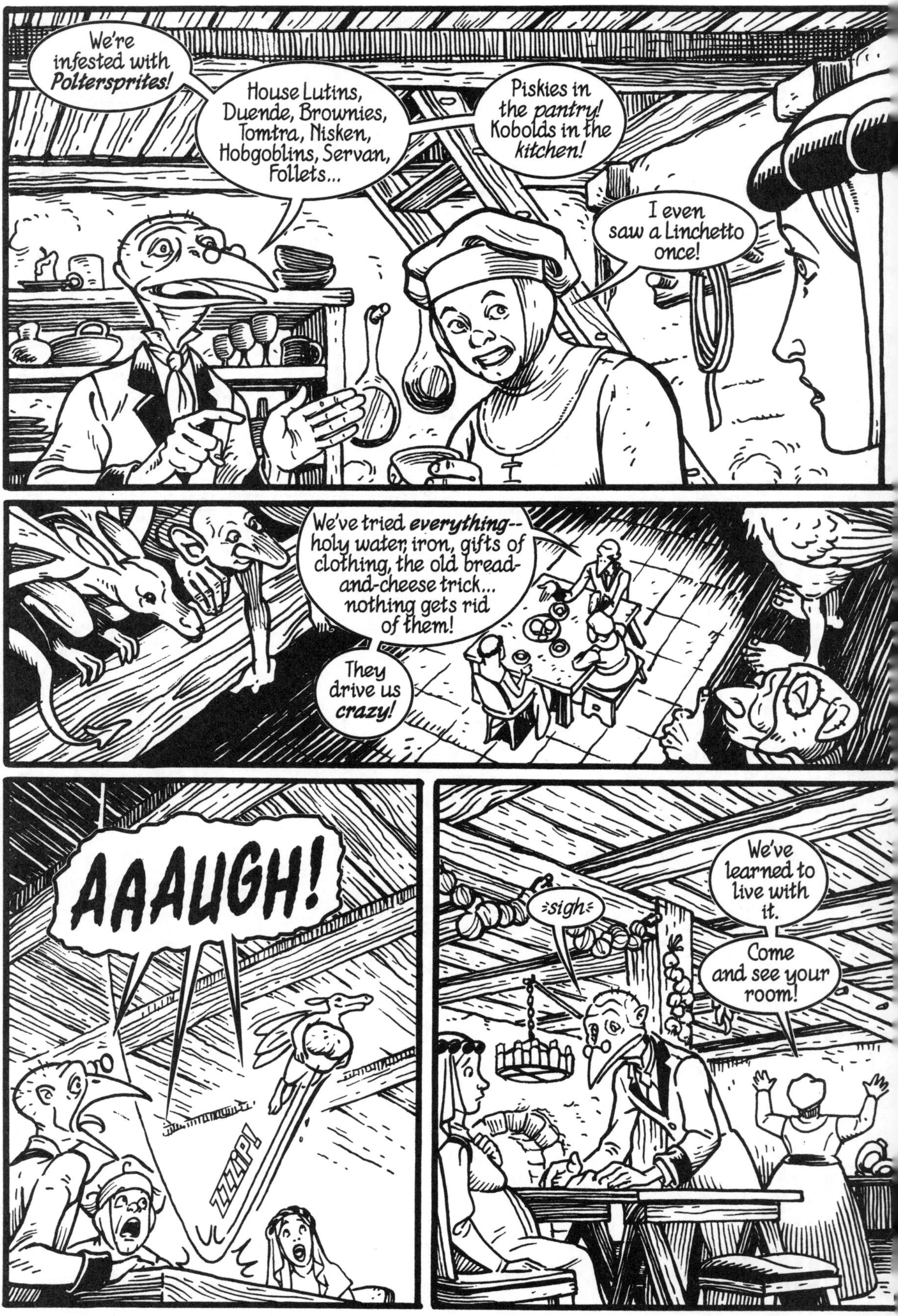
We're infested with *Poltersprites!*
House Lutins, Duende, Brownies, Tomtra, Nisken, Hobgoblins, Servan, Follets...
Piskies in the *pantry!* Kobolds in the *kitchen!*
I even saw a Linchetto once!
We've tried ***everything***--holy water, iron, gifts of clothing, the old bread-and-cheese trick... nothing gets rid of them!
They drive us ***crazy!***
AAAUGH!
ZZZIP!
sigh
We've learned to live with it.
Come and see your room!

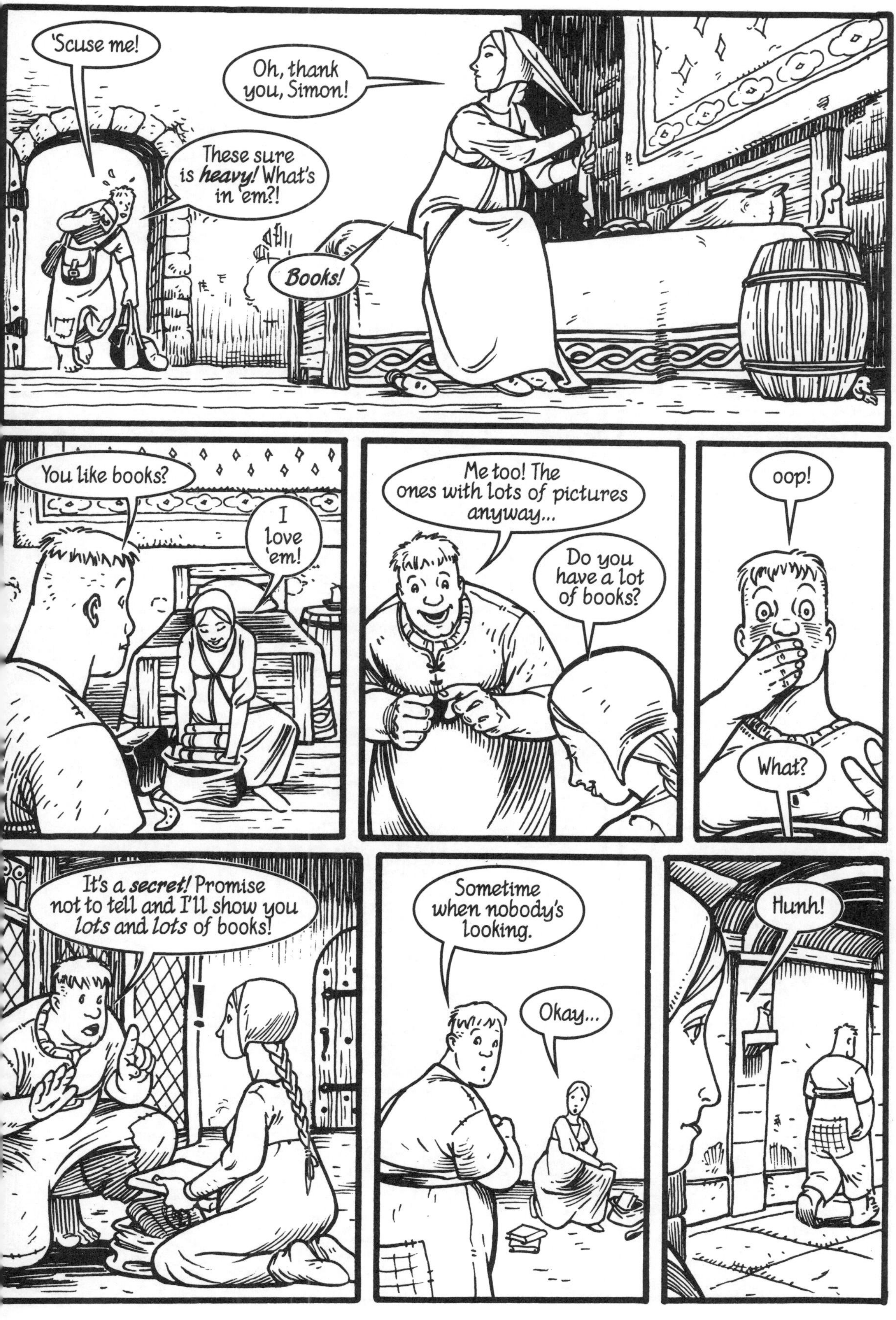
'Scuse me!
Oh, thank you, Simon!
These sure is *heavy!* What's in 'em?!
Books!
You like books?
I love 'em!
Me too! The ones with lots of pictures anyway...
Do you have a lot of books?
oop!
What?
It's a *secret!* Promise not to tell and I'll show you *lots and lots* of books!
Sometime when nobody's looking.
Okay...
Hunh!

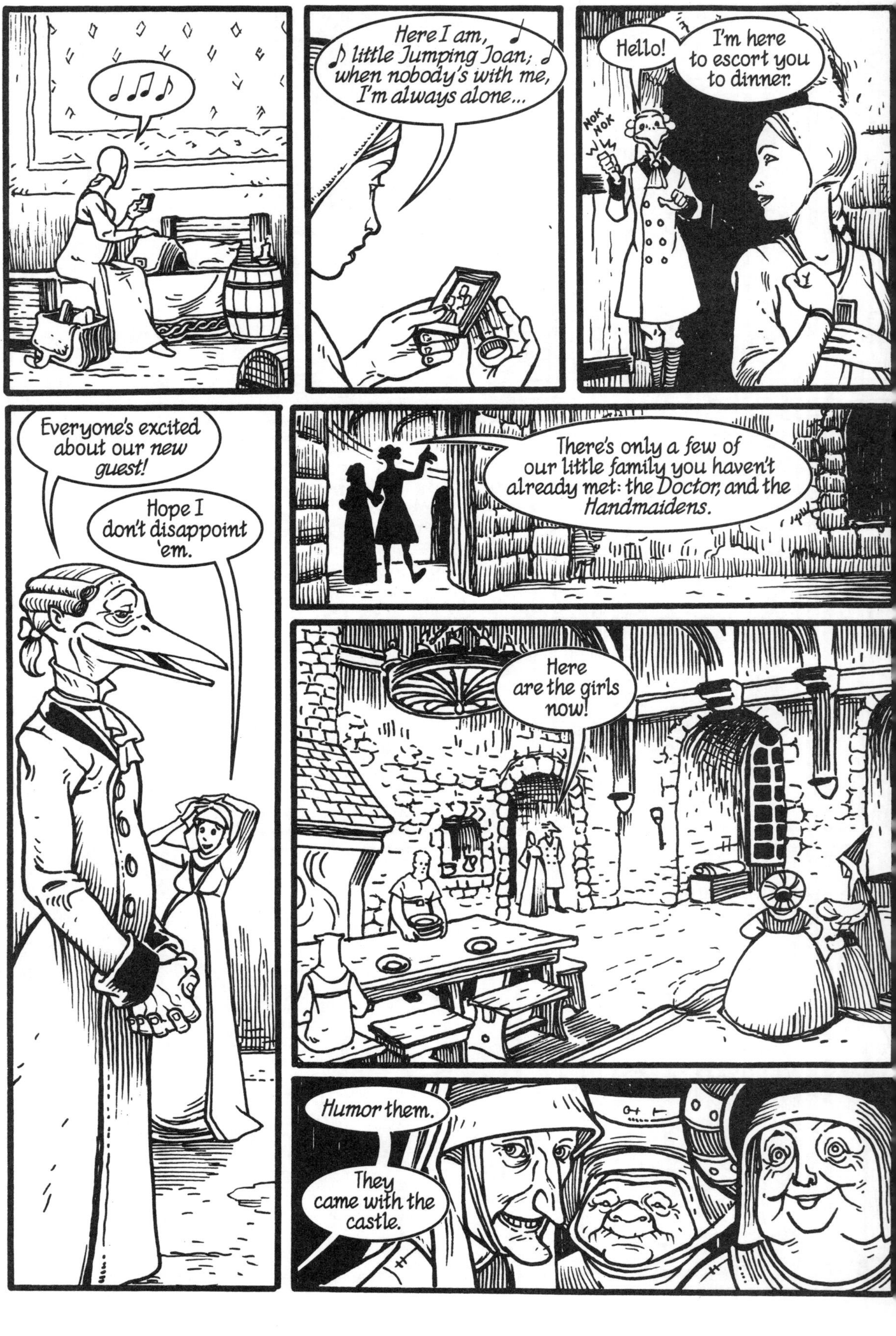
♩♫♪
Here I am, ♩ ♪ little Jumping Joan; ♩ when nobody's with me, I'm always alone...
Hello!
I'm here to escort you to dinner.
NOK NOK
Everyone's excited about our *new guest!*
Hope I don't disappoint 'em.
There's only a few of our little family you haven't already met: the *Doctor,* and the *Handmaidens.*
Here are the girls now!
Humor them.
They came with the castle.

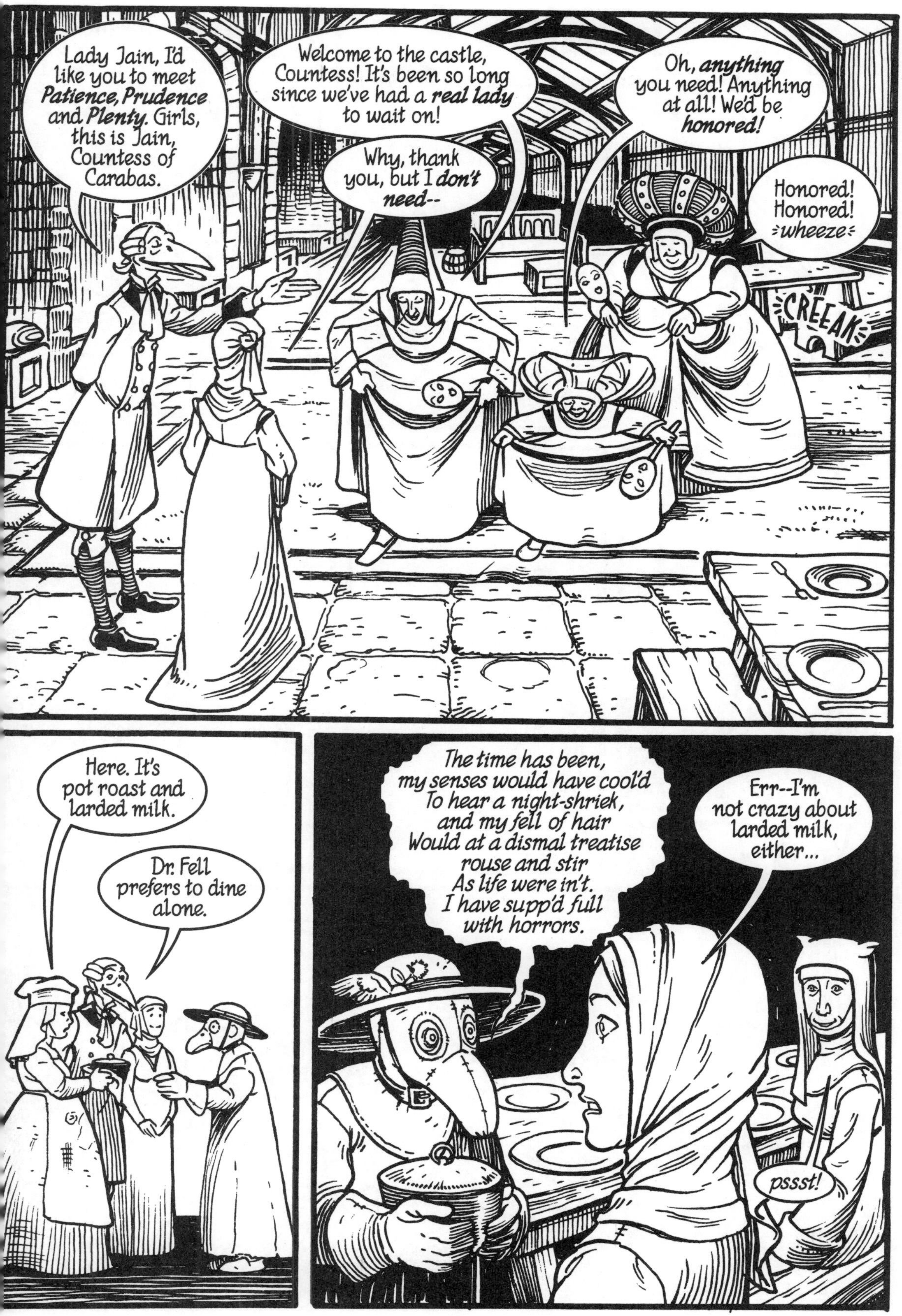
Lady Jain, I'd like you to meet **Patience, Prudence** and **Plenty**. Girls, this is Jain, Countess of Carabas.
Welcome to the castle, Countess! It's been so long since we've had a **real lady** to wait on!
Why, thank you, but I ***don't need***--
Oh, ***anything*** you need! Anything at all! We'd be ***honored!***
Honored! Honored! *wheeze*
CREEAK
Here. It's pot roast and larded milk.
Dr. Fell prefers to dine alone.
The time has been, my senses would have cool'd To hear a night-shriek, and my fell of hair Would at a dismal treatise rouse and stir As life were in't. I have supp'd full with horrors.
Err--I'm not crazy about larded milk, either...
pssst!

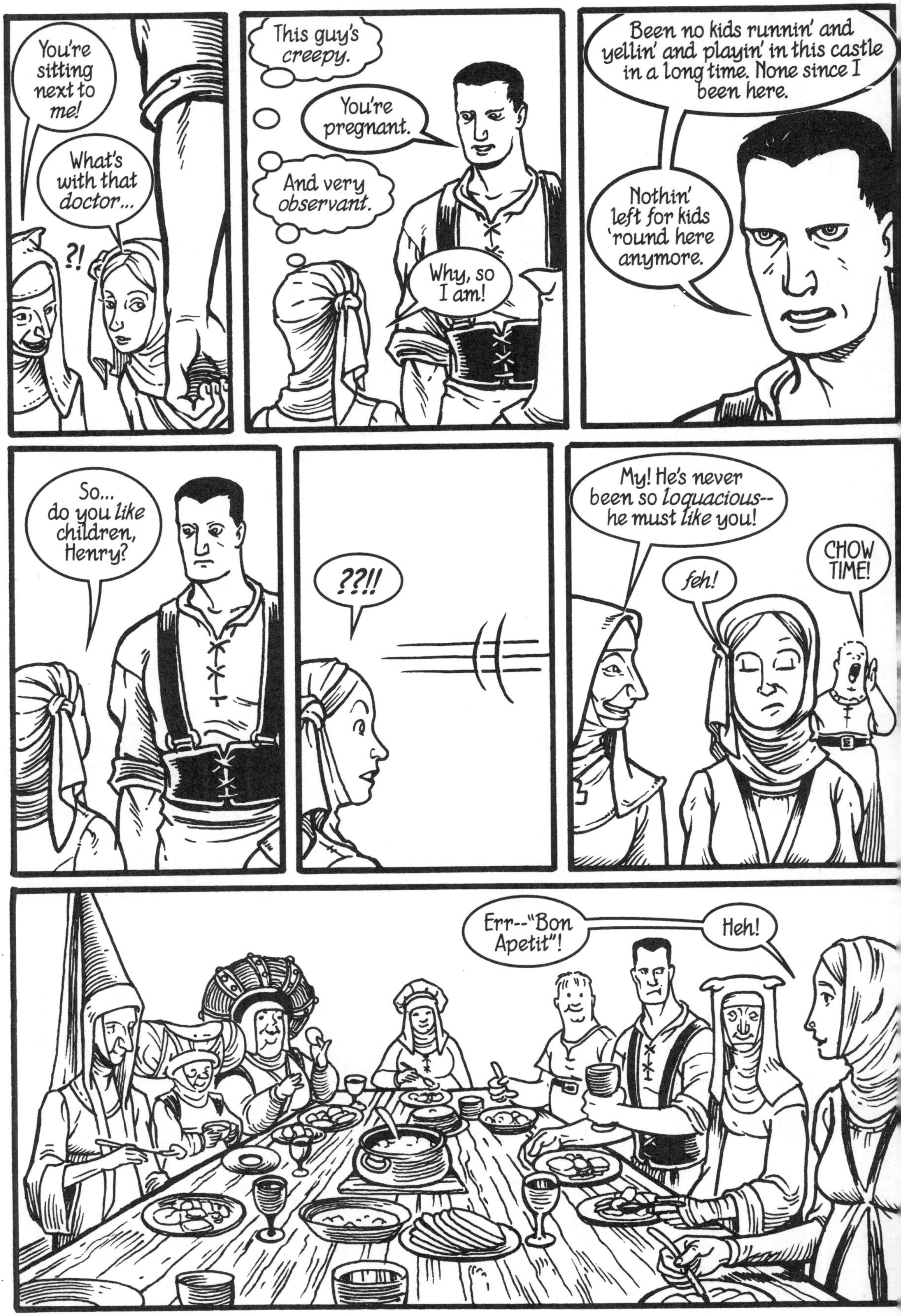
You're sitting next to *me!*
What's with that doctor...
?!
This guy's *creepy.*
You're pregnant.
And very *observant.*
Why, so I am!
Been no kids runnin' and yellin' and playin' in this castle in a long time. None since I been here.
Nothin' left for kids 'round here anymore.
So... do you *like* children, Henry?
??!!
My! He's never been so *loquacious*-- he must *like* you!
feh!
CHOW TIME!
Err--"Bon Apetit"!
Heh!

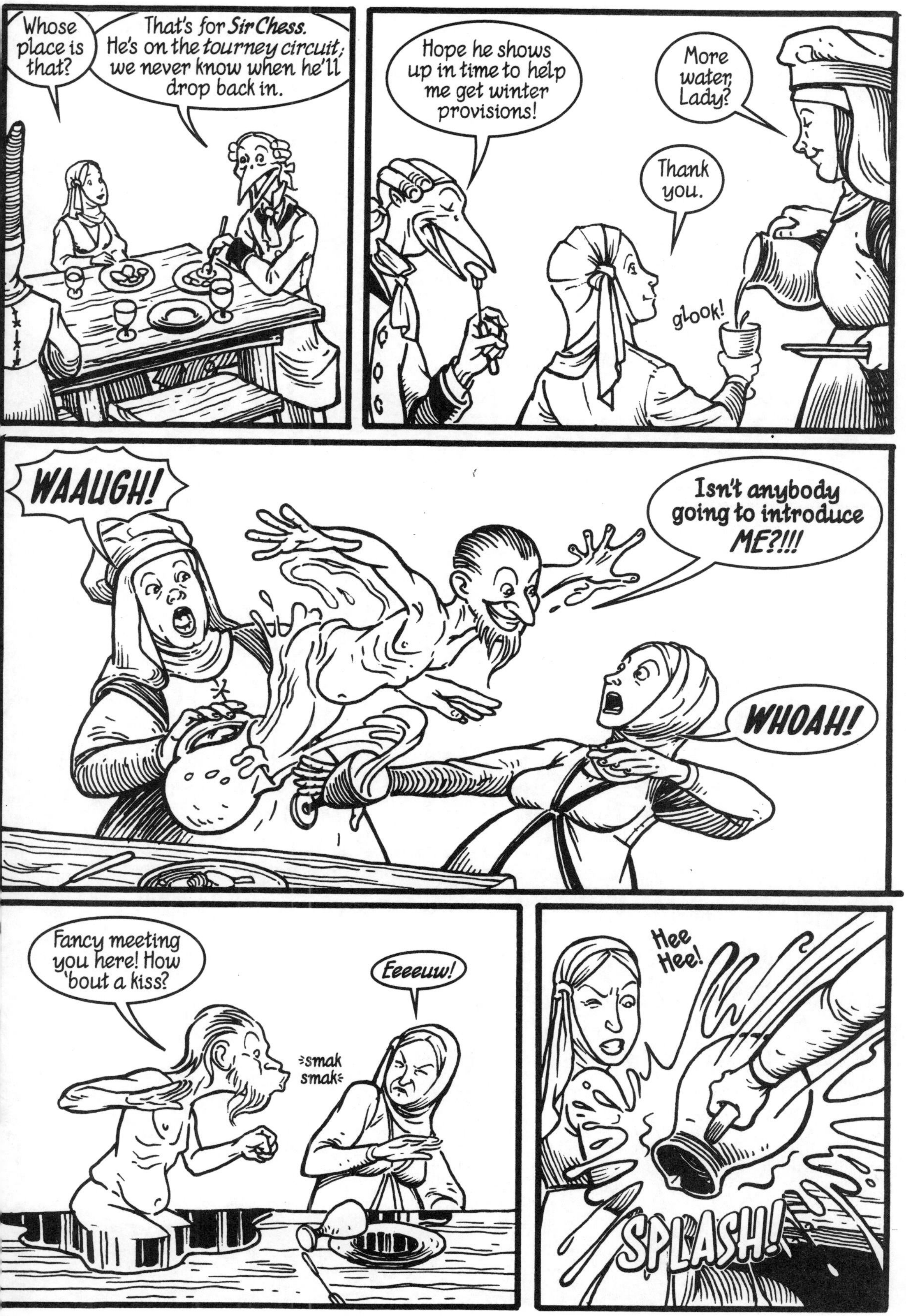

Whose place is that?
That's for *Sir Chess.* He's on the *tourney circuit;* we never know when he'll drop back in.
Hope he shows up in time to help me get winter provisions!
More water, Lady?
Thank you.
glook!
WAAUGH!
Isn't anybody going to introduce *ME?!!!*
WHOAH!
Fancy meeting you here! How 'bout a kiss?
smak smak
Eeeeuw!
Hee Hee!
SPLASH!

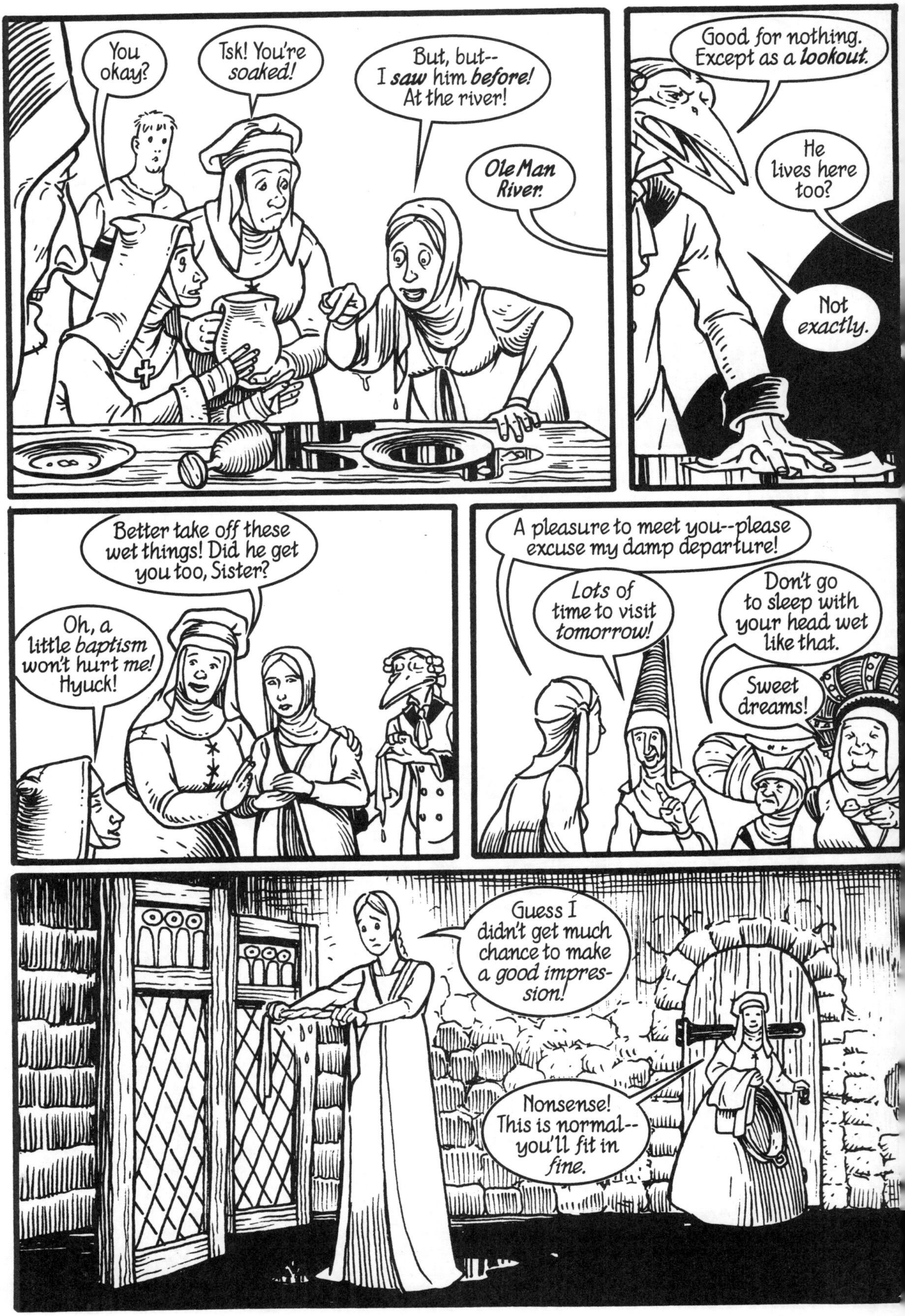
You okay?
Tsk! You're soaked!
But, but-- I saw him before! At the river!
Ole Man River.
Good for nothing. Except as a lookout.
He lives here too?
Not exactly.
Better take off these wet things! Did he get you too, Sister?
Oh, a little baptism won't hurt me! Hyuck!
A pleasure to meet you--please excuse my damp departure!
Lots of time to visit tomorrow!
Don't go to sleep with your head wet like that.
Sweet dreams!
Guess I didn't get much chance to make a good impres-sion!
Nonsense! This is normal-- you'll fit in fine.

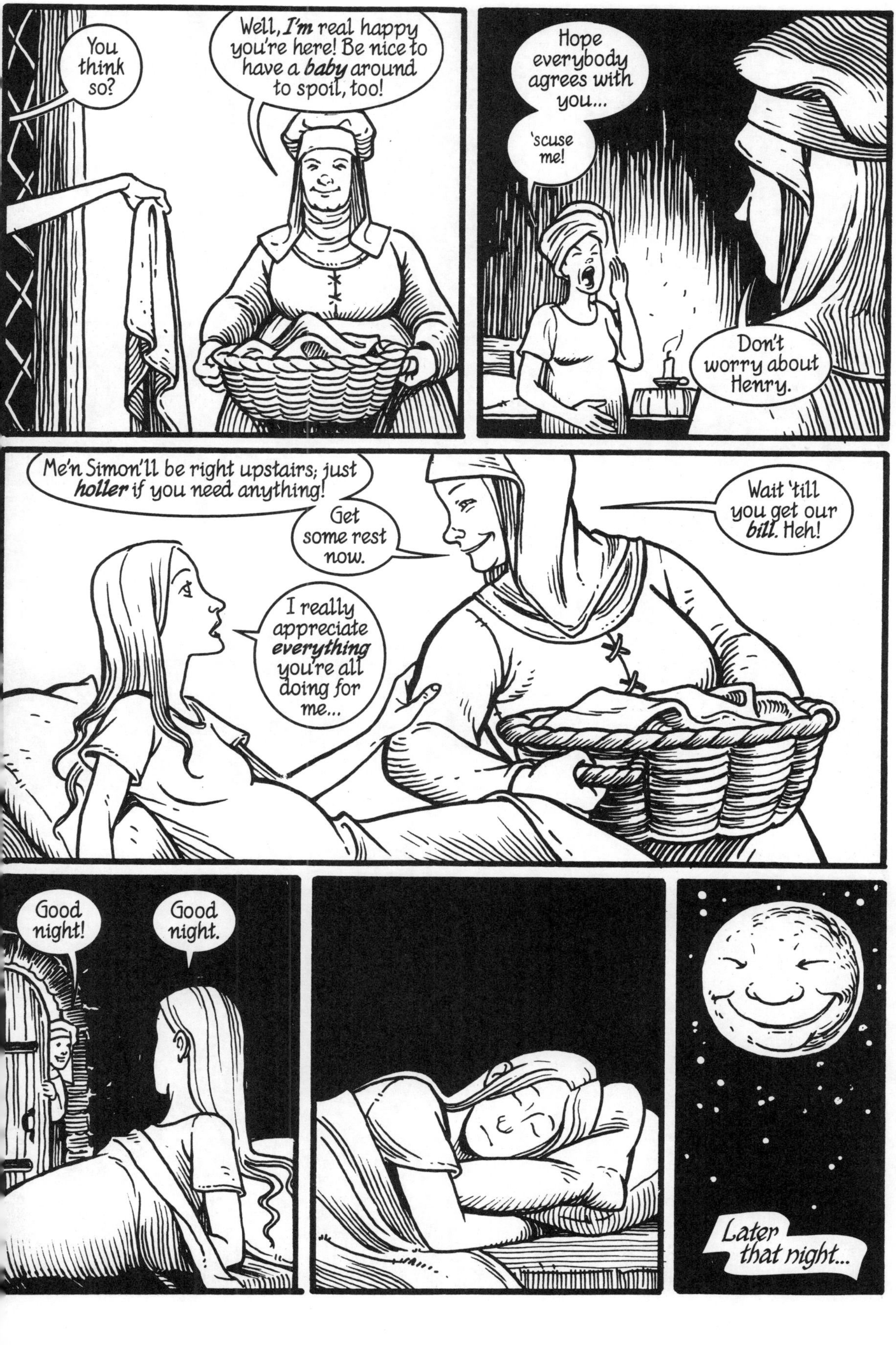

You think so?
Well, *I'm* real happy you're here! Be nice to have a ***baby*** around to spoil, too!
Hope everybody agrees with you...
'scuse me!
Don't worry about Henry.
Me'n Simon'll be right upstairs; just ***holler*** if you need anything!
Get some rest now.
Wait 'till you get our ***bill***. Heh!
I really appreciate ***everything*** you're all doing for me...
Good night!
Good night.
Later that night...

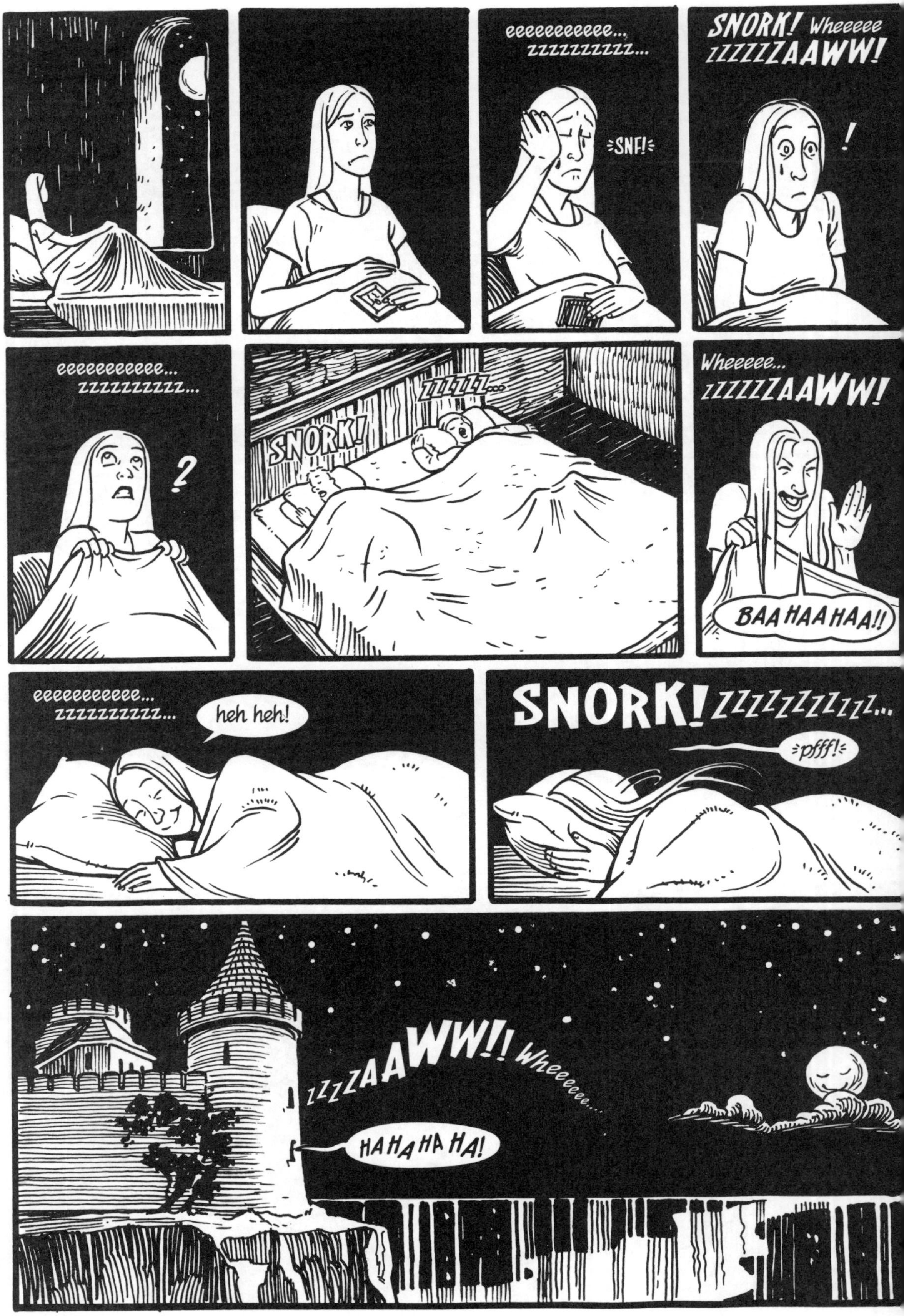

eeeeeeeeeee...,
zzzzzzzzzz...
SNF!
SNORK! Wheeeee
zzzzzZAAWW!
!
eeeeeeeeeee...
zzzzzzzzzz...
?
zzzzzz...
SNORK!
Wheeeee...
zzzzzZAAWW!
BAAHAAHAA!!
eeeeeeeeeee...
zzzzzzzzzz...
heh heh!
SNORK! zzzzzzzzzzz...
pfff!
zzzzAAWW!! wheeeeee...
HAHAHAHA!

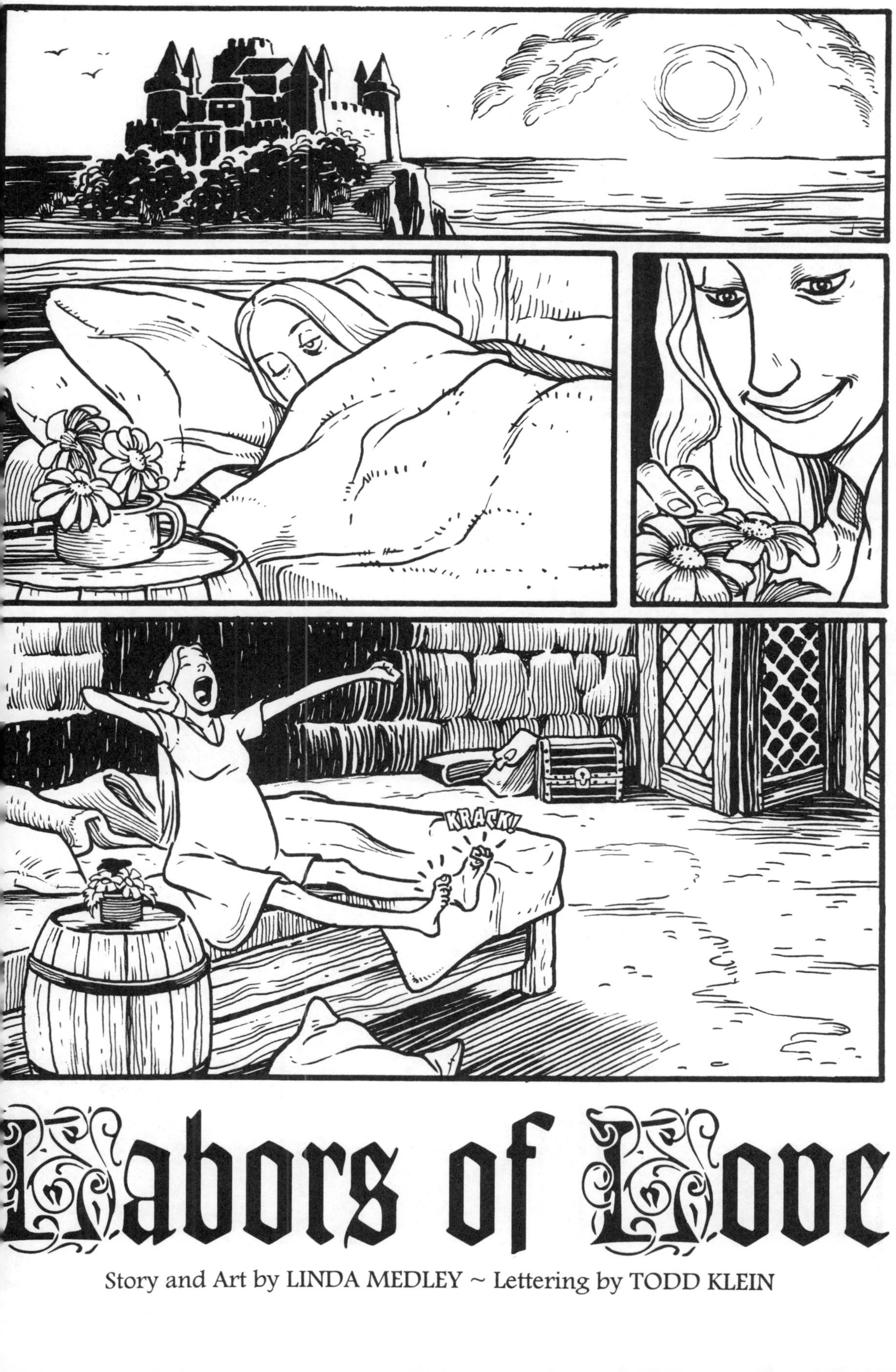
KRACK!

Labors of Love

Story and Art by LINDA MEDLEY ~ Lettering by TODD KLEIN

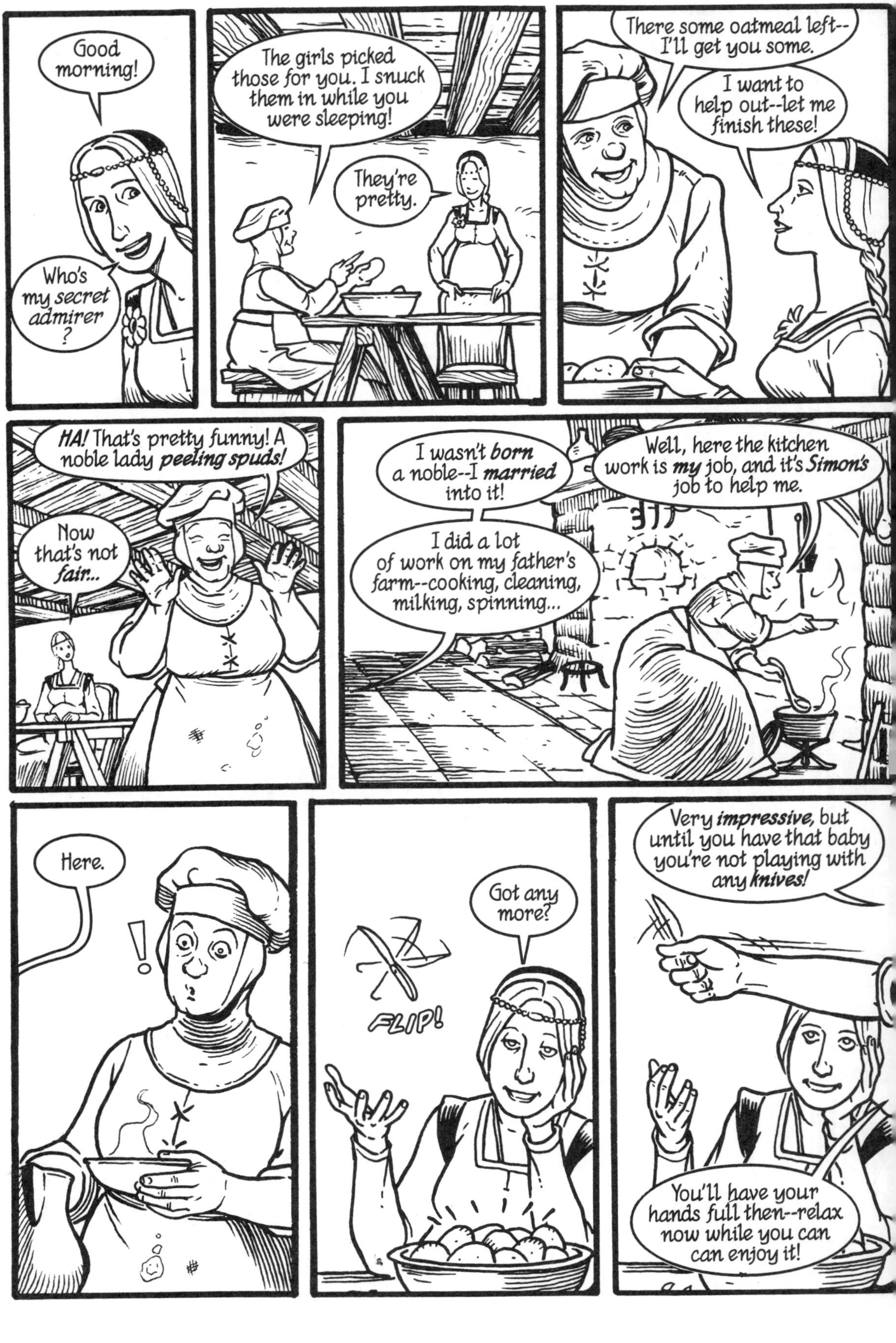
Good morning!
Who's my *secret* admirer?
The girls picked those for you. I snuck them in while you were sleeping!
They're pretty.
There some oatmeal left--I'll get you some.
I want to help out--let me finish these!
HA! That's pretty funny! A noble lady ***peeling spuds!***
Now that's not ***fair...***
I wasn't ***born*** a noble--I ***married*** into it!
I did a lot of work on my father's farm--cooking, cleaning, milking, spinning...
Well, here the kitchen work is ***my*** job, and it's ***Simon's*** job to help me.
Here.
!
FLIP!
Got any more?
Very ***impressive***, but until you have that baby you're not playing with any ***knives!***
You'll have your hands full then--relax now while you can can enjoy it!

Rackham will eventually find *something* for you to do, but I doubt it'll be *peeling vegetables.*

Everyone pitches in and helps with the work. Well, except Dr. Fell--he keeps to *himself...*

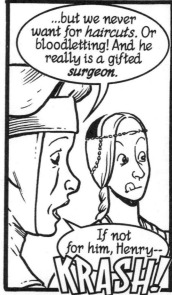

...but we never want for *haircuts.* Or *bloodletting!* And he really is a gifted *surgeon.*

If not for him, Henry--

KRASH!

#@$%!!

*$@+!! #&-%!!

Shoo!

Excuuuse *me!*

Go get some *fresh* air!

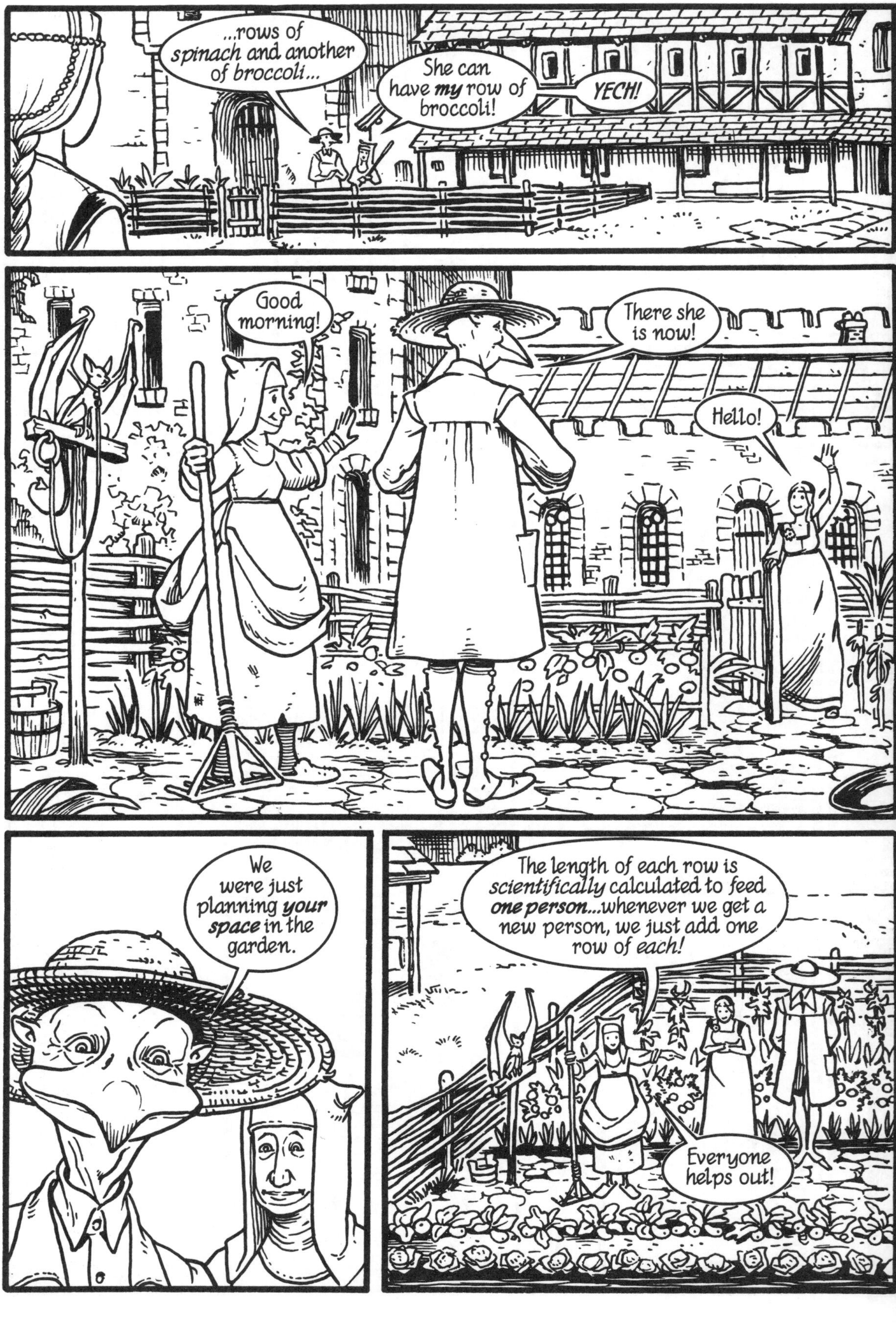
...rows of *spinach* and another of *broccoli*...
She can have ***my*** row of broccoli!
YECH!
Good morning!
There she is now!
Hello!
We were just planning ***your space*** in the garden.
The length of each row is *scientifically* calculated to feed ***one person***...whenever we get a new person, we just add one row of *each!*
Everyone helps out!

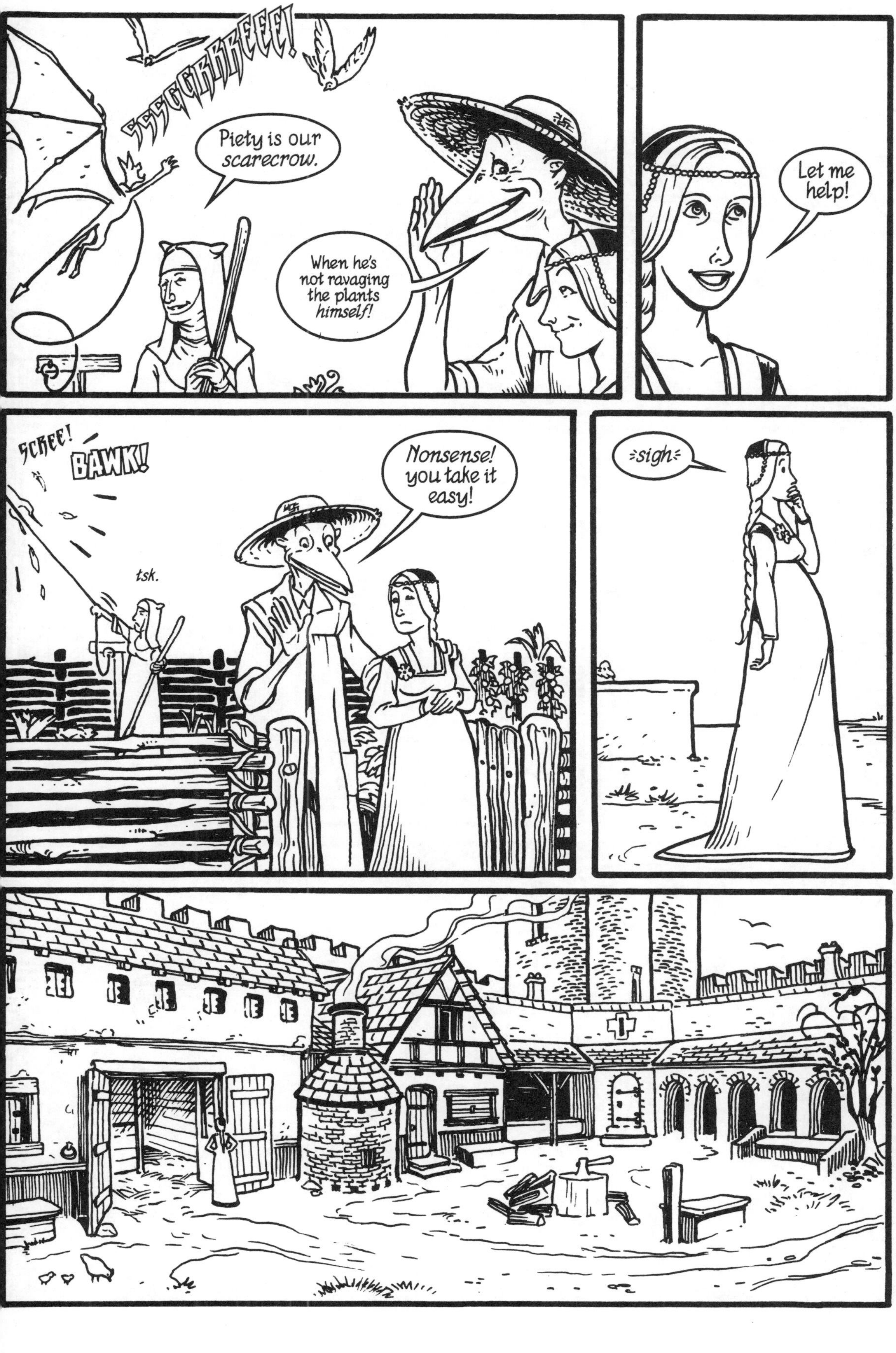
SSSCRRREEE!
Piety is our scarecrow.
When he's not ravaging the plants himself!
Let me help!
SCREE!
BAWK!
tsk.
Nonsense! you take it easy!
sigh

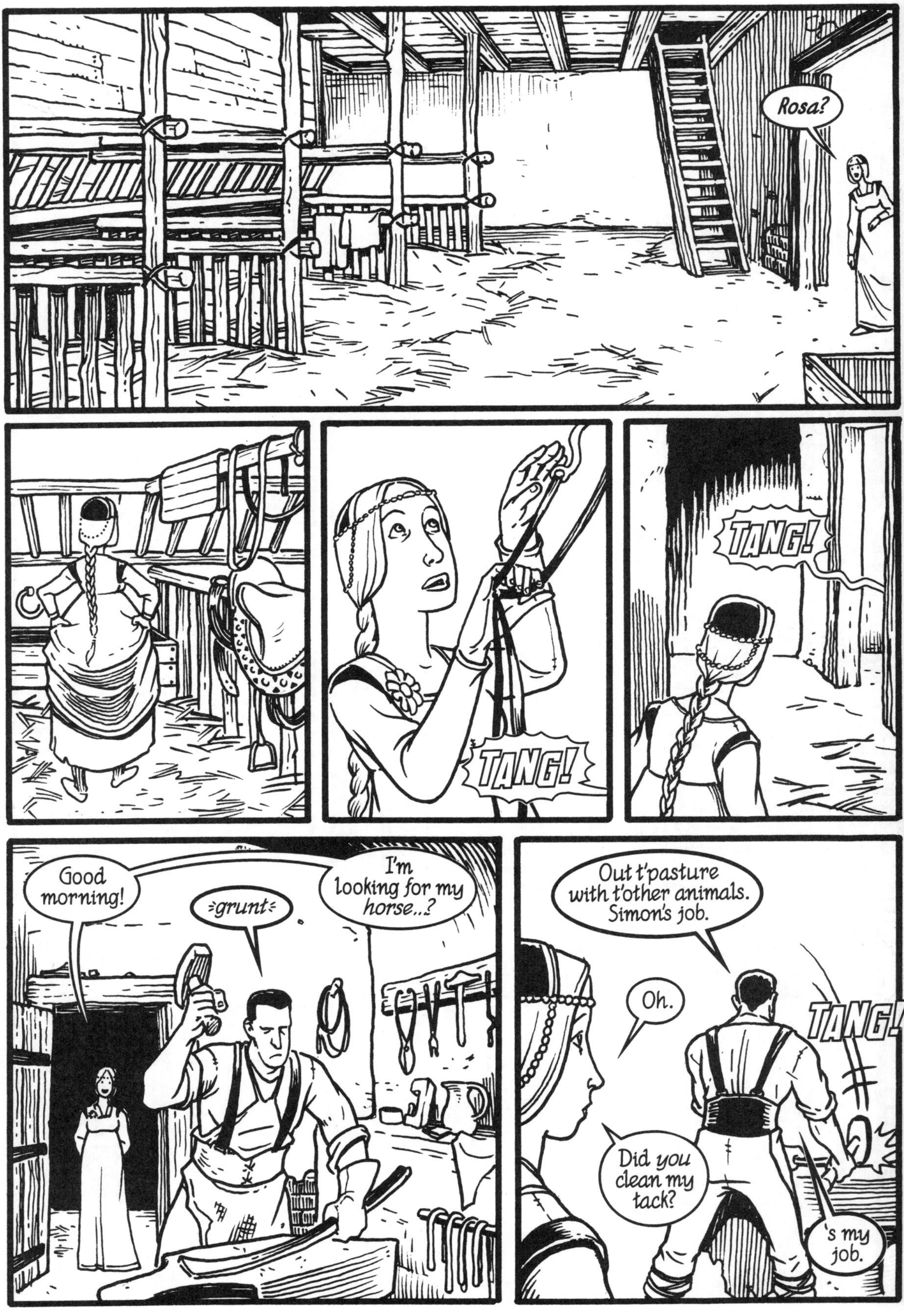
Rosa?
TANG!
TANG!
Good morning!
I'm looking for my horse...?
grunt
Out t'pasture with t'other animals. Simon's job.
Oh.
TANG!
Did you clean my tack?
's my job.

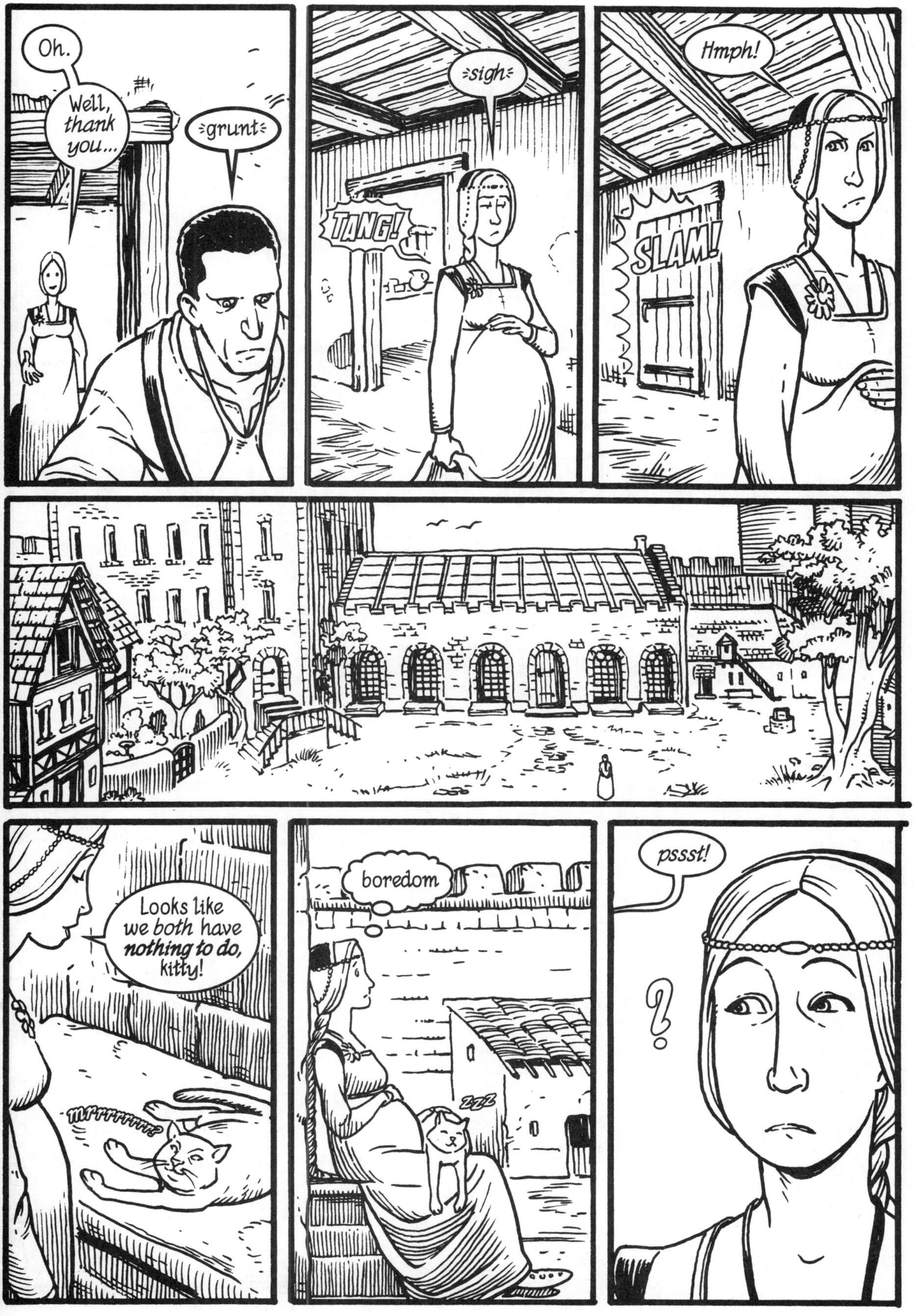
Oh.
Well, thank you...
grunt
sigh
TANG!
Hmph!
SLAM!
Looks like we both have *nothing to do,* kitty!
mrrrrrrrrr?
boredom
zzz
pssst!
?

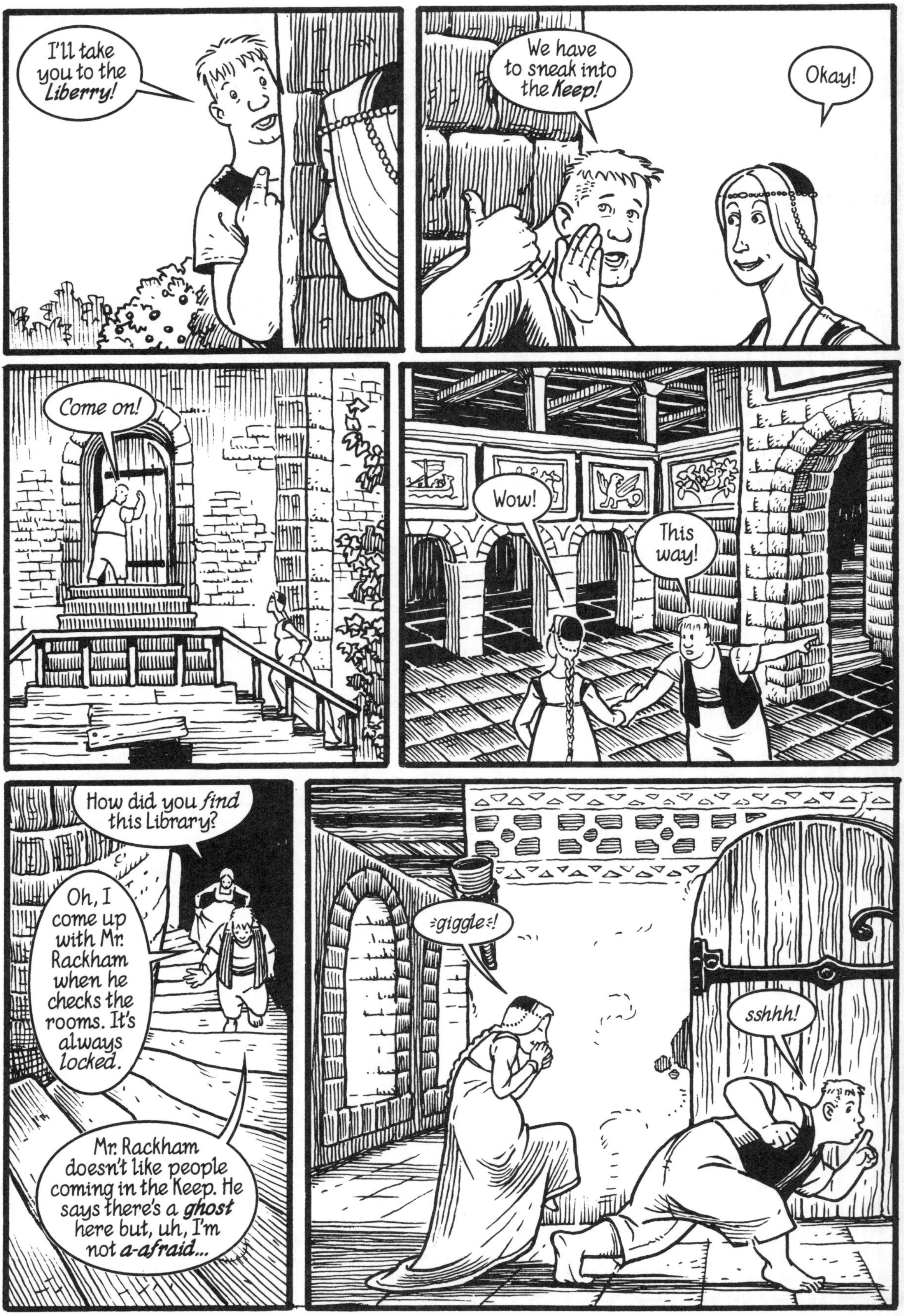
I'll take you to the *Liberry!*
We have to sneak into the *Keep!*
Okay!
Come on!
Wow!
This way!
How did you *find* this Library?
Oh, I come up with Mr. Rackham when he checks the rooms. It's always locked.
Mr. Rackham doesn't like people coming in the Keep. He says there's a ***ghost*** here but, uh, I'm not ***a-afraid...***
giggle!
sshhh!

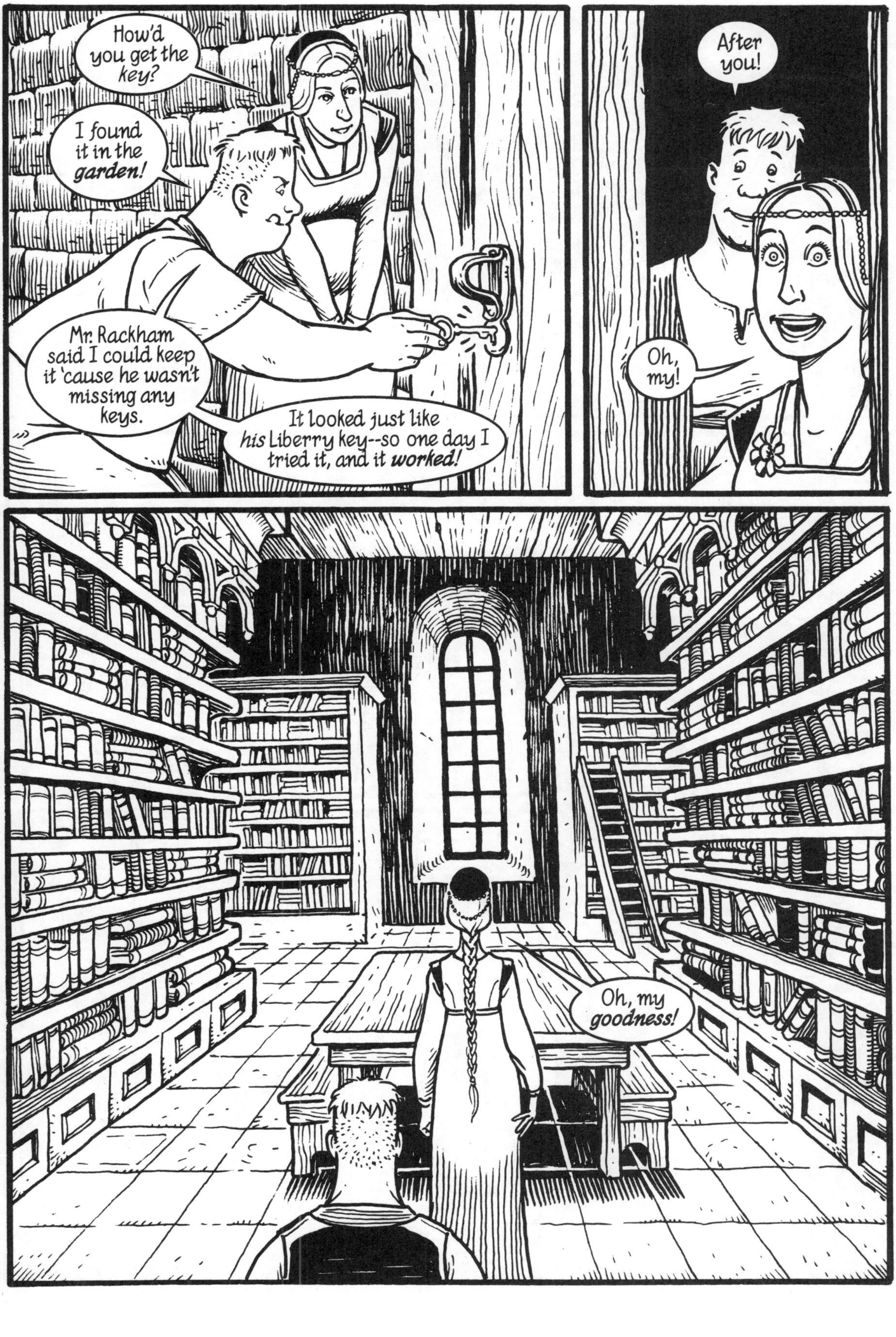
How'd you get the key?
I found it in the garden!
Mr. Rackham said I could keep it 'cause he wasn't missing any keys.
It looked just like his Liberry key--so one day I tried it, and it worked!
After you!
Oh, my!
Oh, my goodness!

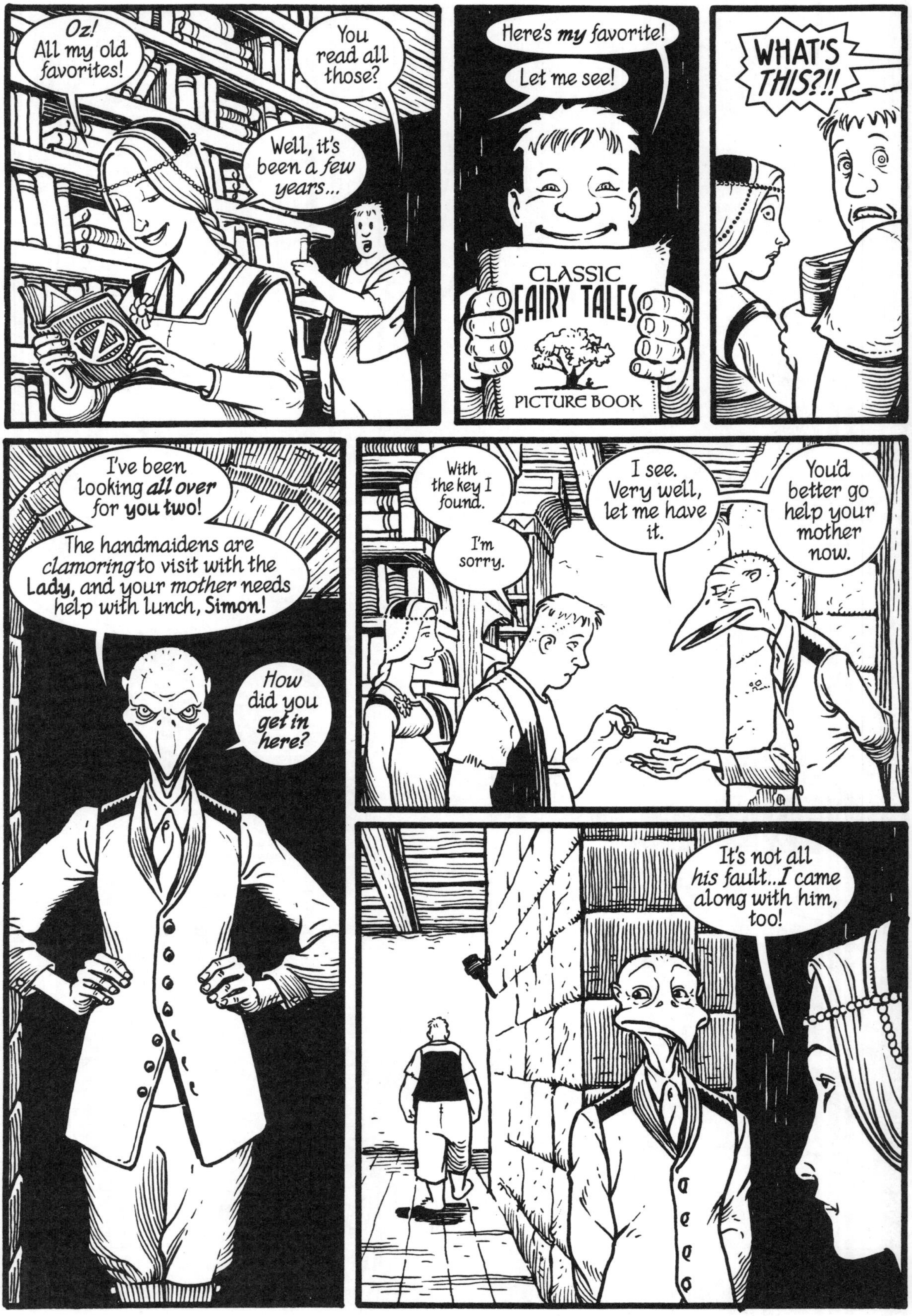
Oz! All my old favorites!
You read all those?
Well, it's been a few years...
Here's my favorite!
Let me see!
CLASSIC FAIRY TALES PICTURE BOOK
WHAT'S THIS?!!
I've been looking all over for you two!
The handmaidens are clamoring to visit with the Lady, and your mother needs help with lunch, Simon!
How did you get in here?
With the key I found.
I'm sorry.
I see. Very well, let me have it.
You'd better go help your mother now.
It's not all his fault...I came along with him, too!

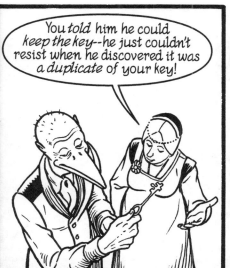

You *told* him he could *keep the key*--he just couldn't resist when he discovered it was a *duplicate* of your key!

There's only *one* key to this room, Lady.

This castle is a lonely place for a lad like Simon.

I knew he liked it *up* here...

...so I "planted" the key where he was sure to *find* it.

You *planted...!!* You knew it all along!

Oh, yes.

Why not just *give* him the key and let him come and go as he *pleased?!!*

Because that's not as much fun as sneaking in to someplace *forbidden*, now, is it?

You *sly dog!*

I get my laughs.

Besides! Simon's chores keep him very *busy*. We couldn't have him spending *all day* in here.

It's really a fine old Library. Pity there's *nobody to take care of it.*

73

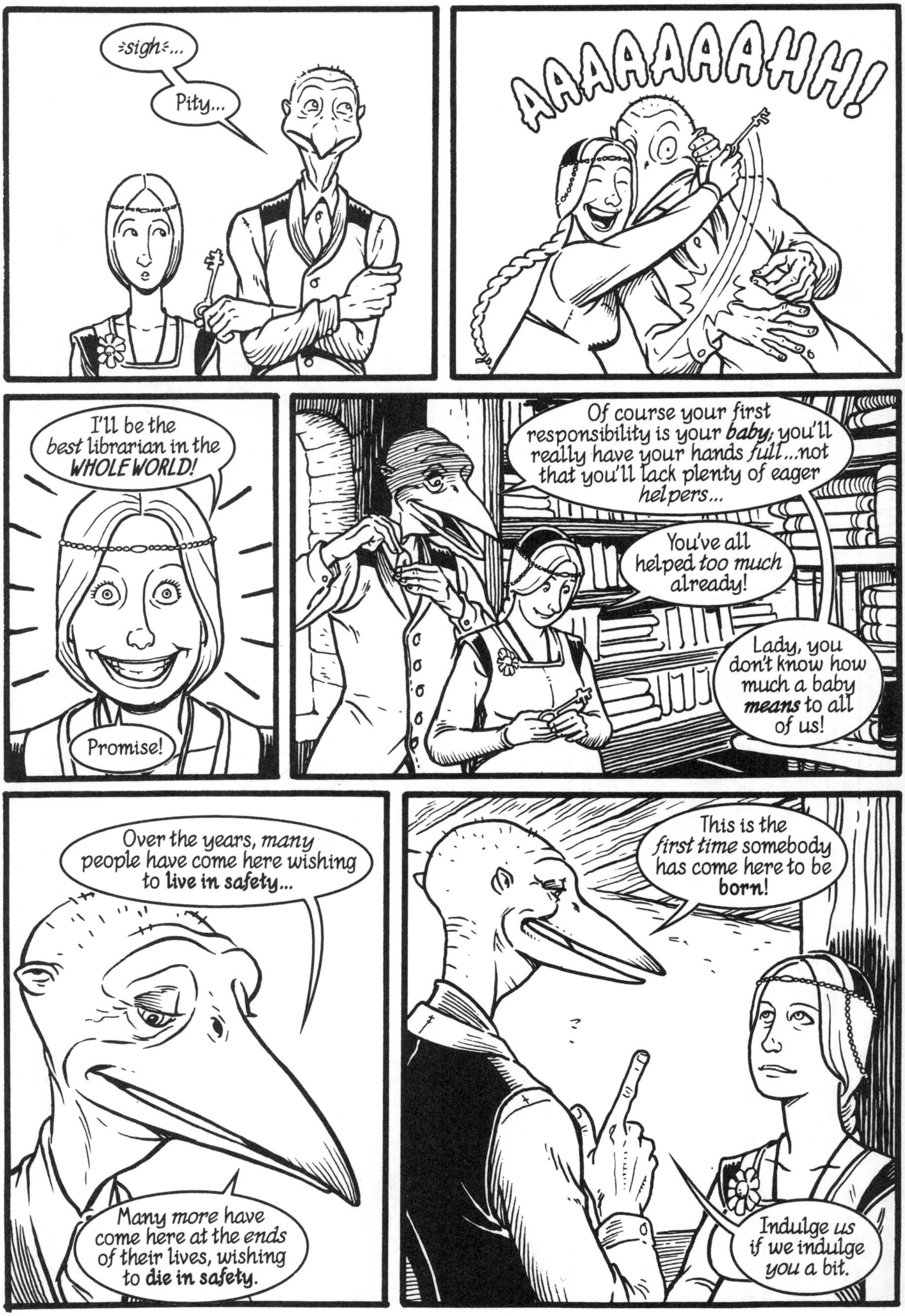

sigh...
Pity...
AAAAAAAHH!
I'll be the *best* librarian in the **WHOLE WORLD!**
Promise!
Of course your first responsibility is your ***baby***; you'll really have your hands *full*...not that you'll lack plenty of eager *helpers*...
You've all helped *too much* already!
Lady, you don't know how much a baby ***means*** to all of us!
Over the years, *many* people have come here wishing to **live in safety...**
Many *more* have come here at the *ends* of their lives, wishing to **die in safety.**
This is the *first time* somebody has come here to be **born**!
Indulge *us* if we indulge *you* a bit.

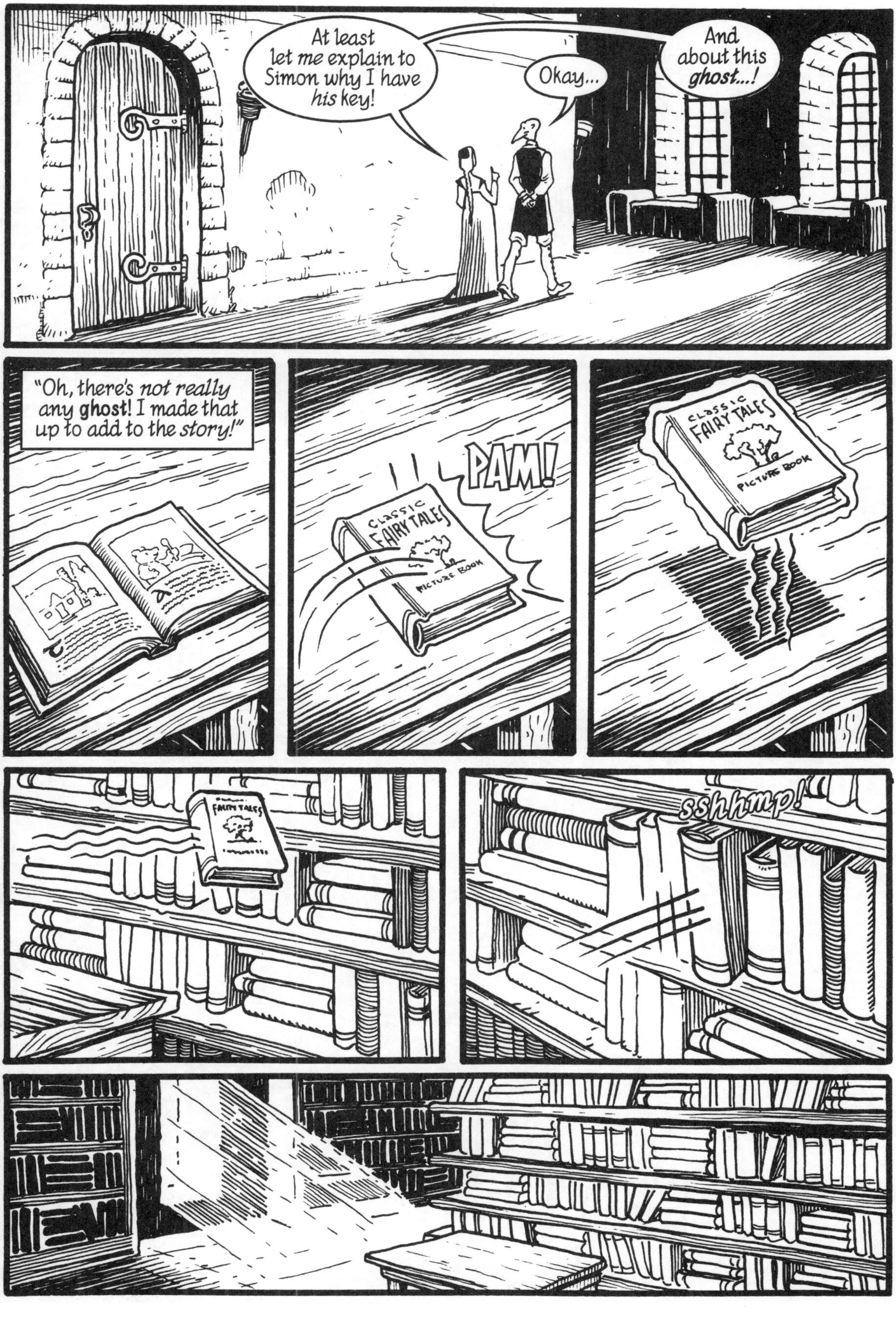
At least let me explain to Simon why I have his key!
Okay...
And about this ghost...!
"Oh, there's not really any ghost! I made that up to add to the story!"
PAM!
CLASSIC FAIRY TALES PICTURE BOOK
CLASSIC FAIRY TALES PICTURE BOOK
FAIRY TALES
sshhmp!

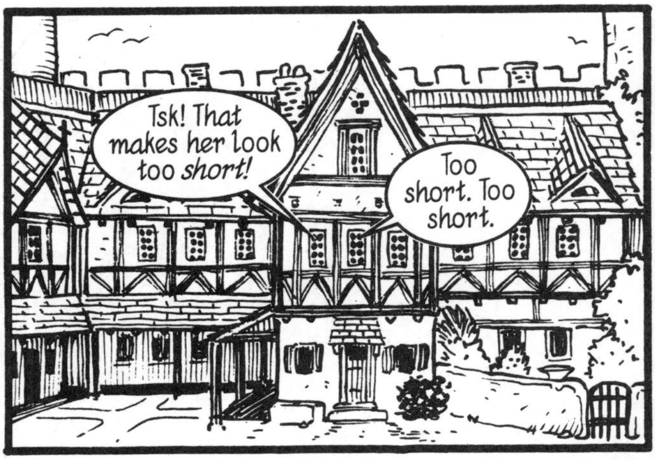
Tsk! That makes her look too *short!*
Too short. Too short.

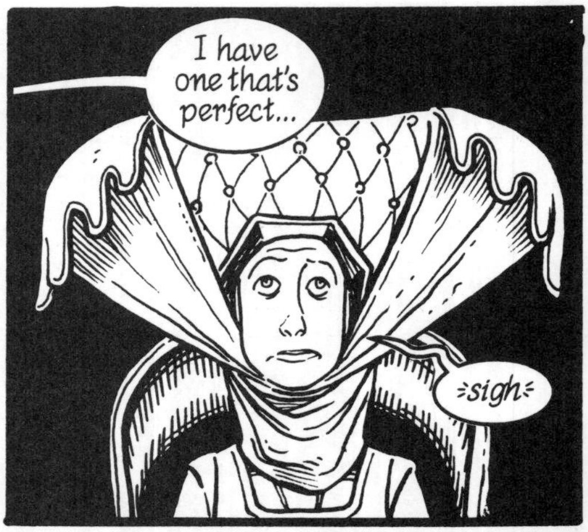
I have one that's perfect...
sigh

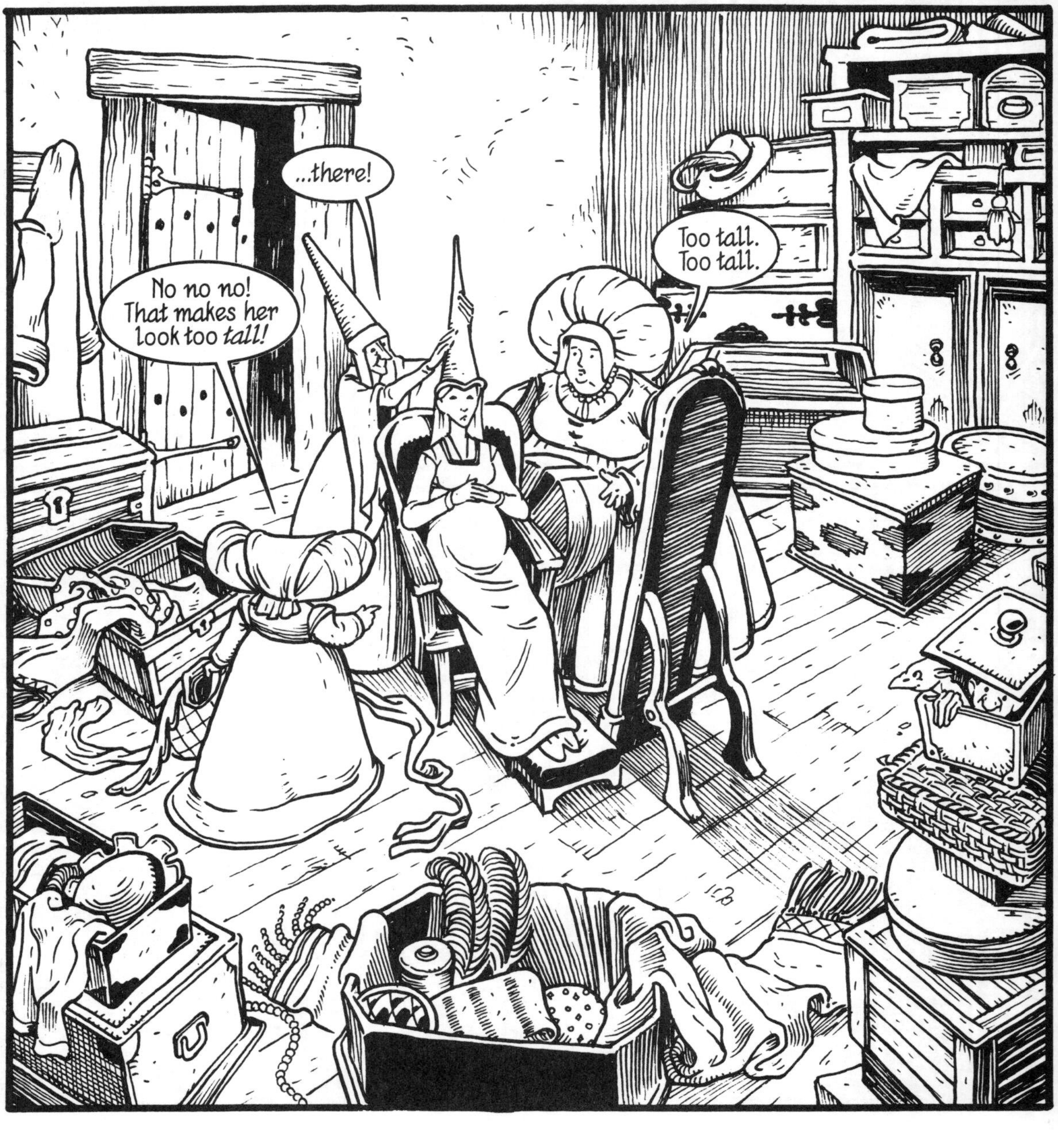
...there!
No no no! That makes her look too *tall!*
Too tall. Too tall.

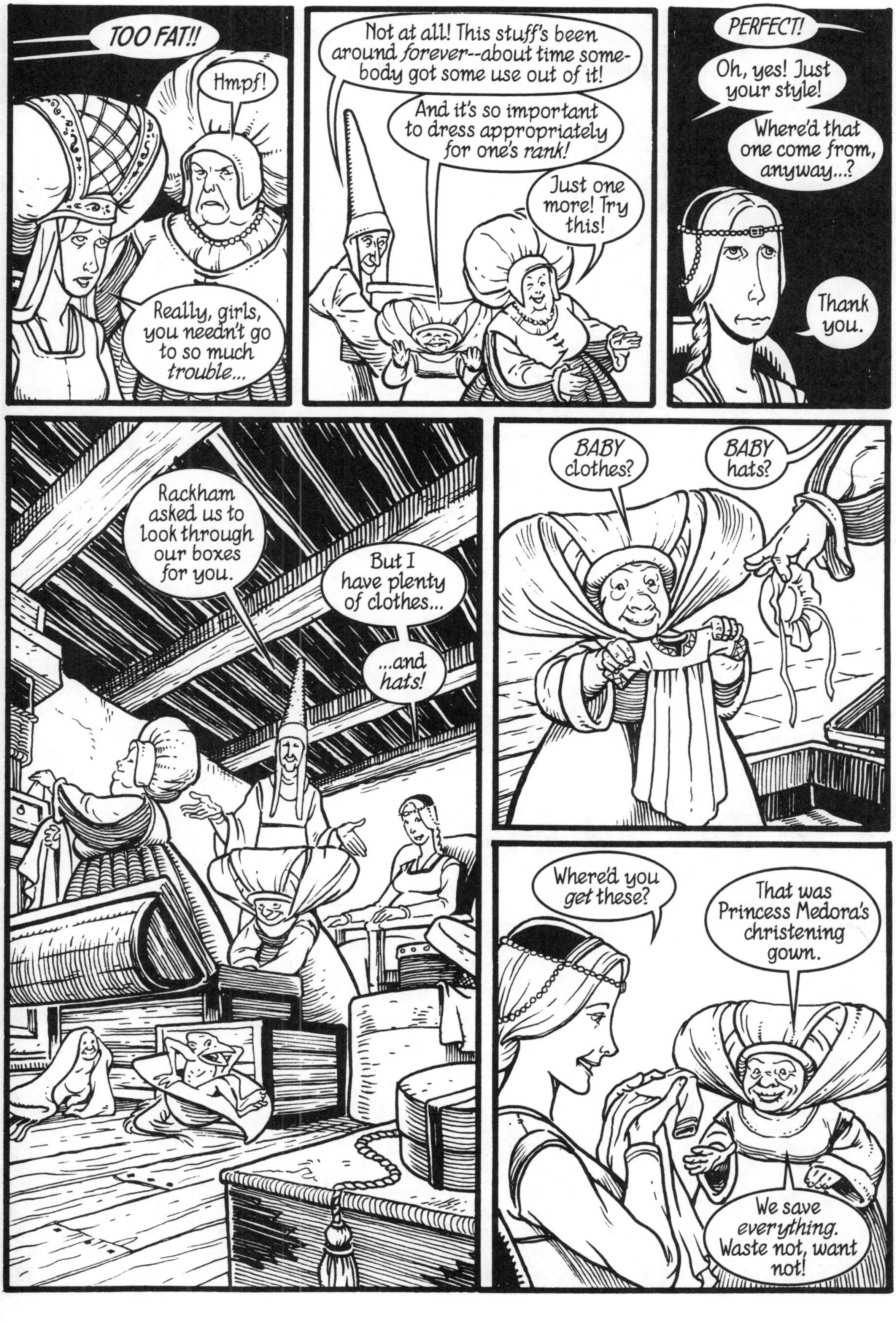
TOO FAT!!
Hmpf!
Really, girls, you needn't go to so much *trouble*...
Not at all! This stuff's been around *forever*--about time somebody got some use out of it!
And it's so important to dress appropriately for one's *rank*!
Just one more! Try this!
PERFECT!
Oh, yes! Just your style!
Where'd that one come from, anyway...?
Thank you.
Rackham asked us to look through our boxes for you.
But I have plenty of clothes...
...and *hats!*
BABY clothes?
BABY hats?
Where'd you *get* these?
That was Princess Medora's christening gown.
We save *everything*. Waste not, want not!

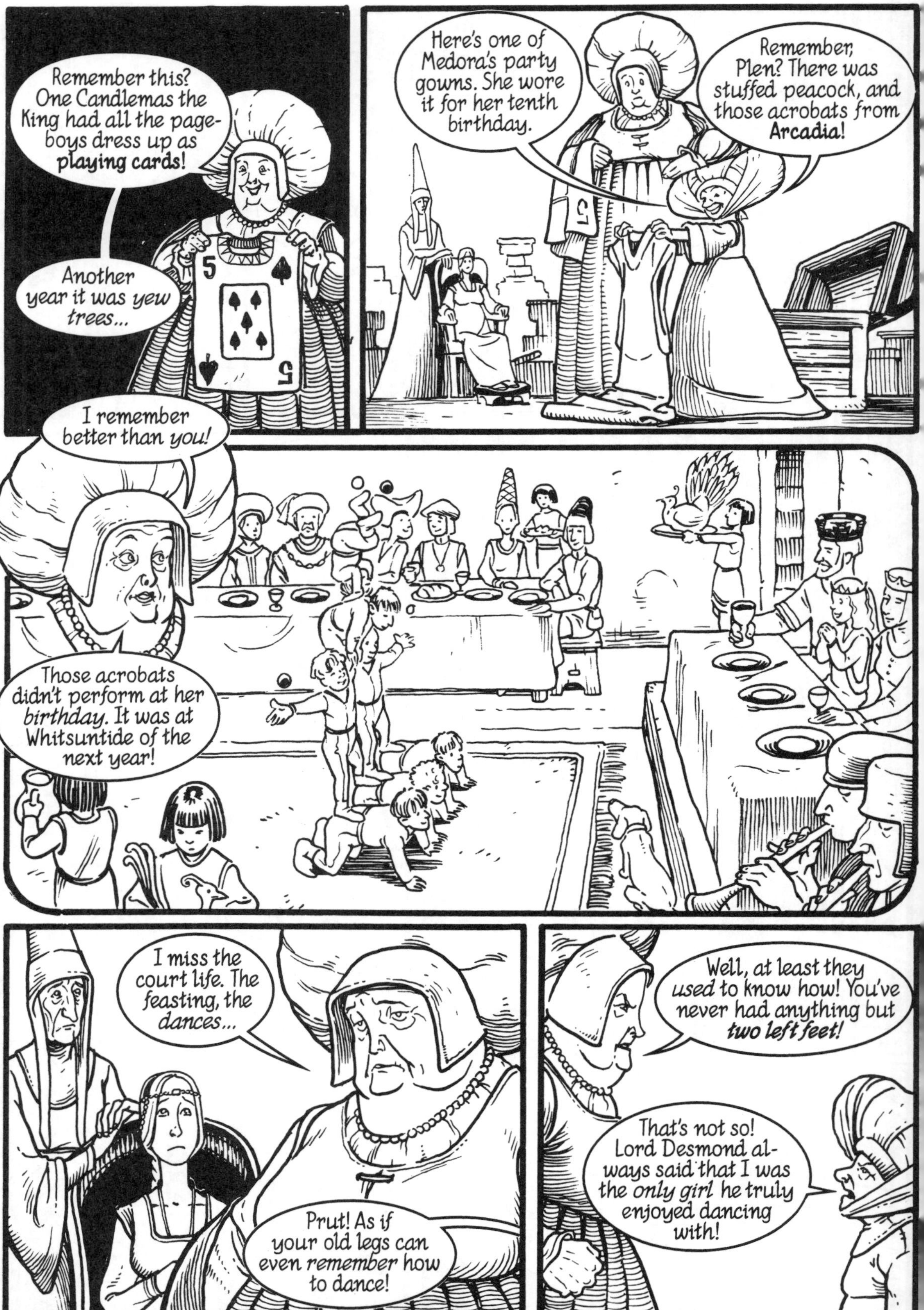
Remember this? One Candlemas the King had all the page-boys dress up as **playing cards**!
Another year it was *yew trees*...
Here's one of Medora's party gowns. She wore it for her tenth birthday.
Remember, Plen? There was stuffed peacock, and those acrobats from **Arcadia**!
I remember better than *you*!
Those acrobats didn't perform at her *birthday*. It was at Whitsuntide of the next year!
I miss the court life. The feasting, the *dances*...
Prut! As if your old legs can even *remember* how to dance!
Well, at least they *used* to know how! You've never had anything but ***two left feet!***
That's not so! Lord Desmond al-ways said that I was the *only girl* he truly enjoyed dancing with!

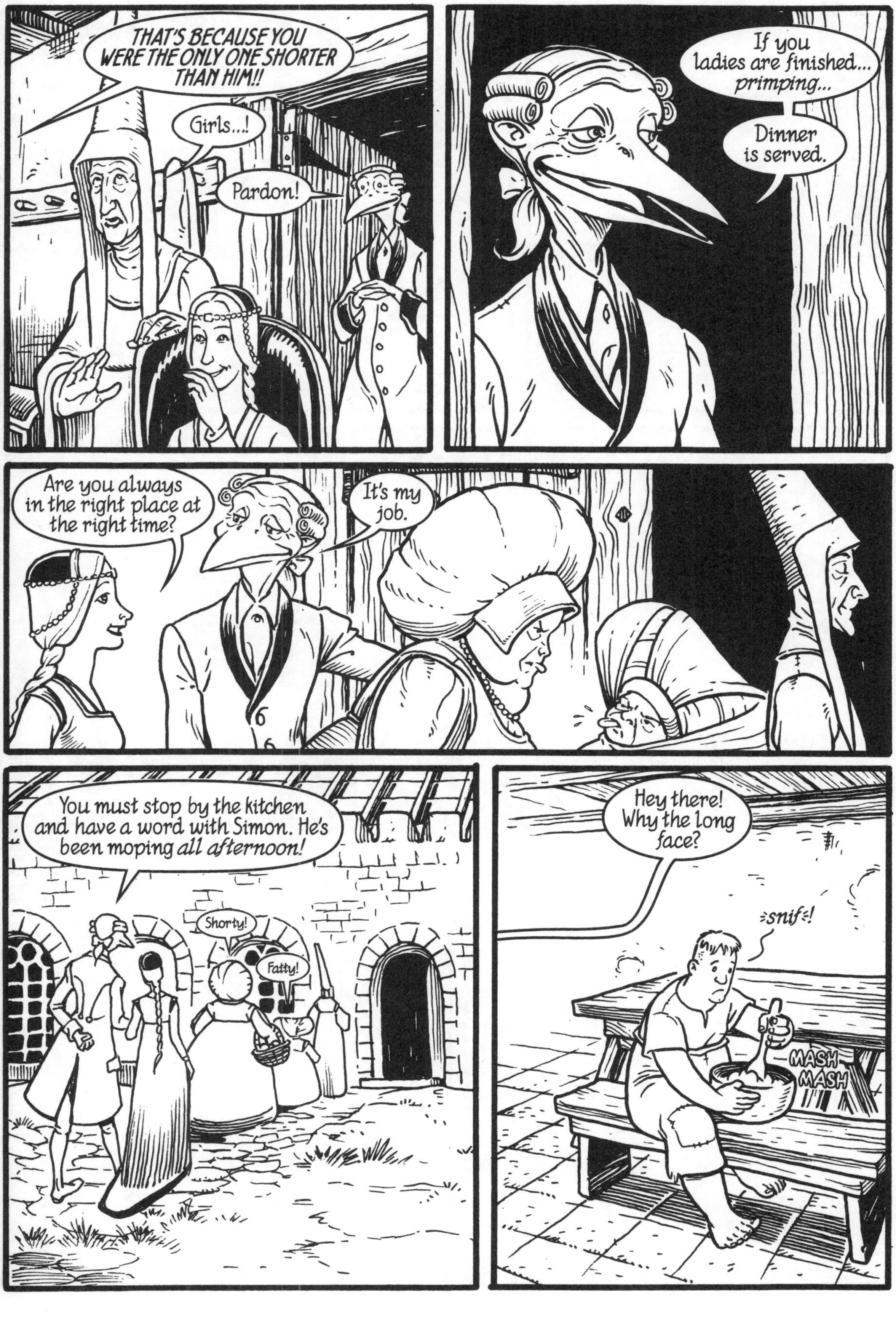
THAT'S BECAUSE YOU WERE THE ONLY ONE SHORTER THAN HIM!!
Girls...!
Pardon!
If you ladies are finished... primping...
Dinner is served.
Are you always in the right place at the right time?
It's my job.
You must stop by the kitchen and have a word with Simon. He's been moping all afternoon!
Shorty!
Fatty!
Hey there! Why the long face?
snif!
MASH MASH

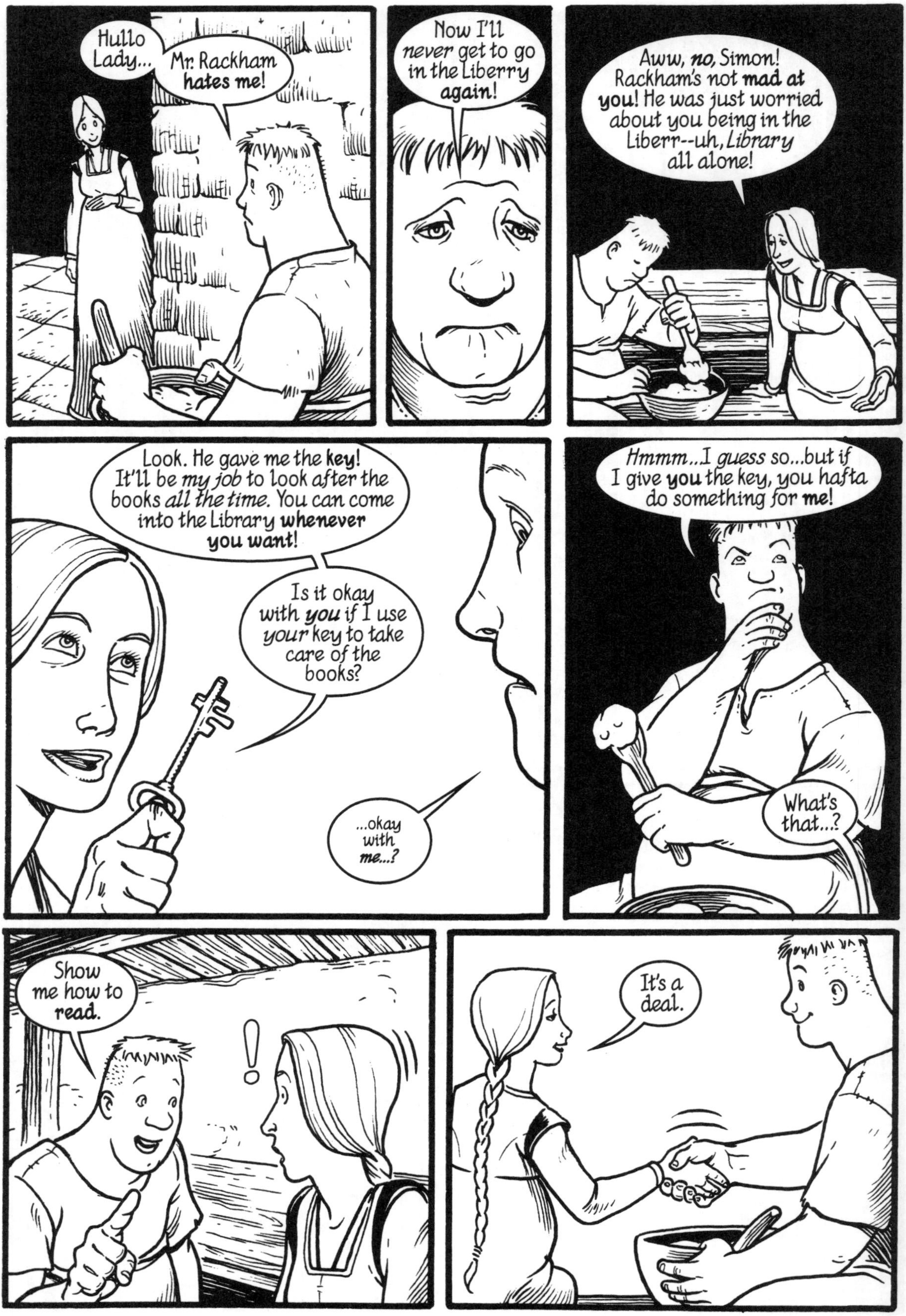

Hullo Lady...
Mr. Rackham **hates me**!
Now I'll *never* get to go in the Liberry **again**!
Aww, ***no***, Simon! Rackham's not **mad at you**! He was just worried about you being in the Liberr--uh, *Library* all alone!
Look. He gave me the **key**! It'll be *my job* to look *after* the books *all the time*. You can come into the Library **whenever you want**!
Is it okay with ***you*** if I use *your* key to take care of the books?
...okay with ***me...?***
Hmmm...I *guess* so...but if I give **you** the key, you hafta do something for **me**!
What's that...?
Show me how to **read**.
!
It's a deal.

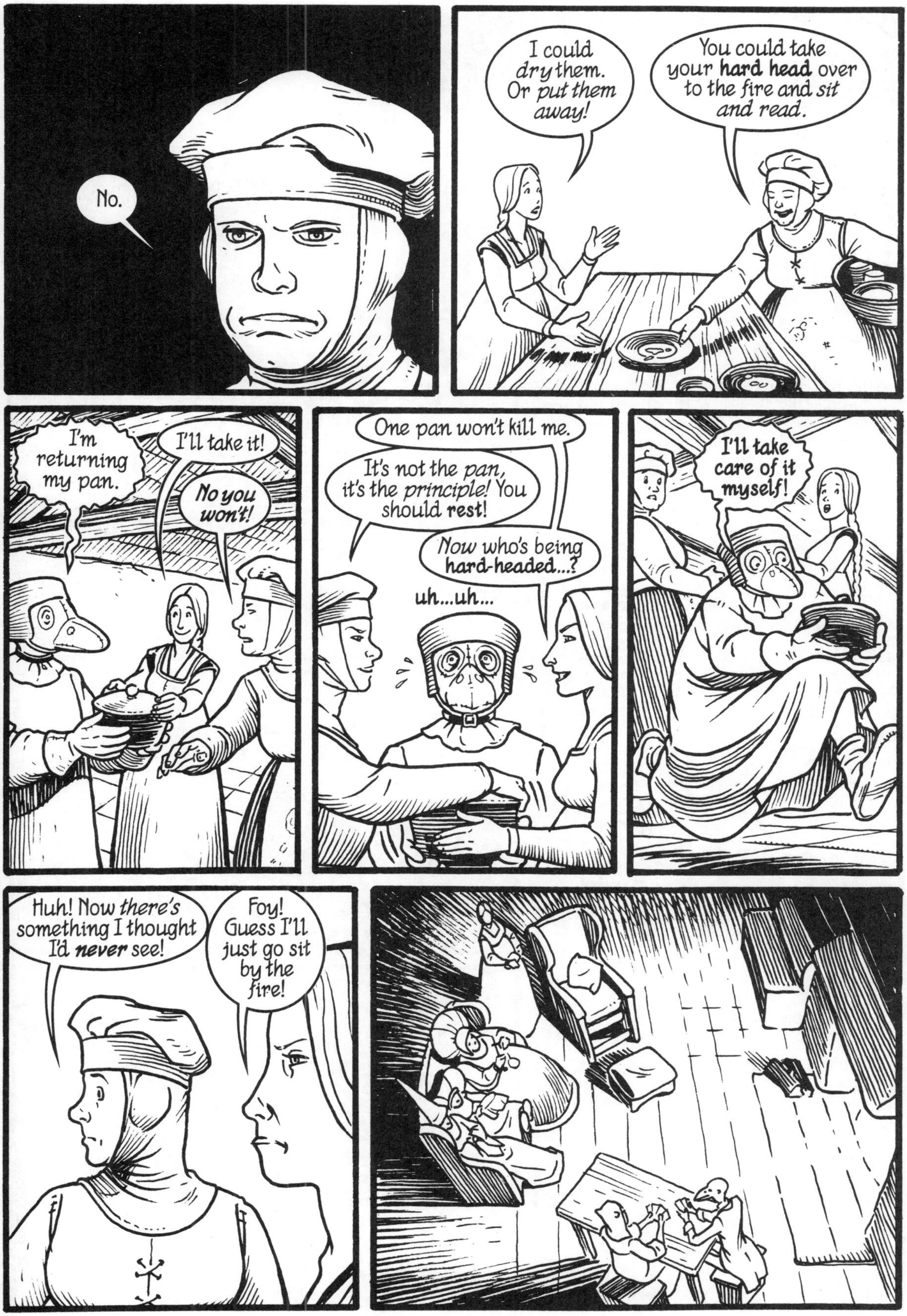
No.
I could dry them. Or put them away!
You could take your **hard head** over to the fire and sit and read.
I'm returning my pan.
I'll take it!
No you won't!
One pan won't kill me.
It's not the pan, it's the principle! You should rest!
Now who's being hard-headed...?
uh...uh...
I'll take care of it myself!
Huh! Now there's something I thought I'd **never** see!
Foy! Guess I'll just go sit by the fire!

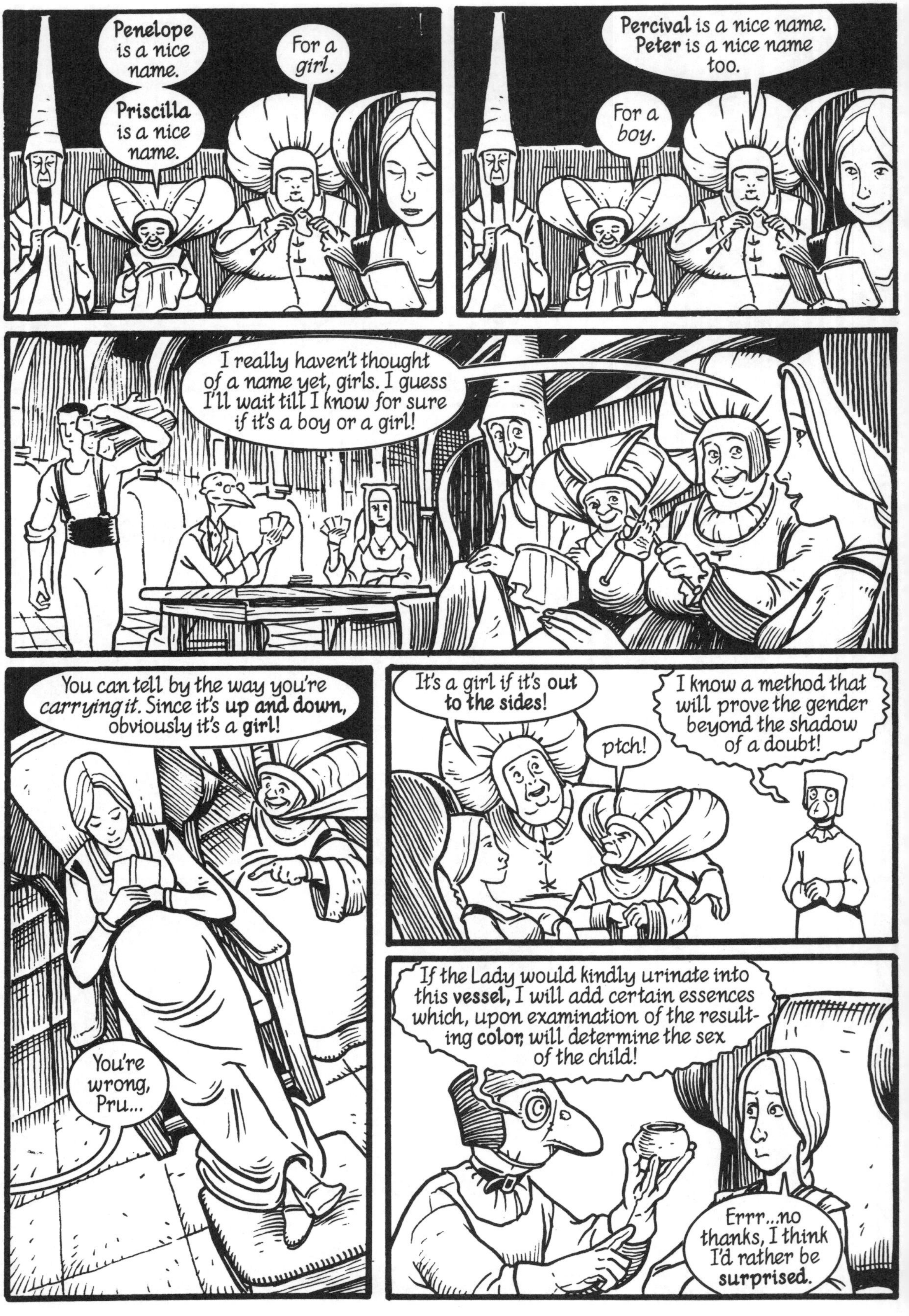
Penelope is a nice name.
Priscilla is a nice name.
For a girl.
Percival is a nice name. Peter is a nice name too.
For a boy.
I really haven't thought of a name yet, girls. I guess I'll wait till I know for sure if it's a boy or a girl!
You can tell by the way you're carrying it. Since it's up and down, obviously it's a girl!
You're wrong, Pru...
It's a girl if it's out to the sides!
ptch!
I know a method that will prove the gender beyond the shadow of a doubt!
If the Lady would kindly urinate into this vessel, I will add certain essences which, upon examination of the resulting color, will determine the sex of the child!
Errr...no thanks, I think I'd rather be surprised.

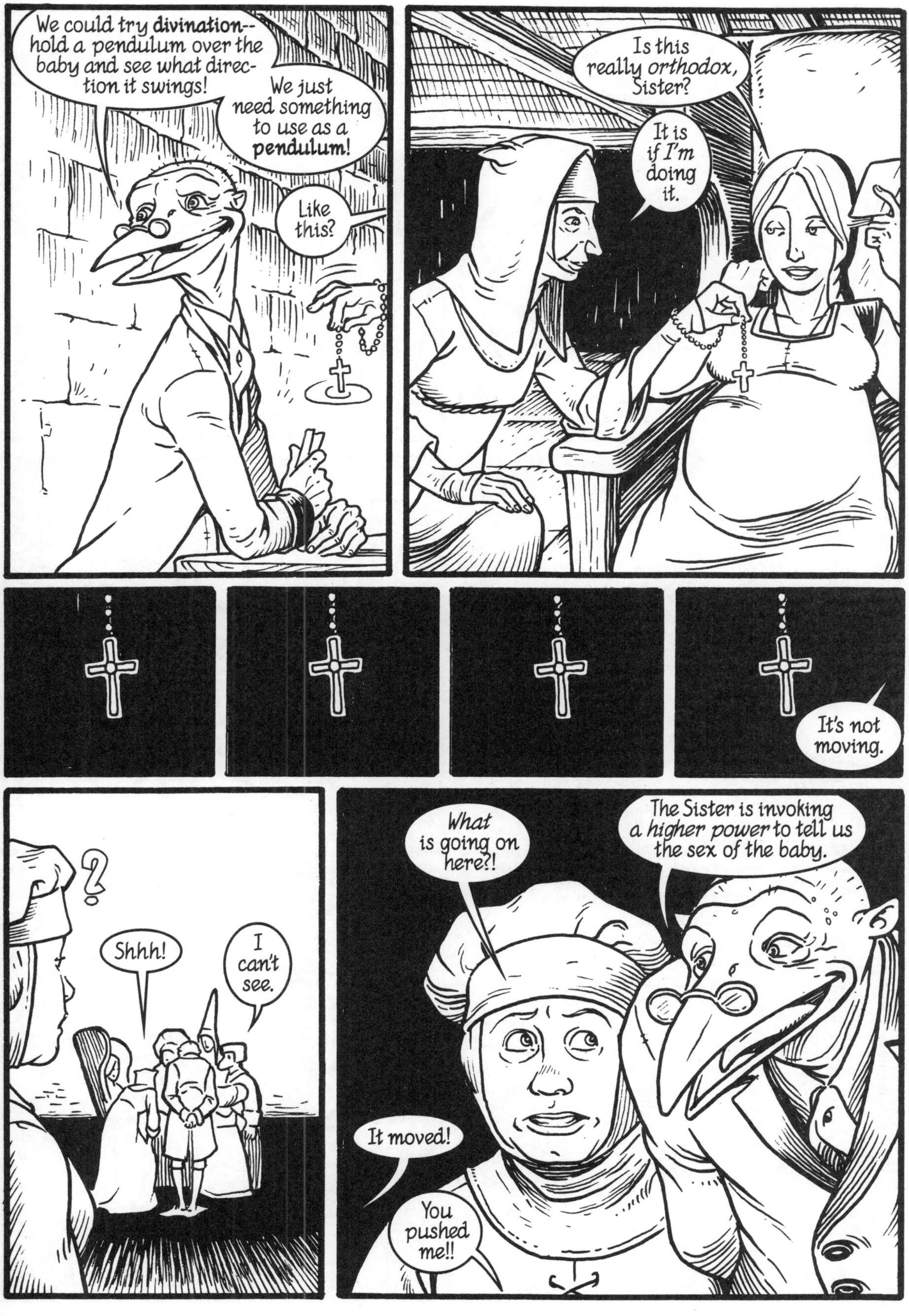
We could try divination--hold a pendulum over the baby and see what direction it swings!
We just need something to use as a pendulum!
Like this?
Is this really orthodox, Sister?
It is if I'm doing it.
It's not moving.
Shhh!
I can't see.
What is going on here?!
The Sister is invoking a higher power to tell us the sex of the baby.
It moved!
You pushed me!!

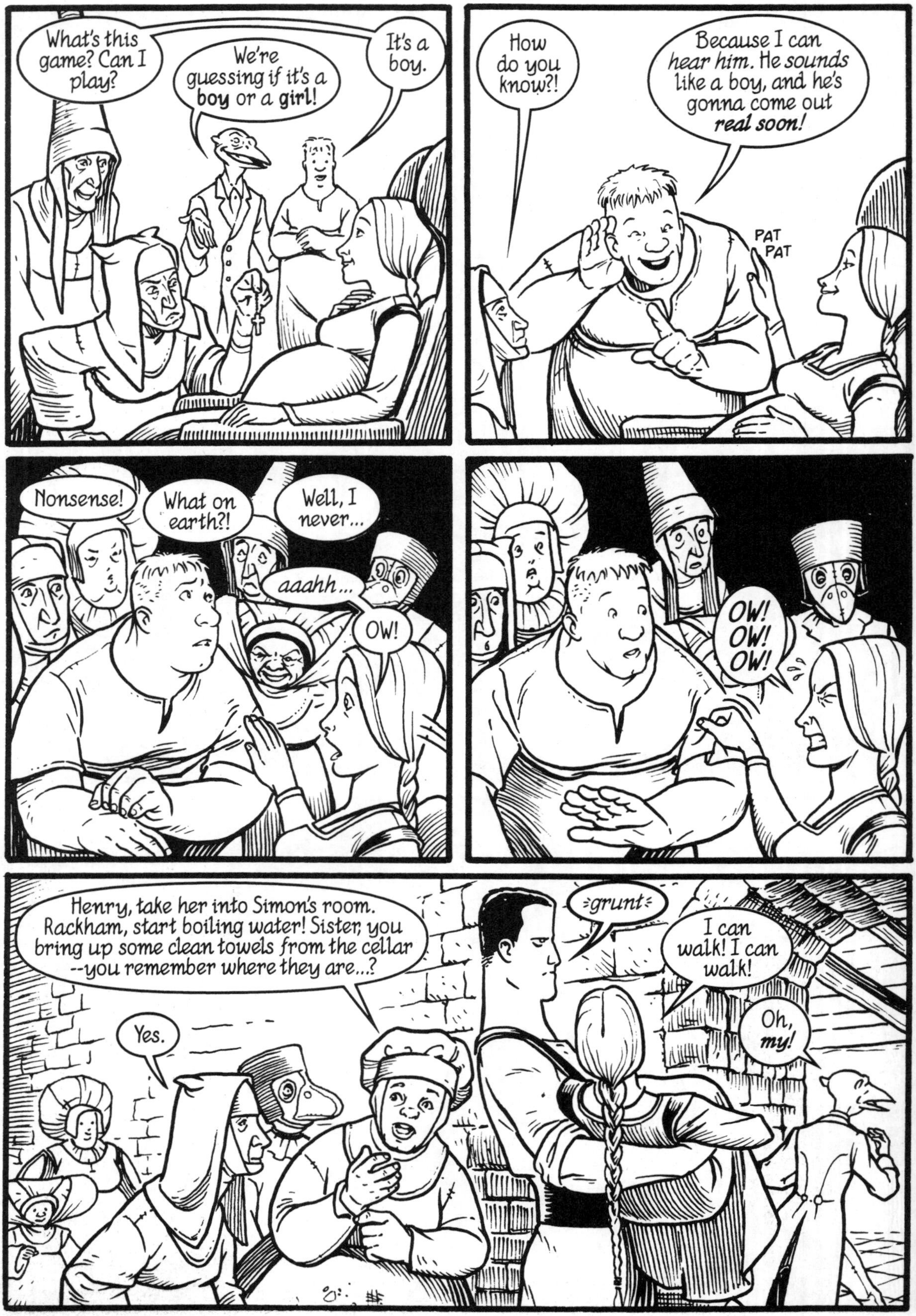
What's this game? Can I play?
We're guessing if it's a **boy** or a **girl**!
It's a boy.
How do you know?!
Because I can *hear him*. He *sounds* like a boy, and he's gonna come out ***real soon!***
PAT PAT
Nonsense!
What on earth?!
Well, I never...
aaahh...
OW!
OW! OW! OW!
Henry, take her into Simon's room. Rackham, start boiling water! Sister, you bring up some clean towels from the cellar --you remember where they are...?
grunt
I can walk! I can walk!
Yes.
Oh, *my*!

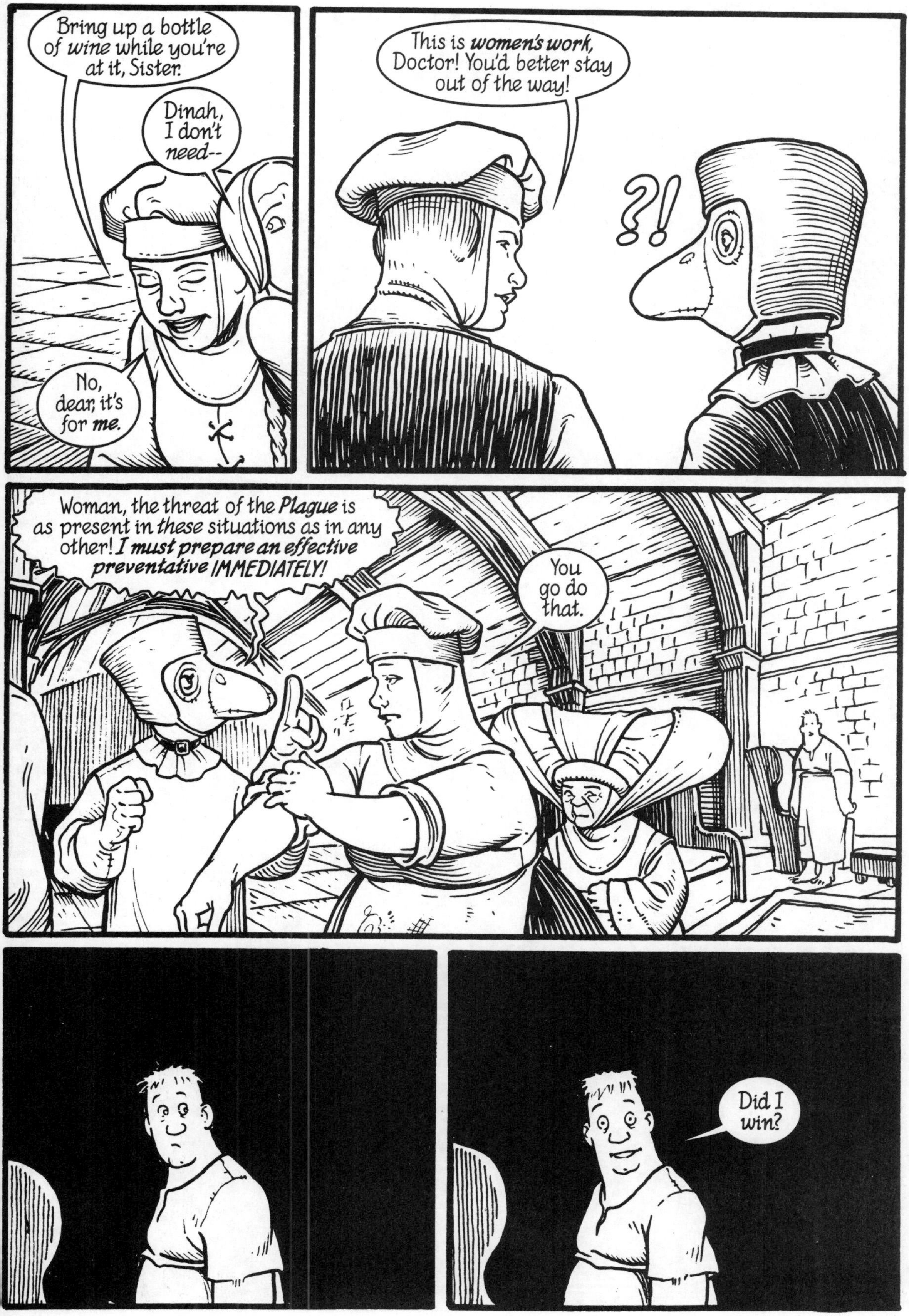
Bring up a bottle of wine while you're at it, Sister.
Dinah, I don't need--
No, dear, it's for me.
This is women's work, Doctor! You'd better stay out of the way!
?!
Woman, the threat of the Plague is as present in these situations as in any other! I must prepare an effective preventative IMMEDIATELY!
You go do that.
Did I win?

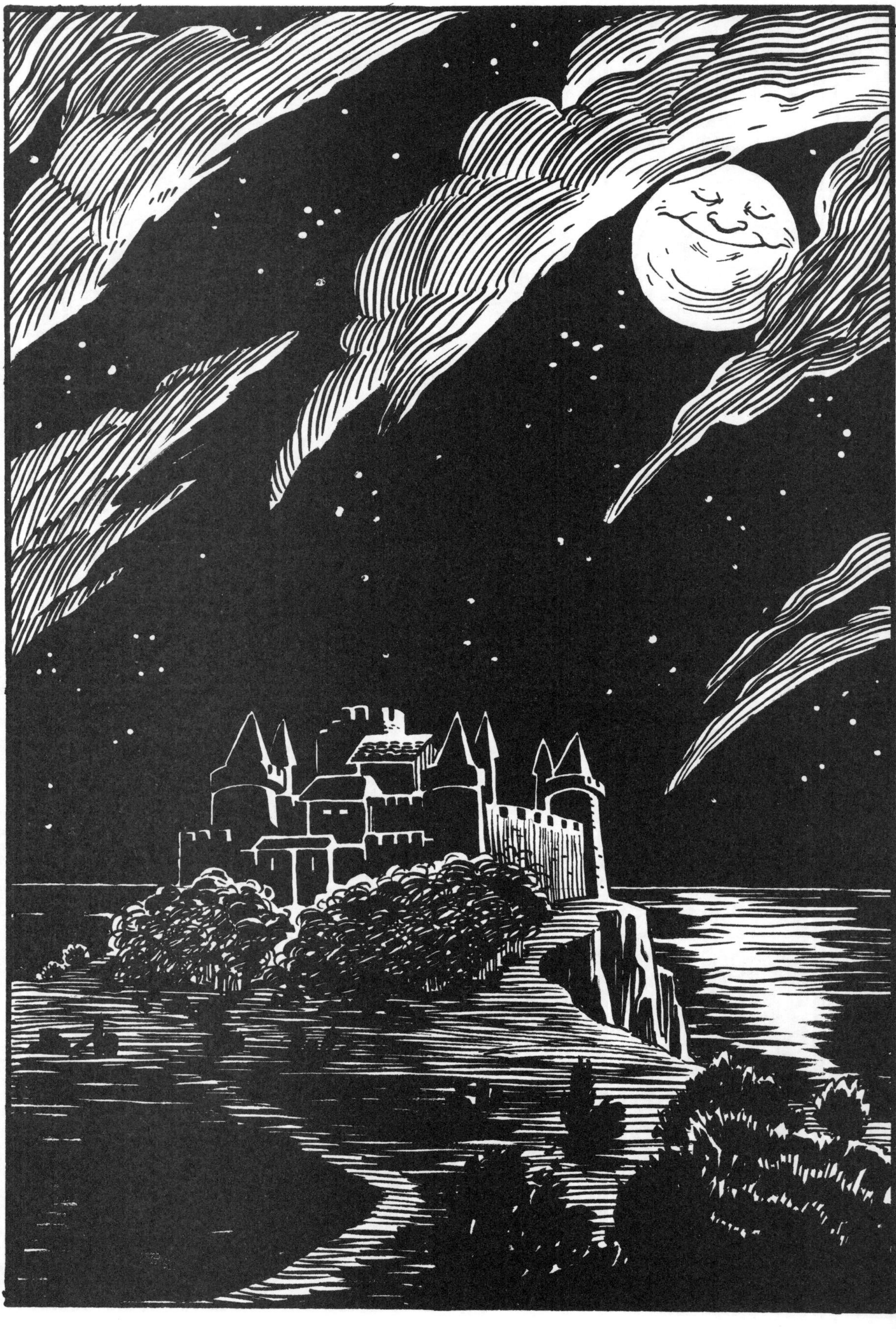

The Caged Heart

Story and Art by Linda Medley - Lettering by Todd Klein

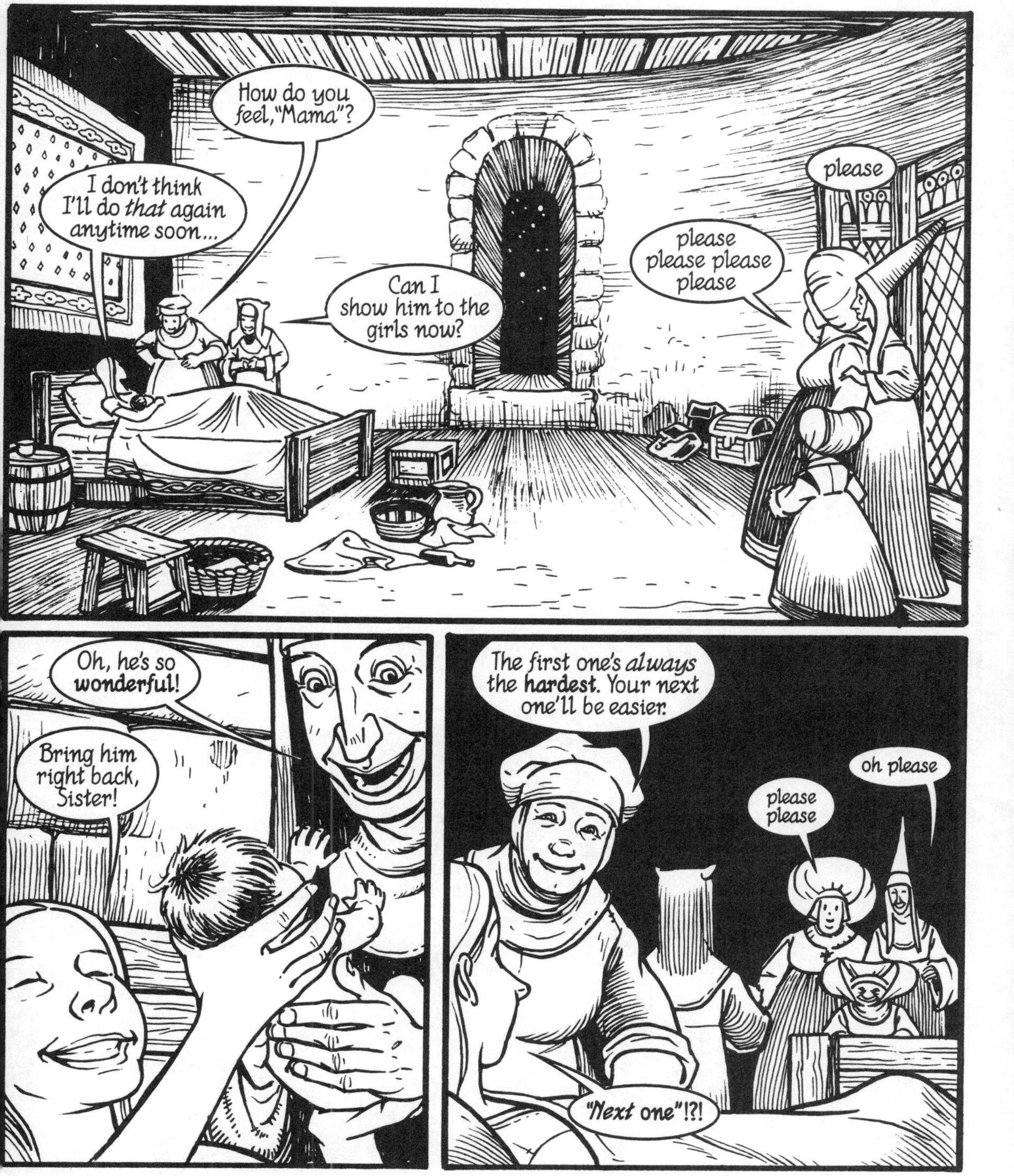
How do you feel, "Mama"?
I don't think I'll do *that* again anytime soon...
Can I show him to the girls now?
please
please please please please
Oh, he's so **wonderful**!
Bring him right back, Sister!
The first one's *always* the **hardest**. Your next one'll be easier.
oh please
please please
"*Next one*"!?!

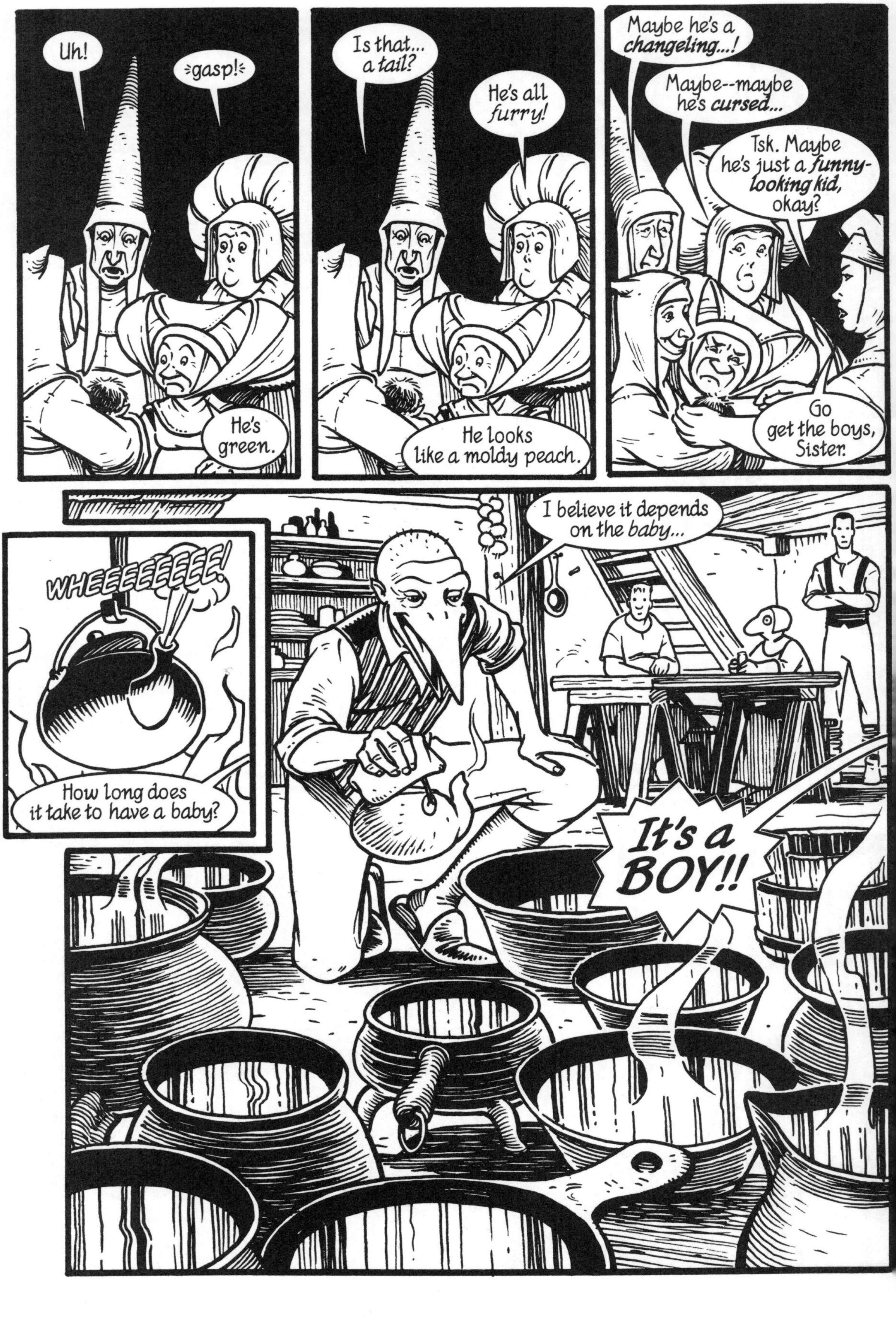
Uh!
gasp!
He's green.
Is that... a tail?
He's all furry!
He looks like a moldy peach.
Maybe he's a changeling...!
Maybe--maybe he's cursed...
Tsk. Maybe he's just a funny-looking kid, okay?
Go get the boys, Sister.
WHEEEEEEEEE!
How long does it take to have a baby?
I believe it depends on the baby...
It's a BOY!!

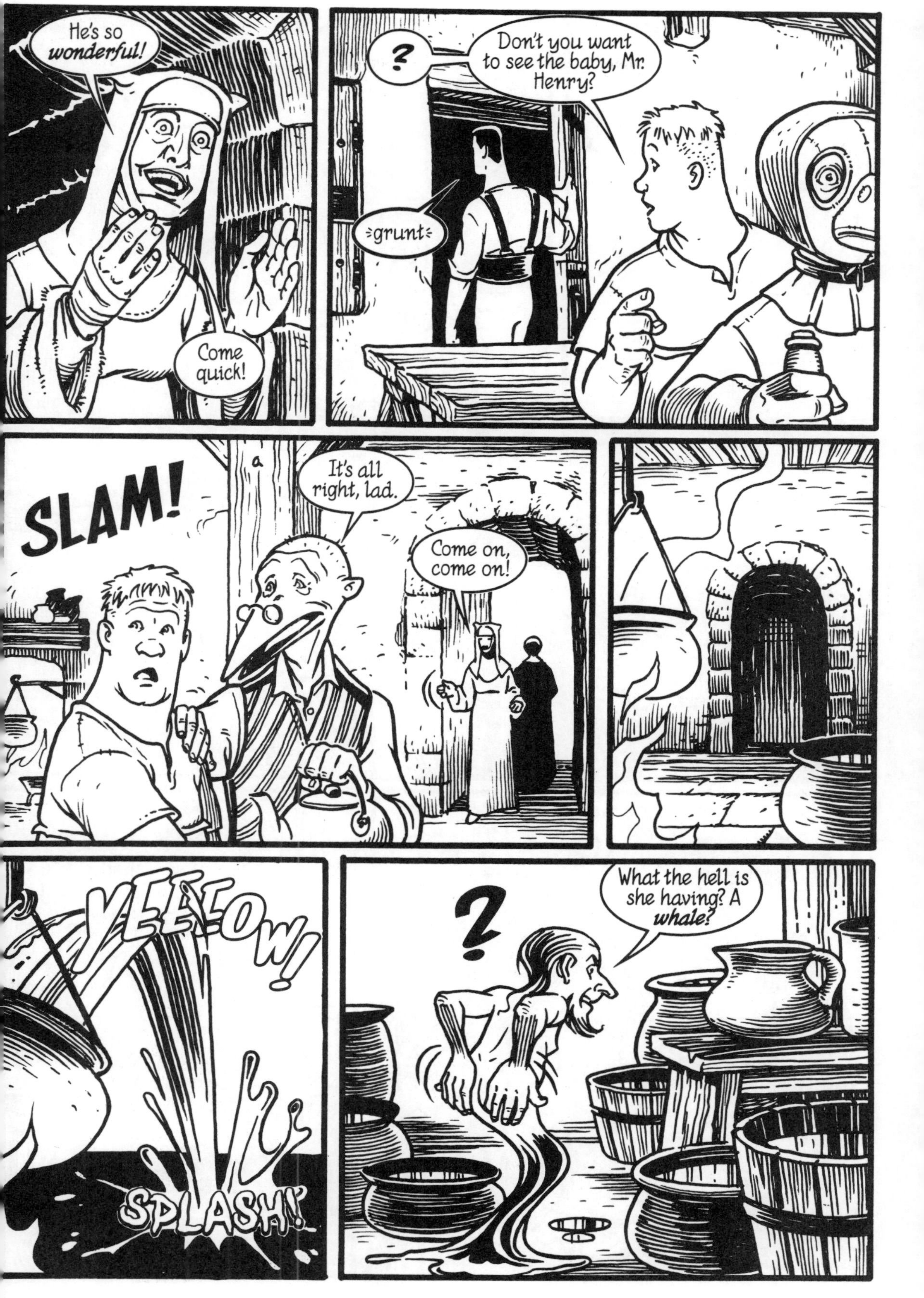
He's so *wonderful!*
Come quick!
?
Don't you want to see the baby, Mr. Henry?
grunt
SLAM!
It's all right, lad.
Come on, come on!
YEEEOW!
SPLASH!
?
What the hell is she having? A *whale?*

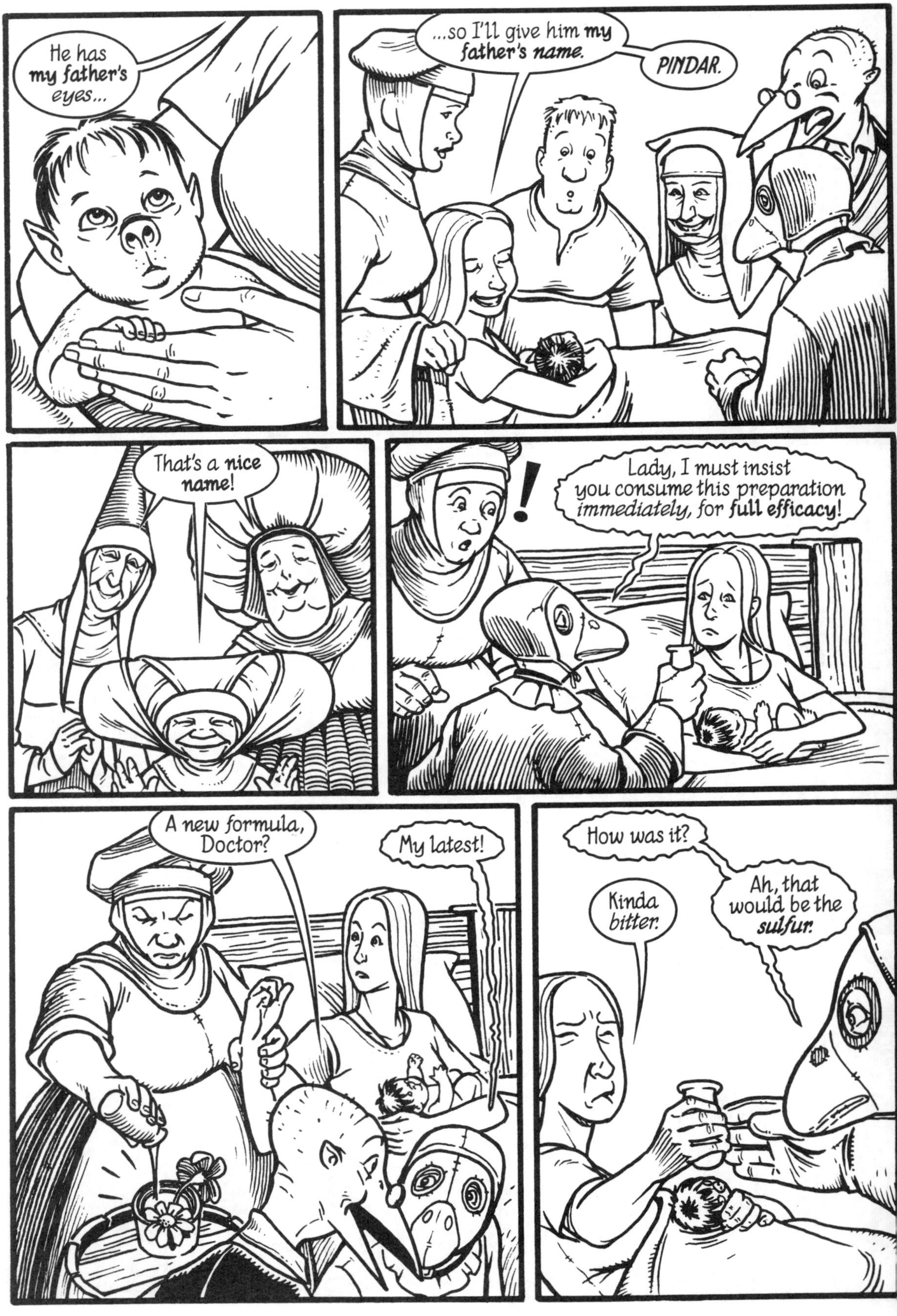
He has my father's eyes...
...so I'll give him my father's name.
PINDAR.
That's a nice name!
!
Lady, I must insist you consume this preparation immediately, for full efficacy!
A new formula, Doctor?
My latest!
How was it?
Kinda bitter.
Ah, that would be the sulfur.

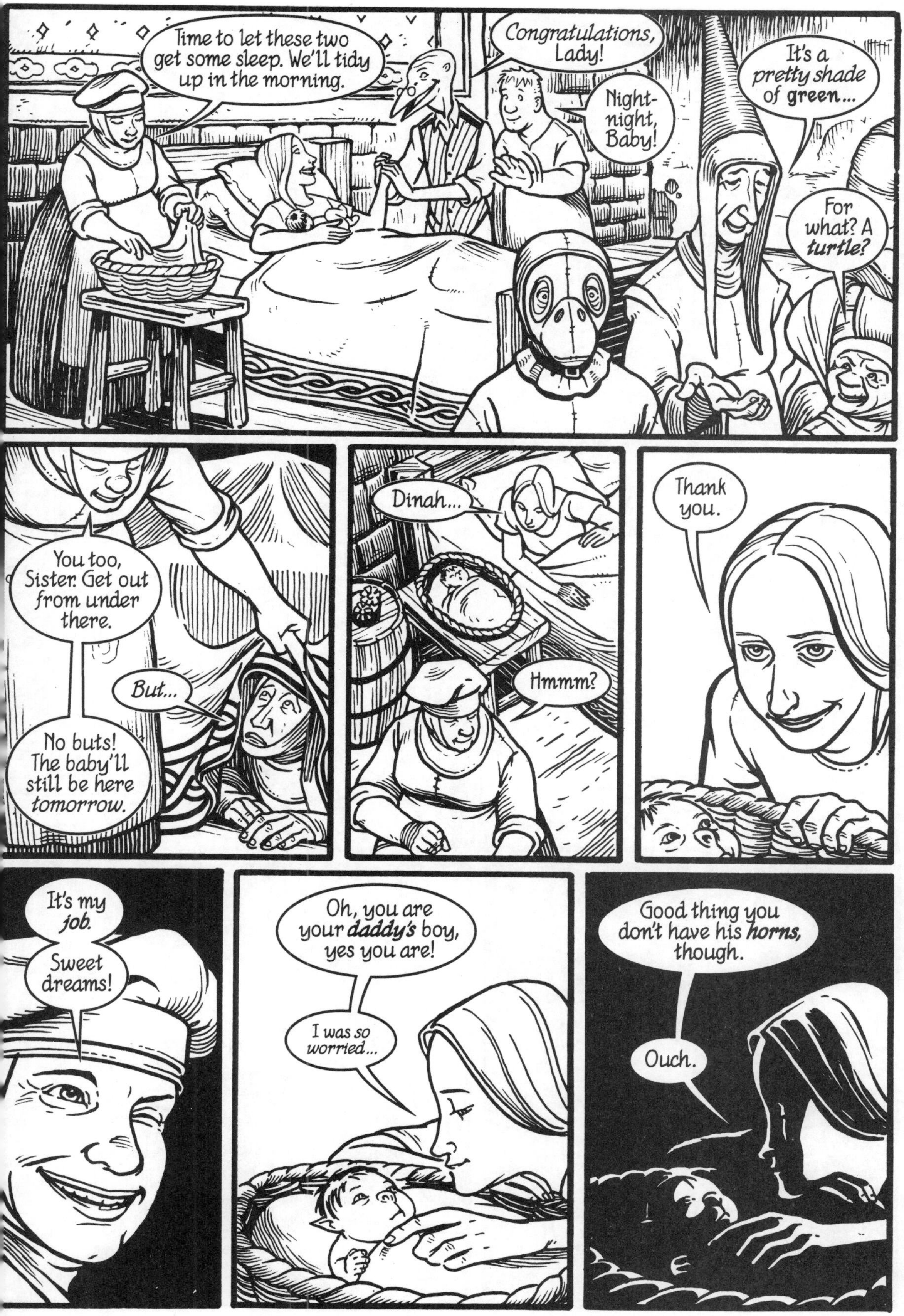
Time to let these two get some sleep. We'll tidy up in the morning.
Congratulations, Lady!
Night-night, Baby!
It's a pretty shade of **green...**
For what? A *turtle?*
You too, Sister. Get out from under there.
But...
No buts! The baby'll still be here *tomorrow.*
Dinah...
Hmmm?
Thank you.
It's my *job.*
Sweet dreams!
Oh, you are your ***daddy's*** boy, yes you are!
I was so worried...
Good thing you don't have his ***horns,*** though.
Ouch.

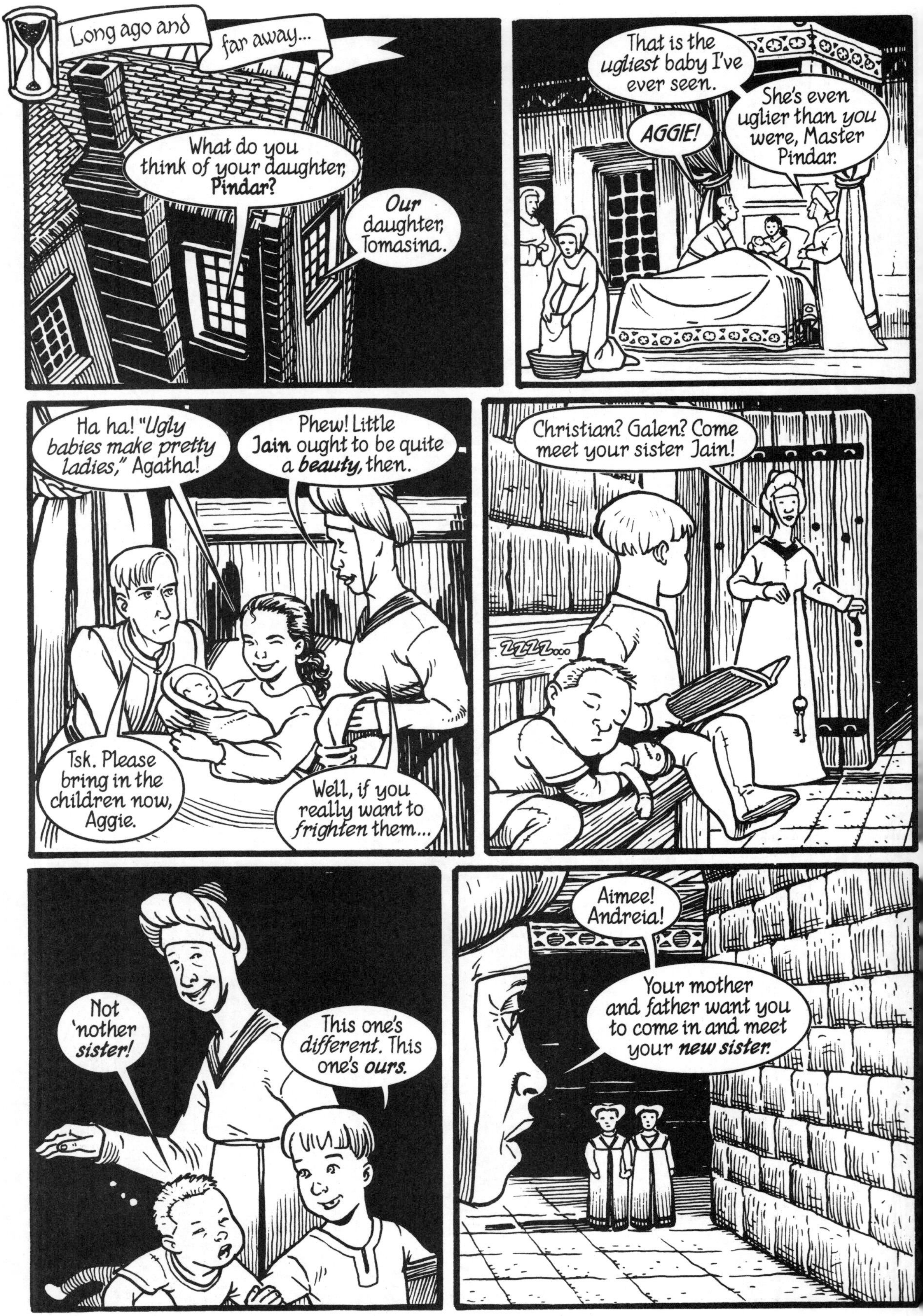

Long ago and
far away...
What do you think of your daughter, **Pindar?**
Our daughter, Tomasina.
That is the *ugliest* baby I've ever seen.
AGGIE!
She's even uglier than *you* were, Master Pindar.
Ha ha! "*Ugly babies make pretty ladies,*" Agatha!
Phew! Little **Jain** ought to be quite a ***beauty,*** then.
Tsk. Please bring in the children now, Aggie.
Well, if you really want to *frighten* them...
Christian? Galen? Come meet your sister Jain!
ZZZZ...
Not 'nother ***sister!***
This one's *different*. This one's ***ours.***
Aimee! Andreia!
Your mother and father want you to come in and meet your ***new sister.***

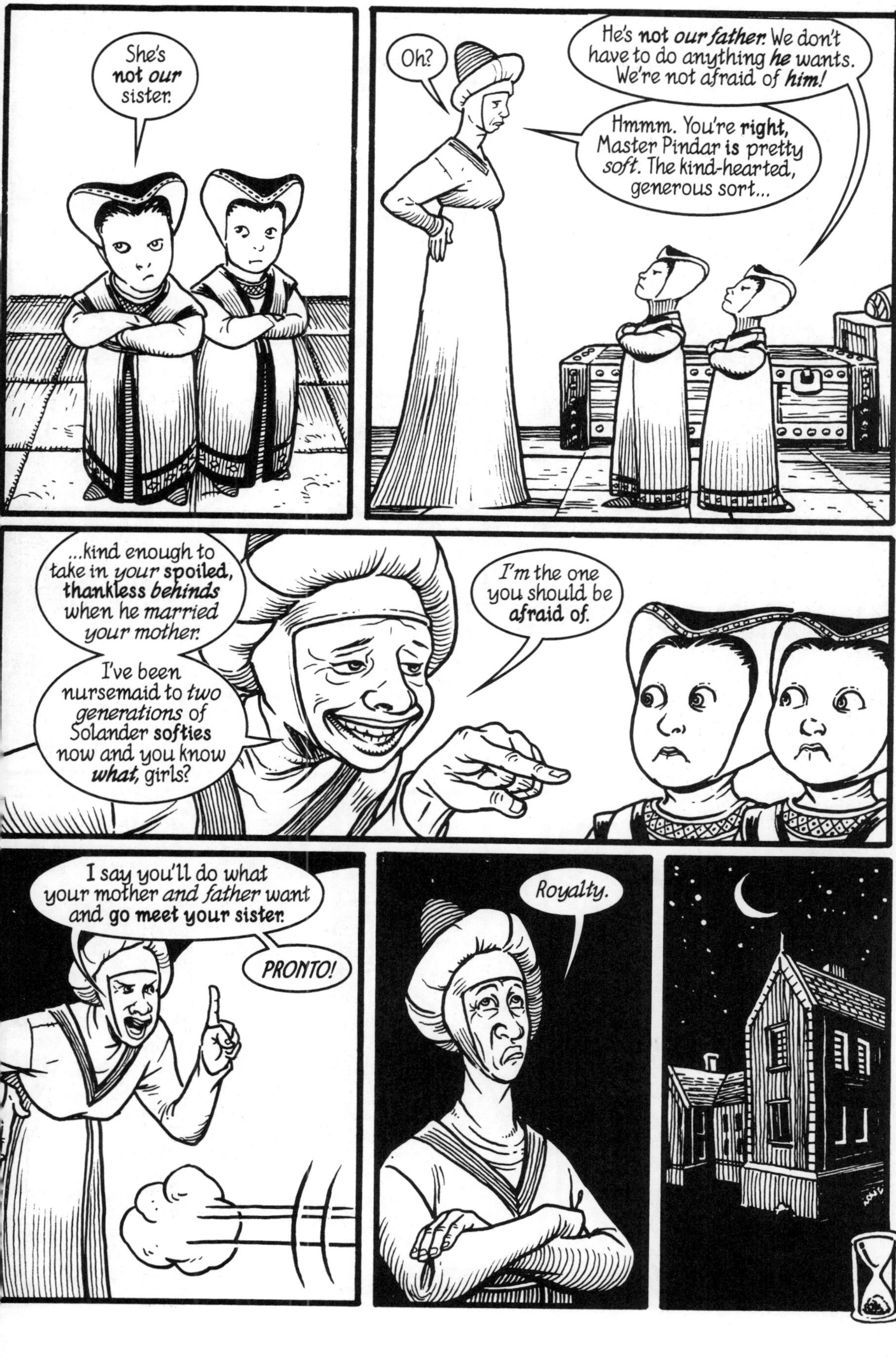
She's not our sister.
Oh?
He's not our father. We don't have to do anything he wants. We're not afraid of him!
Hmmm. You're right, Master Pindar is pretty soft. The kind-hearted, generous sort...
...kind enough to take in your spoiled, thankless behinds when he married your mother.
I've been nursemaid to two generations of Solander softies now and you know what, girls?
I'm the one you should be afraid of.
I say you'll do what your mother and father want and go meet your sister.
PRONTO!
Royalty.

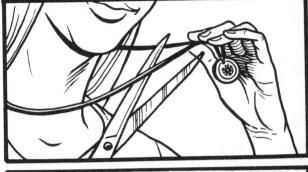

Knock, knock! Just me 'n' Simon!

Feel up to a jaunt into the *kitchen?*

Sure!

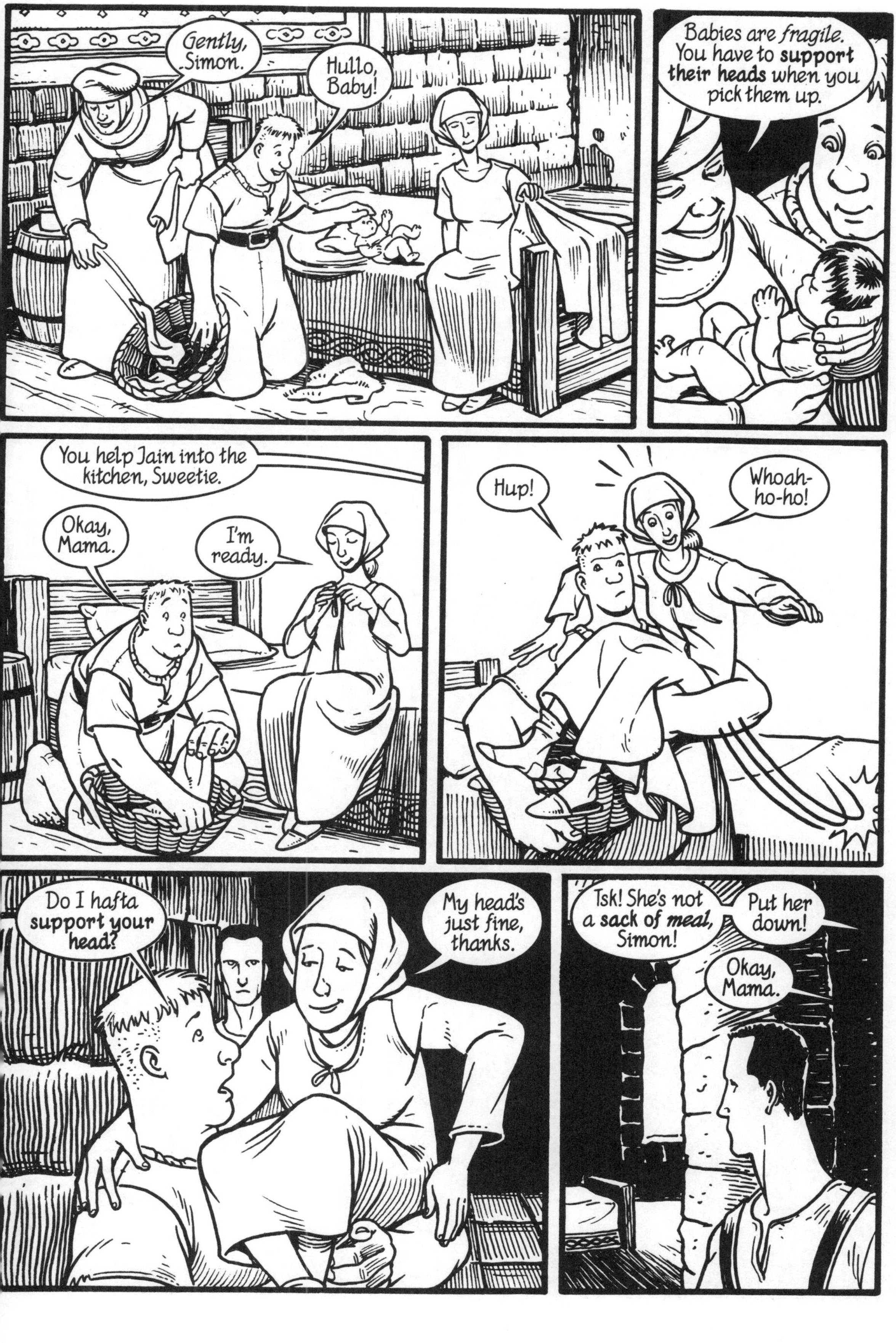
Gently, Simon.
Hullo, Baby!
Babies are *fragile.* You have to **support their heads** when you pick them up.
You help Jain into the kitchen, Sweetie.
Okay, Mama.
I'm ready.
Hup!
Whoah-ho-ho!
Do I hafta **support your head?**
My head's just fine, thanks.
Tsk! She's not a **sack of *meal*,** Simon!
Put her down!
Okay, Mama.

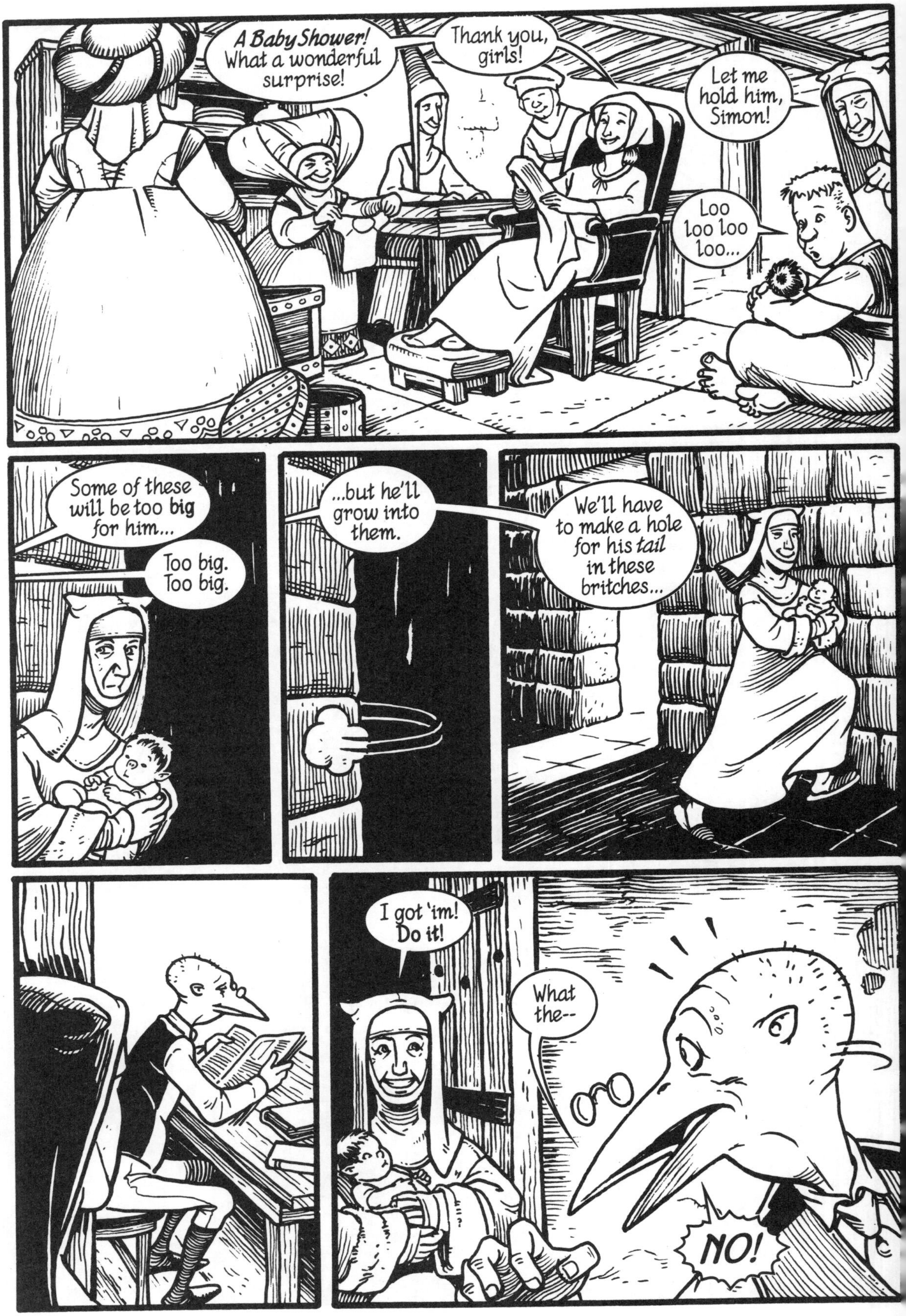
A Baby Shower! What a wonderful surprise!
Thank you, girls!
Let me hold him, Simon!
Loo loo loo loo...
Some of these will be too big for him...
Too big. Too big.
...but he'll grow into them.
We'll have to make a hole for his tail in these britches...
I got 'im! Do it!
What the--
NO!

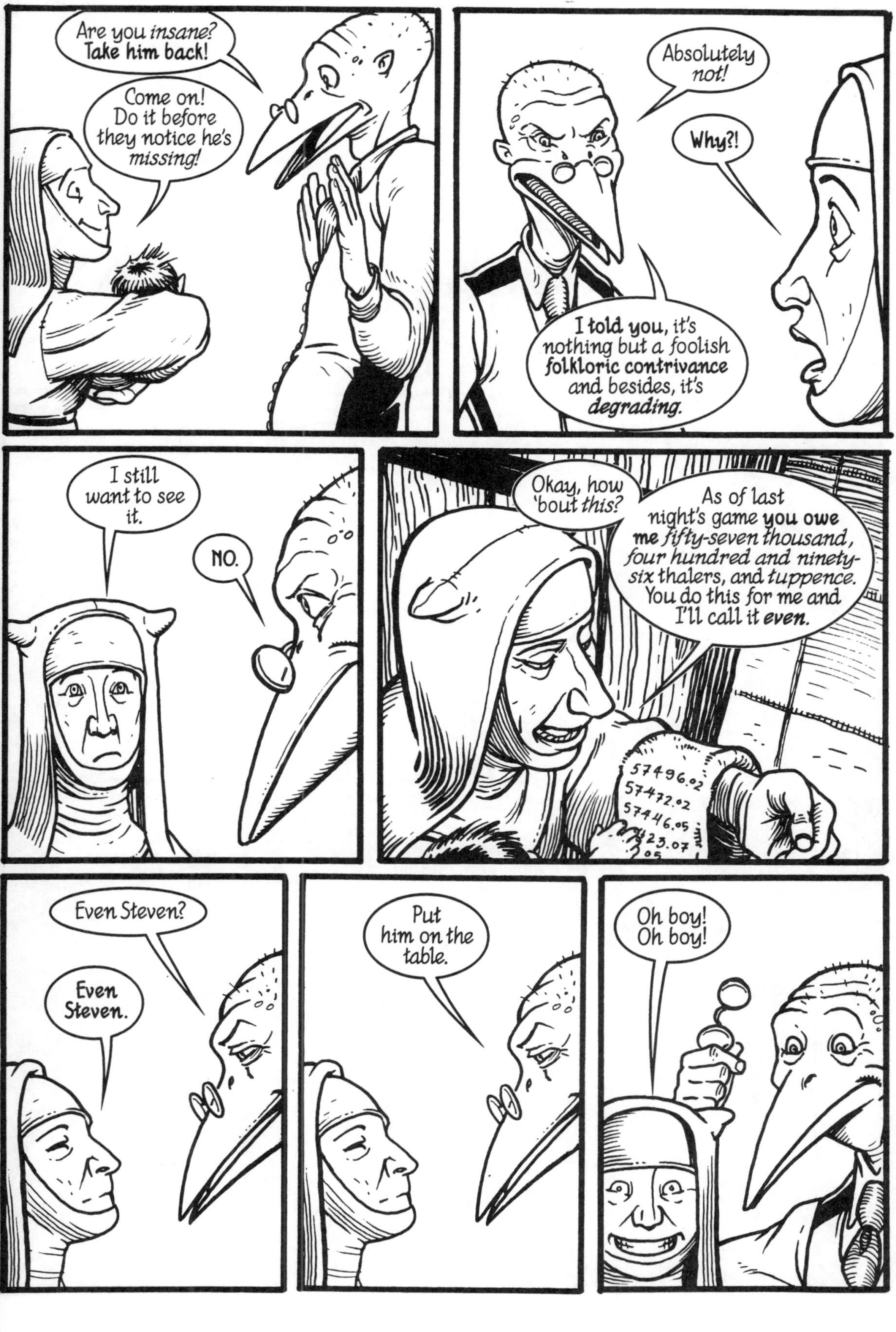

Are you *insane?* **Take him back!**
Come on! Do it before they notice he's *missing!*
Absolutely *not!*
Why?!
I told you, it's nothing but a foolish **folkloric contrivance** and besides, it's ***degrading***.
I still want to see it.
NO.
Okay, how 'bout *this?*
As of last night's game **you owe me** *fifty-seven thousand, four hundred and ninety-six* thalers, and *tuppence*. You do this for me and I'll call it ***even***.
57496.02
57472.02
57446.05
Even Steven?
Even Steven.
Put him on the table.
Oh boy! Oh boy!

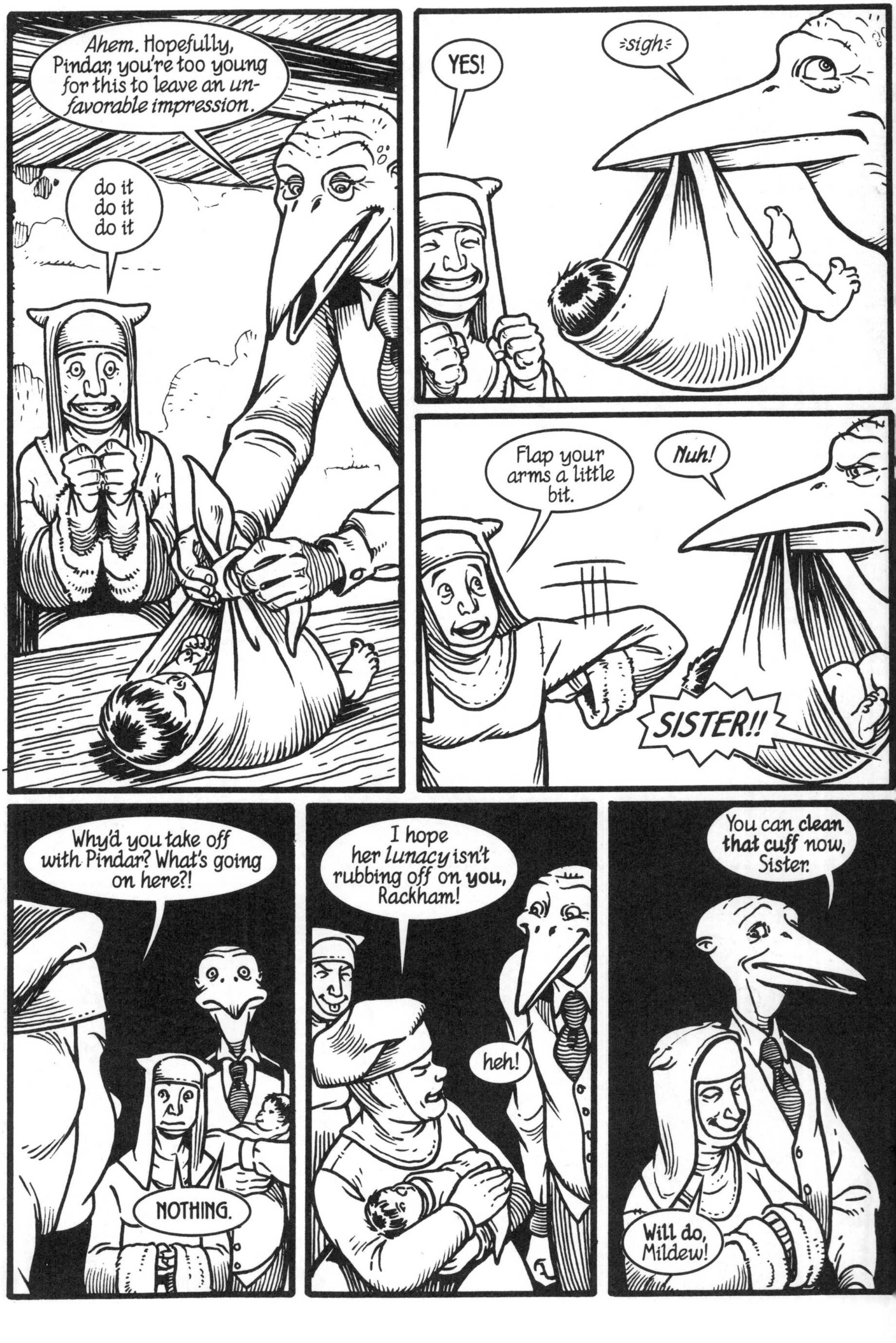
Ahem. Hopefully, Pindar, you're too young for this to leave an unfavorable impression.
do it do it do it
YES!
=sigh=
Flap your arms a little bit.
Nuh!
SISTER!!
Why'd you take off with Pindar? What's going on here?!
NOTHING.
I hope her lunacy isn't rubbing off on you, Rackham!
heh!
You can clean that cuff now, Sister.
Will do, Mildew!

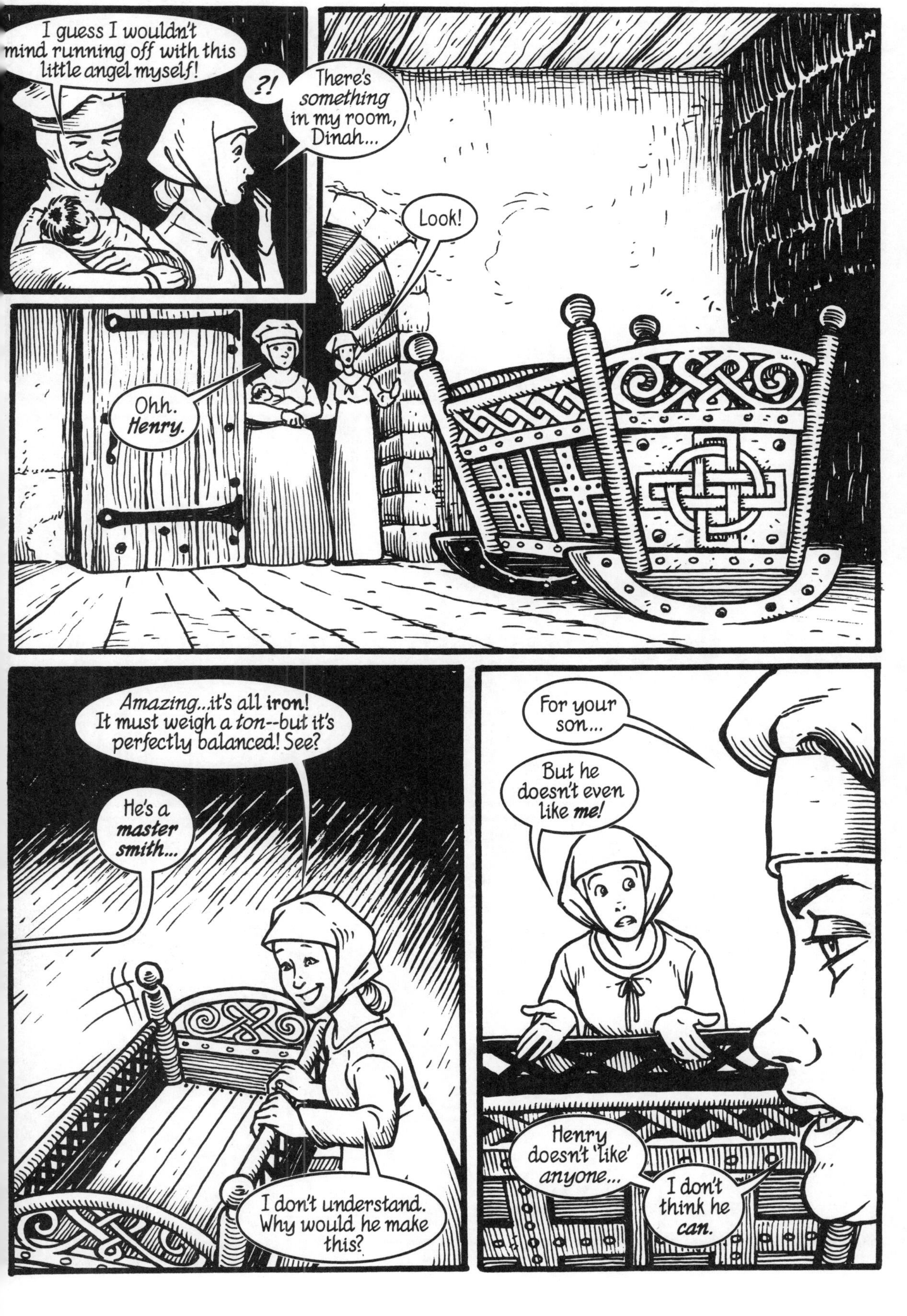

I guess I wouldn't mind running off with this little angel myself!
?!
There's *something* in my room, Dinah...
Look!
Ohh. **Henry.**
Amazing...it's all **iron**! It must weigh a *ton*--but it's perfectly balanced! See?
He's a ***master smith...***
I don't understand. Why would he make this?
For your son...
But he doesn't even like ***me!***
Henry doesn't 'like' *anyone*...
I don't think he ***can***.

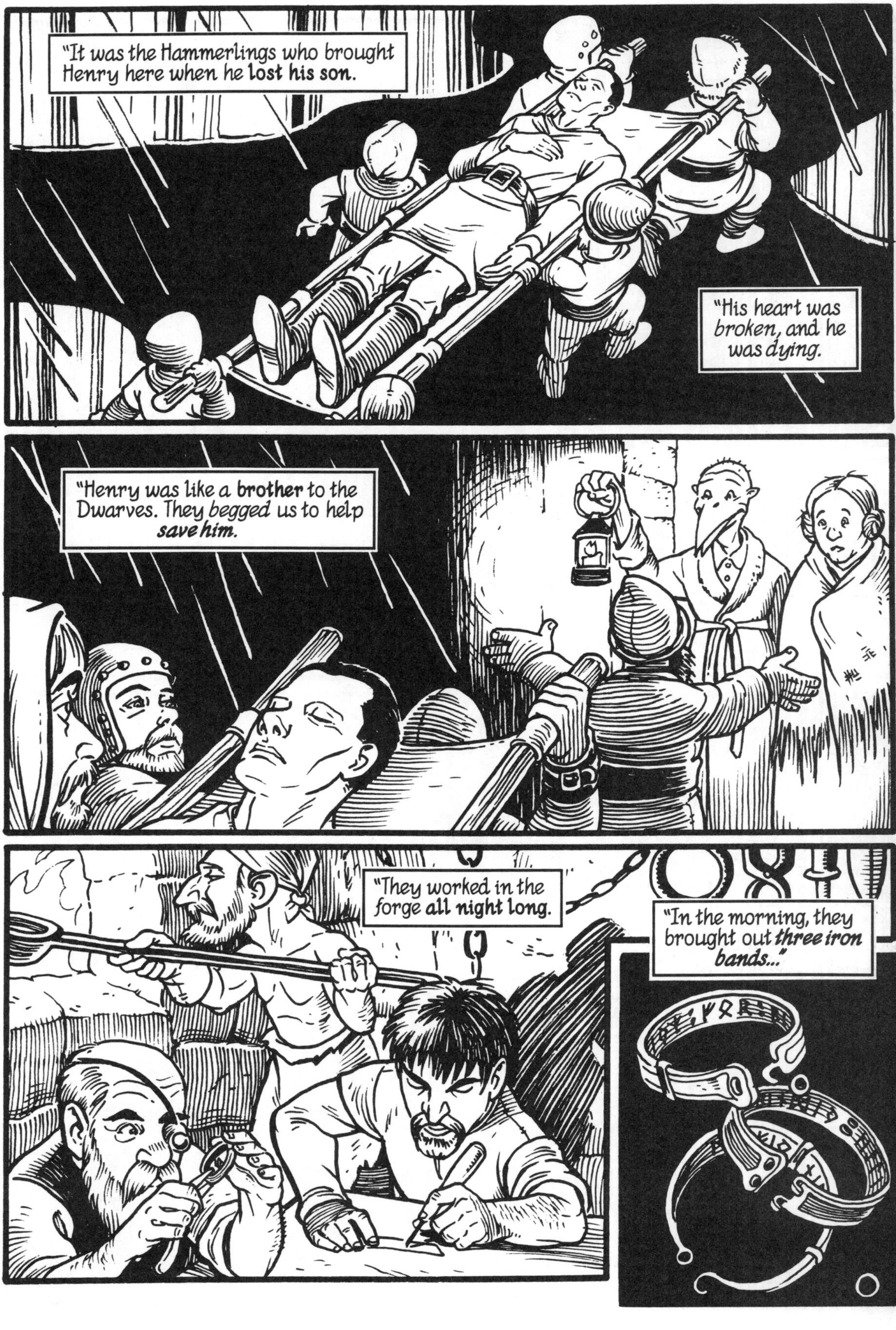
"It was the Hammerlings who brought Henry here when he **lost his son**.
"His heart was *broken*, and he was *dying*.
"Henry was like a **brother** to the Dwarves. They *begged* us to help ***save him***.
"They worked in the forge **all night long**.
"In the morning, they brought out ***three iron bands...***"

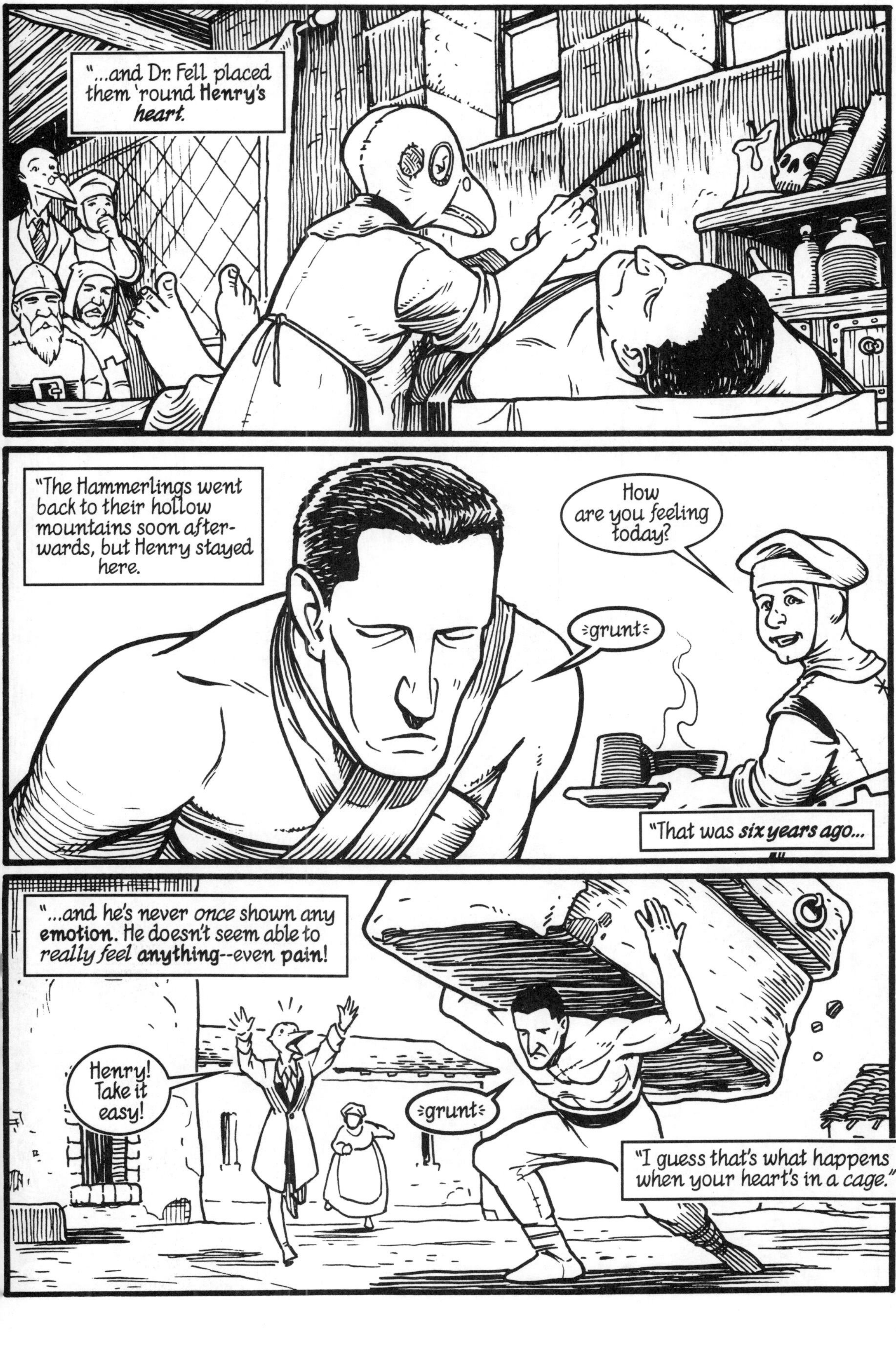
"...and Dr. Fell placed them 'round Henry's *heart*.
"The Hammerlings went back to their hollow mountains soon afterwards, but Henry stayed here.
How are you feeling today?
grunt
"That was **six years ago...**"
"...and he's never *once* shown any **emotion**. He doesn't seem able to *really feel* **anything**--even **pain**!
Henry! Take it easy!
grunt
"I guess that's what happens when your heart's in a cage."

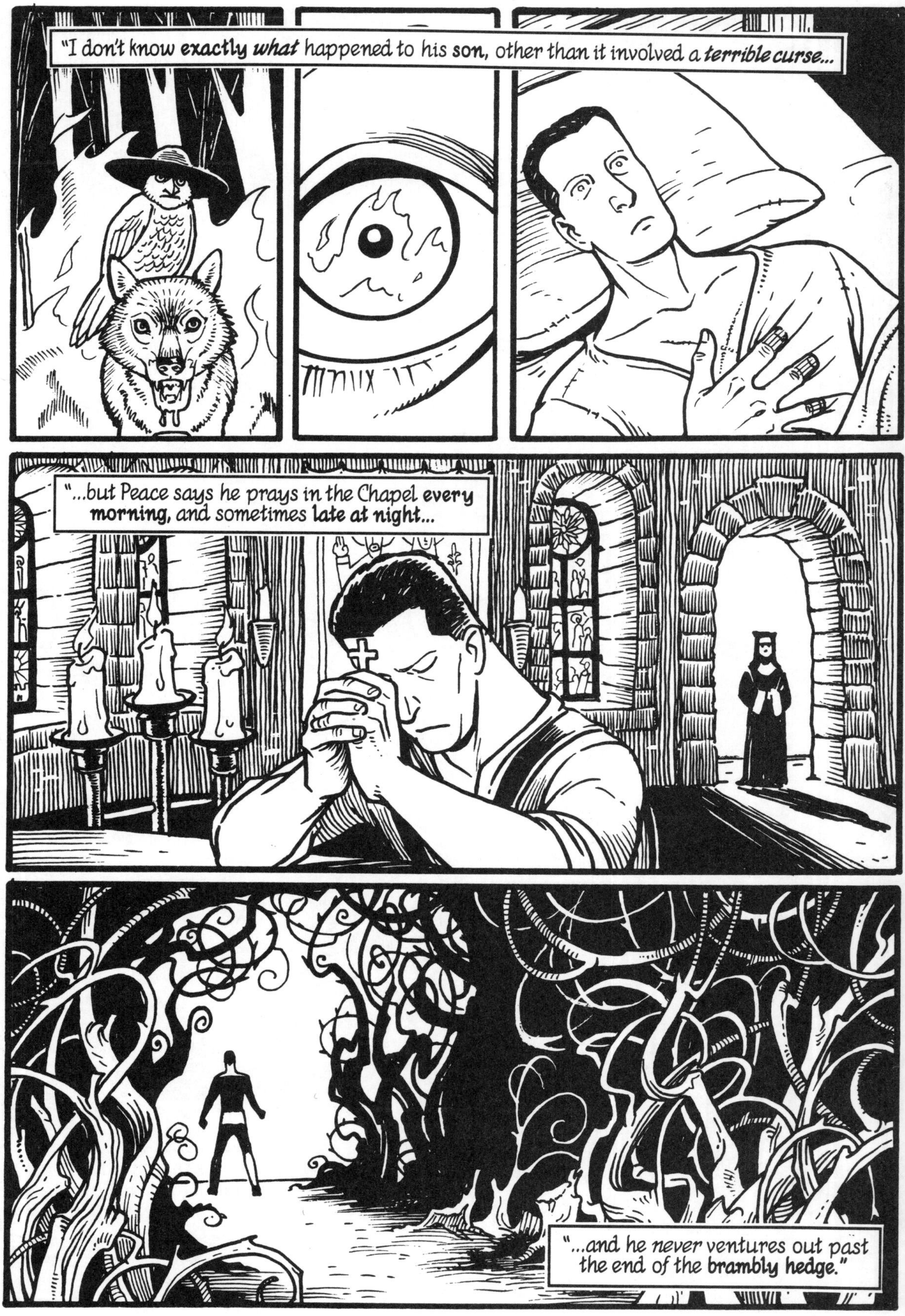
"I don't know exactly what happened to his son, other than it involved a terrible curse...
"...but Peace says he prays in the Chapel every morning, and sometimes late at night...
"...and he never ventures out past the end of the brambly hedge."

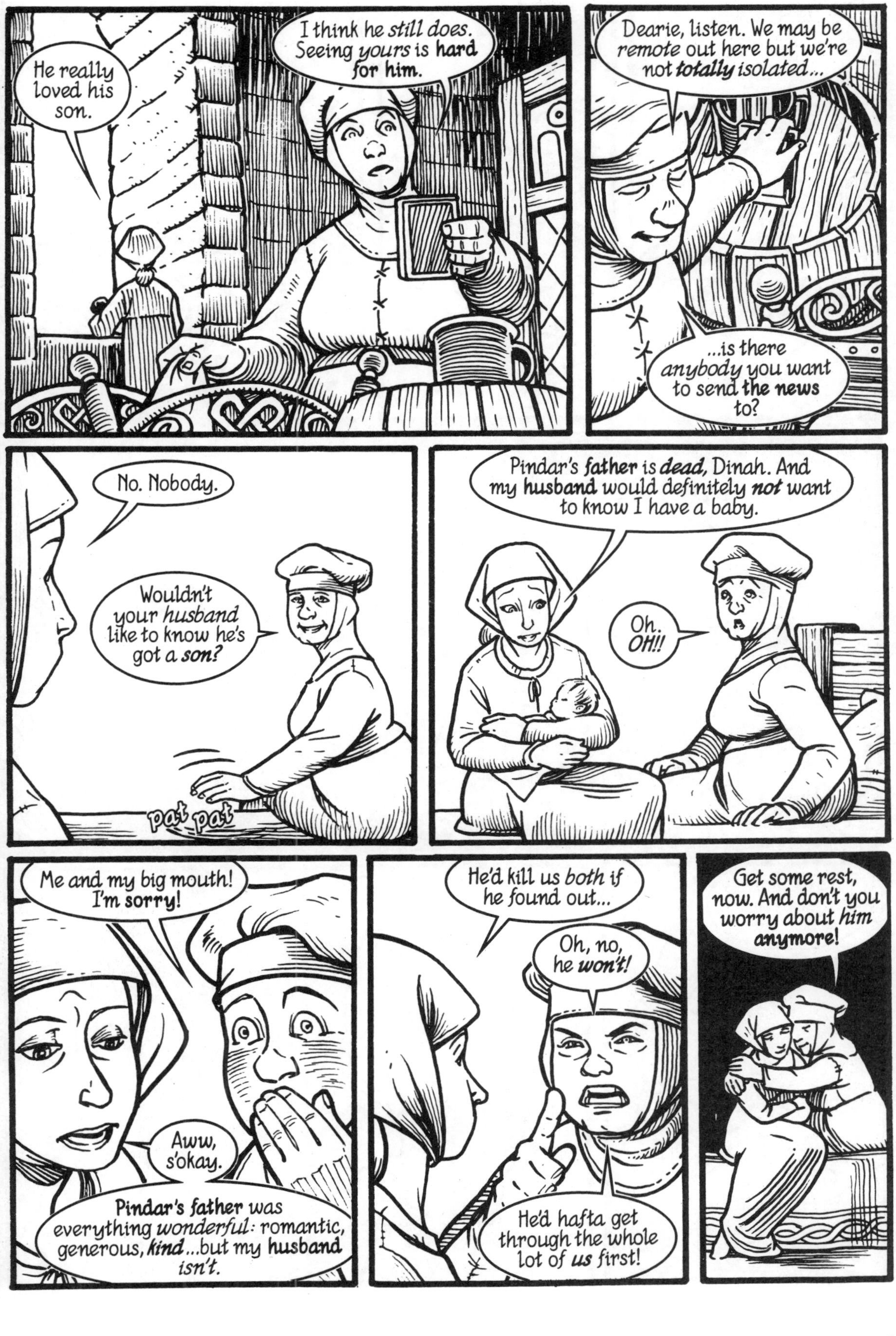
He really loved his son.
I think he *still does.* Seeing *yours* is **hard for him.**
Dearie, listen. We may be *remote* out here but we're not ***totally*** *isolated...*
...is there *anybody* you want to send **the news** to?
No. Nobody.
Wouldn't your *husband* like to know he's got a *son?*
pat pat
Pindar's **father** is ***dead,*** Dinah. And my **husband** would definitely ***not*** want to know I have a baby.
Oh. *OH!!*
Me and my big mouth! I'm **sorry**!
Aww, s'okay.
Pindar's father was everything *wonderful*: romantic, generous, ***kind***...but my **husband** *isn't.*
He'd kill us *both* if he found out...
Oh, no, he ***won't!***
He'd hafta get through the whole lot of ***us*** first!
Get some rest, now. And don't you worry about *him* **anymore**!

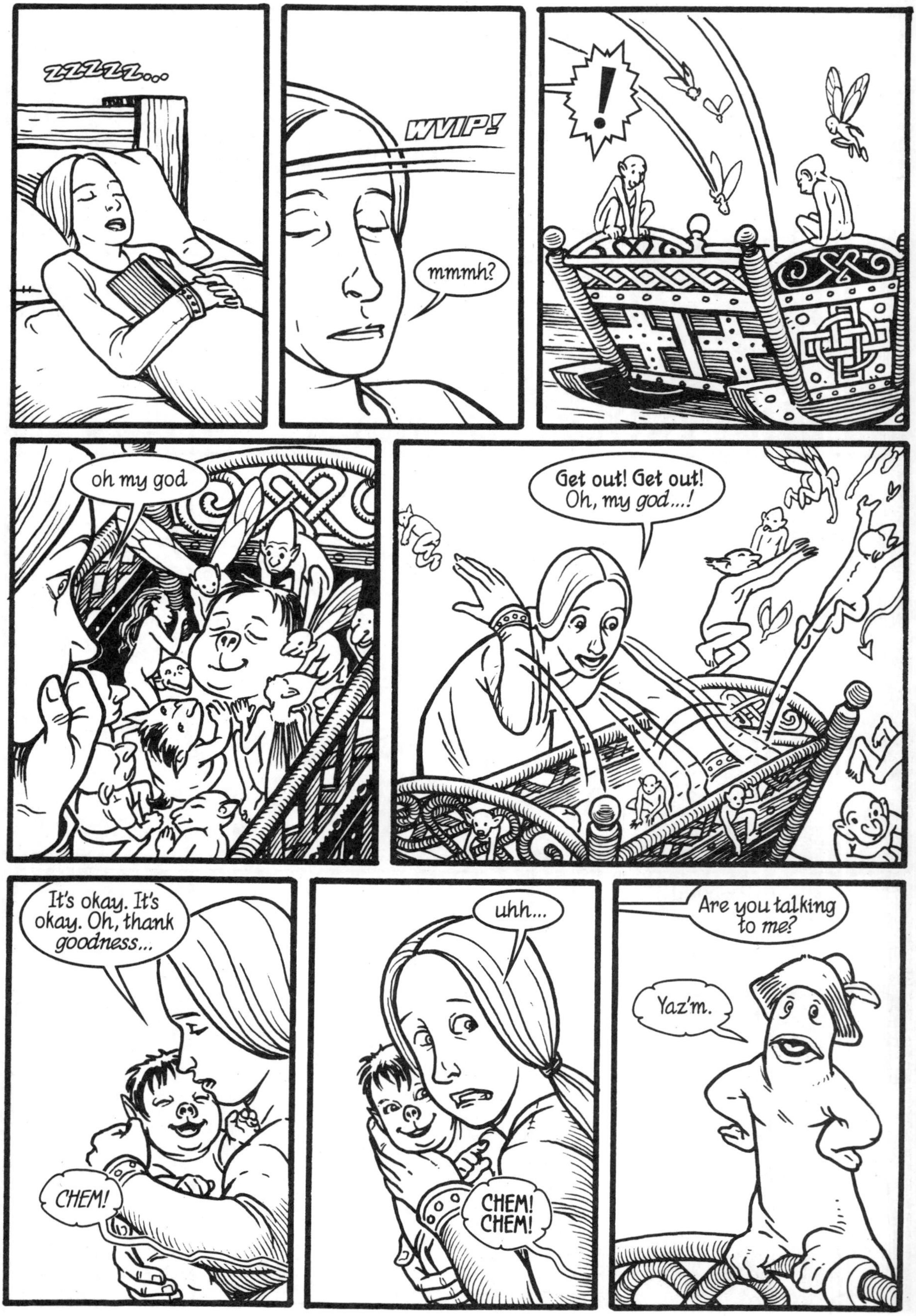
ZZZZZZ...
WVIP!
mmmh?
!
oh my god
Get out! Get out! Oh, my god...!
It's okay. It's okay. Oh, thank goodness...
CHEM!
uhh...
CHEM! CHEM!
Are you talking to me?
Yaz'm.

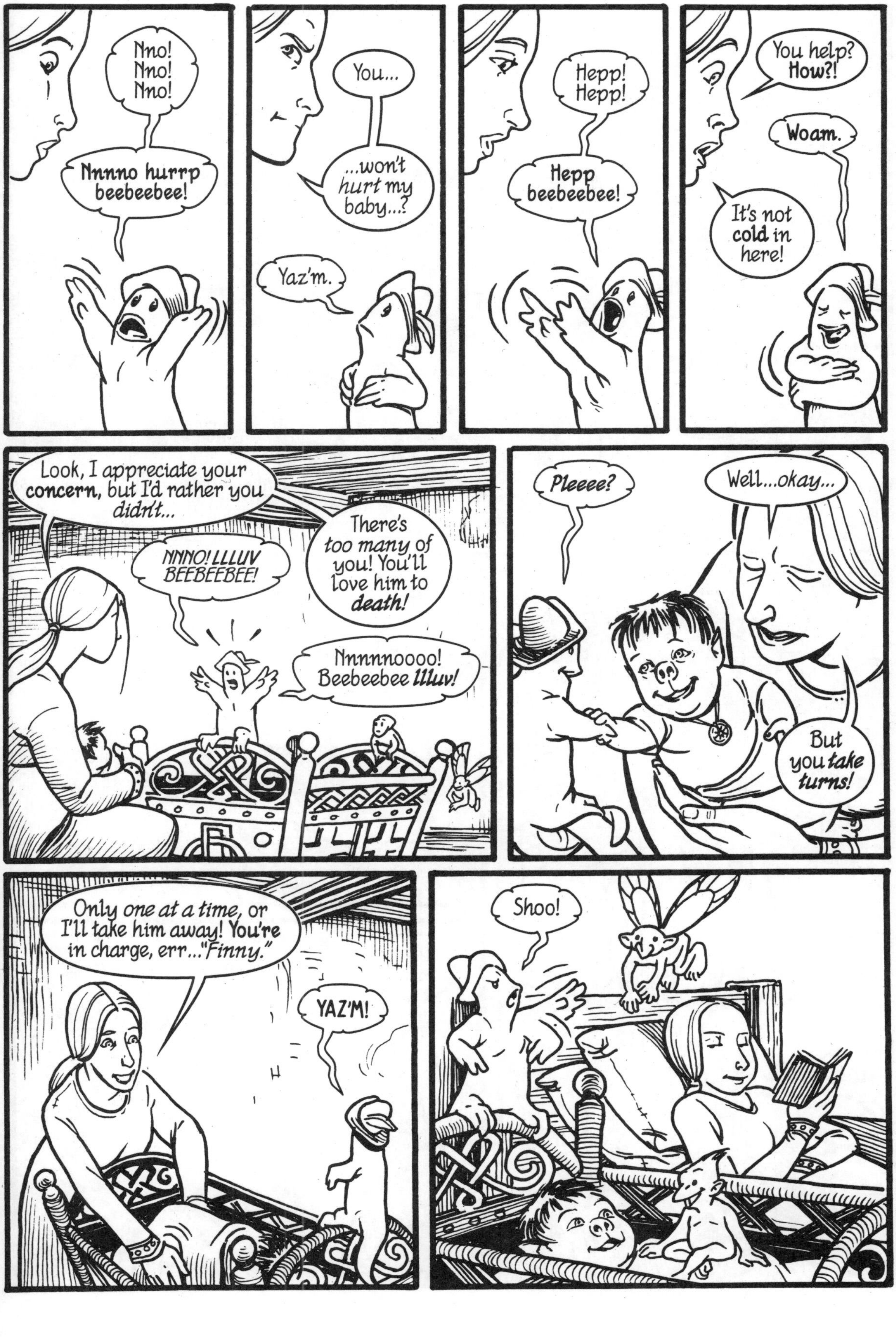
Nno! Nno! Nno!
Nnnno hurrp beebeebee!
You...
...won't hurt my baby...?
Yaz'm.
Hepp! Hepp!
Hepp beebeebee!
You help? How?!
Woam.
It's not cold in here!
Look, I appreciate your concern, but I'd rather you didn't...
NNNO! LLLUV BEEBEEBEE!
There's too many of you! You'll love him to death!
Nnnnnoooo! Beebeebee llluv!
Pleeee?
Well...okay...
But you take turns!
Only one at a time, or I'll take him away! You're in charge, err..."Finny."
YAZ'M!
Shoo!

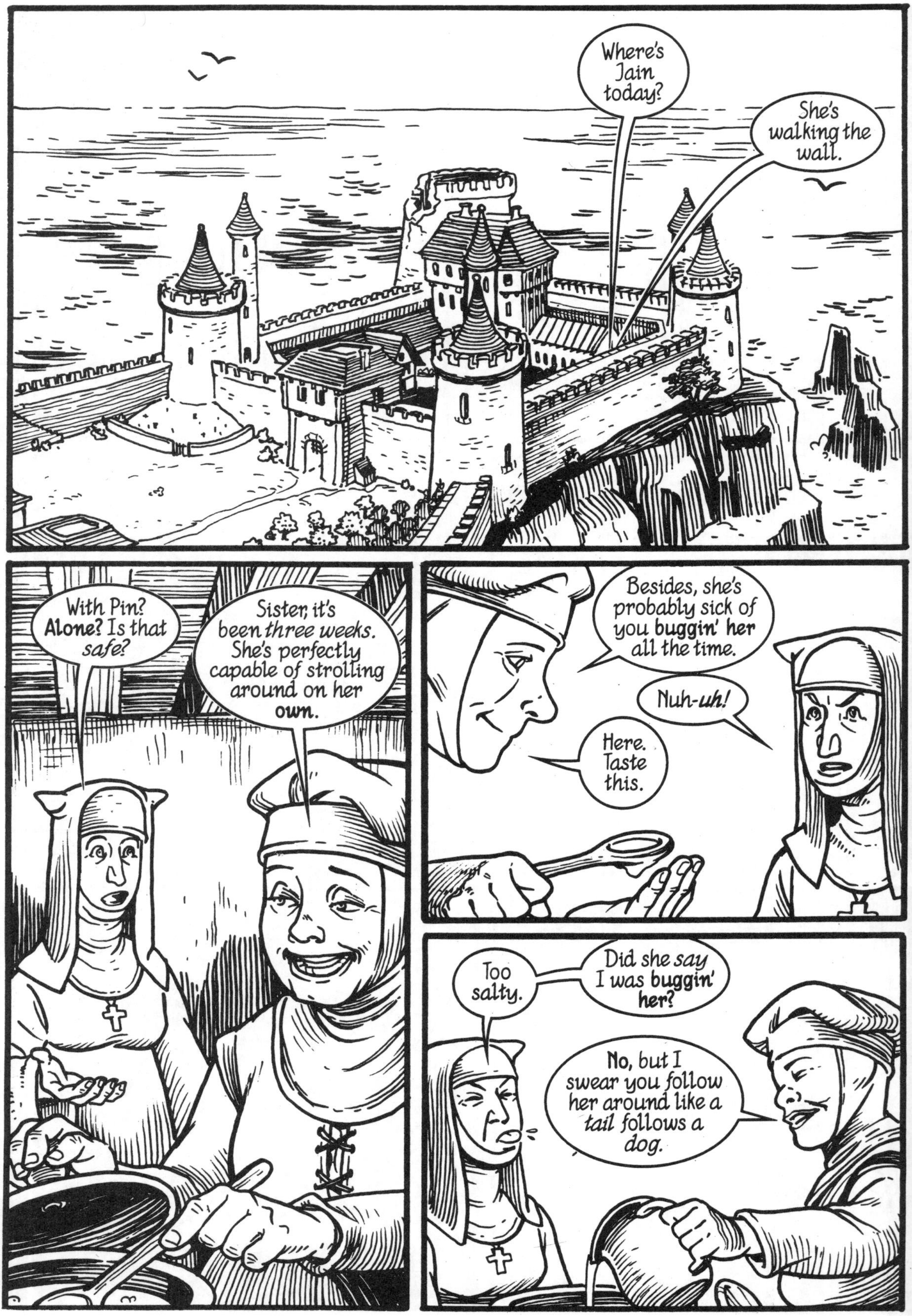

Where's Jain today?
She's walking the wall.
With Pin? Alone? Is that safe?
Sister, it's been three weeks. She's perfectly capable of strolling around on her own.
Besides, she's probably sick of you buggin' her all the time.
Nuh-uh!
Here. Taste this.
Too salty.
Did she say I was buggin' her?
No, but I swear you follow her around like a tail follows a dog.

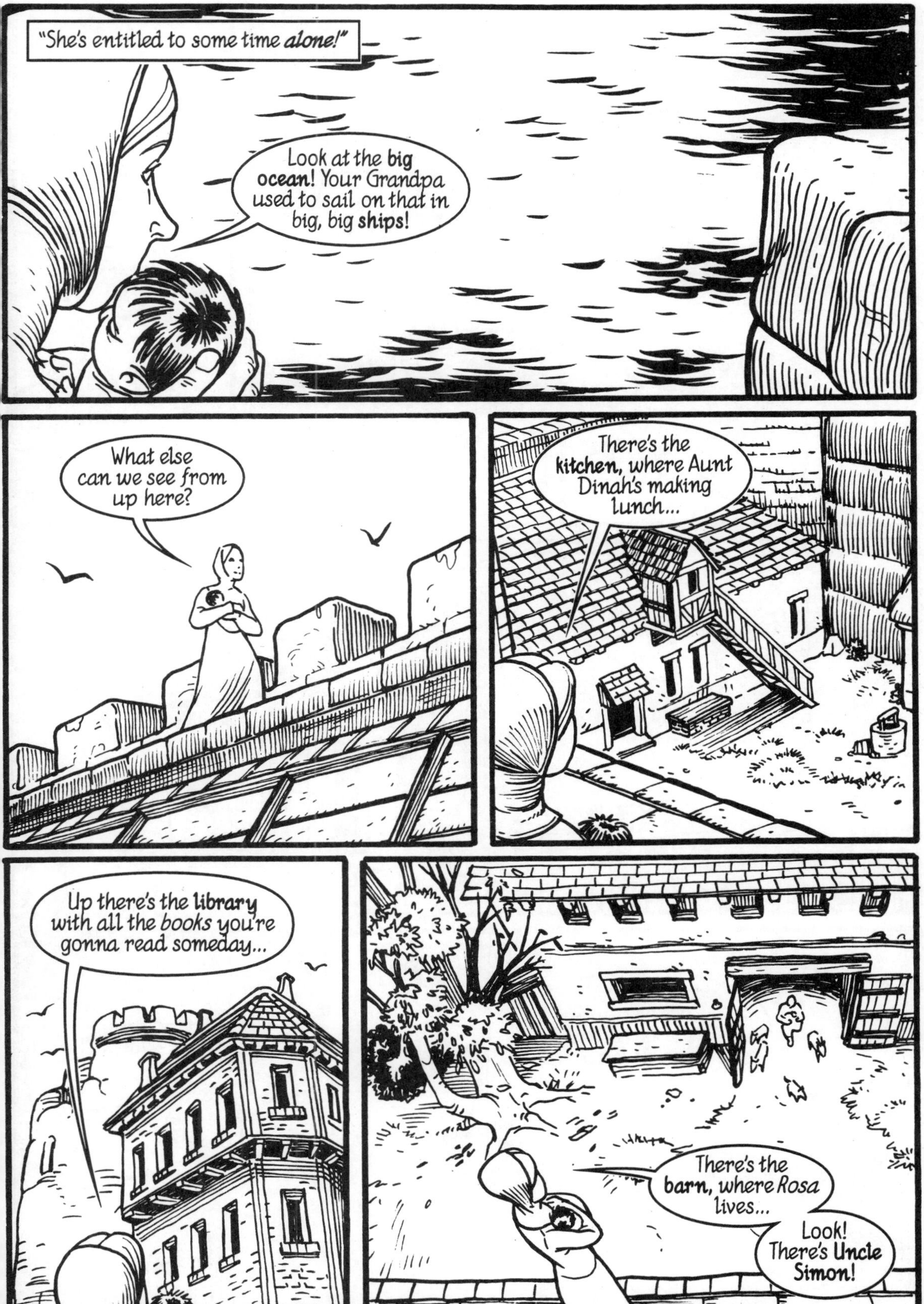
"She's entitled to some time *alone!*"
Look at the **big ocean**! Your Grandpa used to sail on that in big, big **ships**!
What else can we see from up here?
There's the **kitchen**, where Aunt Dinah's making lunch...
Up there's the **library** with all the *books* you're gonna read someday...
There's the **barn**, where *Rosa* lives...
Look! There's **Uncle Simon**!

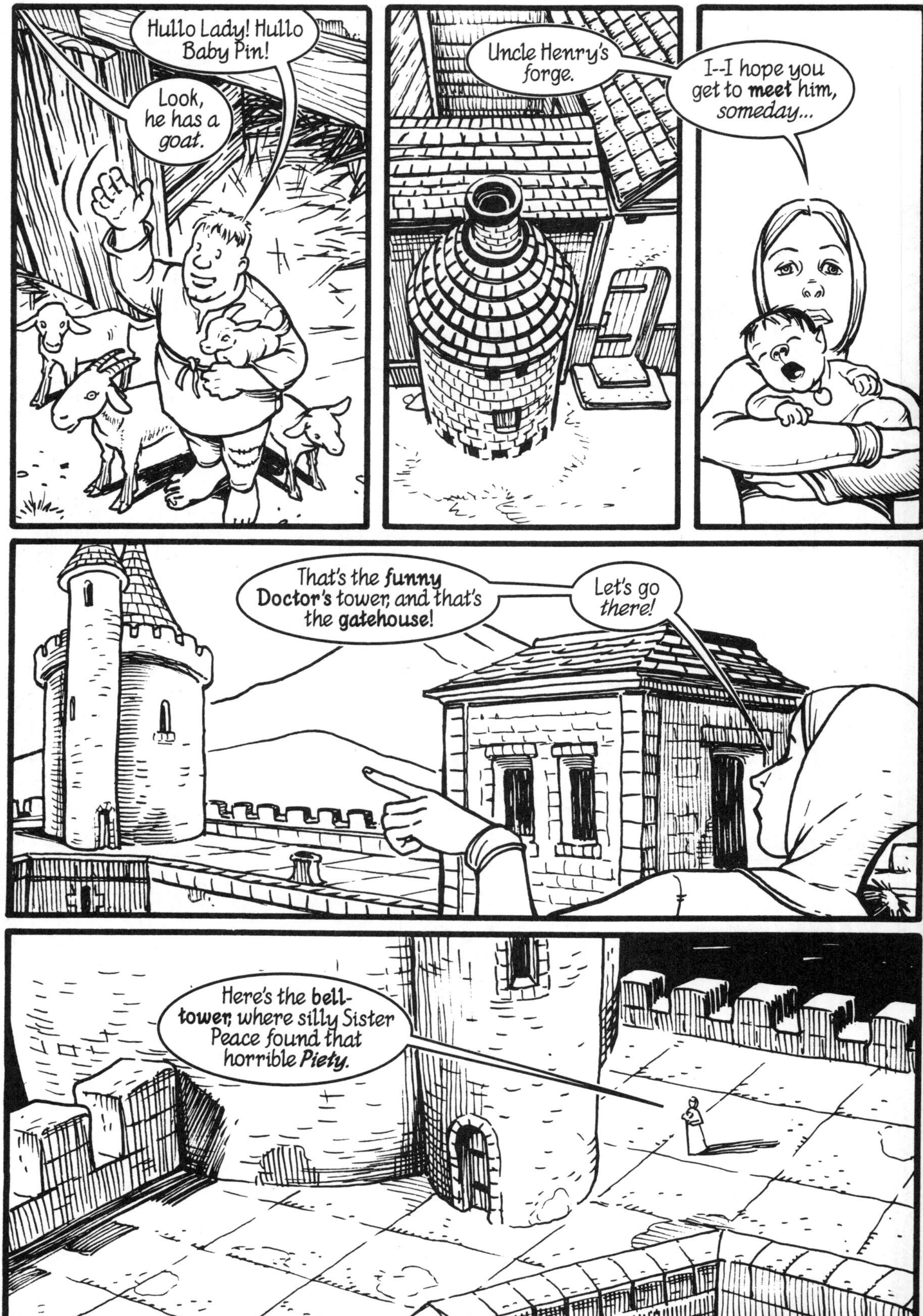
Hullo Lady! Hullo Baby Pin!
Look, he has a *goat.*
Uncle Henry's forge.
I--I hope you get to **meet** him, *someday...*
That's the **funny Doctor's** tower, and that's the **gatehouse**!
Let's go *there!*
Here's the **bell-tower**, where silly Sister Peace found that horrible ***Piety***.

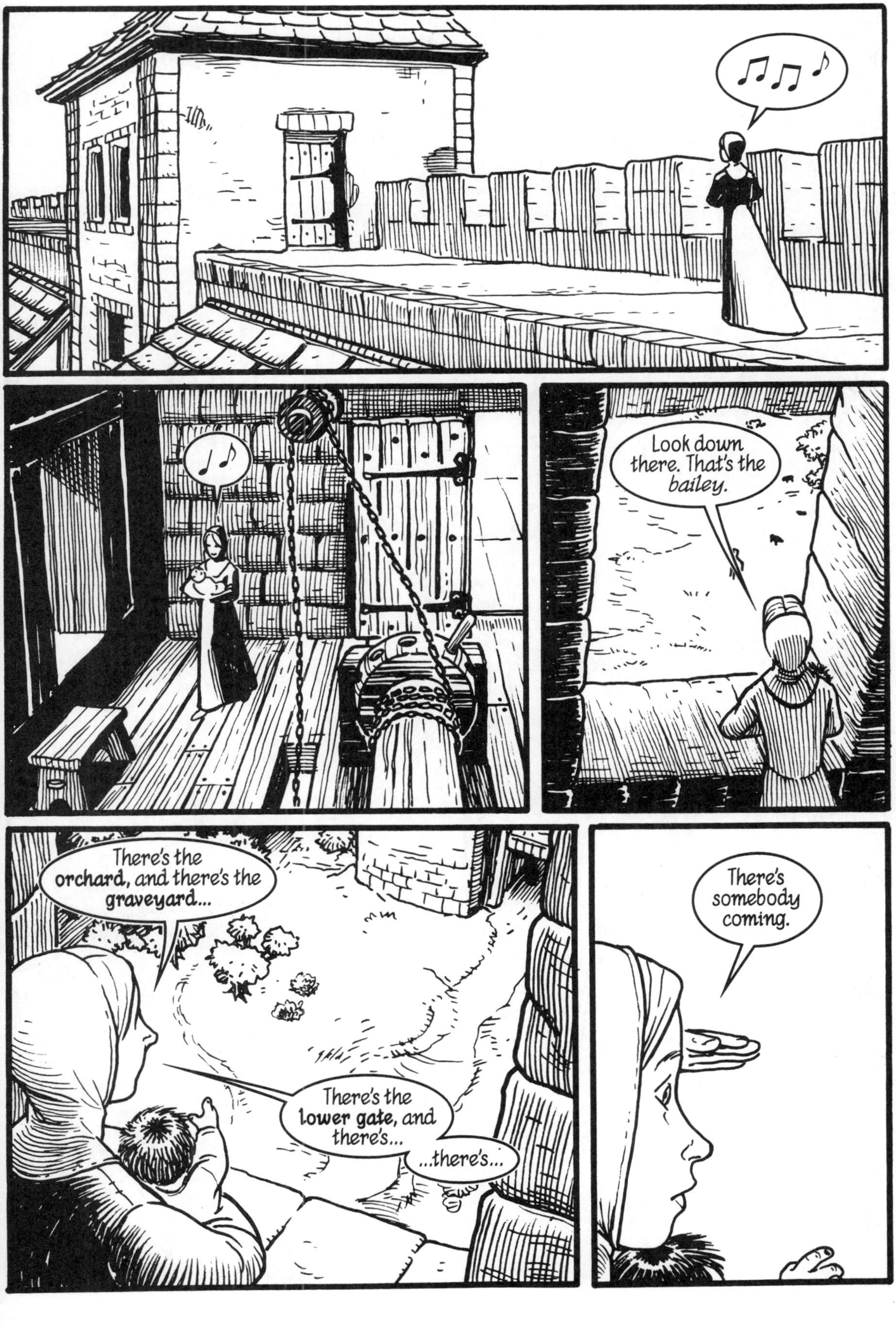
Look down there. That's the *bailey.*
There's the **orchard**, and there's the **graveyard**...
There's the **lower gate**, and there's...
...there's...
There's somebody coming.

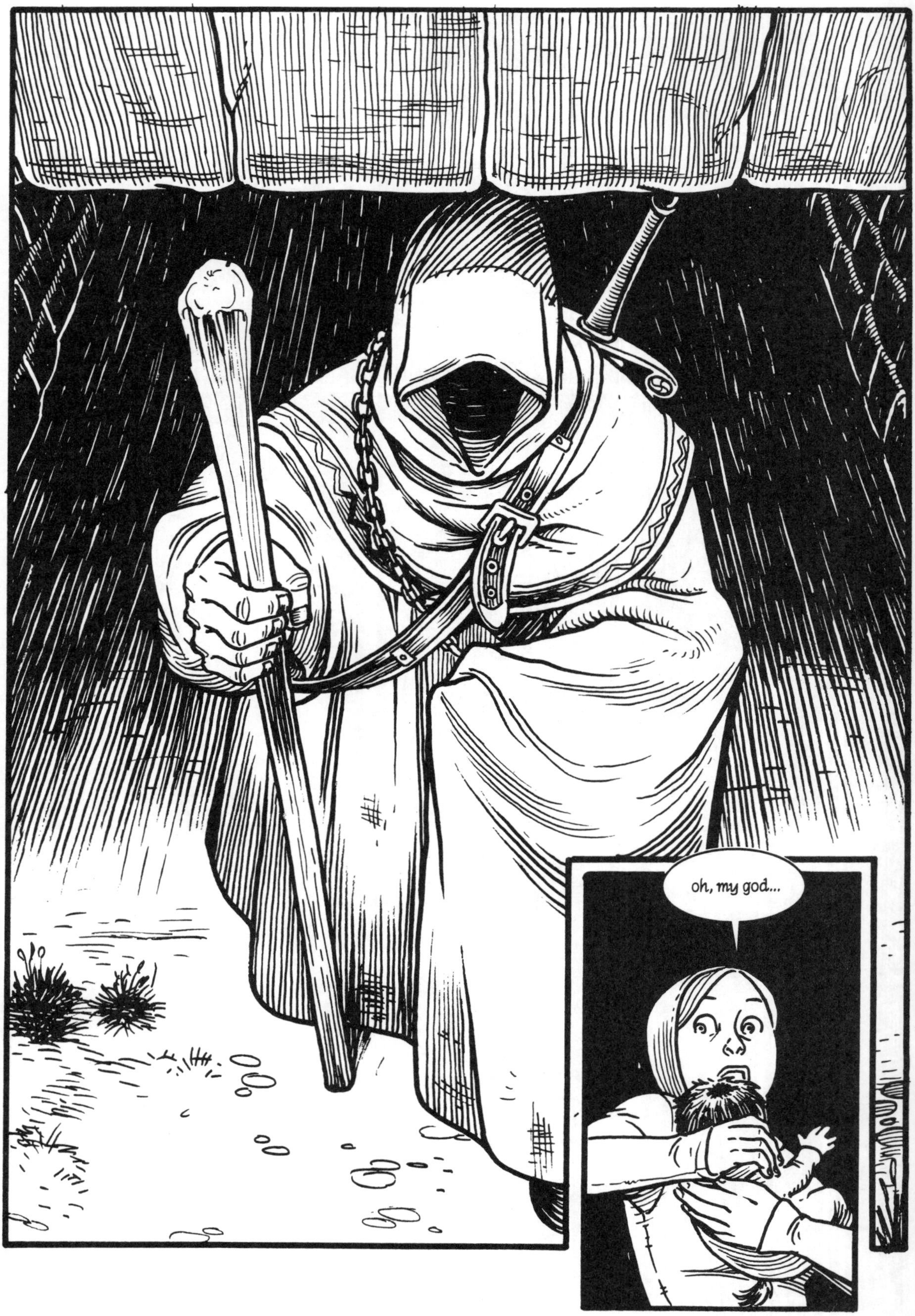
oh, my god...

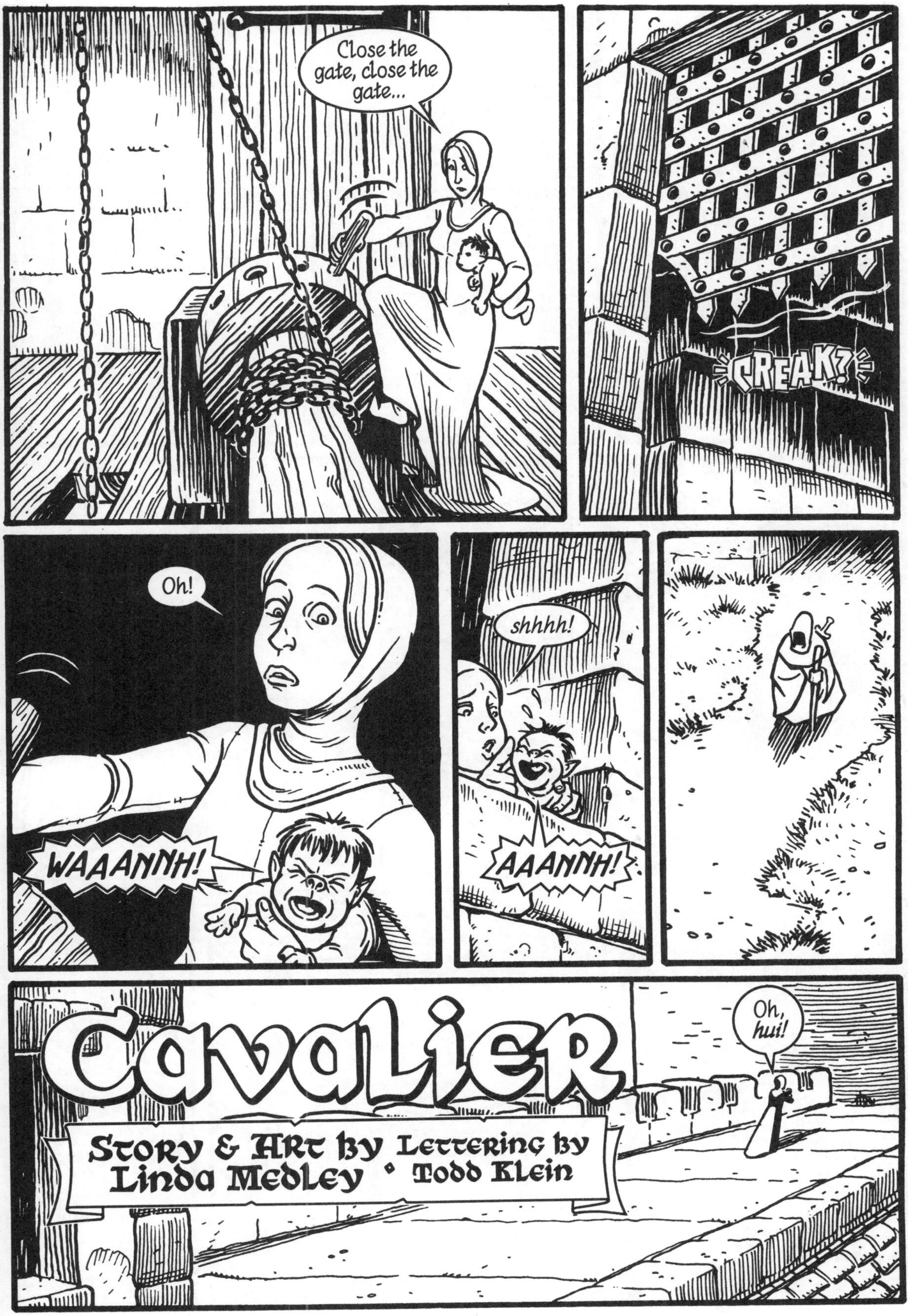
Close the gate, close the gate...
CREAK!
Oh!
WAAANNH!
shhhh!
AAANNH!
Cavalier
Oh, hui!
Story & Art by Linda Medley
Lettering by Todd Klein

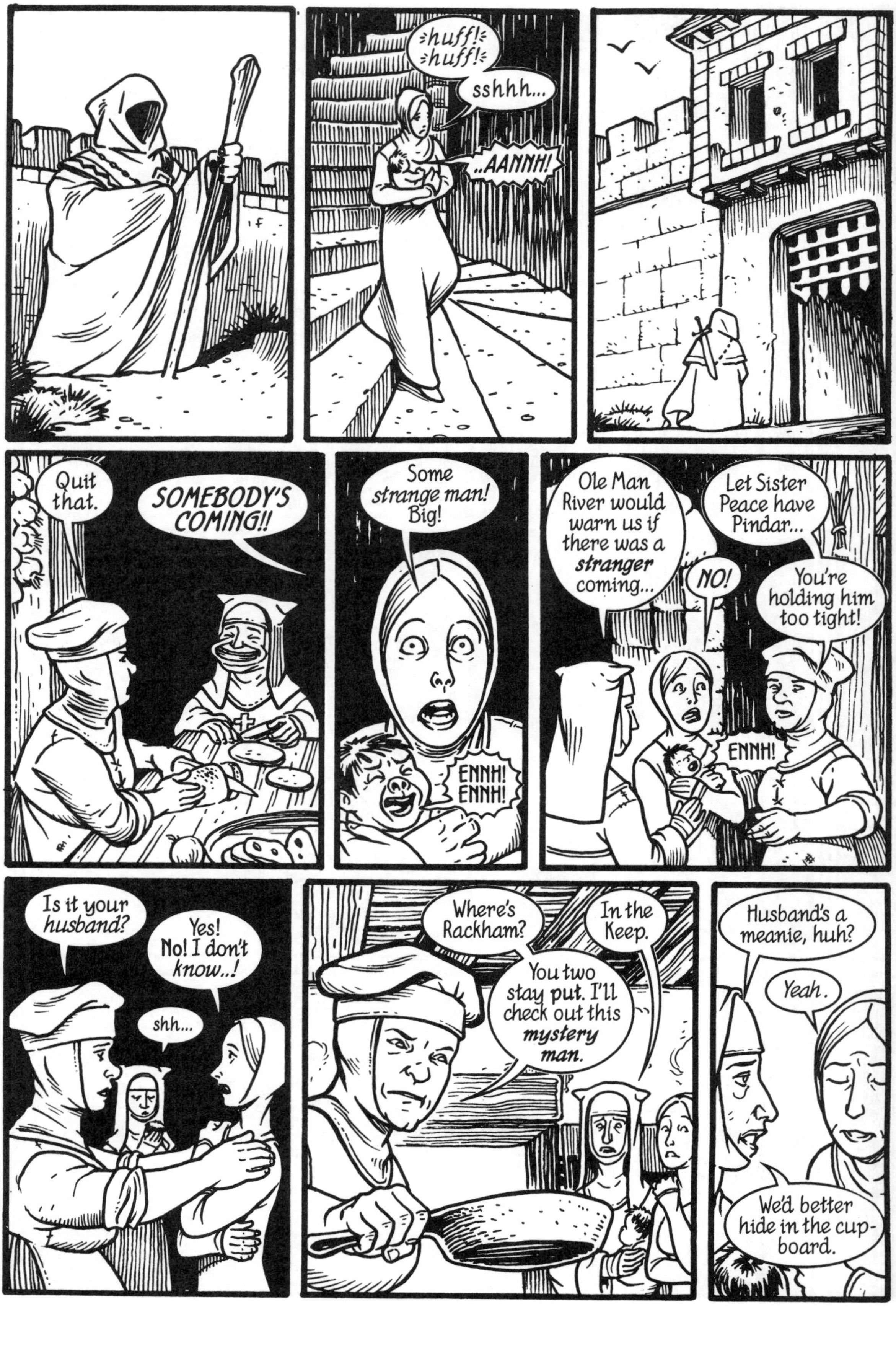
huff! huff!
sshhh...
..AANNH!
Quit that.
SOMEBODY'S COMING!!
Some strange man! Big!
ENNH! ENNH!
Ole Man River would warn us if there was a stranger coming...
Let Sister Peace have Pindar...
NO!
You're holding him too tight!
ENNH!
Is it your husband?
Yes! No! I don't know..!
shh...
Where's Rackham?
In the Keep.
You two stay put. I'll check out this mystery man.
Husband's a meanie, huh?
Yeah.
We'd better hide in the cupboard.

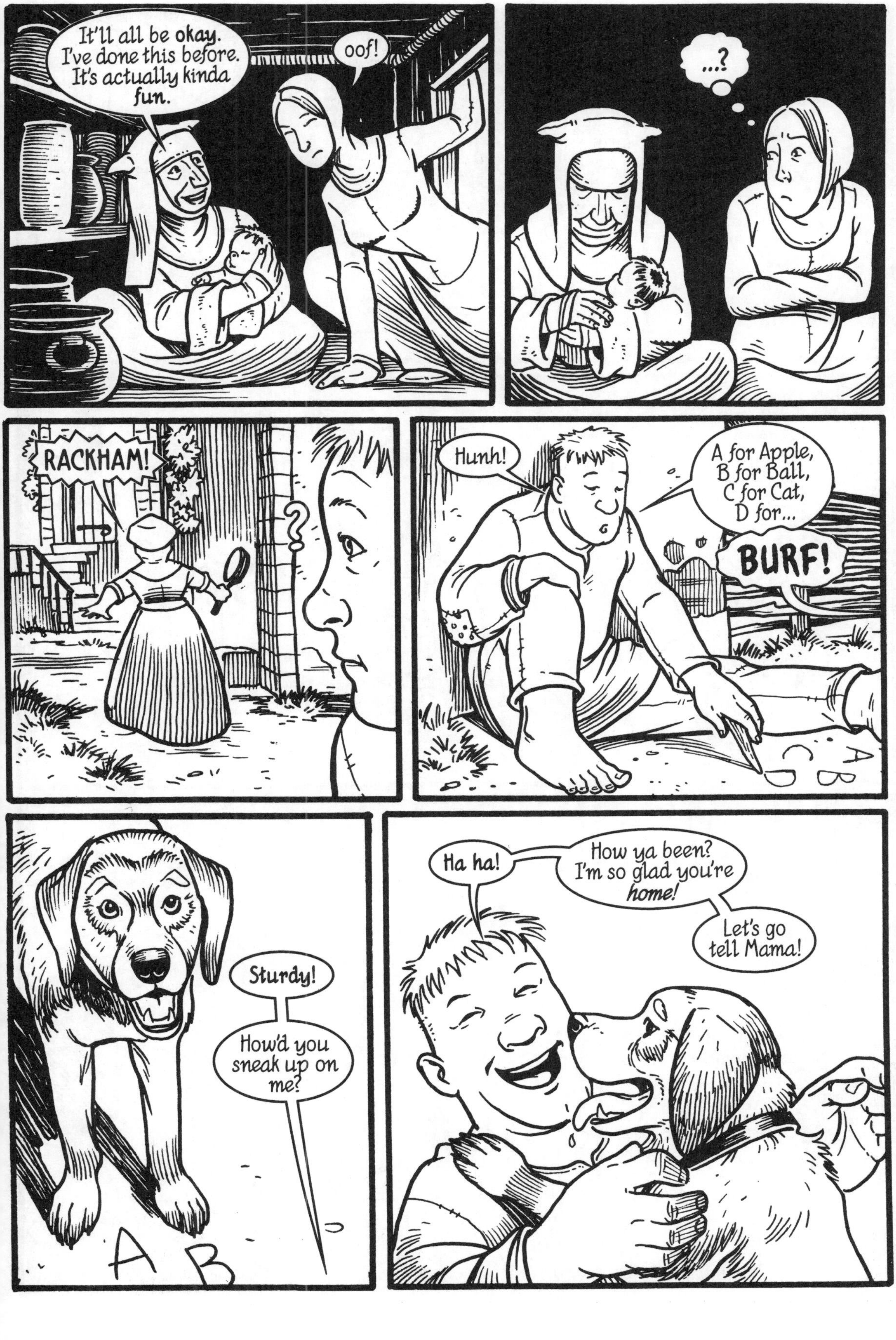
It'll all be okay. I've done this before. It's actually kinda fun.
oof!
...?
RACKHAM!
?
Hunh!
A for Apple, B for Ball, C for Cat, D for...
BURF!
Sturdy!
How'd you sneak up on me?
Ha ha!
How ya been? I'm so glad you're *home!*
Let's go tell Mama!

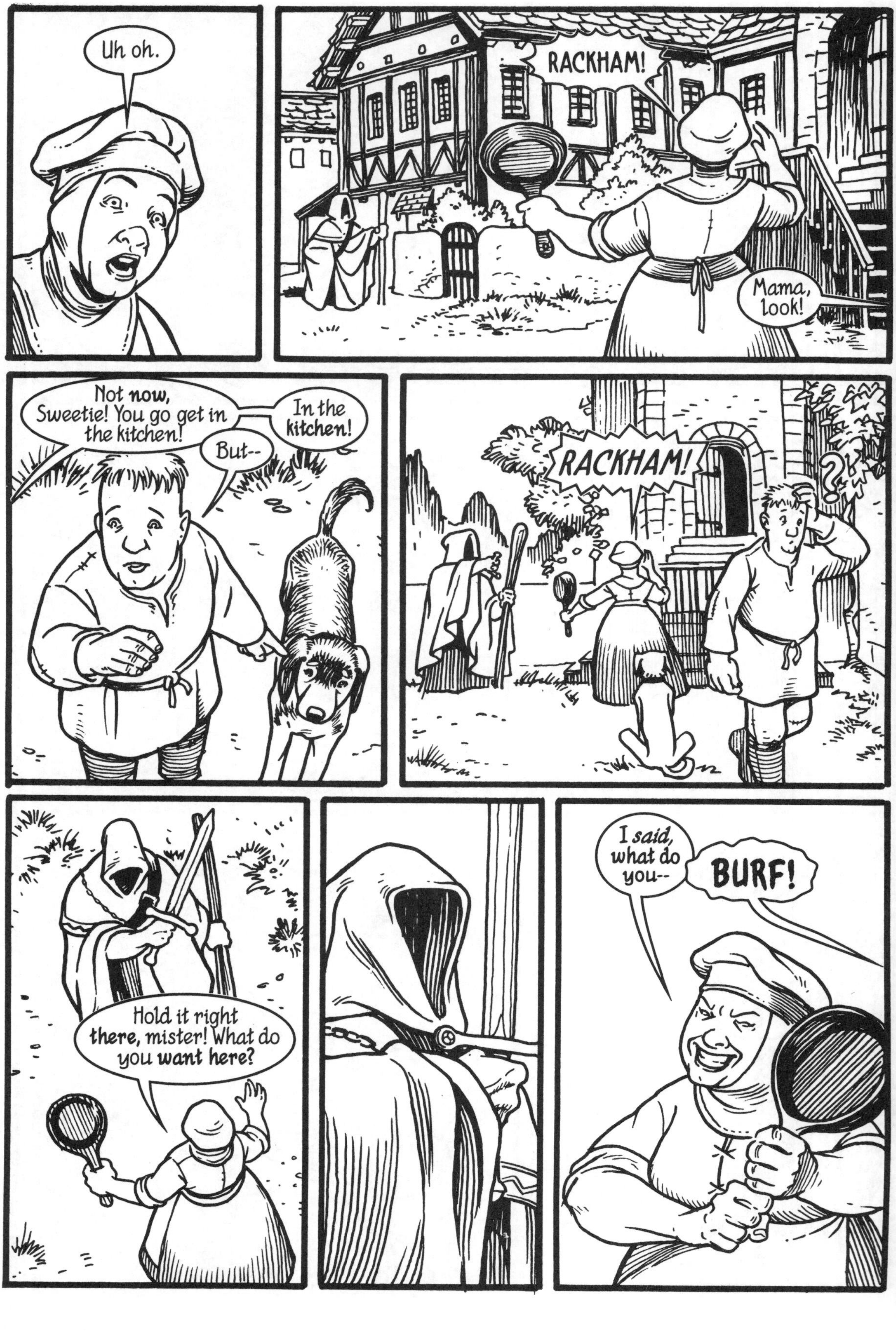
Uh oh.
RACKHAM!
Mama, look!
Not now, Sweetie! You go get in the kitchen!
In the kitchen!
But--
RACKHAM!
?
Hold it right there, mister! What do you want here?
I said, what do you--
BURF!

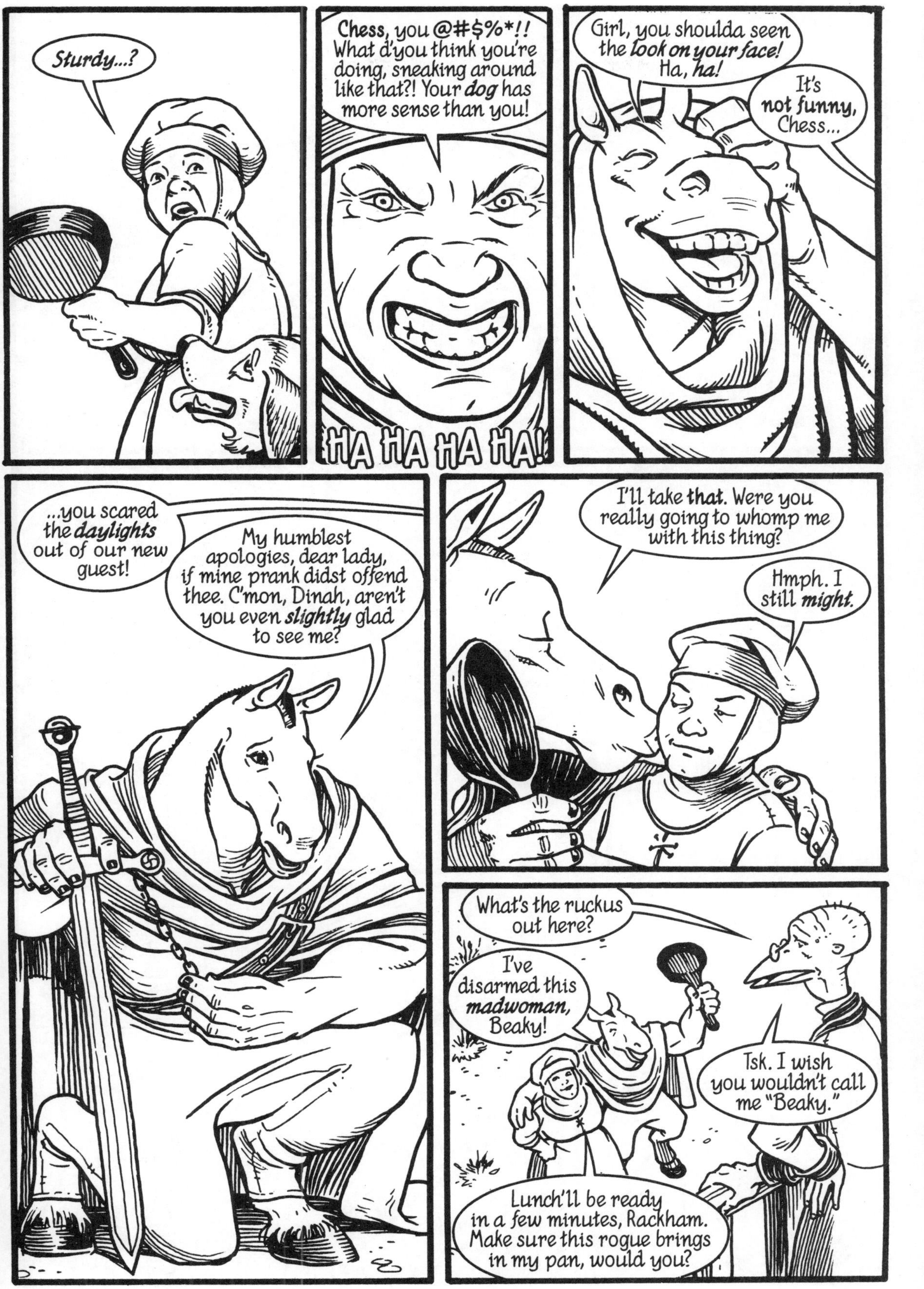
Sturdy...?
Chess, you @#$%*!! What d'you think you're doing, sneaking around like that?! Your dog has more sense than you!
HA HA HA HA!
Girl, you shoulda seen the look on your face! Ha, ha!
It's not funny, Chess...
...you scared the daylights out of our new guest!
My humblest apologies, dear lady, if mine prank didst offend thee. C'mon, Dinah, aren't you even slightly glad to see me?
I'll take that. Were you really going to whomp me with this thing?
Hmph. I still might.
What's the ruckus out here?
I've disarmed this madwoman, Beaky!
Tsk. I wish you wouldn't call me "Beaky."
Lunch'll be ready in a few minutes, Rackham. Make sure this rogue brings in my pan, would you?

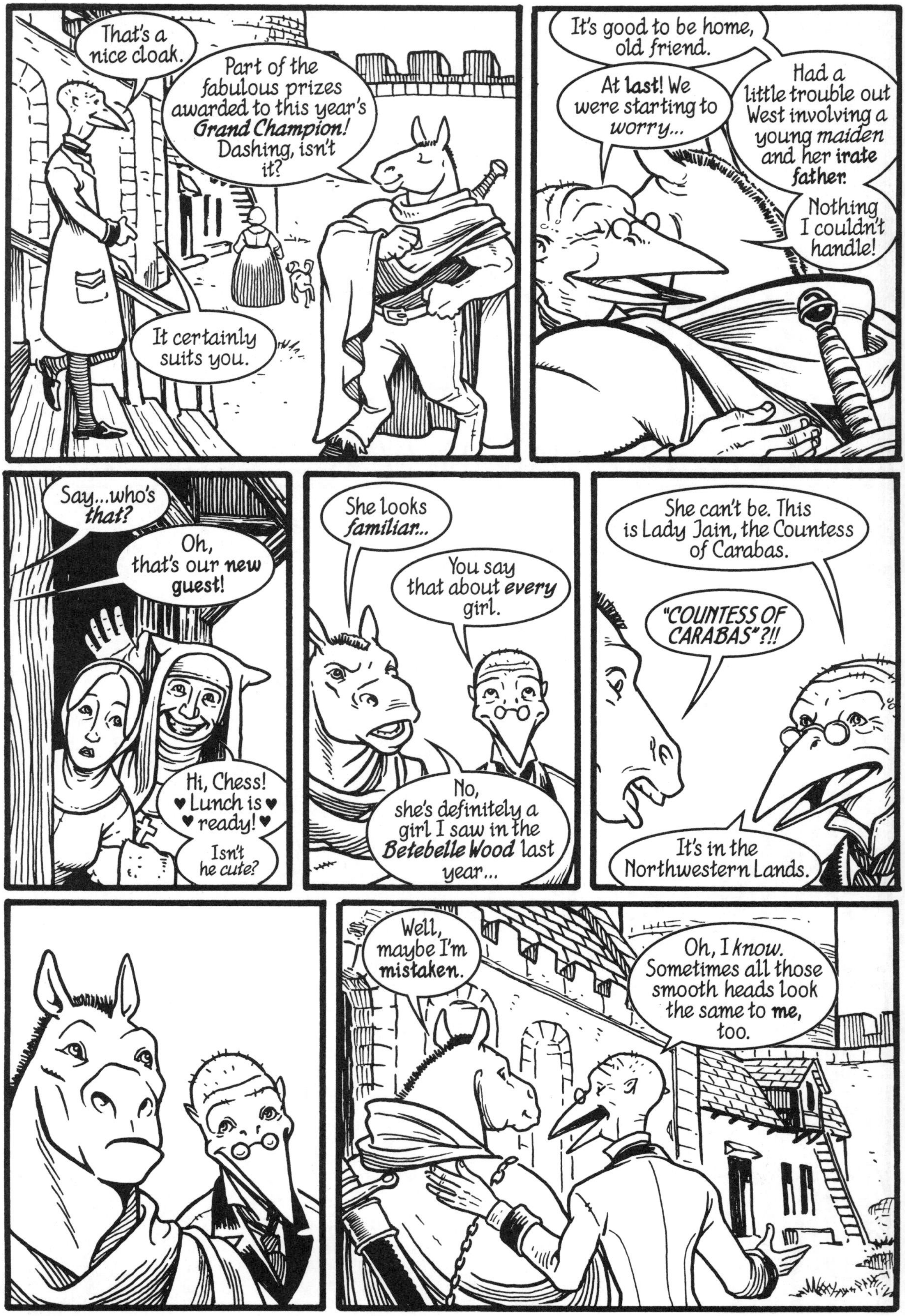

That's a nice cloak.
Part of the fabulous prizes awarded to this year's *Grand Champion!* Dashing, isn't it?
It certainly suits you.
It's good to be home, old friend.
At **last**! We were starting to *worry*...
Had a little trouble out West involving a young *maiden* and her **irate father**.
Nothing I couldn't handle!
Say...who's *that?*
Oh, that's our **new guest**!
Hi, Chess! ♥ Lunch is ♥ ♥ ready! ♥
Isn't he cute?
She looks *familiar*...
You say that about *every* girl.
No, she's definitely a girl I saw in the ***Betebelle Wood*** last year...
She can't be. This is Lady Jain, the Countess of Carabas.
"COUNTESS OF CARABAS"?!!
It's in the Northwestern Lands.
Well, maybe I'm **mistaken**.
Oh, I *know*. Sometimes all those smooth heads look the same to **me**, too.

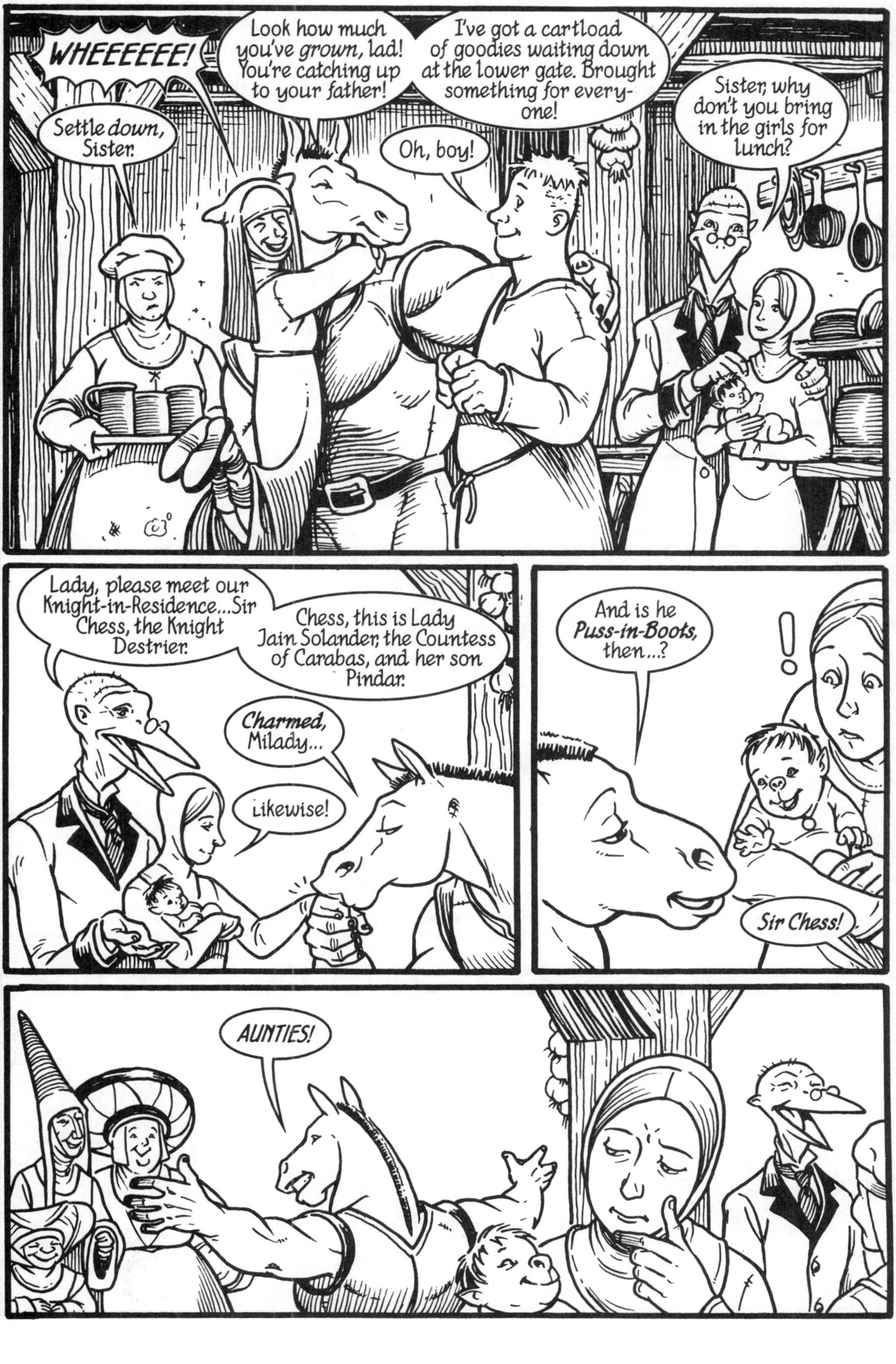
WHEEEEEEE!
Settle down, Sister.
Look how much you've grown, lad! You're catching up to your father!
I've got a cartload of goodies waiting down at the lower gate. Brought something for every-one!
Oh, boy!
Sister, why don't you bring in the girls for lunch?
Lady, please meet our Knight-in-Residence...Sir Chess, the Knight Destrier.
Chess, this is Lady Jain Solander, the Countess of Carabas, and her son Pindar.
Charmed, Milady...
Likewise!
And is he Puss-in-Boots, then...?
!
Sir Chess!
AUNTIES!

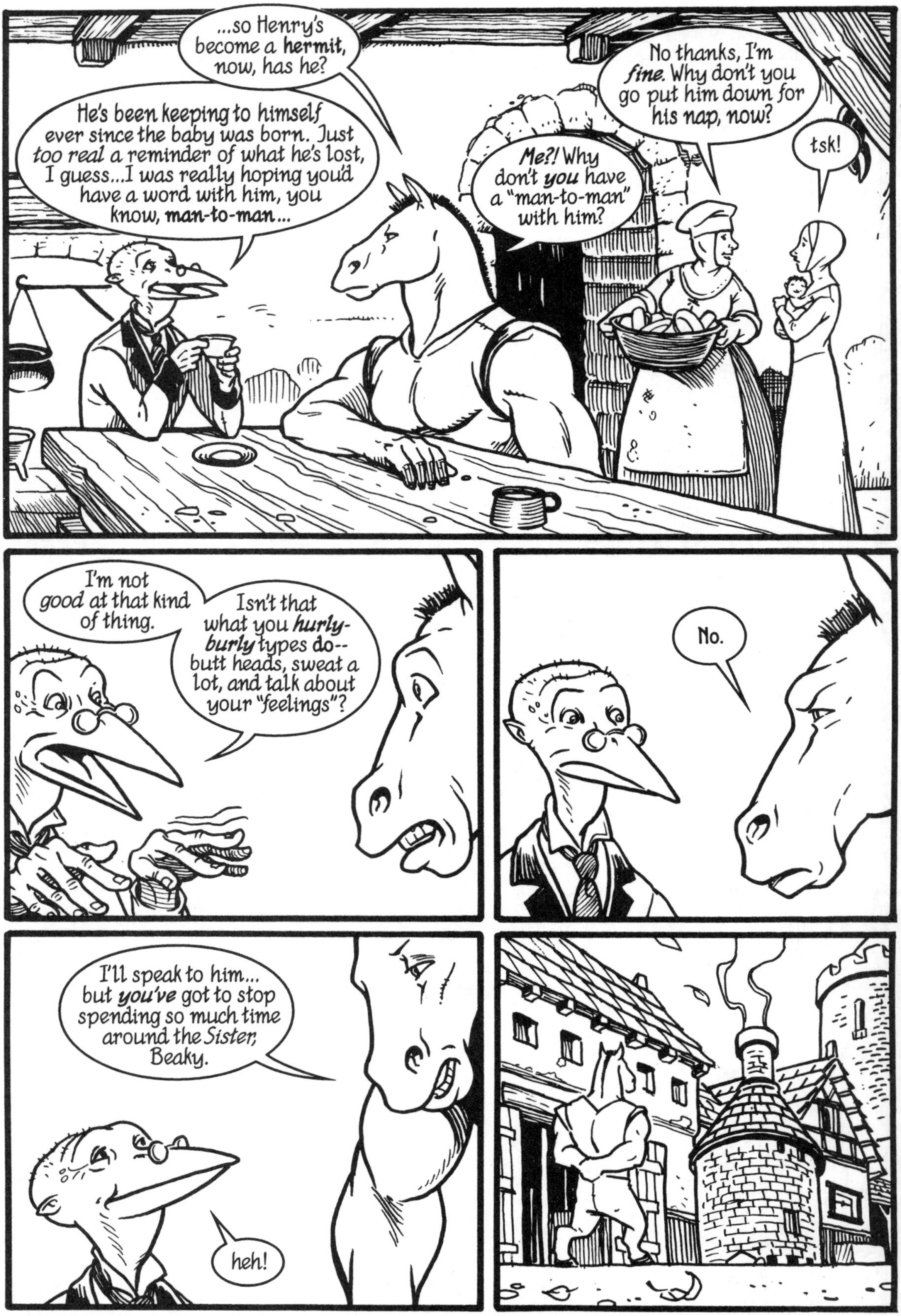

...so Henry's become a **hermit**, now, has he?
He's been keeping to himself ever since the baby was born. Just *too real* a reminder of what he's lost, I guess...I was really hoping you'd have a word with him, you know, **man-to-man**...
Me?! Why don't *you* have a "man-to-man" with him?
No thanks, I'm *fine*. Why don't you go put him down for his nap, now?
tsk!
I'm not *good* at that kind of thing.
Isn't that what you *hurly-burly* types **do**-- butt heads, sweat a lot, and talk about your "feelings"?
No.
I'll speak to him... but *you've* got to stop spending so much time around the *Sister*, Beaky.
heh!

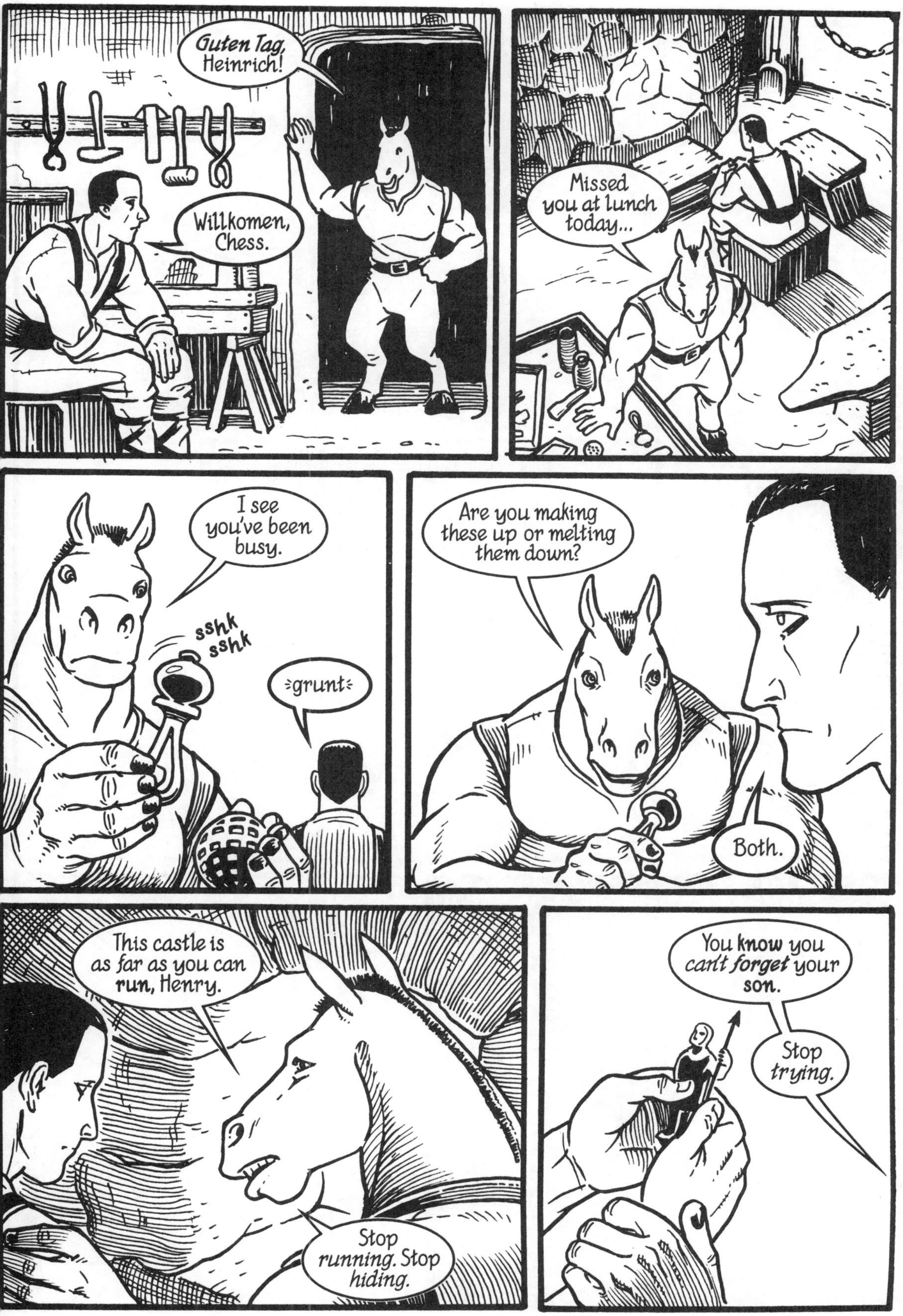
Guten Tag, Heinrich!
Willkomen, Chess.
Missed you at lunch today...
I see you've been busy.
sshk sshk
grunt
Are you making these up or melting them down?
Both.
This castle is as far as you can run, Henry.
Stop running. Stop hiding.
You know you can't forget your son.
Stop trying.

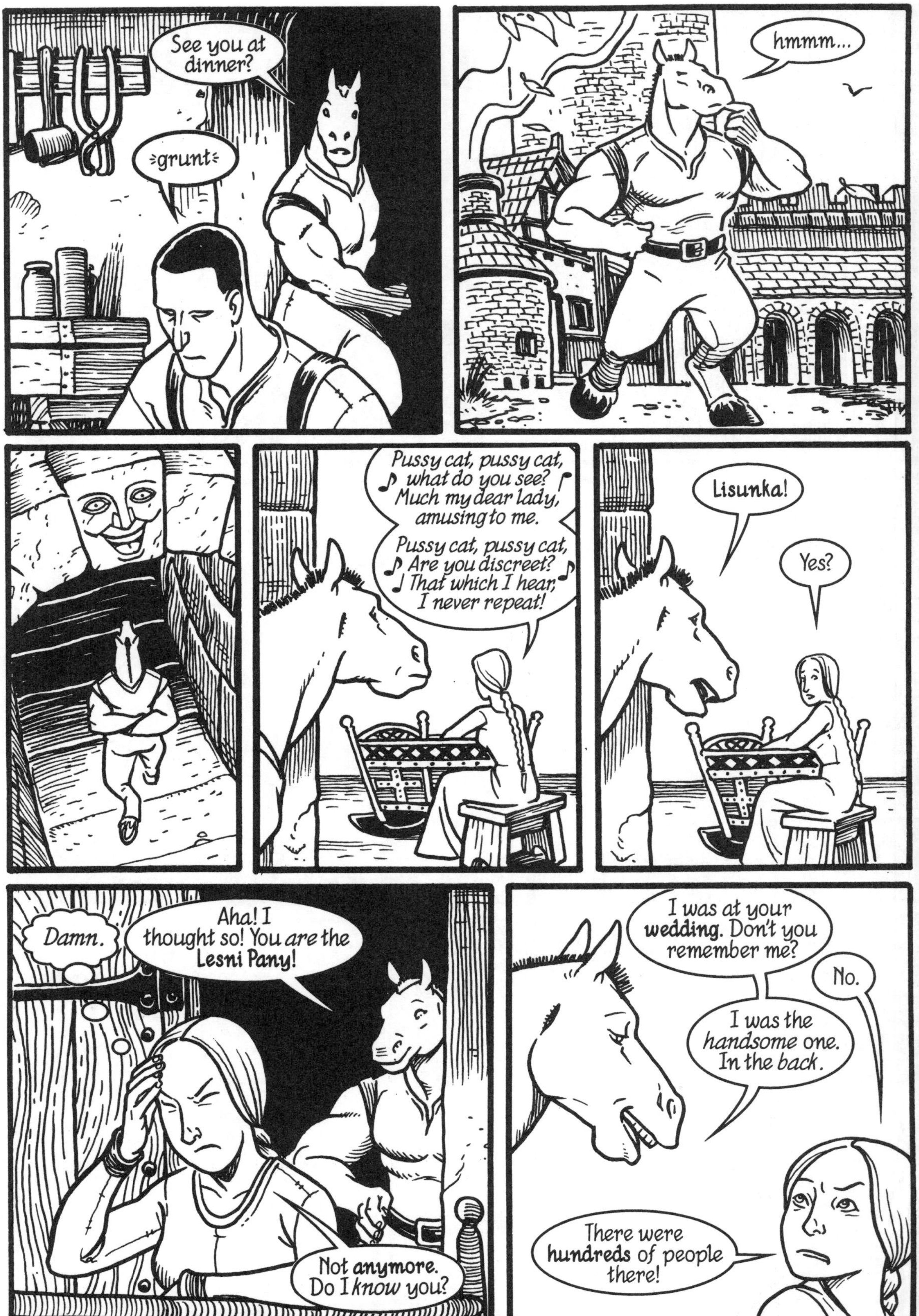
See you at dinner?
grunt
hmmm...
Pussy cat, pussy cat, what do you see? Much my dear lady, amusing to me.
Pussy cat, pussy cat, Are you discreet? That which I hear, I never repeat!
Lisunka!
Yes?
Damn.
Aha! I thought so! You *are* the **Lesni Pany**!
Not **anymore**. Do I *know* you?
I was at your **wedding**. Don't you remember me?
No.
I was the *handsome* one. In the *back*.
There were **hundreds** of people there!

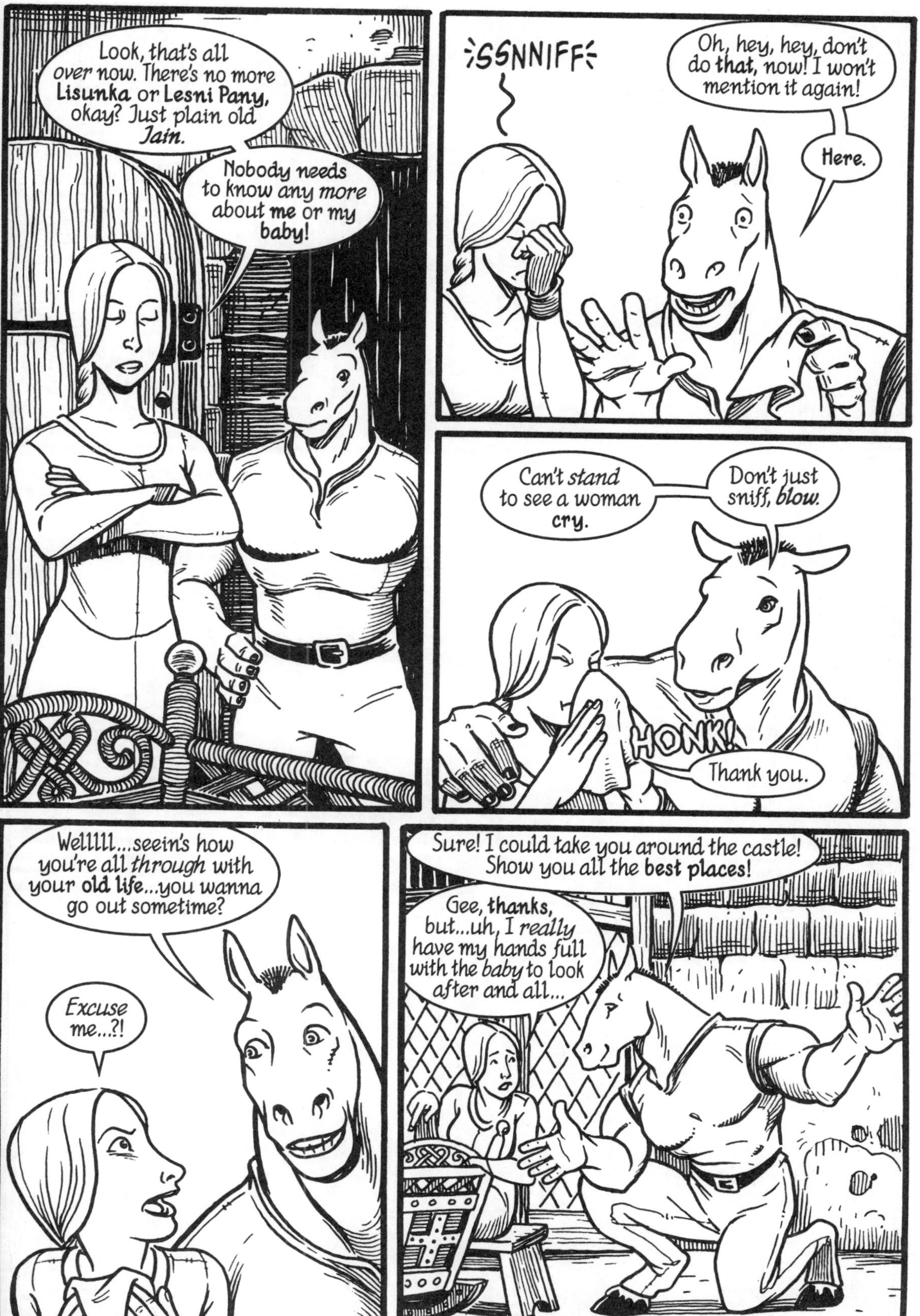

Look, that's all over now. There's no more **Lisunka** or **Lesni Pany**, okay? Just plain old ***Jain***.
Nobody needs to know any *more* about **me** or my **baby**!
SSNNIFF
Oh, hey, hey, don't do **that**, now! I won't mention it again!
Here.
Can't *stand* to see a woman **cry**.
Don't just sniff, *blow*.
HONK!
Thank you.
Wellllll...seein's how you're all *through* with your **old life**...you wanna go out sometime?
Excuse me...?!
Sure! I could take you around the castle! Show you all the **best places**!
Gee, **thanks**, but...uh, I *really* have my hands full with the *baby* to look after and all...

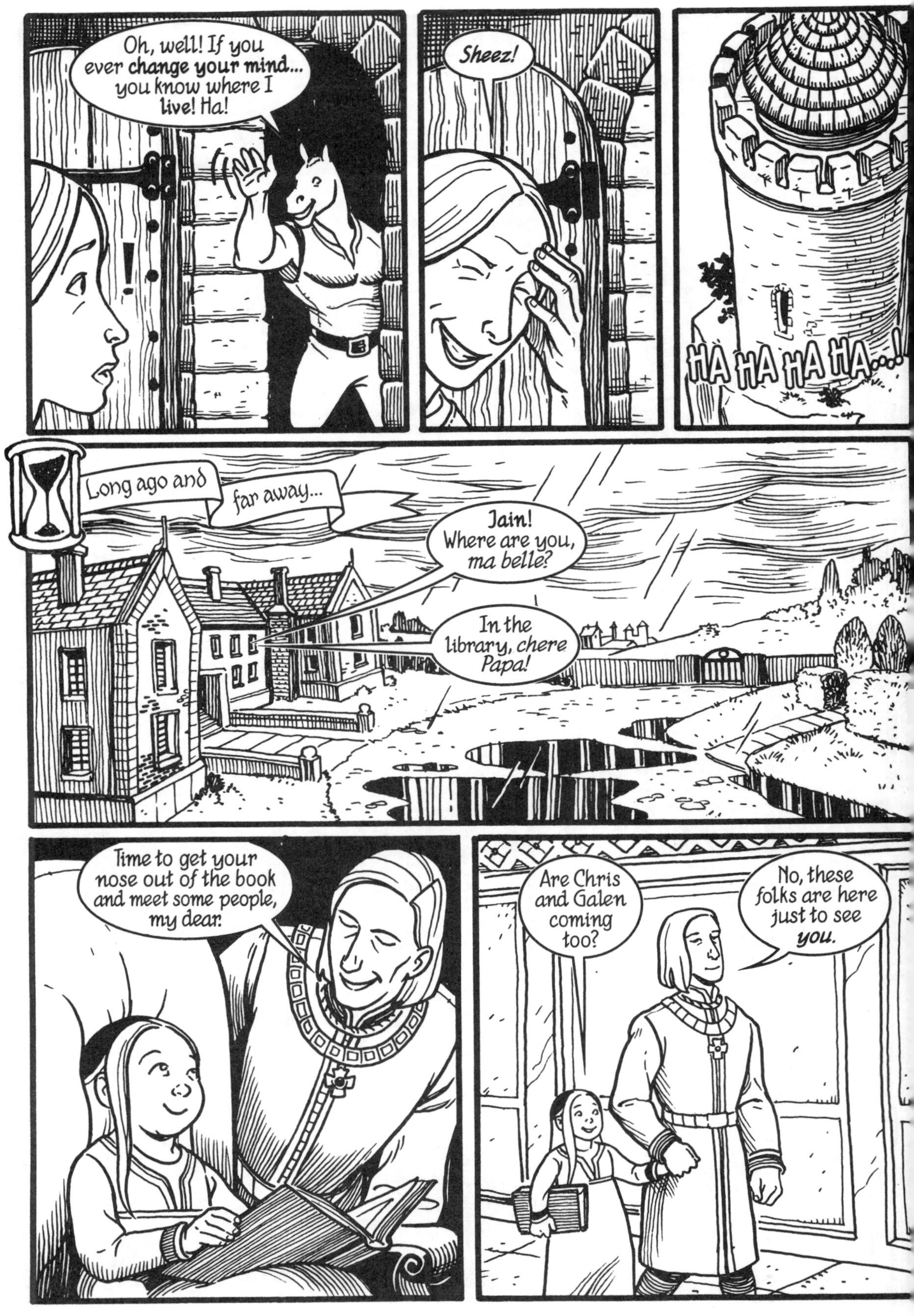
Oh, well! If you ever change your mind... you know where I live! Ha!
!
Sheez!
HA HA HA HA...!
Long ago and
far away...
Jain! Where are you, ma belle?
In the library, chere Papa!
Time to get your nose out of the book and meet some people, my dear.
Are Chris and Galen coming too?
No, these folks are here just to see you.

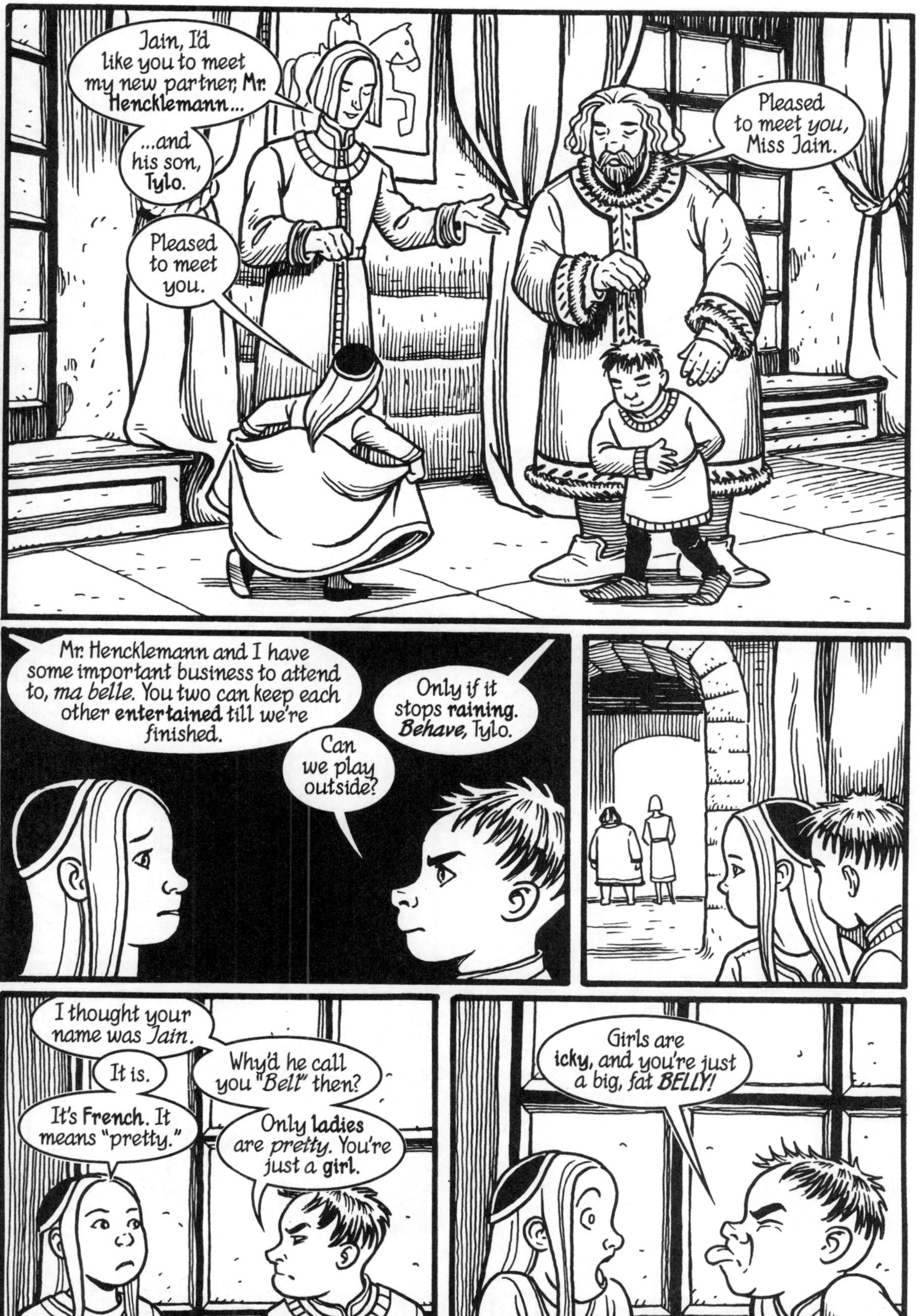

Jain, I'd like you to meet my new partner, Mr. Hencklemann...
...and his son, Tylo.
Pleased to meet you, Miss Jain.
Pleased to meet you.
Mr. Hencklemann and I have some important business to attend to, *ma belle*. You two can keep each other **entertained** till we're finished.
Can we play outside?
Only if it stops **raining**. ***Behave***, Tylo.
I thought your name was *Jain*.
It is.
Why'd he call you "*Bell*" then?
It's **French**. It means "pretty."
Only **ladies** are *pretty*. You're just a **girl**.
Girls are **icky**, and you're just a big, fat ***BELLY!***

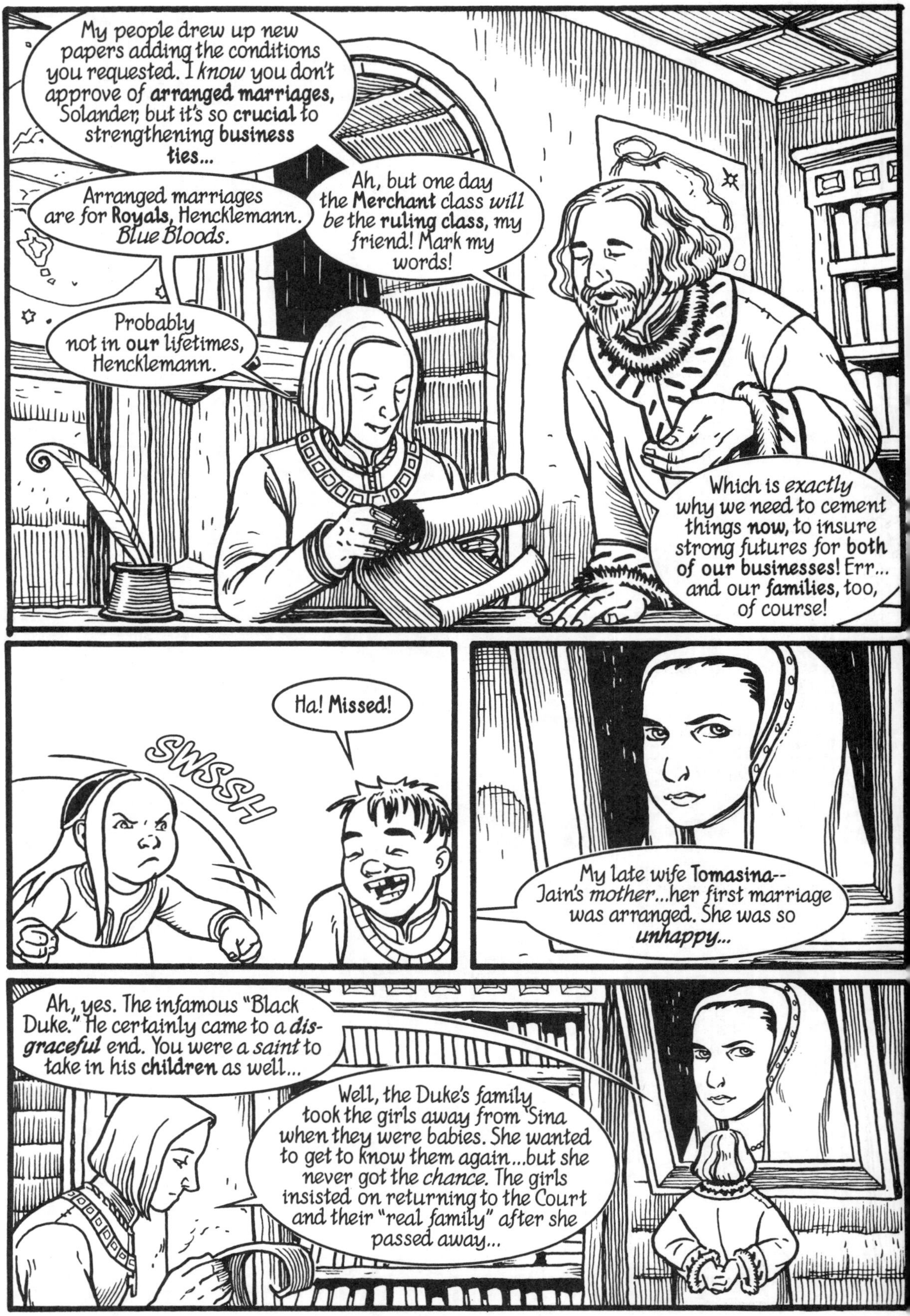
My people drew up new papers adding the conditions you requested. I *know* you don't approve of **arranged marriages**, Solander, but it's so **crucial** to strengthening **business ties**...
Arranged marriages are for **Royals**, Henckleman. *Blue Bloods*.
Ah, but one day the **Merchant** class *will be* the **ruling class**, my friend! Mark my words!
Probably not in **our** lifetimes, Henckleman.
Which is *exactly* why we need to cement things **now**, to insure strong futures for **both of our businesses**! Err... and our **families**, too, of course!
SWSSH
Ha! **Missed!**
My late wife **Tomasina**--Jain's *mother*...her first marriage was arranged. She was so ***unhappy***...
Ah, yes. The infamous "Black Duke." He certainly came to a ***disgraceful*** end. You were a *saint* to take in his **children** as well...
Well, the Duke's family took the girls away from 'Sina when they were babies. She wanted to get to know them again...but she never got the *chance*. The girls insisted on returning to the Court and their "real family" after she passed away...

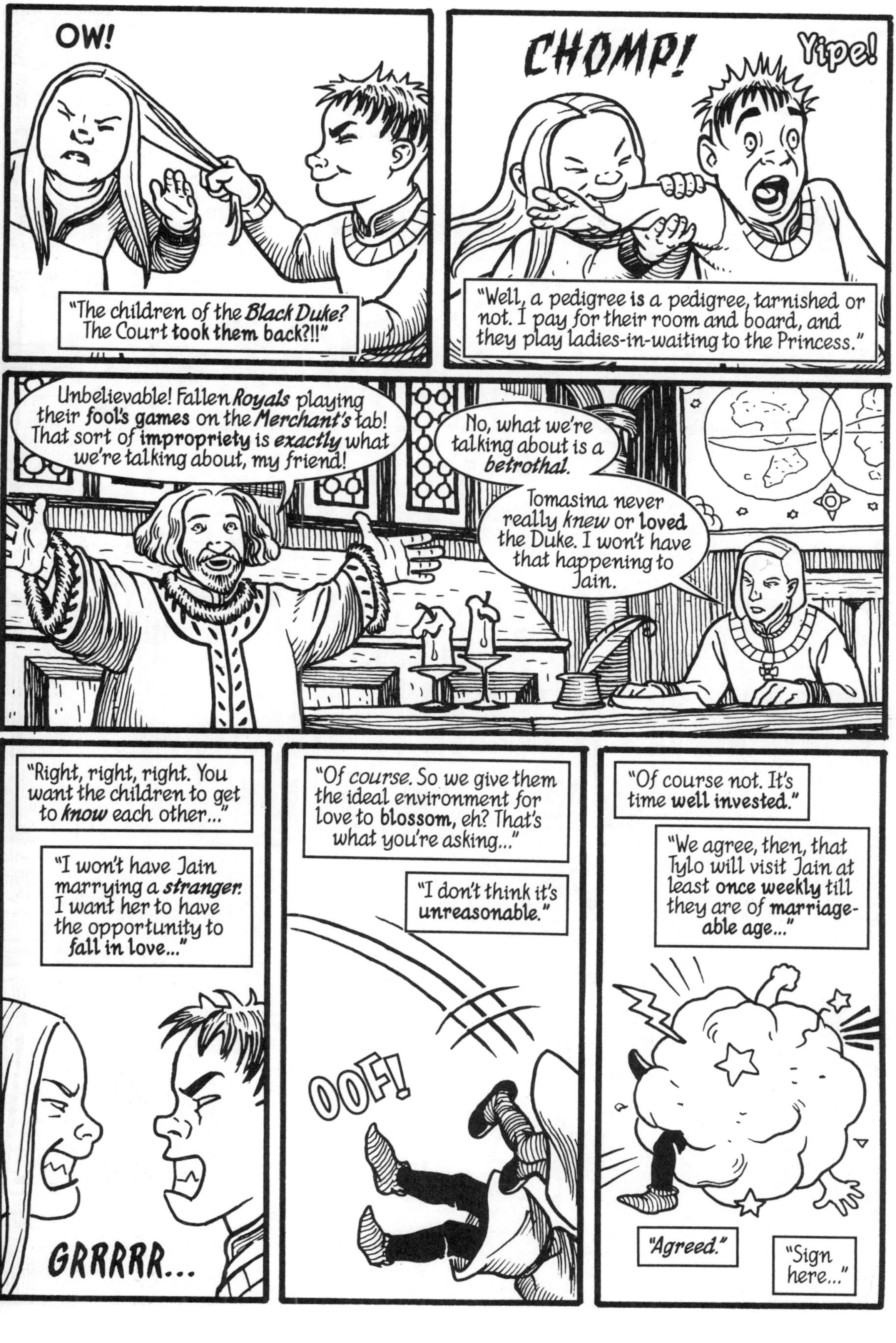
OW!
"The children of the Black Duke? The Court took them back?!!"
CHOMP!
Yipe!
"Well, a pedigree is a pedigree, tarnished or not. I pay for their room and board, and they play ladies-in-waiting to the Princess."
Unbelievable! Fallen Royals playing their fool's games on the Merchant's tab! That sort of impropriety is exactly what we're talking about, my friend!
No, what we're talking about is a betrothal.
Tomasina never really knew or loved the Duke. I won't have that happening to Jain.
"Right, right, right. You want the children to get to know each other..."
"I won't have Jain marrying a stranger. I want her to have the opportunity to fall in love..."
GRRRRR...
"Of course. So we give them the ideal environment for love to blossom, eh? That's what you're asking..."
"I don't think it's unreasonable."
OOF!
"Of course not. It's time well invested."
"We agree, then, that Tylo will visit Jain at least once weekly till they are of marriage-able age..."
"Agreed."
"Sign here..."

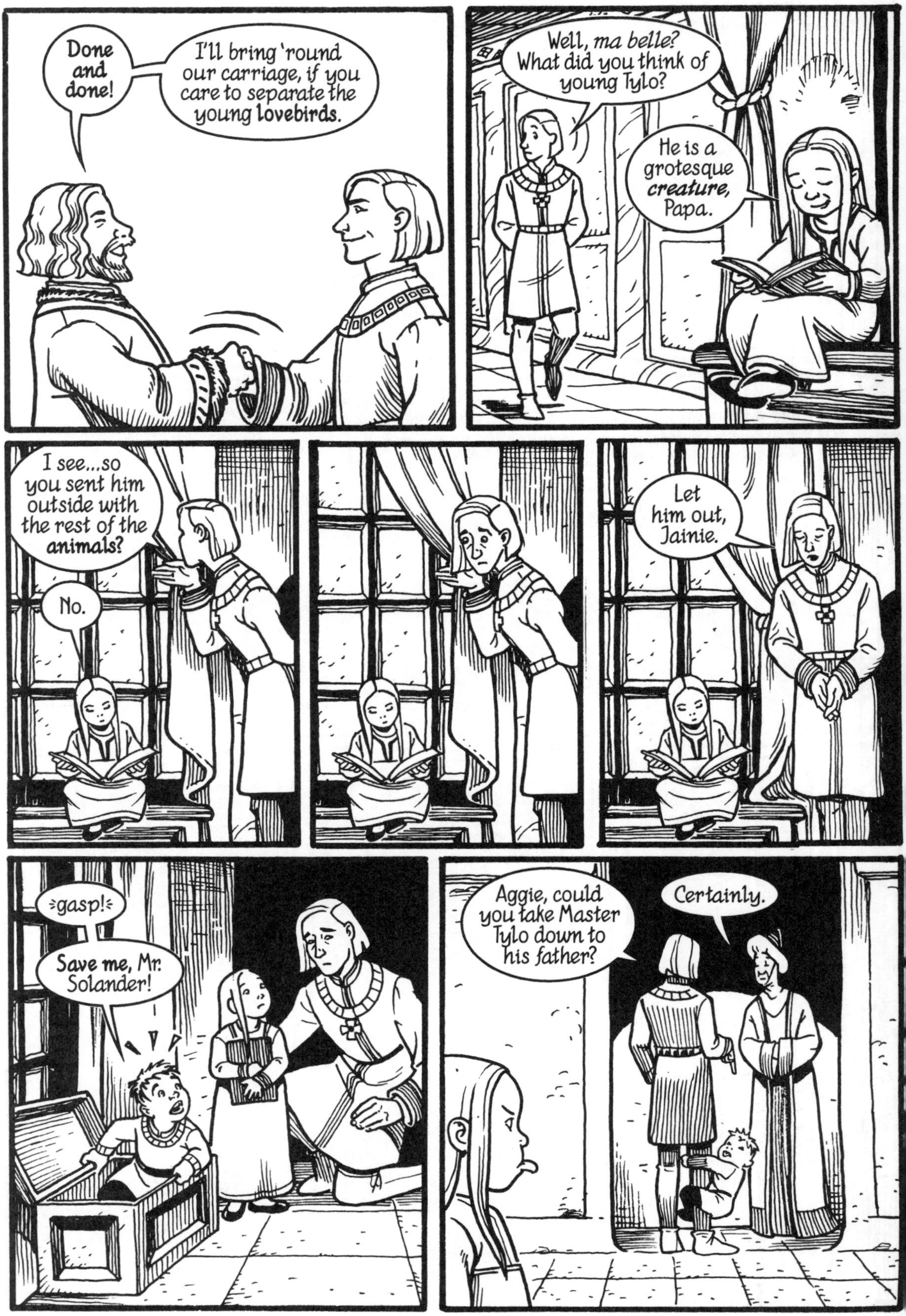
Done and done!
I'll bring 'round our carriage, if you care to separate the young lovebirds.
Well, ma belle? What did you think of young Tylo?
He is a grotesque creature, Papa.
I see...so you sent him outside with the rest of the animals?
No.
Let him out, Jainie.
gasp!
Save me, Mr. Solander!
Aggie, could you take Master Tylo down to his father?
Certainly.

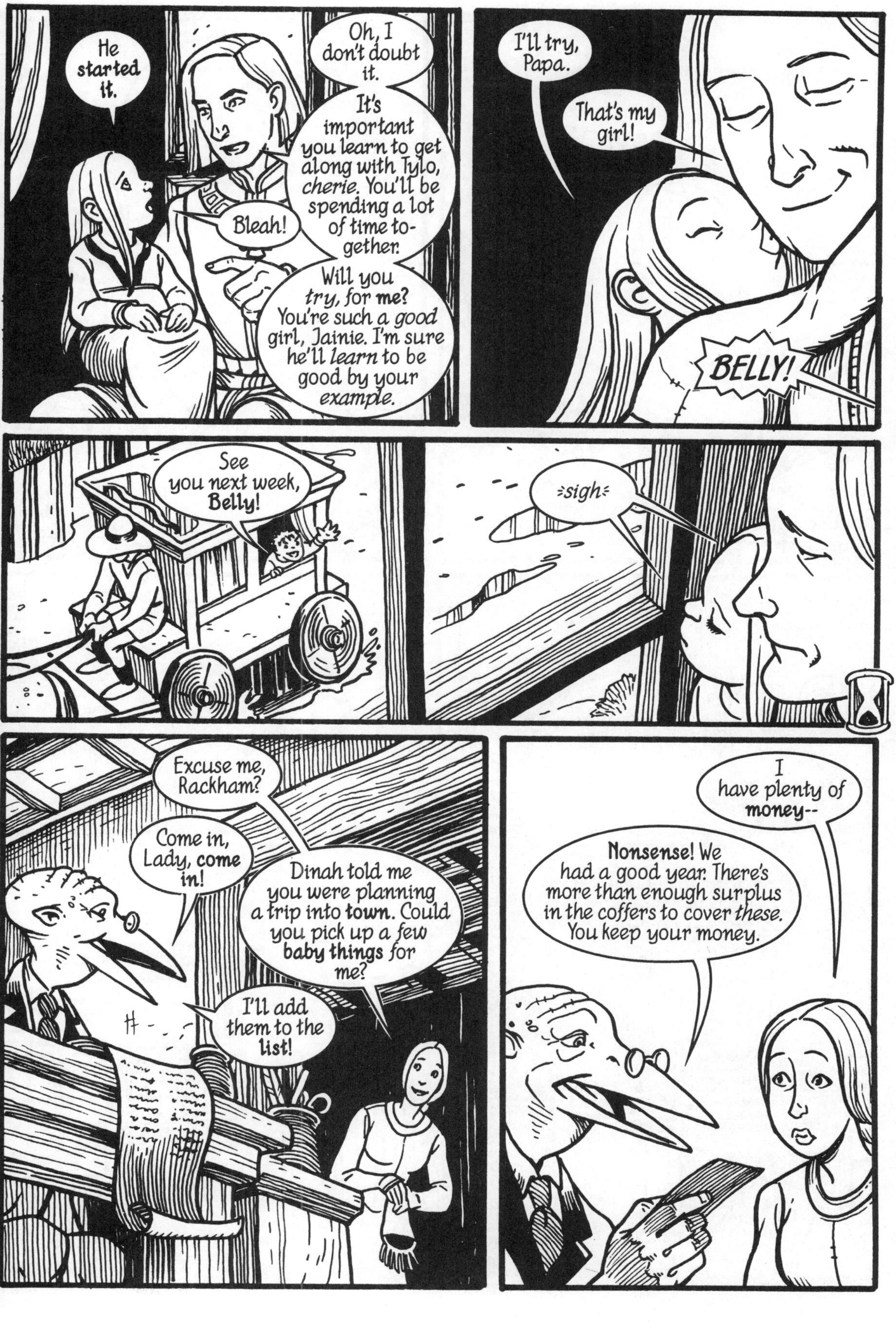
He started it.
Oh, I don't doubt it.
It's important you learn to get along with Tylo, cherie. You'll be spending a lot of time together.
Bleah!
Will you try, for me? You're such a good girl, Jainie. I'm sure he'll learn to be good by your example.
I'll try, Papa.
That's my girl!
BELLY!
See you next week, Belly!
sigh
Excuse me, Rackham?
Come in, Lady, come in!
Dinah told me you were planning a trip into town. Could you pick up a few baby things for me?
I'll add them to the list!
I have plenty of money--
Nonsense! We had a good year. There's more than enough surplus in the coffers to cover these. You keep your money.

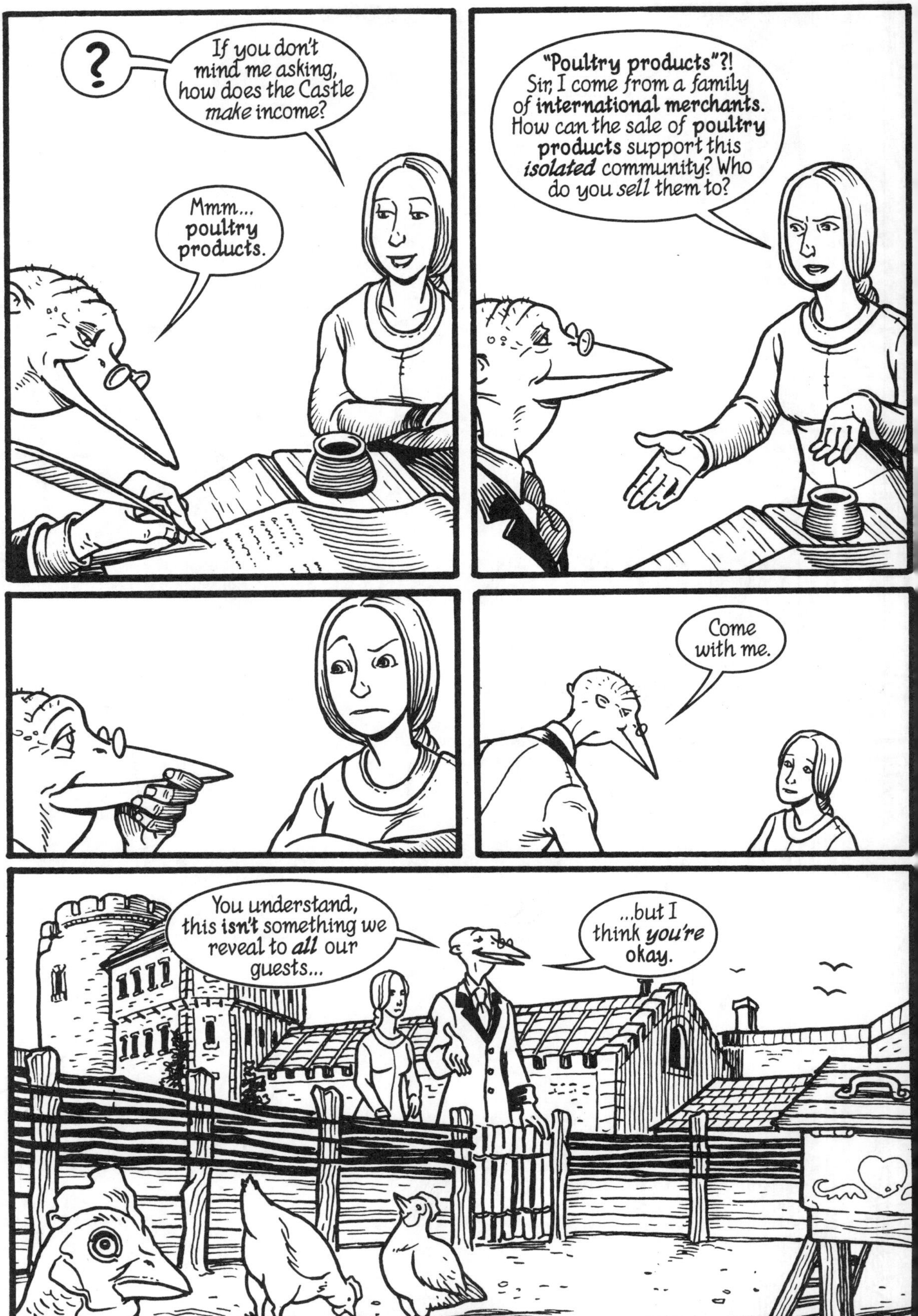
?
If you don't mind me asking, how does the Castle *make* income?
Mmm... **poultry products.**
"Poultry products"?! Sir, I come from a family of **international merchants.** How can the sale of **poultry products** support this ***isolated*** community? Who do you *sell* them to?
Come with me.
You understand, this **isn't** something we reveal to ***all*** our guests...
...but I think ***you're*** **okay.**

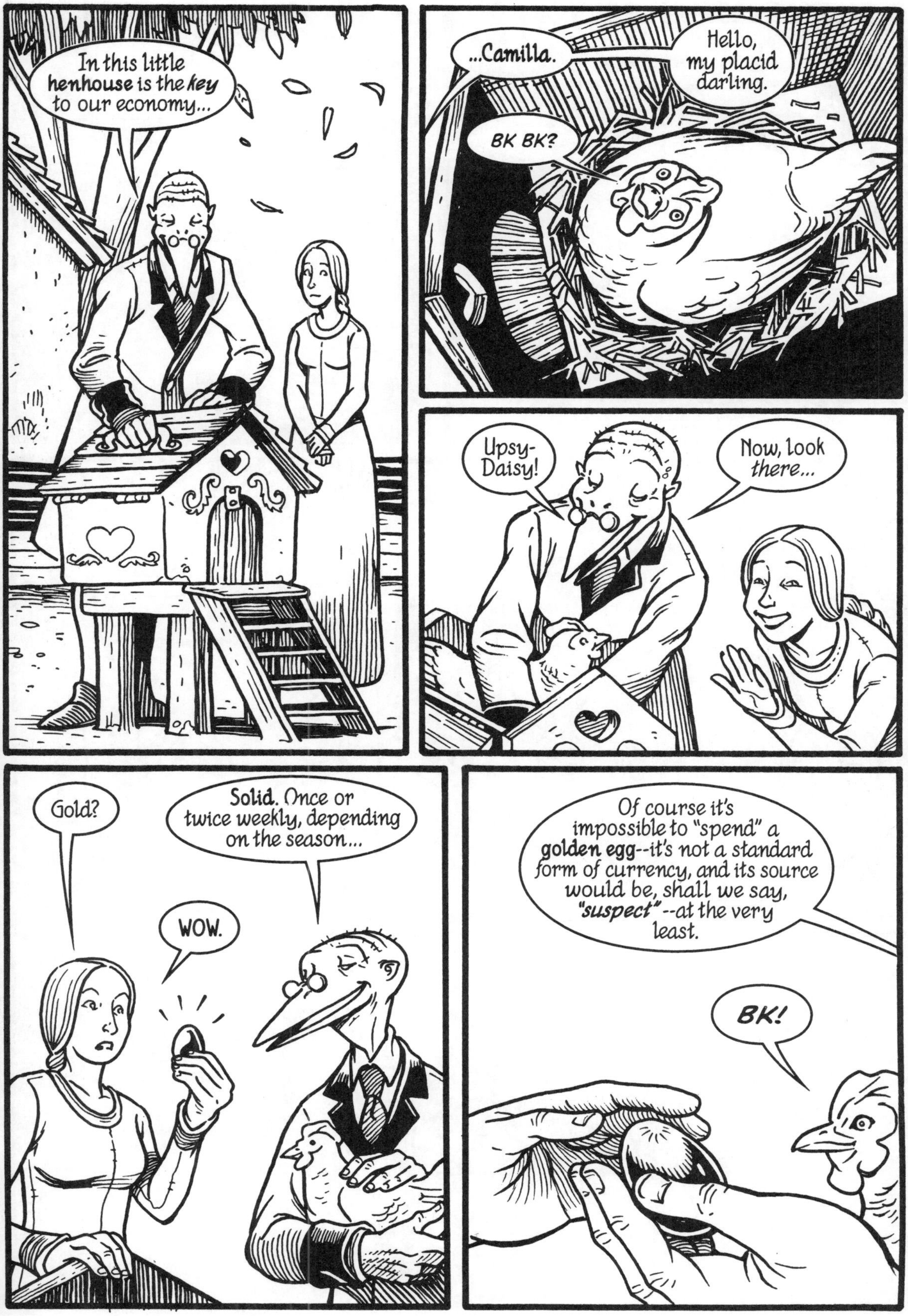
In this little **henhouse** is the ***key*** to our economy...
...**Camilla**.
Hello, my placid darling.
BK BK?
Upsy-Daisy!
Now, look *there*...
Gold?
Solid. Once or twice weekly, depending on the season...
WOW.
Of course it's impossible to "spend" a **golden egg**--it's not a standard form of currency, and its source would be, shall we say, ***"suspect"***--at the very least.
BK!

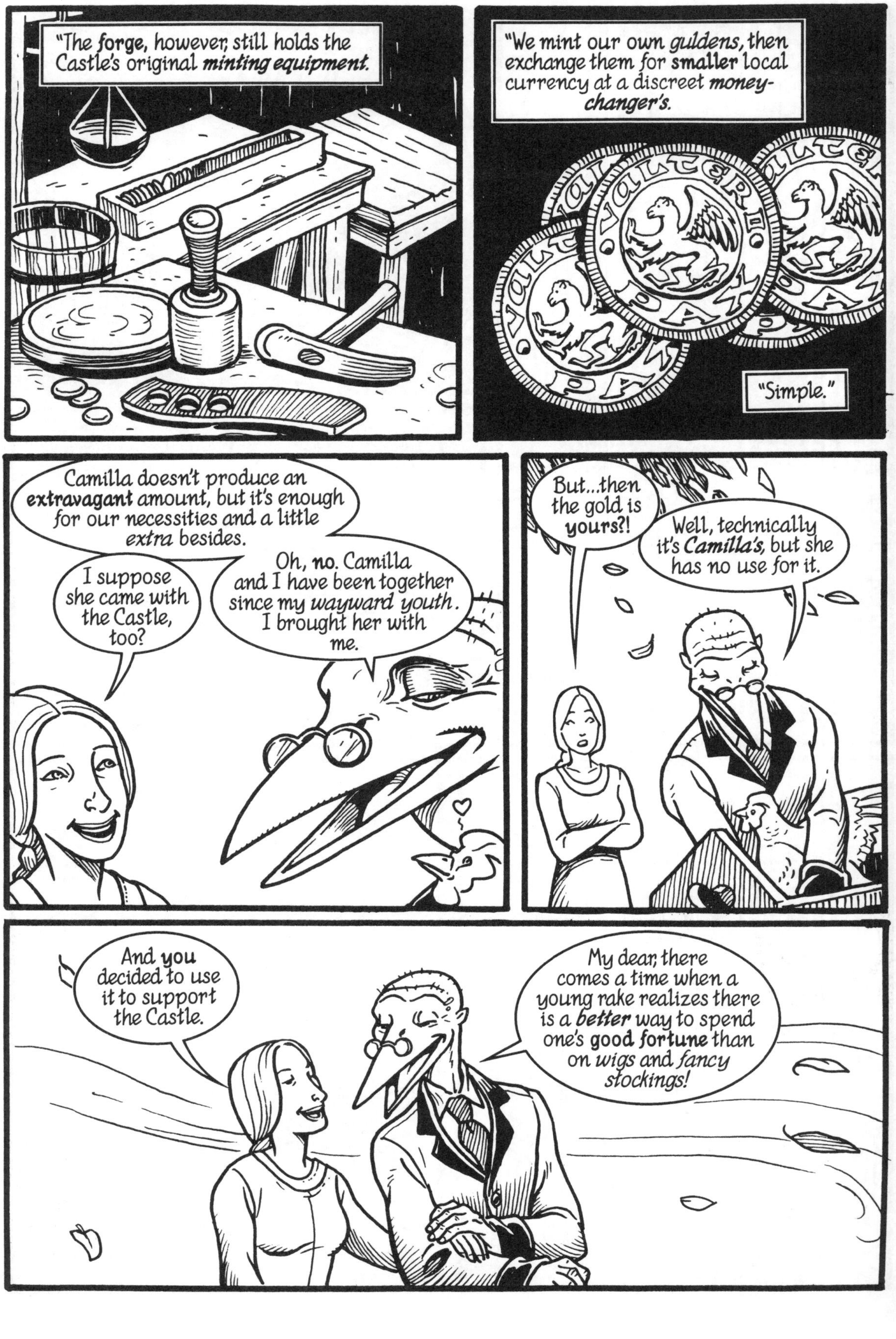
"The forge, however, still holds the Castle's original minting equipment.
"We mint our own guldens, then exchange them for smaller local currency at a discreet money-changer's.
"Simple."
Camilla doesn't produce an extravagant amount, but it's enough for our necessities and a little extra besides.
I suppose she came with the Castle, too?
Oh, no. Camilla and I have been together since my wayward youth. I brought her with me.
But...then the gold is yours?!
Well, technically it's Camilla's, but she has no use for it.
And you decided to use it to support the Castle.
My dear, there comes a time when a young rake realizes there is a better way to spend one's good fortune than on wigs and fancy stockings!

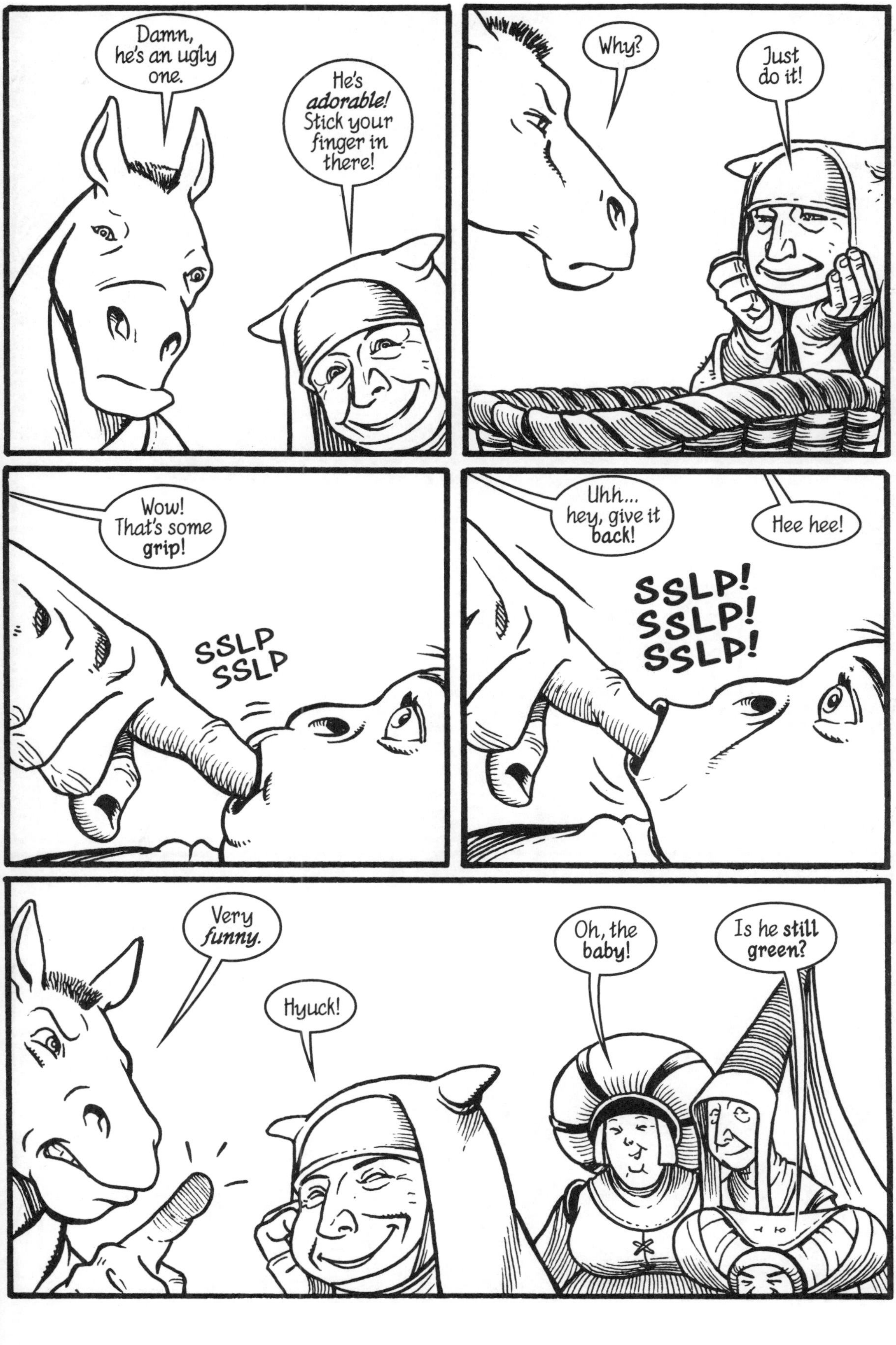
Damn, he's an ugly one.
He's *adorable!* Stick your finger in there!
Why?
Just do it!
Wow! That's some **grip!**
SSLP SSLP
Uhh... hey, give it back!
Hee hee!
SSLP! SSLP! SSLP!
Very *funny.*
Hyuck!
Oh, the **baby!**
Is he **still green?**

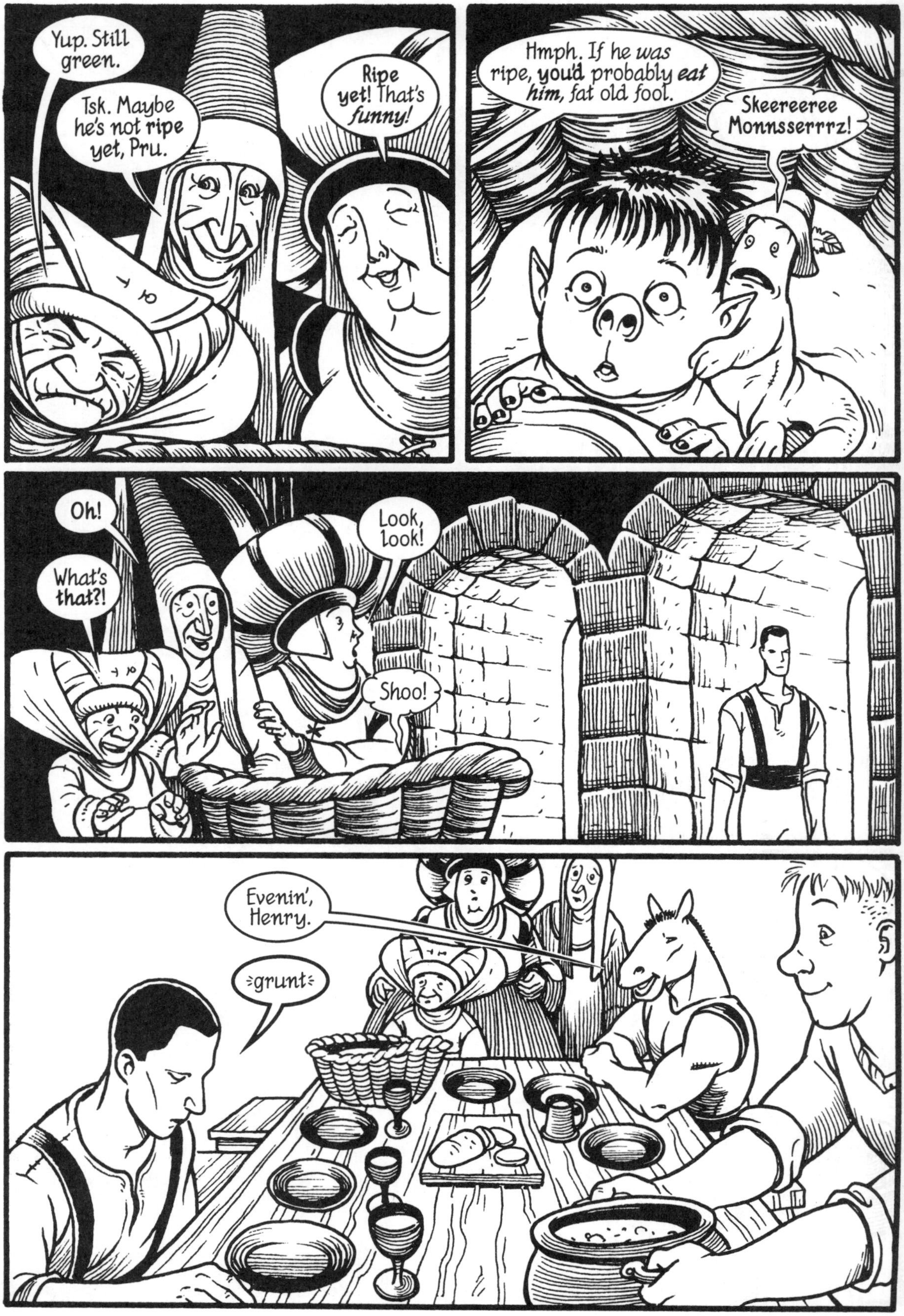

Yup. Still green.
Tsk. Maybe he's not ripe yet, Pru.
Ripe yet! That's funny!
Hmph. If he was ripe, you'd probably eat him, fat old fool.
Skeereeree Monnsserrrz!
Oh!
What's that?!
Look, look!
Shoo!
Evenin', Henry.
grunt

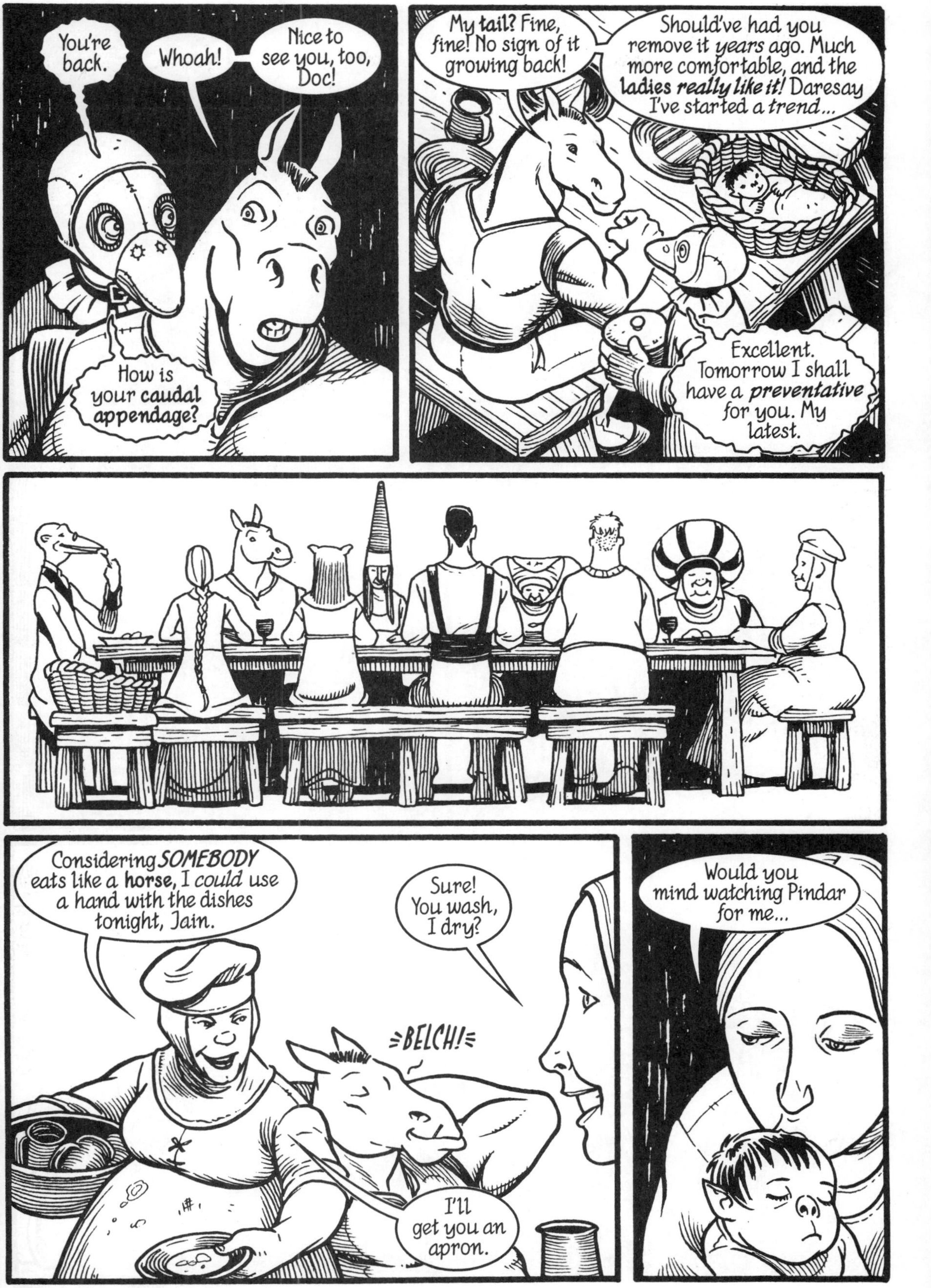
You're back.
Whoah!
Nice to see you, too, Doc!
How is your **caudal appendage**?
My **tail**? Fine, *fine*! No sign of it growing back!
Should've had you remove it *years* ago. Much more comfortable, and the **ladies *really like it!*** Daresay I've started a *trend*...
Excellent. Tomorrow I shall have a ***preventative*** for you. My latest.
Considering *SOMEBODY* eats like a **horse**, I *could* use a hand with the dishes tonight, Jain.
Sure! You wash, I dry?
BELCH!
I'll get you an apron.
Would you mind watching Pindar for me...

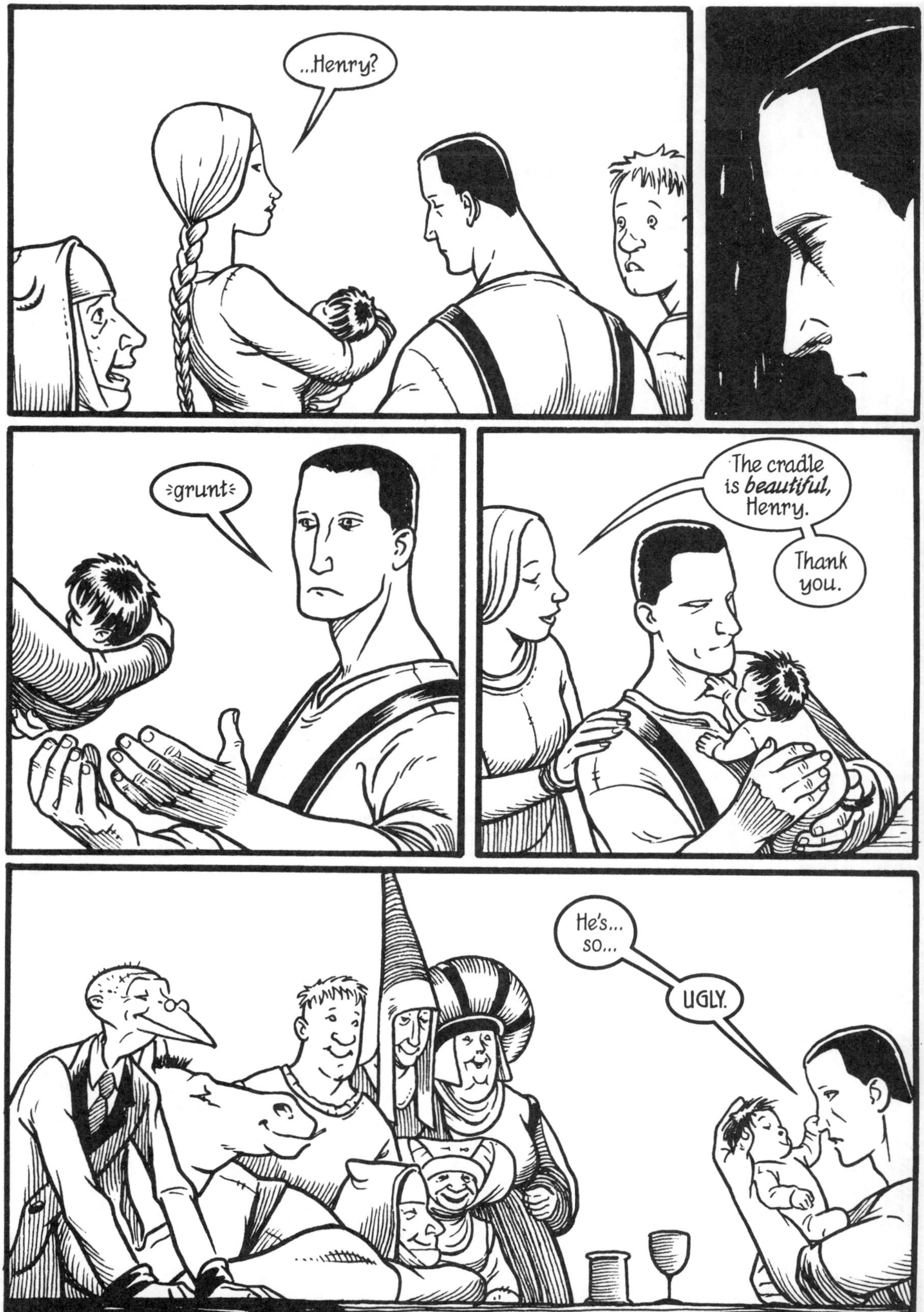
...Henry?
grunt
The cradle is *beautiful,* Henry.
Thank you.
He's... so...
UGLY.

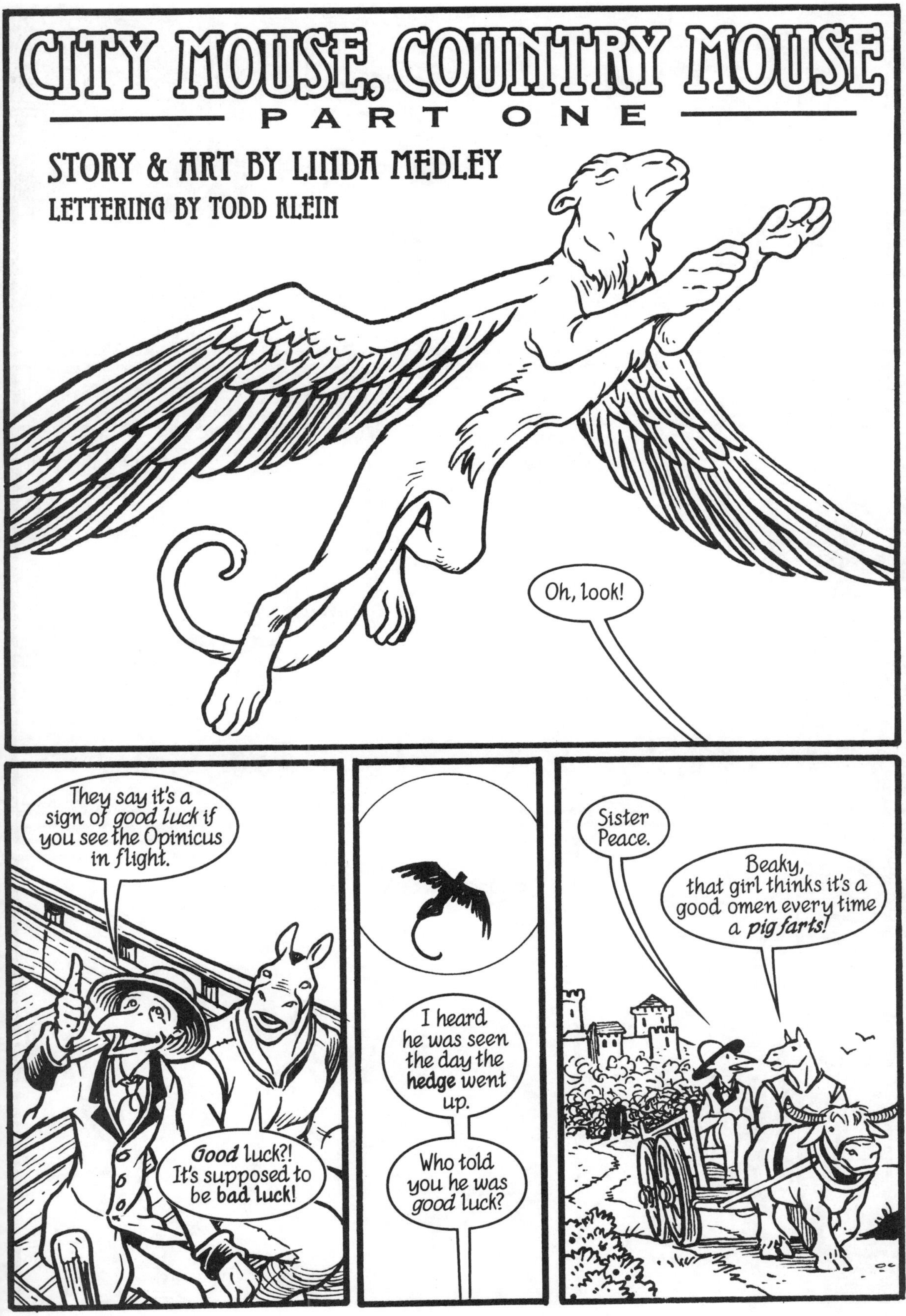
CITY MOUSE, COUNTRY MOUSE
PART ONE
STORY & ART BY LINDA MEDLEY
LETTERING BY TODD KLEIN
Oh, look!
They say it's a sign of *good luck* if you see the Opinicus in flight.
Good luck?! It's supposed to be **bad luck**!
I heard he was seen the day the **hedge** went up.
Who told you he was *good* luck?
Sister Peace.
Beaky, that girl thinks it's a good omen every time a ***pig farts***!

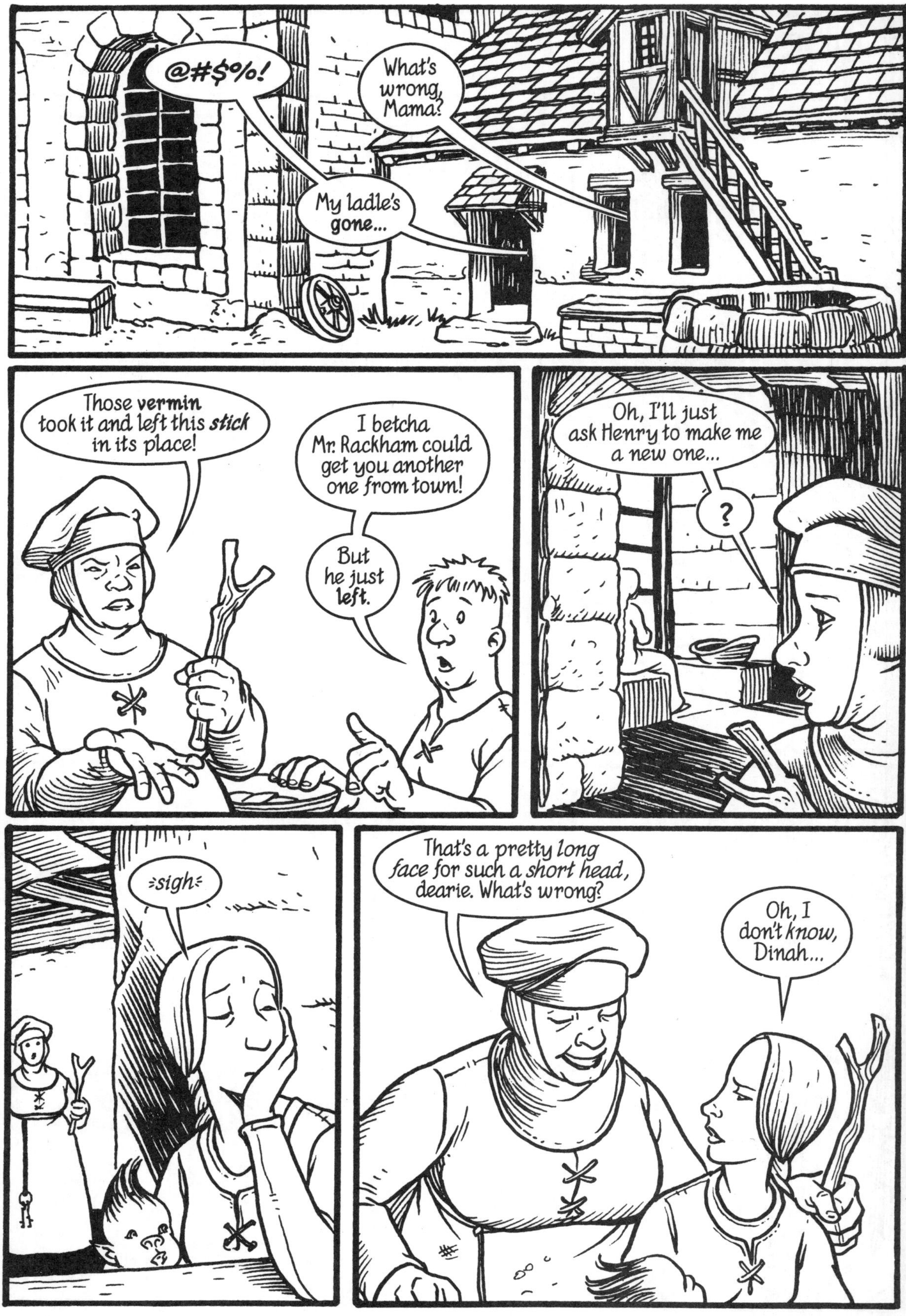
@#$%!
What's wrong, Mama?
My ladle's gone...
Those vermin took it and left this stick in its place!
I betcha Mr. Rackham could get you another one from town!
But he just left.
Oh, I'll just ask Henry to make me a new one...
?
sigh
That's a pretty long face for such a short head, dearie. What's wrong?
Oh, I don't know, Dinah...

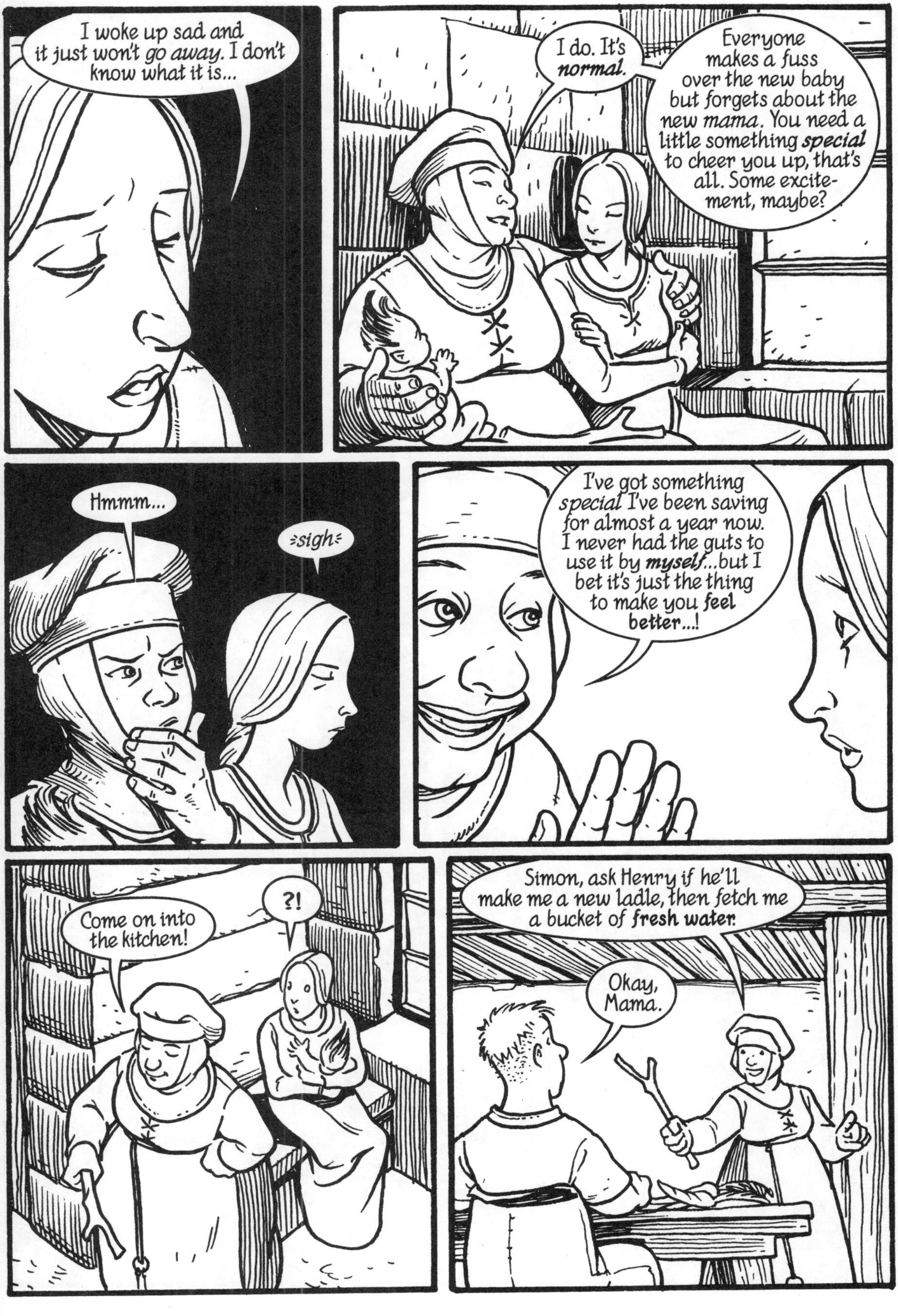
I woke up sad and it just won't *go away*. I don't know what it is...
I do. It's ***normal***.
Everyone makes a fuss over the new baby but forgets about the new *mama*. You need a little something ***special*** to cheer you up, that's all. Some excitement, maybe?
Hmmm...
sigh
I've got something *special* I've been saving for almost a year now. I never had the guts to use it by ***myself***...but I bet it's just the thing to make you **feel better**...!
Come on into the kitchen!
?!
Simon, ask Henry if he'll make me a new ladle, then fetch me a bucket of **fresh water**.
Okay, Mama.

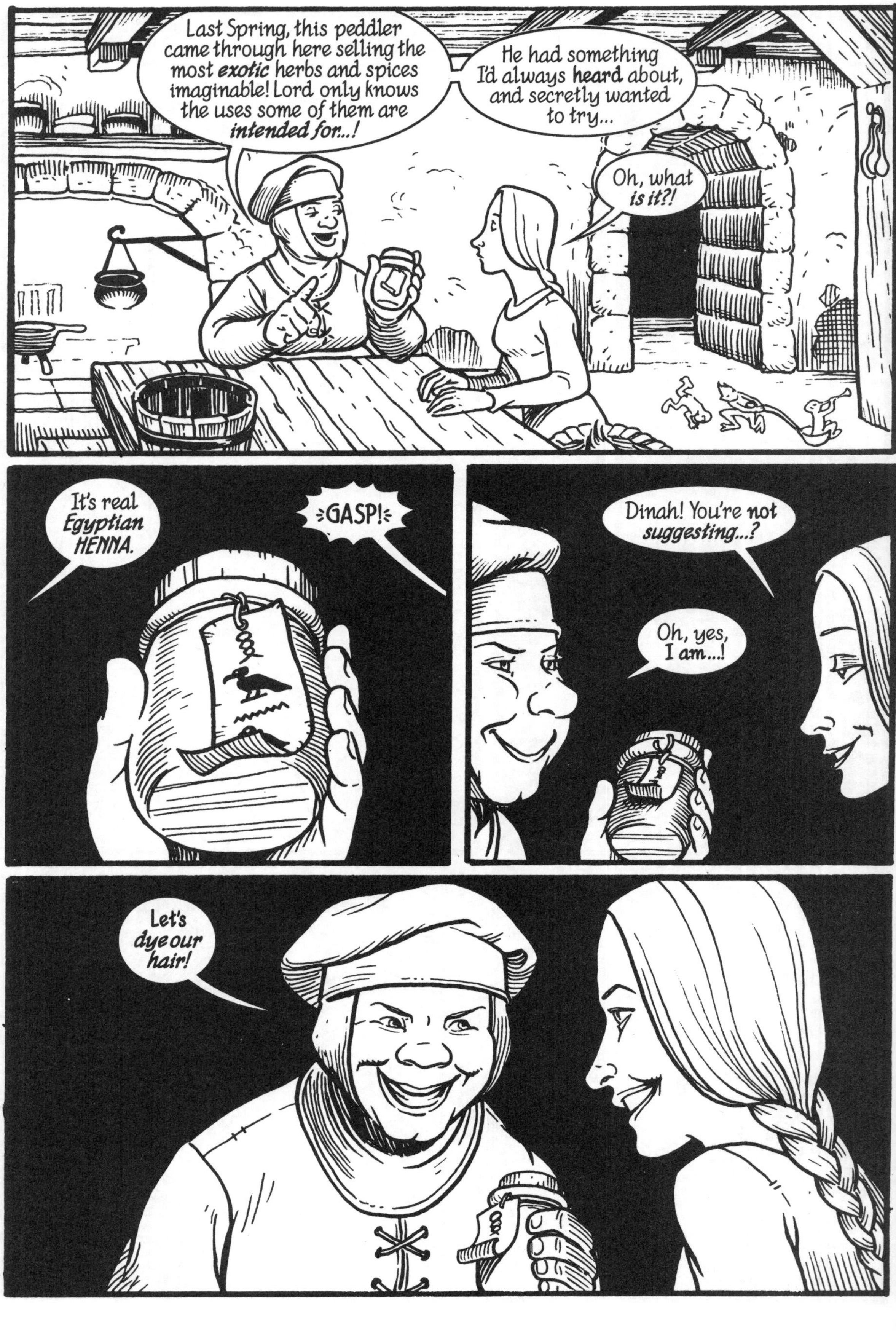

Last Spring, this peddler came through here selling the most *exotic* herbs and spices imaginable! Lord only knows the uses some of them are *intended for...!*
He had something I'd always **heard** about, and secretly wanted to try...
Oh, what *is it?!*
It's real *Egyptian HENNA.*
GASP!
Dinah! You're **not** *suggesting...?*
Oh, yes, I am...!
Let's *dye our hair!*

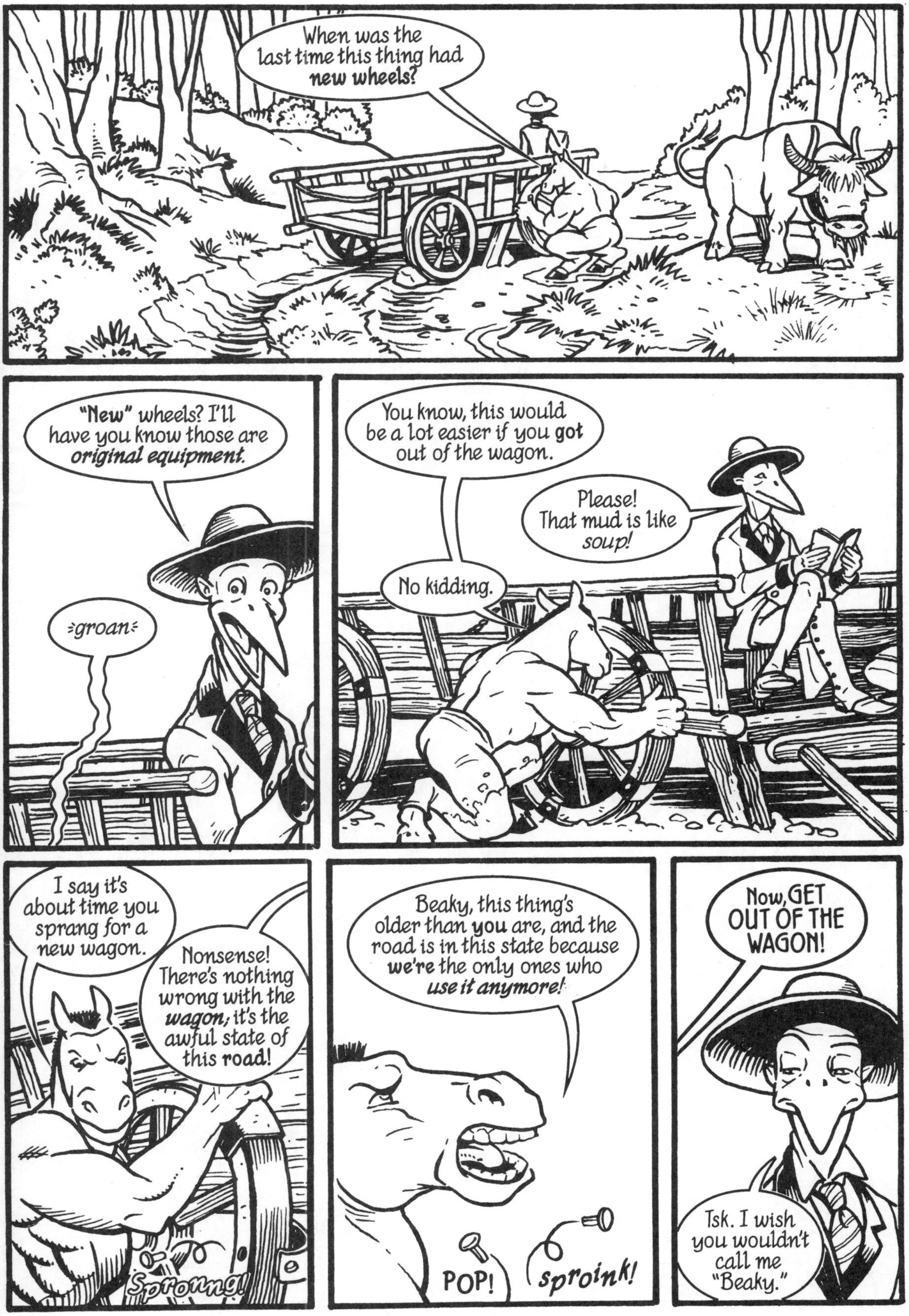

When was the last time this thing had new wheels?
"New" wheels? I'll have you know those are original equipment.
groan
You know, this would be a lot easier if you got out of the wagon.
Please! That mud is like soup!
No kidding.
I say it's about time you sprang for a new wagon.
Nonsense! There's nothing wrong with the wagon; it's the awful state of this road!
Spronng!
Beaky, this thing's older than you are, and the road is in this state because we're the only ones who use it anymore!
POP!
sproink!
Now, GET OUT OF THE WAGON!
Tsk. I wish you wouldn't call me "Beaky."

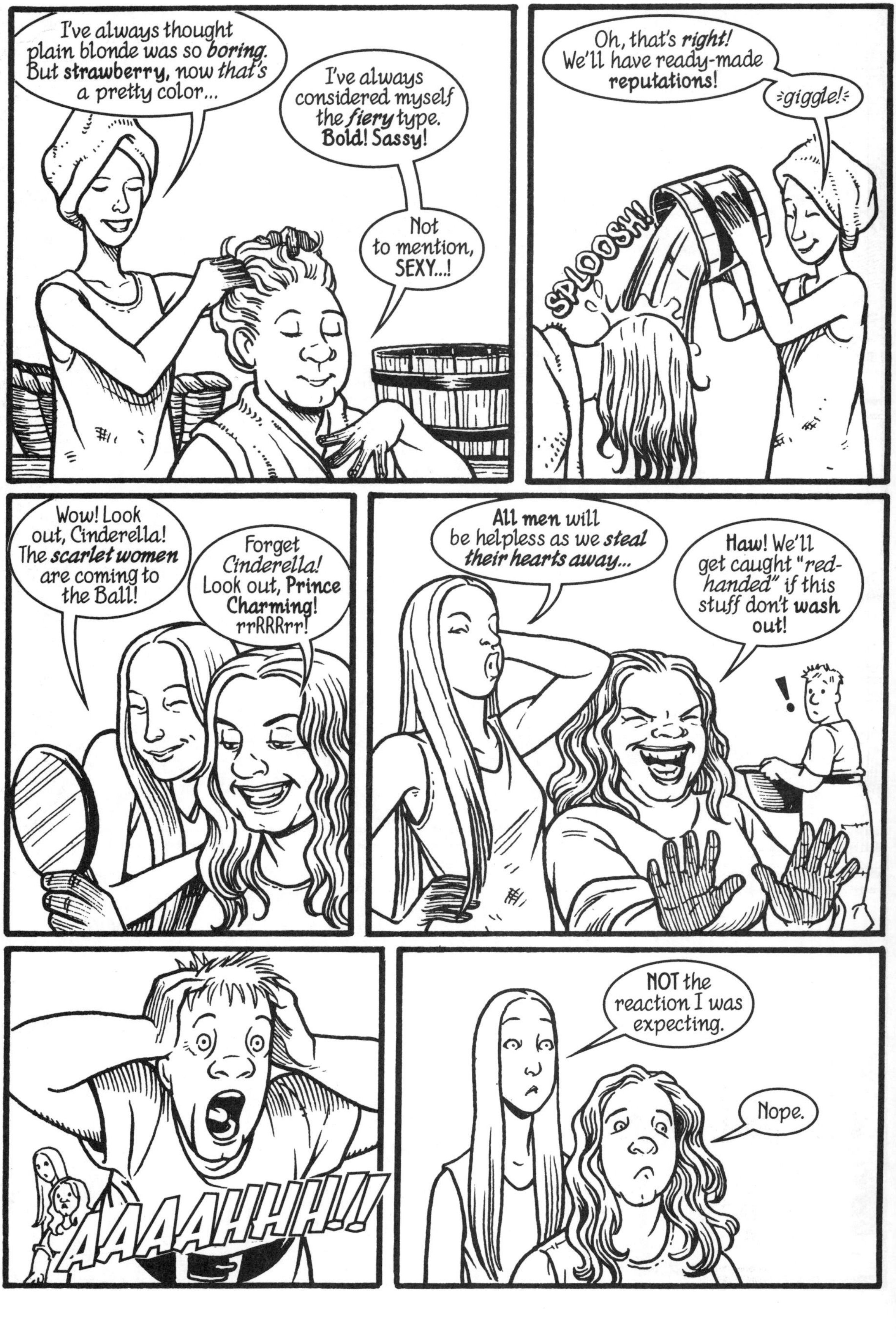

I've always thought plain blonde was so *boring*. But **strawberry**, now *that's* a pretty color...
I've always considered myself the *fiery* type. **Bold! Sassy!**
Not to mention, SEXY...!
Oh, that's *right!* We'll have ready-made **reputations!**
giggle!
SPLOOSH!
Wow! Look out, Cinderella! The ***scarlet women*** are coming to the Ball!
Forget *Cinderella!* Look out, **Prince Charming!** rrRRRrr!
All men will be helpless as we ***steal their hearts away...***
Haw! We'll get caught "*red-handed*" if this stuff don't **wash out!**
!
AAAAAHHHH!!!
NOT the reaction I was expecting.
Nope.

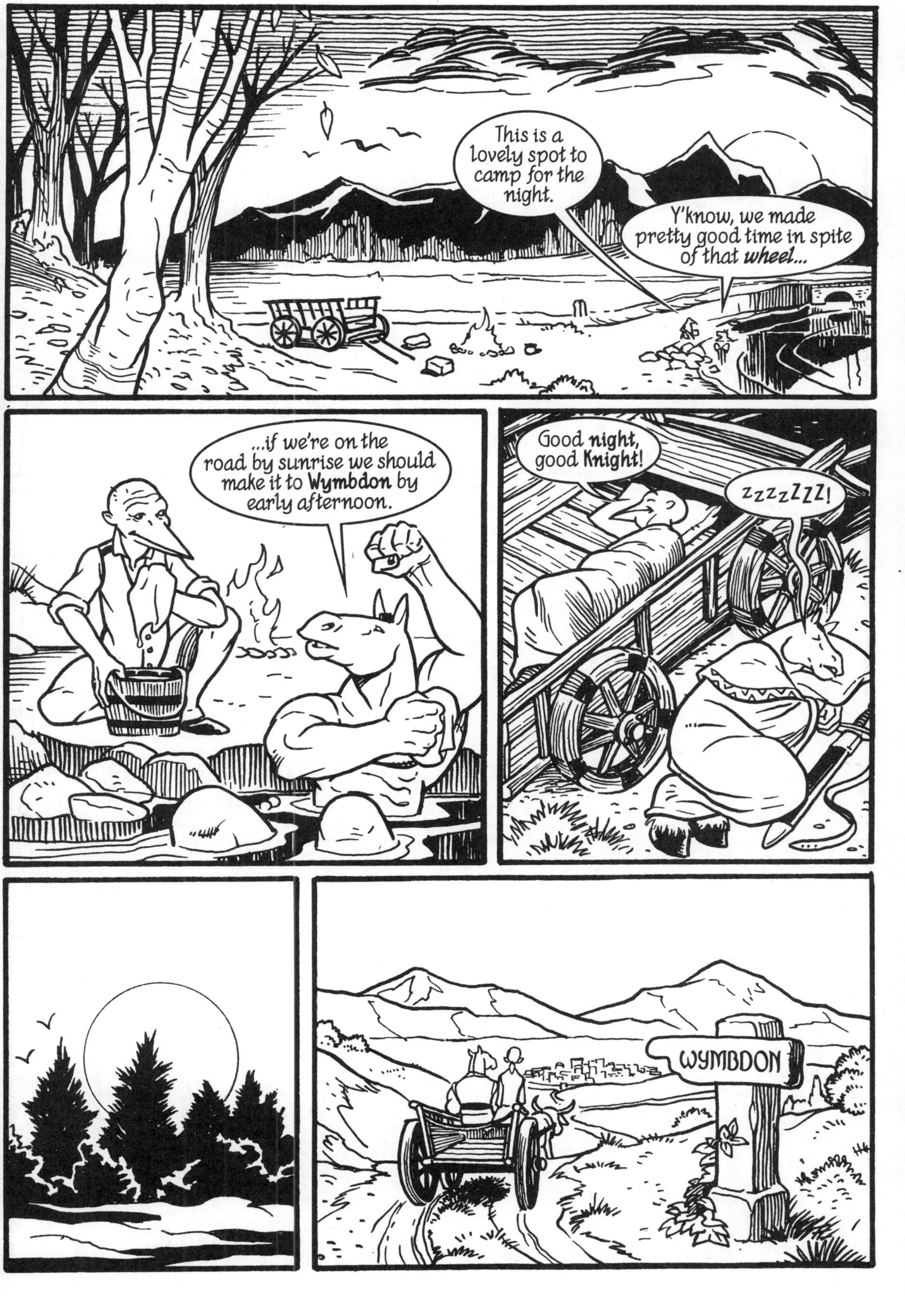
This is a lovely spot to camp for the night.
Y'know, we made pretty good time in spite of that **wheel**...
...if we're on the road by sunrise we should make it to **Wymbdon** by early afternoon.
Good **night**, good **Knight**!
zzzzZZZ!
WYMBDON

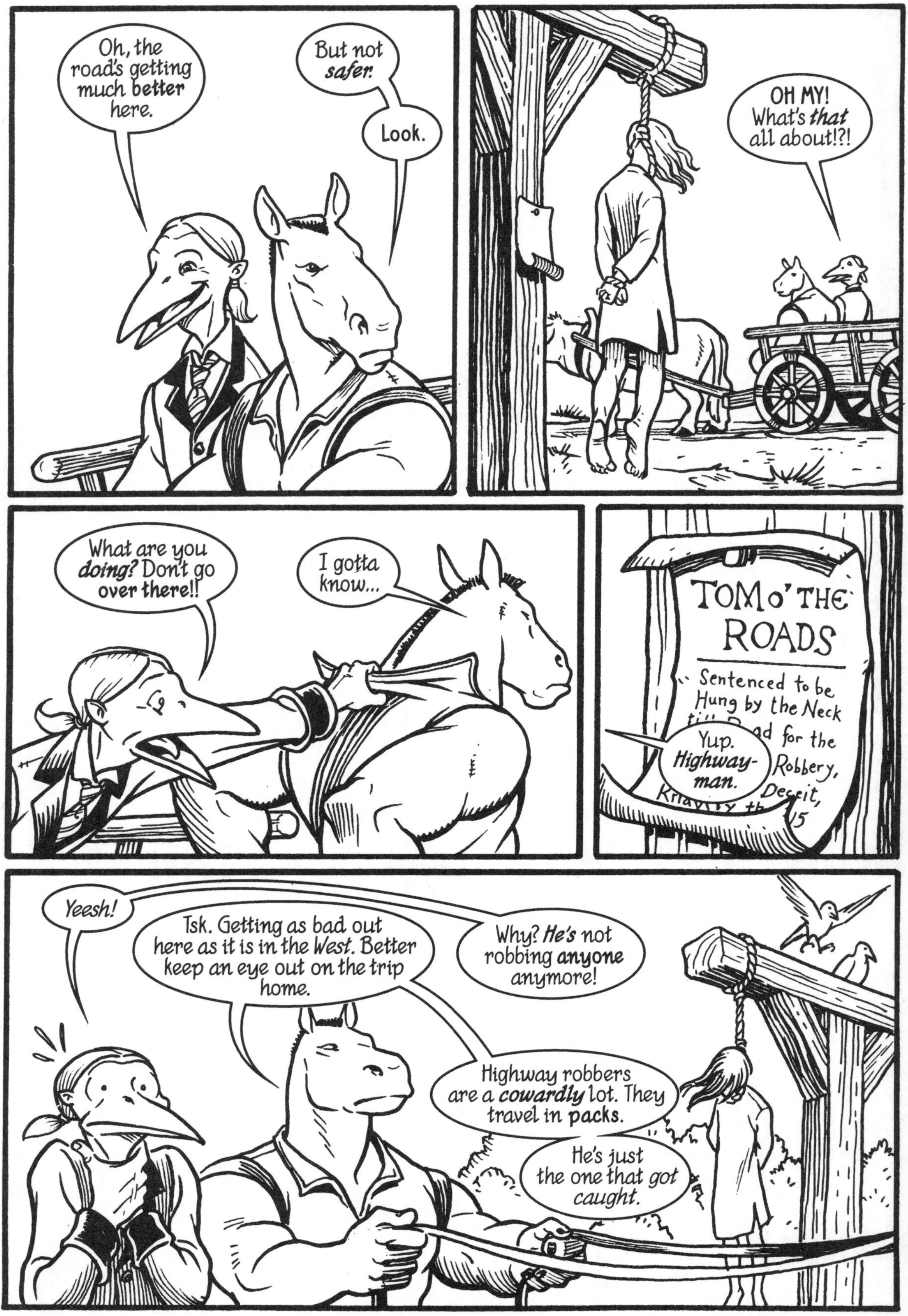
Oh, the road's getting much better here.
But not safer.
Look.
OH MY! What's that all about!?!
What are you doing? Don't go over there!!
I gotta know...
TOM o' THE ROADS
Sentenced to be Hung by the Neck
for the
Robbery,
Deceit,
Yup. Highwayman.
Yeesh!
Tsk. Getting as bad out here as it is in the West. Better keep an eye out on the trip home.
Why? He's not robbing anyone anymore!
Highway robbers are a cowardly lot. They travel in packs.
He's just the one that got caught.

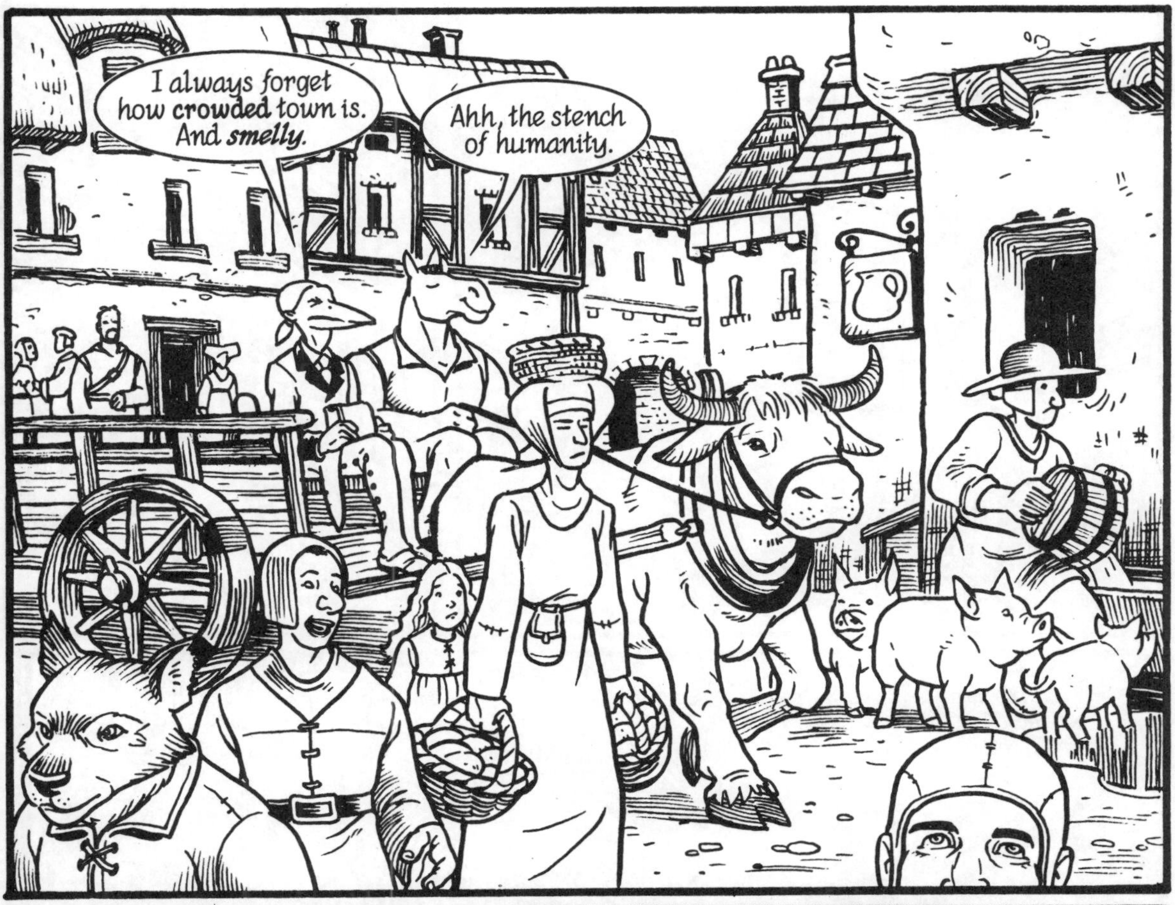
I always forget how **crowded** town is. And ***smelly***.
Ahh, the stench of humanity.

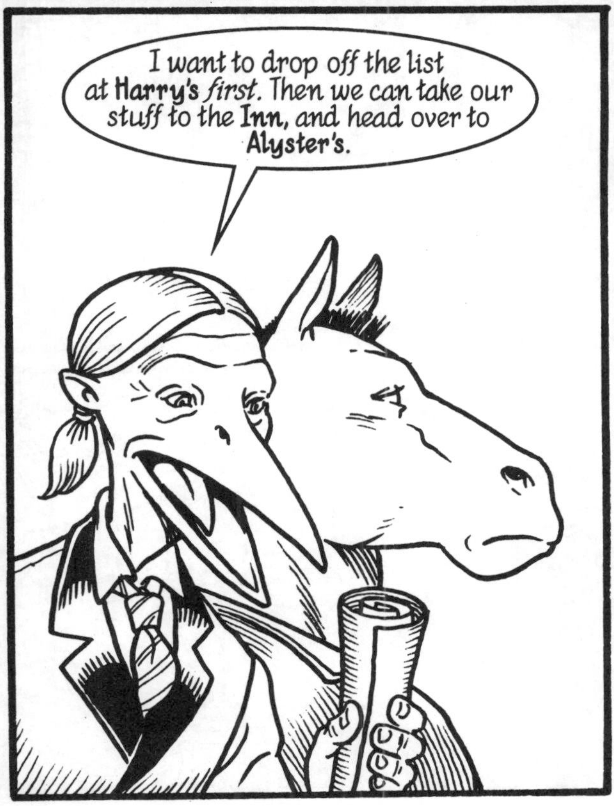
I want to drop off the list at **Harry's** *first*. Then we can take our stuff to the **Inn**, and head over to **Alyster's**.

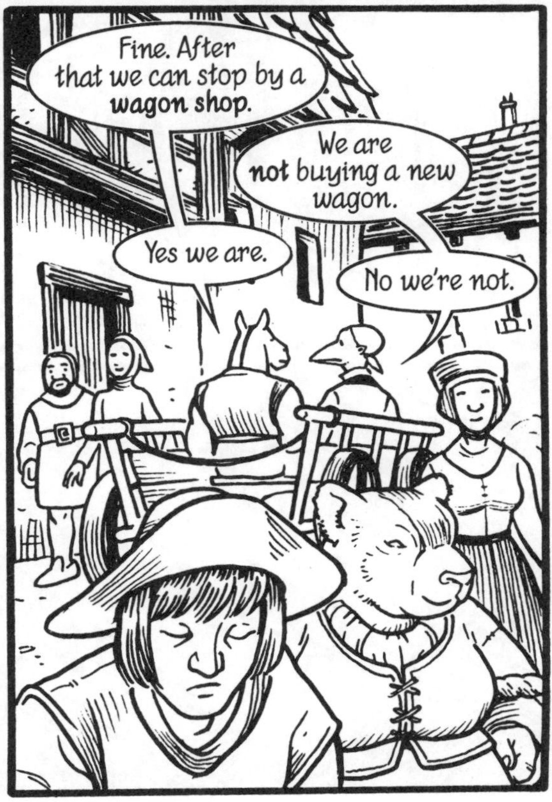
Fine. After that we can stop by a **wagon shop**.
We are **not** buying a new wagon.
Yes we are.
No we're not.

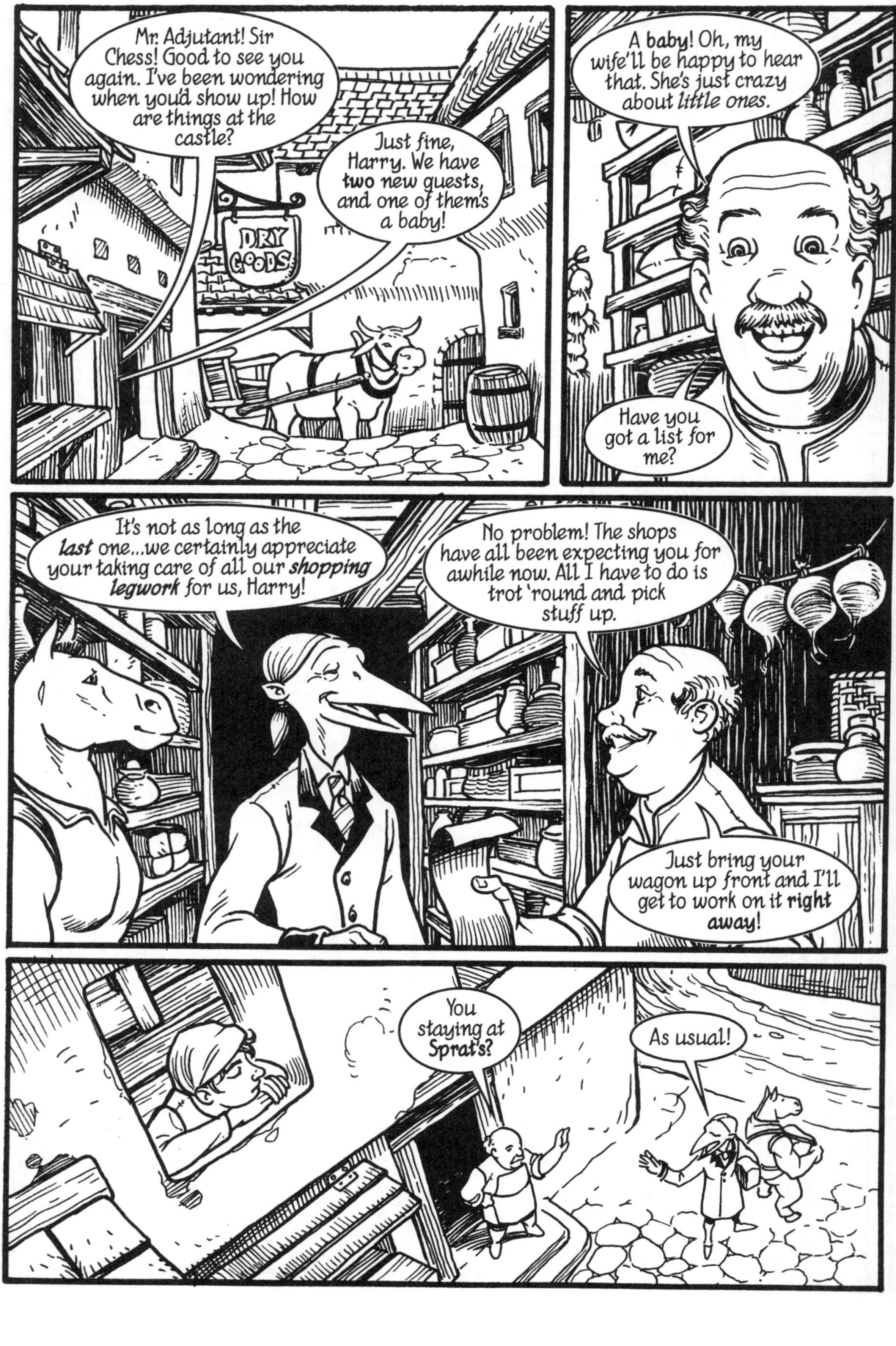

Mr. Adjutant! Sir Chess! Good to see you again. I've been wondering when you'd show up! How are things at the castle?
Just fine, Harry. We have **two** new guests, and one of them's a baby!
DRY GOODS
A **baby**! Oh, my wife'll be happy to hear that. She's just crazy about *little ones*.
Have you got a list for me?
It's not as long as the ***last*** one...we certainly appreciate your taking care of all our ***shopping legwork*** for us, Harry!
No problem! The shops have all been expecting you for awhile now. All I have to do is trot 'round and pick stuff up.
Just bring your wagon up front and I'll get to work on it **right away**!
You staying at **Sprat's**?
As usual!

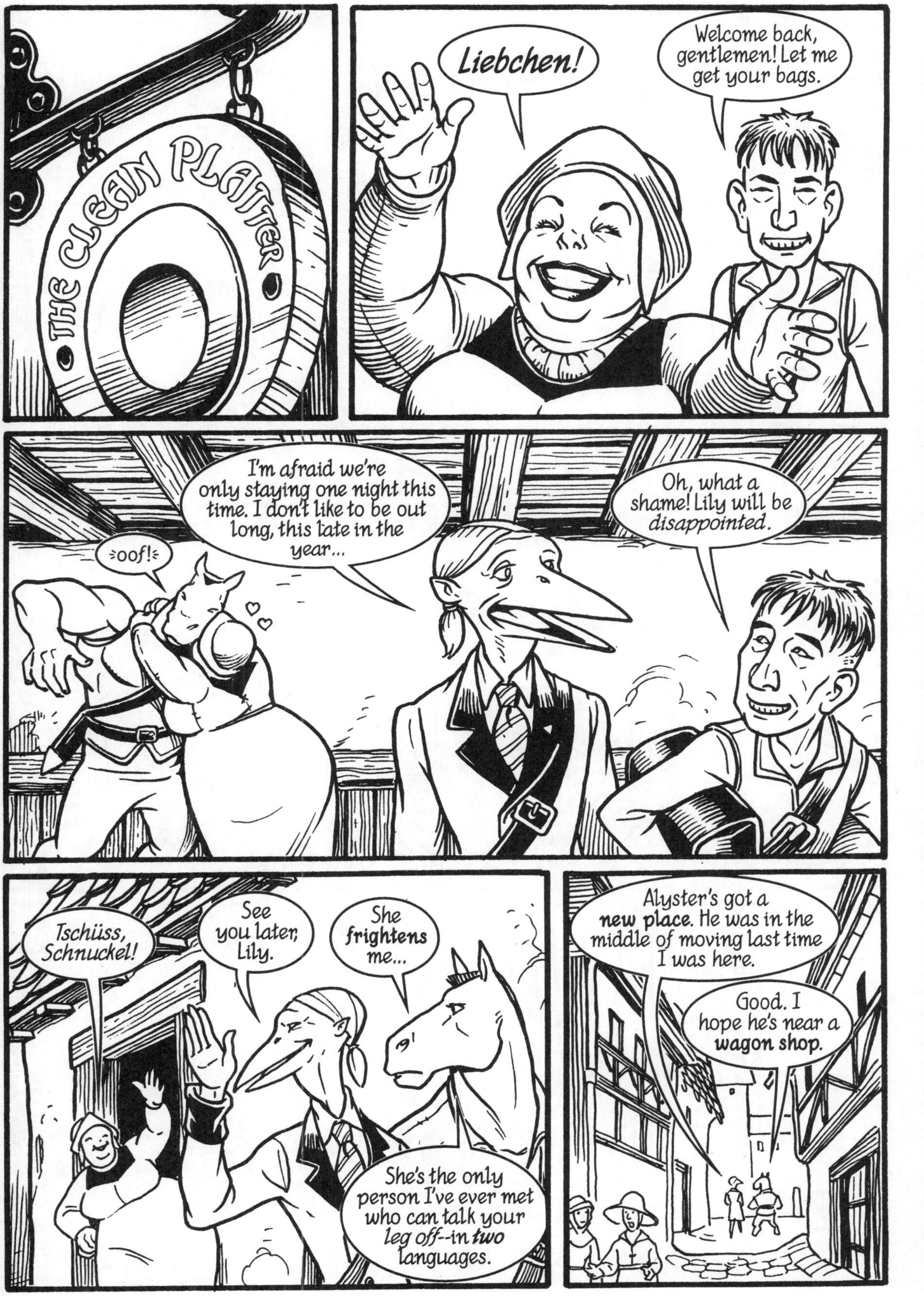
THE CLEAN PLATTER
Liebchen!
Welcome back, gentlemen! Let me get your bags.
I'm afraid we're only staying one night this time. I don't like to be out long, this late in the year...
oof!
Oh, what a shame! Lily will be *disappointed*.
Tschüss, Schnuckel!
See you later, Lily.
She **frightens** me...
She's the only person I've ever met who can talk your *leg off*--in ***two*** languages.
Alyster's got a **new place**. He was in the middle of moving last time I was here.
Good. I hope he's near a **wagon shop**.

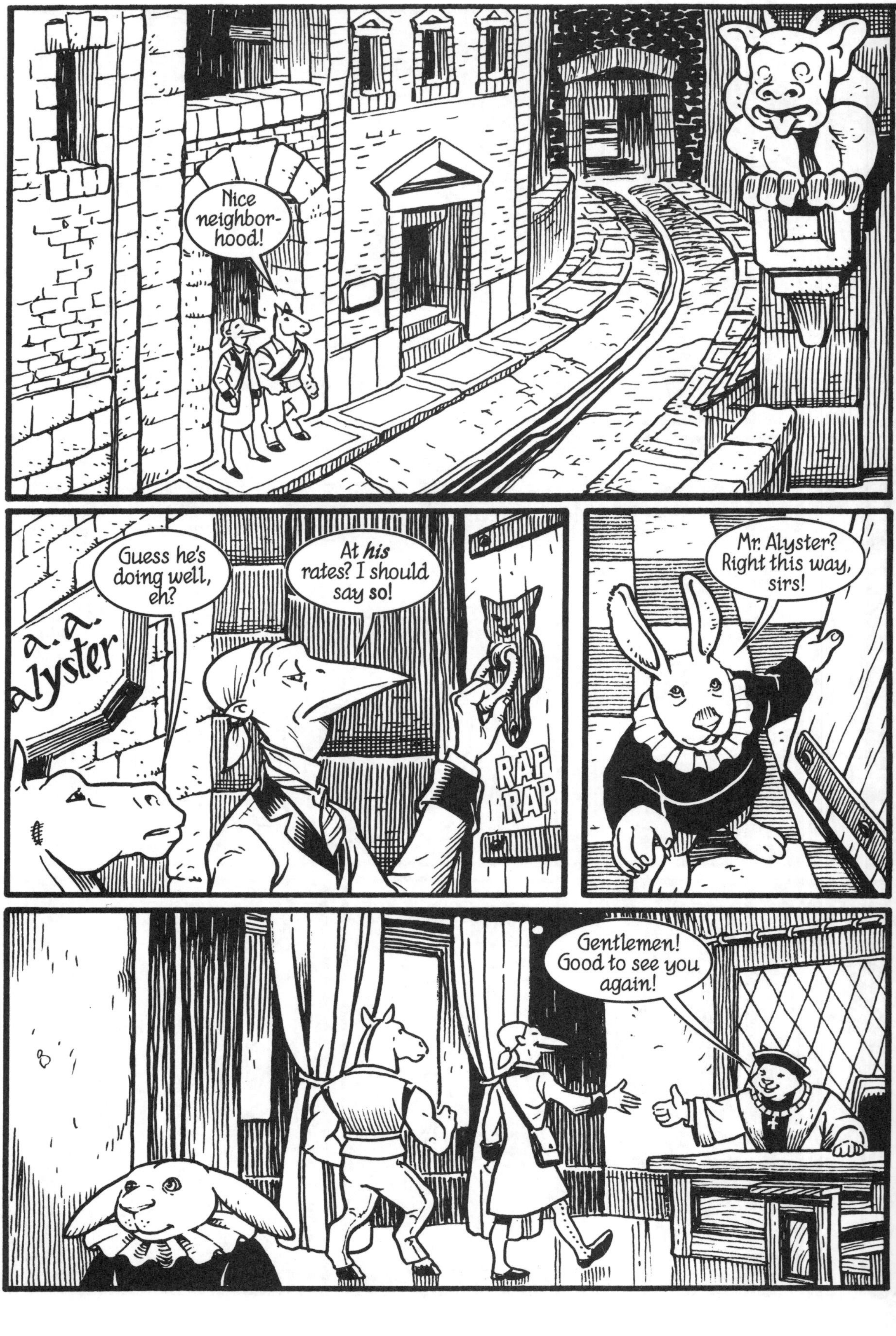
Nice neighbor-hood!
a. a.
alyster
Guess he's doing well, eh?
At *his* rates? I should say so!
RAP RAP
Mr. Alyster? Right this way, sirs!
Gentlemen! Good to see you again!

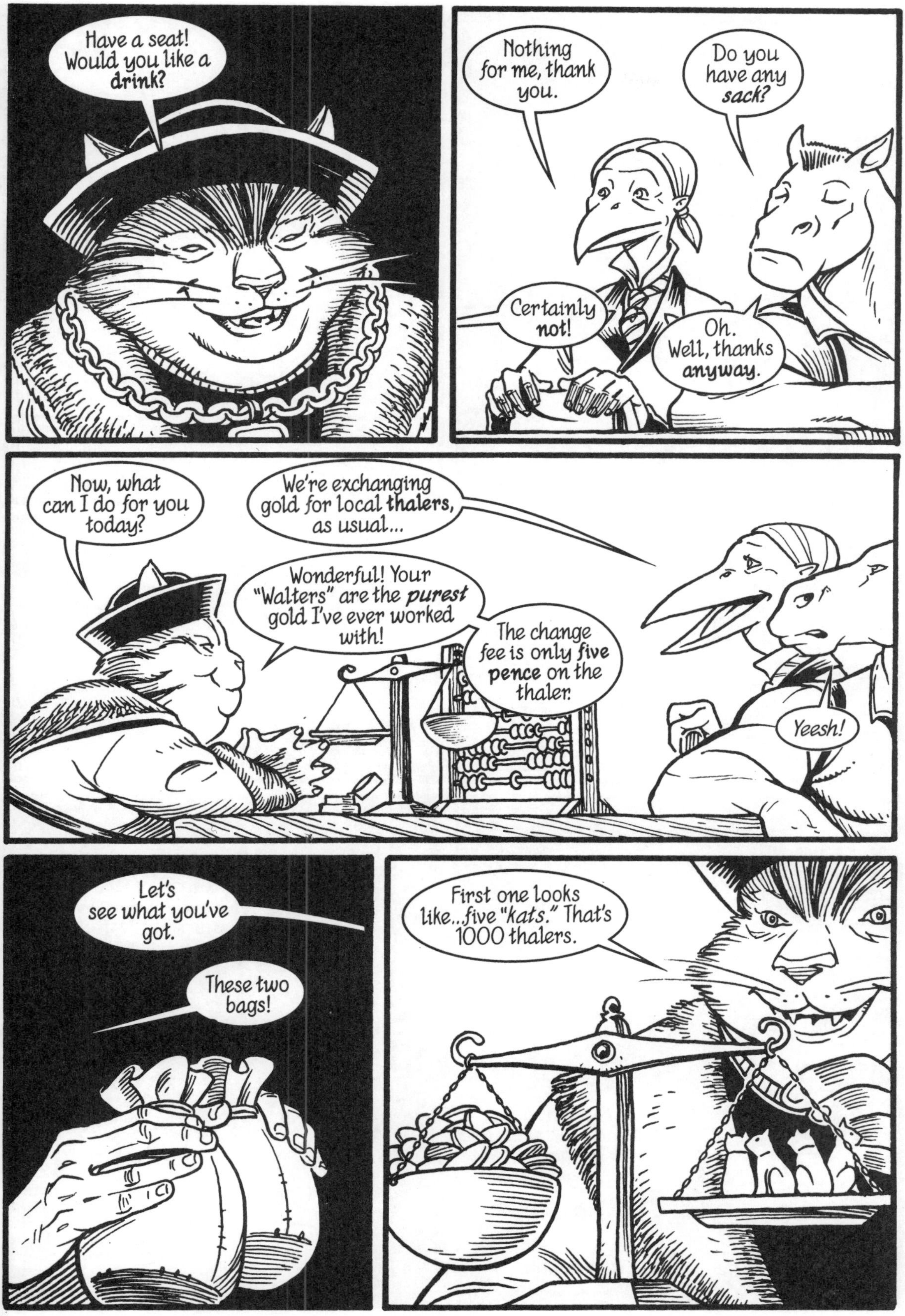
Have a seat! Would you like a **drink?**
Nothing for me, thank you.
Do you have any *sack?*
Certainly **not!**
Oh. Well, thanks **anyway**.
Now, what can I do for you today?
We're exchanging gold for local **thalers**, as usual...
Wonderful! Your "Walters" are the ***purest*** gold I've ever worked with!
The change fee is only **five pence** on the thaler.
Yeesh!
Let's see what you've got.
These two bags!
First one looks like...five "*kats.*" That's 1000 thalers.

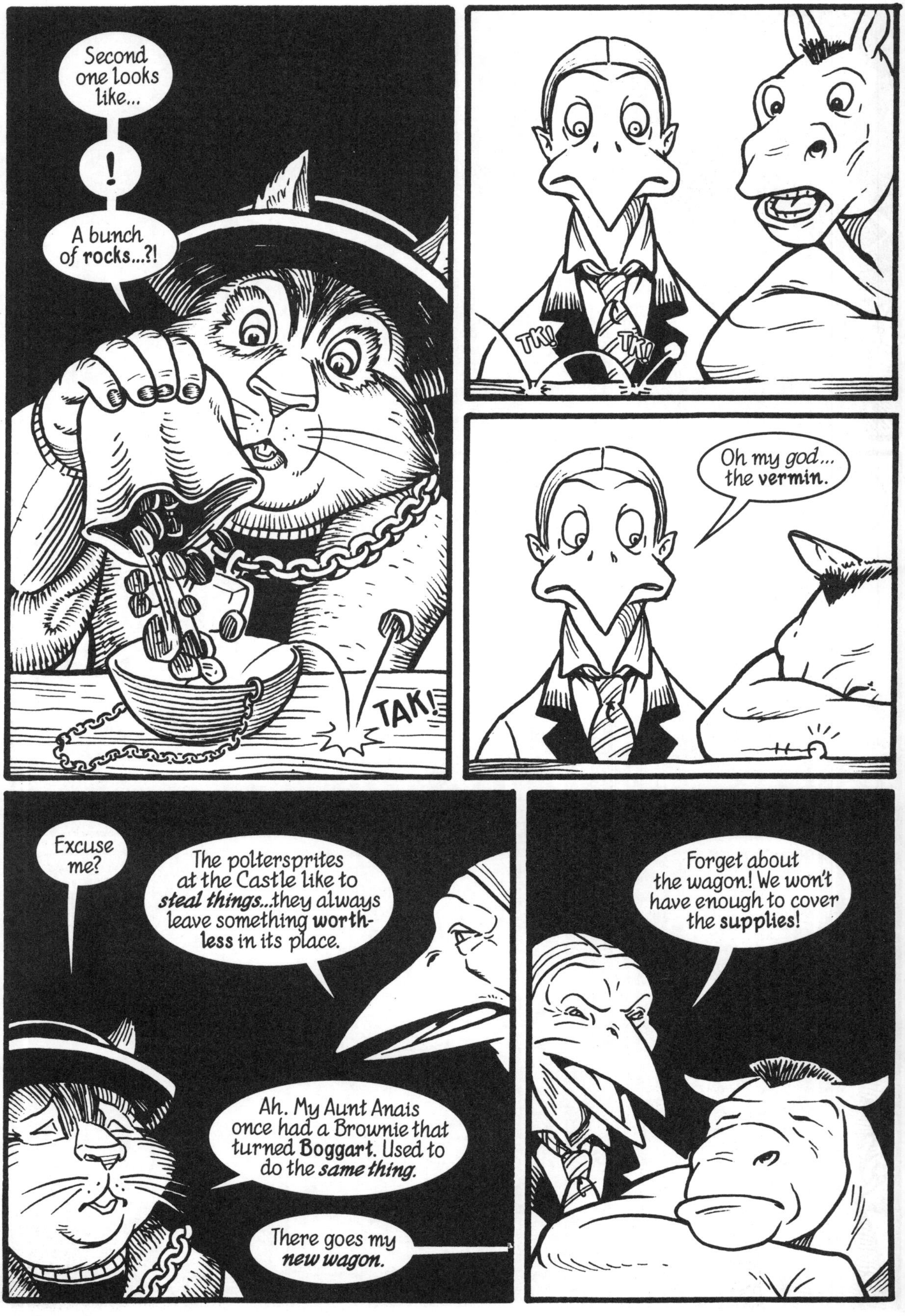
Second one looks like...
!
A bunch of rocks...?!
TAK!
TK!
TK!
Oh my god... the vermin.
Excuse me?
The poltersprites at the Castle like to steal things...they always leave something worthless in its place.
Ah. My Aunt Anais once had a Brownie that turned Boggart. Used to do the same thing.
There goes my new wagon.
Forget about the wagon! We won't have enough to cover the supplies!

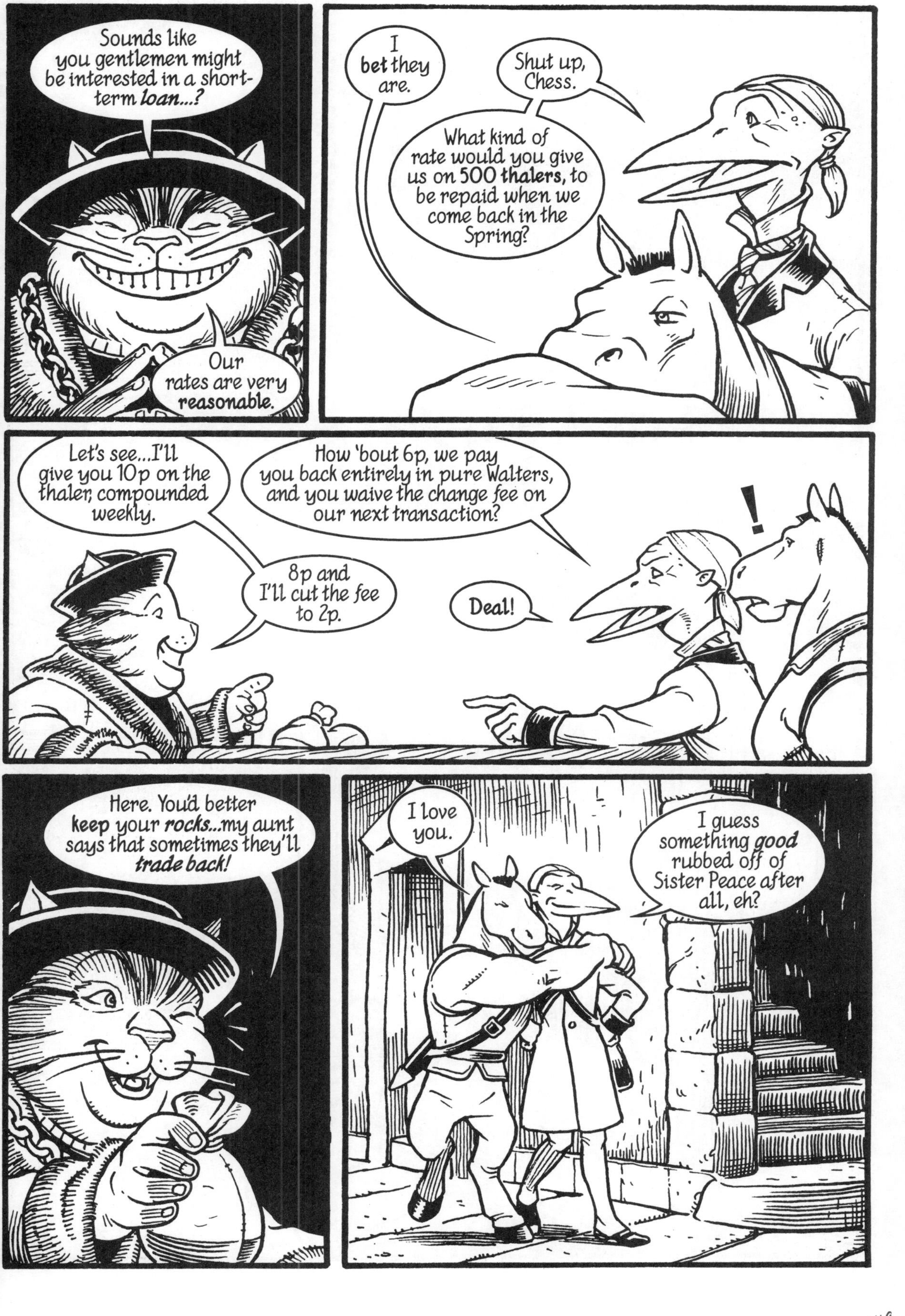
Sounds like you gentlemen might be interested in a short-term *loan...?*
Our rates are very **reasonable.**
I **bet** they are.
Shut up, Chess.
What kind of rate would you give us on **500 thalers**, to be repaid when we come back in the Spring?
Let's see...I'll give you 10p on the thaler, compounded weekly.
How 'bout 6p, we pay you back entirely in pure Walters, and you waive the change fee on our next transaction?
!
8p and I'll cut the fee to 2p.
Deal!
Here. You'd better **keep** your ***rocks...*** my aunt says that sometimes they'll ***trade back!***
I love you.
I guess something ***good*** rubbed off of Sister Peace after all, eh?

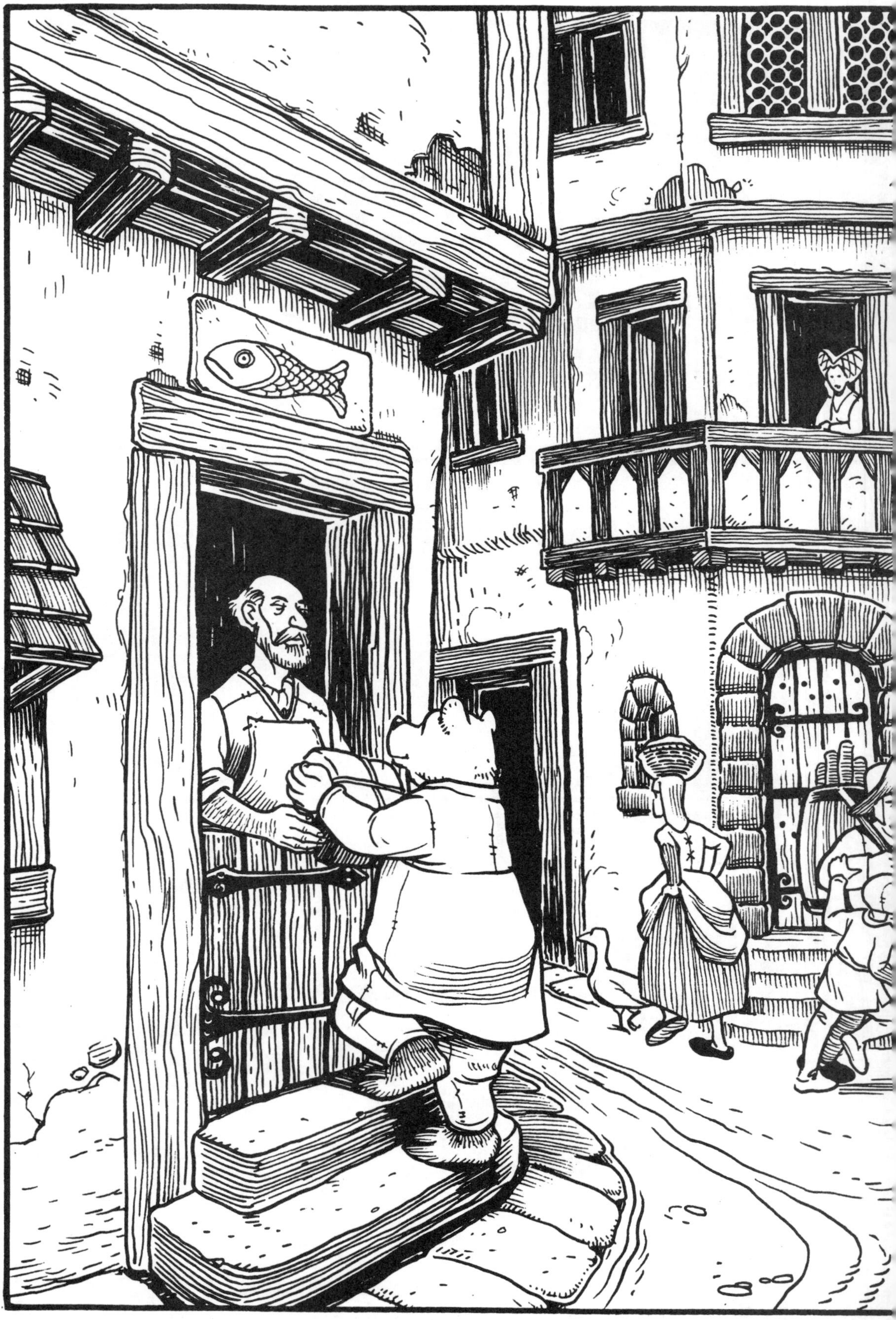

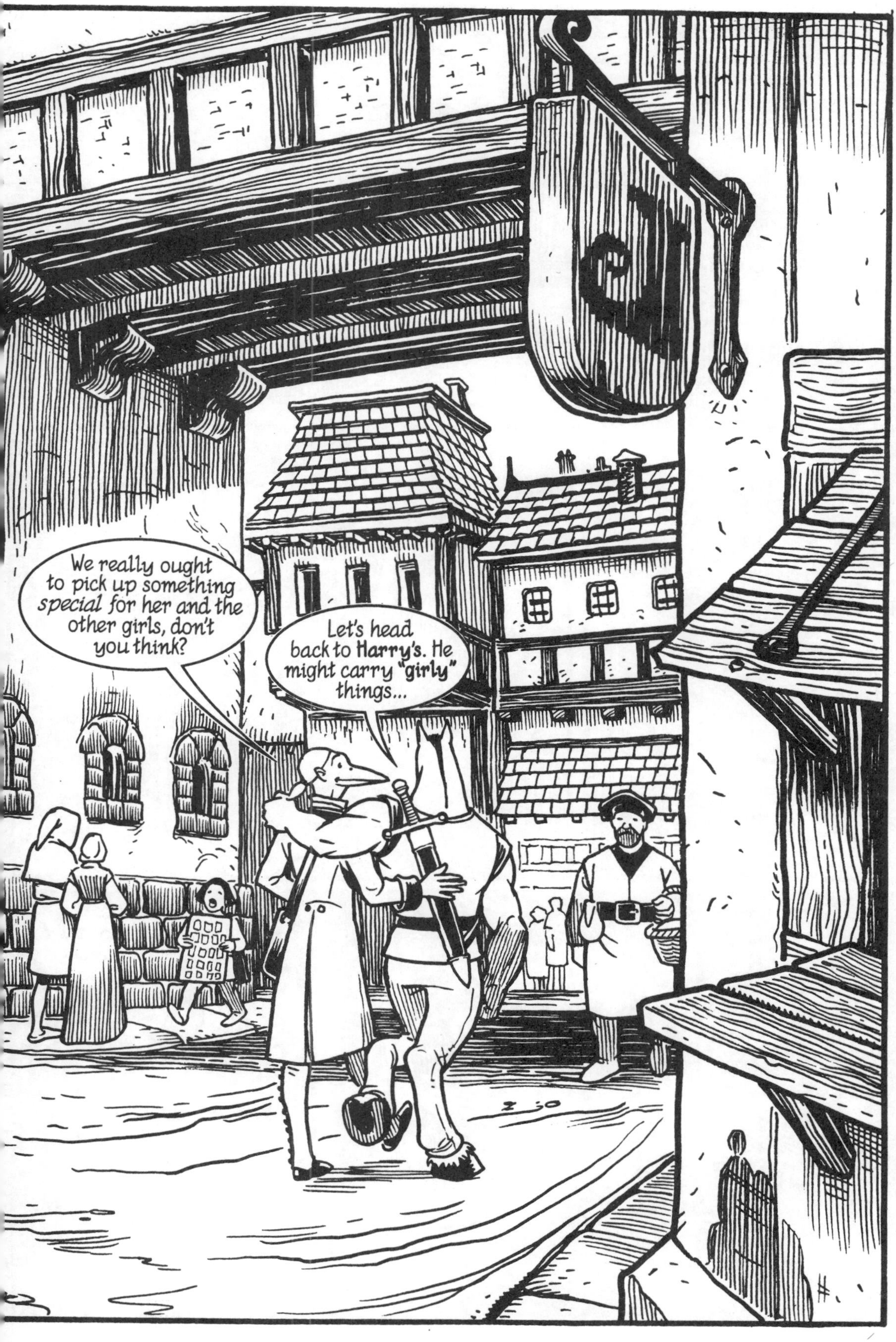
We really ought to pick up something *special* for her and the other girls, don't you think?
Let's head back to **Harry's**. He might carry **"girly"** things...

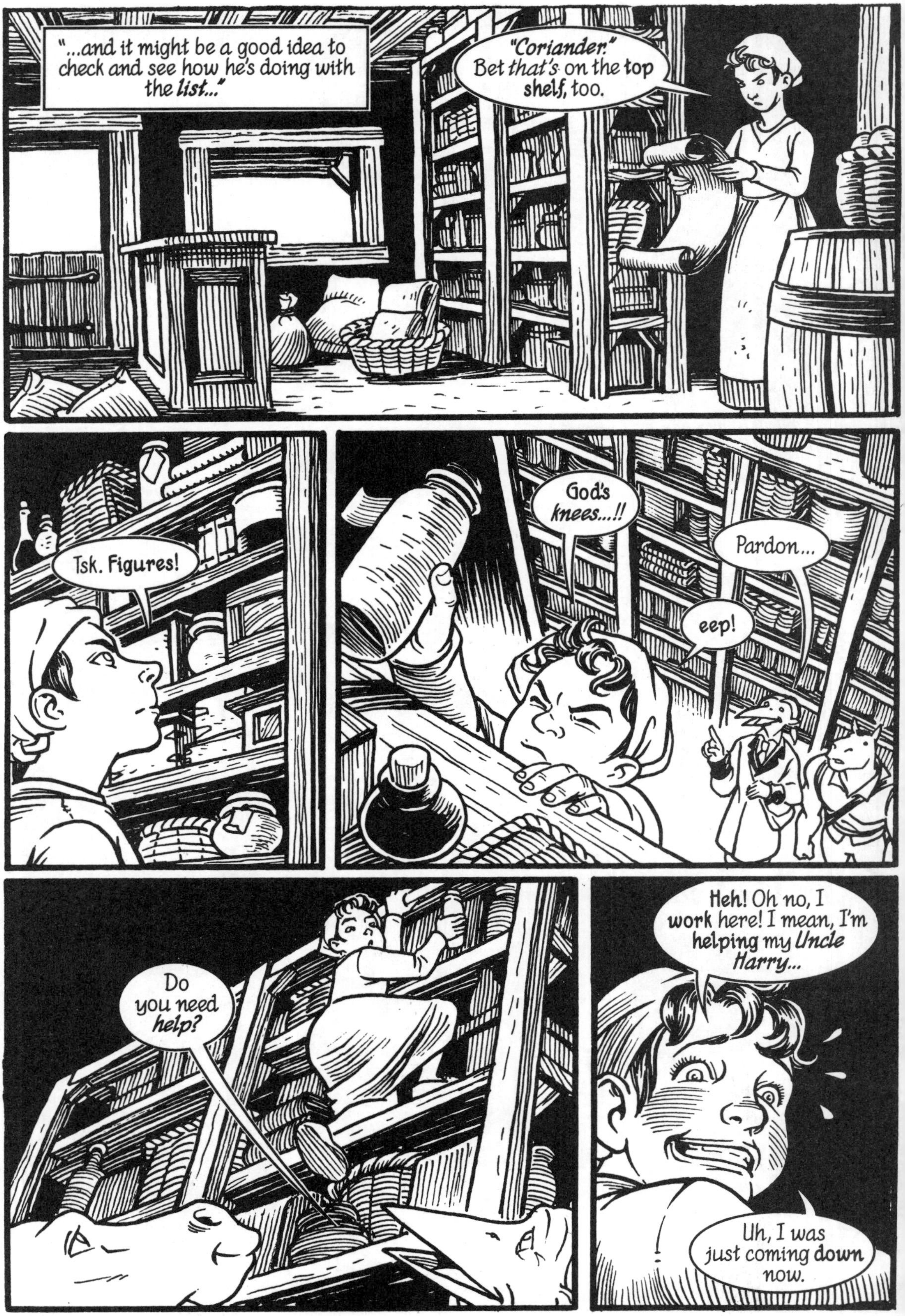
"...and it might be a good idea to check and see how he's doing with the *list*..."
"*Coriander.*" Bet *that's* on the **top shelf**, too.
Tsk. **Figures!**
God's *knees*...!!
Pardon...
eep!
Do you need *help?*
Heh! Oh no, I **work** here! I mean, I'm **helping** my *Uncle Harry*...
Uh, I was just coming **down** now.

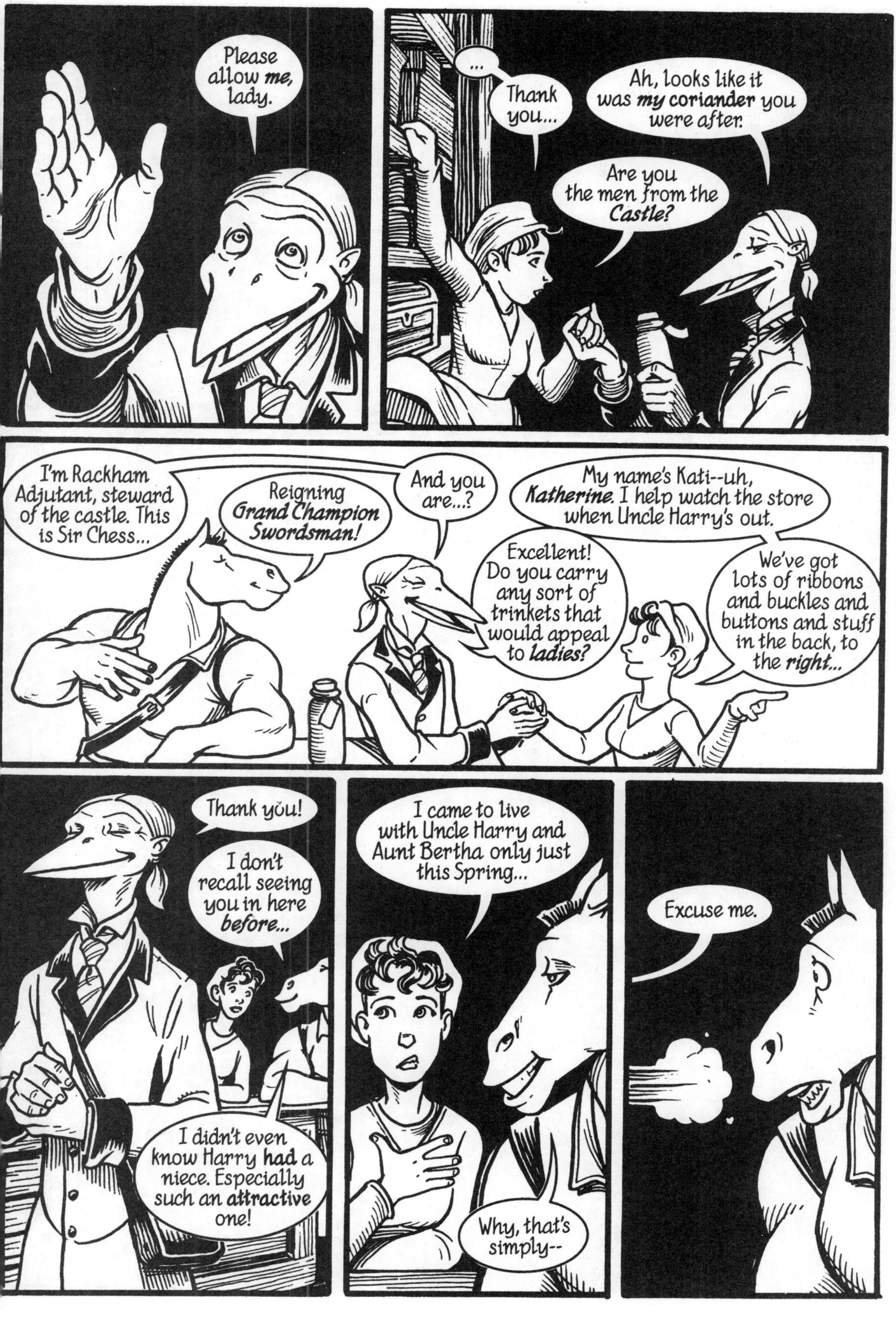
Please allow *me,* lady.
...
Thank you...
Ah, looks like it was ***my coriander*** you were after.
Are you the men from the ***Castle?***
I'm Rackham Adjutant, steward of the castle. This is Sir Chess...
Reigning ***Grand Champion Swordsman!***
And you are...?
My name's Kati--uh, ***Katherine***. I help watch the store when Uncle Harry's out.
Excellent! Do you carry any sort of trinkets that would appeal to ***ladies?***
We've got lots of ribbons and buckles and buttons and stuff in the back, to the ***right...***
Thank you!
I don't recall seeing you in here ***before...***
I didn't even know Harry **had** a niece. Especially such an **attractive** one!
I came to live with Uncle Harry and Aunt Bertha only just this Spring...
Why, that's simply--
Excuse me.

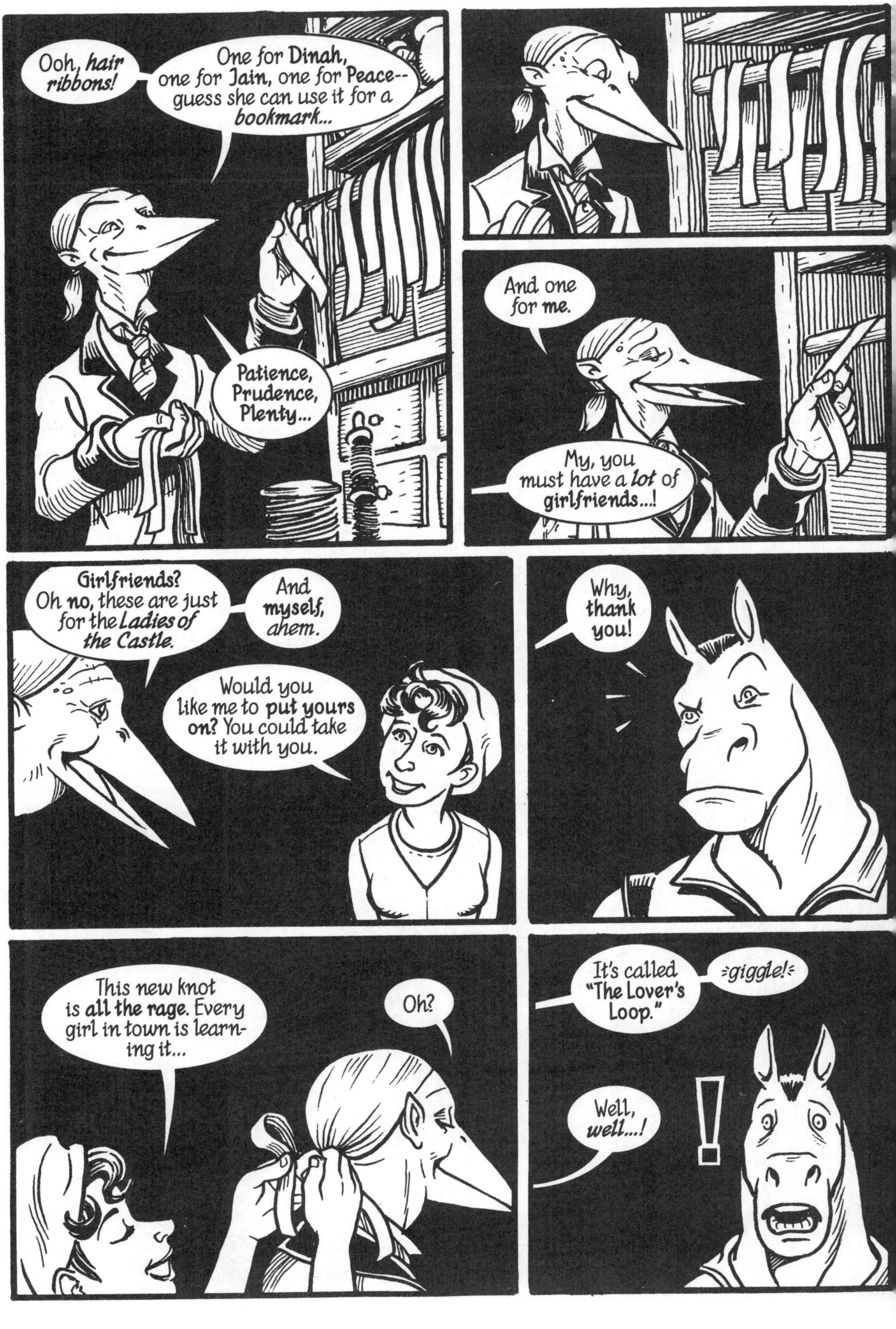
Ooh, *hair ribbons!*
One for **Dinah**, one for **Jain**, one for **Peace**-- guess she can use it for a *bookmark...*
Patience, Prudence, Plenty...
And one for **me**.
My, you must have a *lot* of **girlfriends**...!
Girlfriends? Oh **no**, these are just for the *Ladies of the Castle.*
And **myself**, *ahem*.
Would you like me to **put yours on**? You could take it with you.
Why, **thank** you!
This new knot is **all the rage**. Every girl in town is learning it...
Oh?
It's called **"The Lover's Loop."**
giggle!
Well, ***well***...!
!

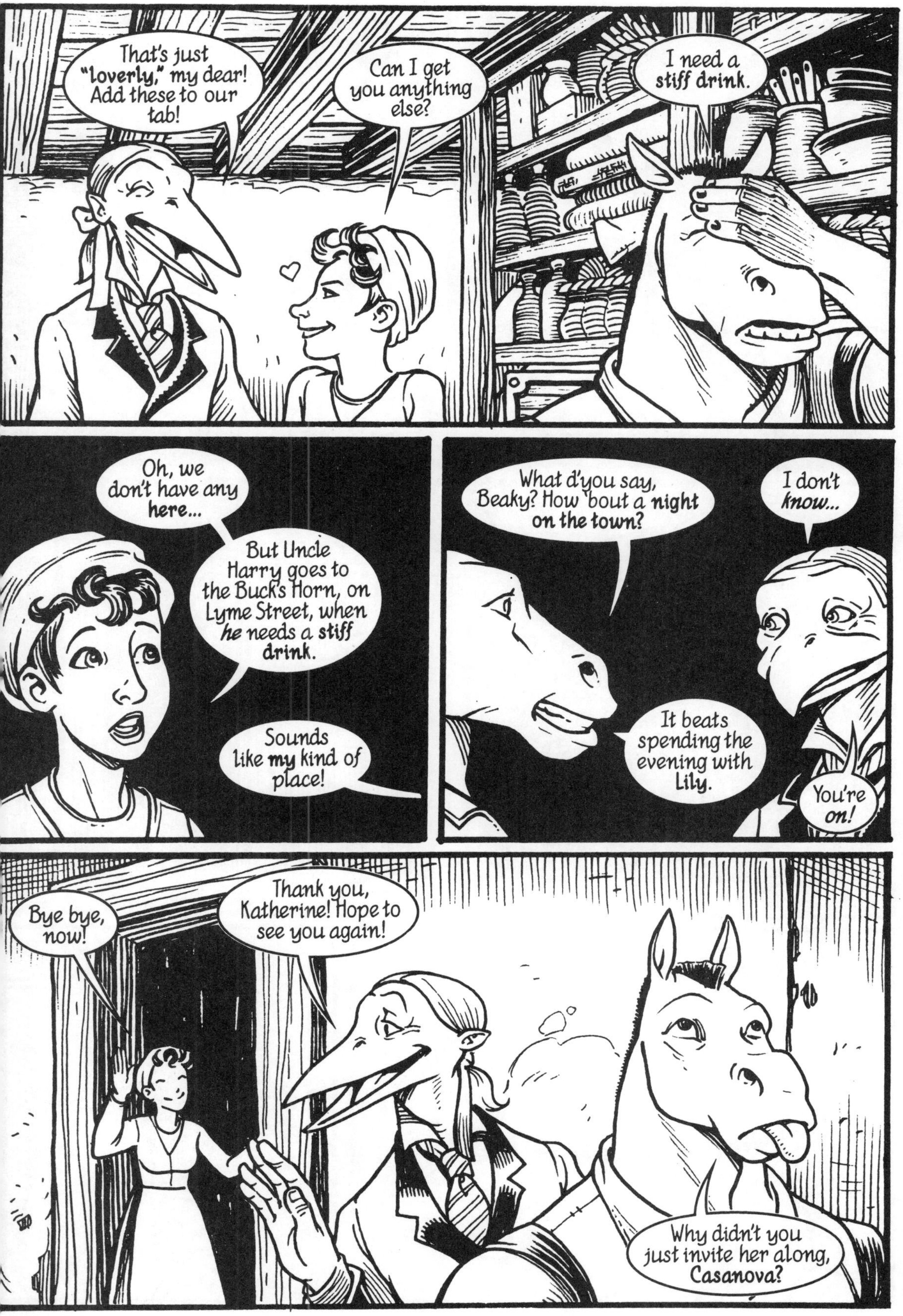

That's just "loverly," my dear! Add these to our tab!
Can I get you anything else?
I need a stiff drink.
Oh, we don't have any here...
But Uncle Harry goes to the Buck's Horn, on Lyme Street, when he needs a stiff drink.
Sounds like my kind of place!
What d'you say, Beaky? How 'bout a night on the town?
I don't know...
It beats spending the evening with Lily.
You're on!
Bye bye, now!
Thank you, Katherine! Hope to see you again!
Why didn't you just invite her along, Casanova?

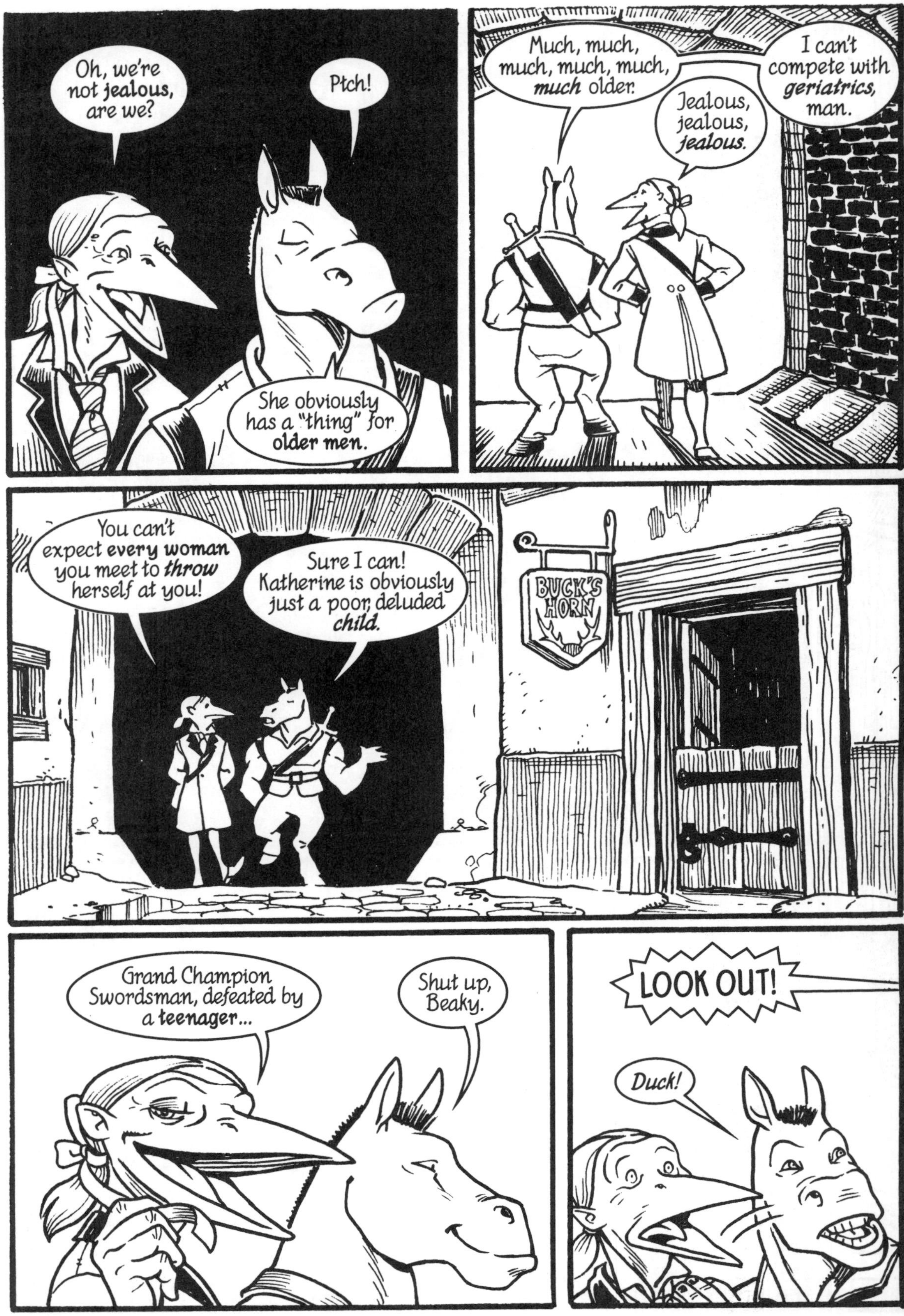
Oh, we're not jealous, are we?
Ptch!
She obviously has a "thing" for older men.
Much, much, much, much, much, much older.
Jealous, jealous, jealous.
I can't compete with geriatrics, man.
You can't expect every woman you meet to throw herself at you!
Sure I can! Katherine is obviously just a poor, deluded child.
BUCK'S HORN
Grand Champion Swordsman, defeated by a teenager...
Shut up, Beaky.
LOOK OUT!
Duck!

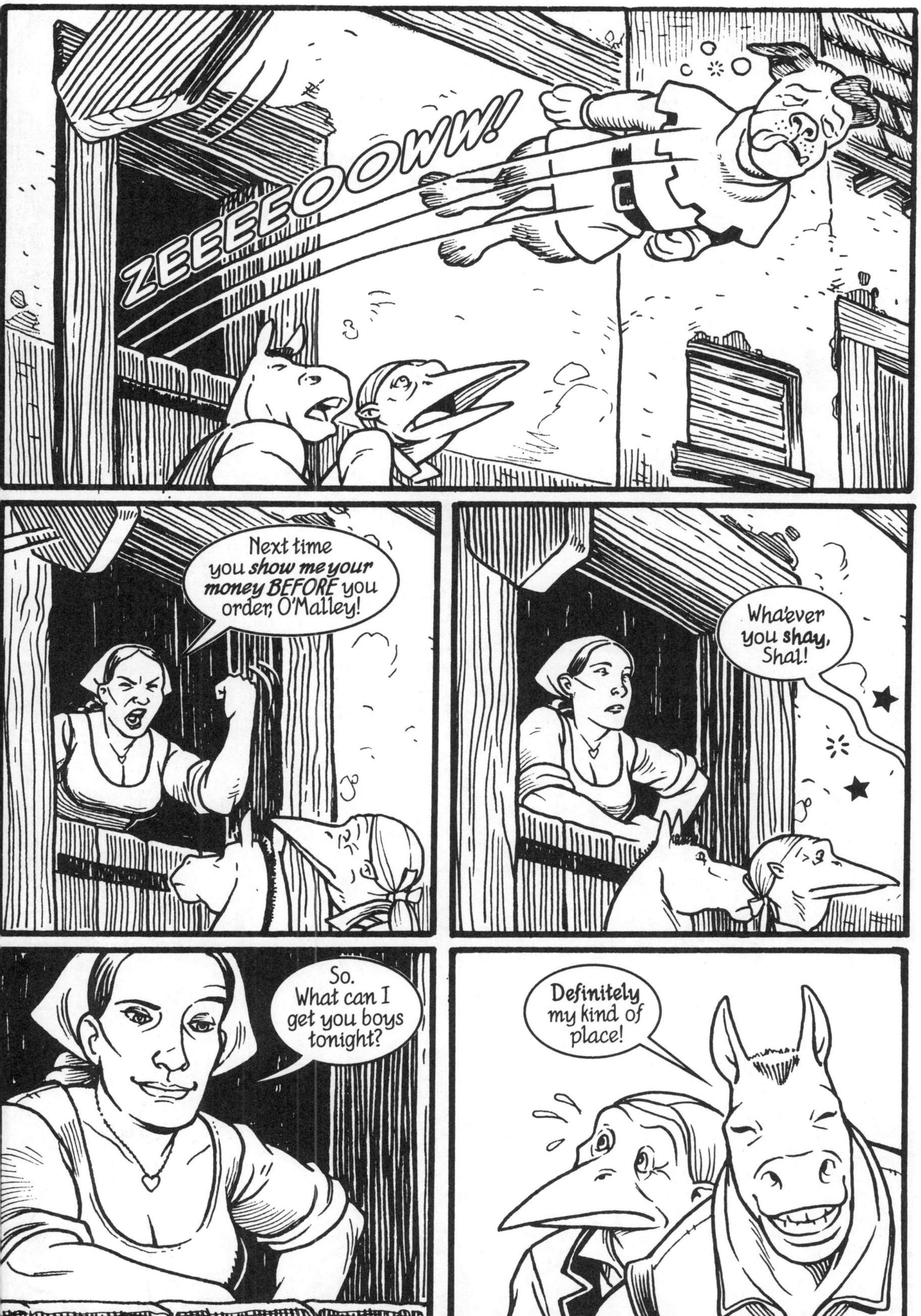
ZEEEEOOOWW!
Next time you show me your money BEFORE you order, O'Malley!
Wha'ever you shay, Shal!
So. What can I get you boys tonight?
Definitely my kind of place!

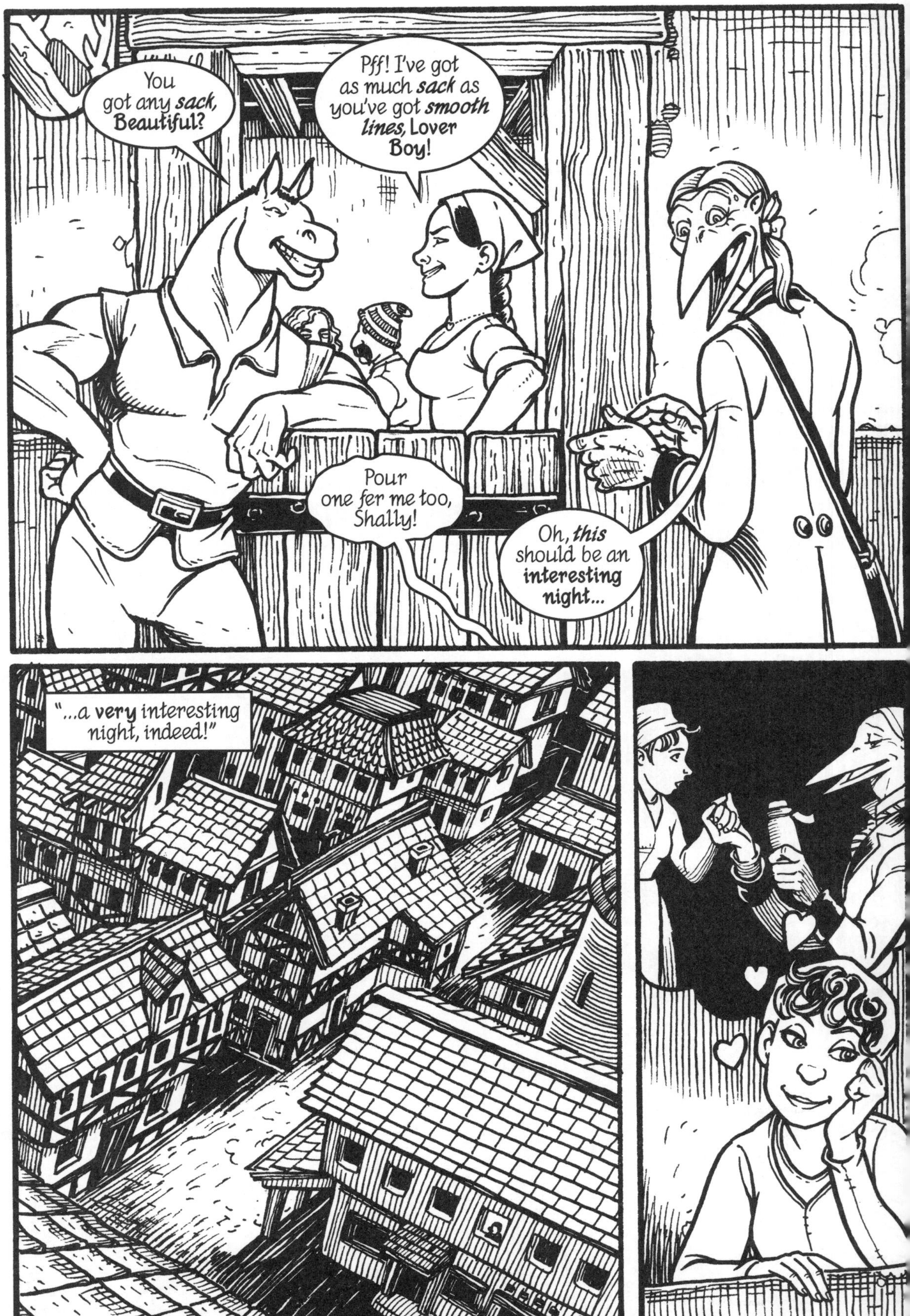
You got any sack, Beautiful?
Pff! I've got as much sack as you've got smooth lines, Lover Boy!
Pour one fer me too, Shally!
Oh, this should be an interesting night...
"...a very interesting night, indeed!"

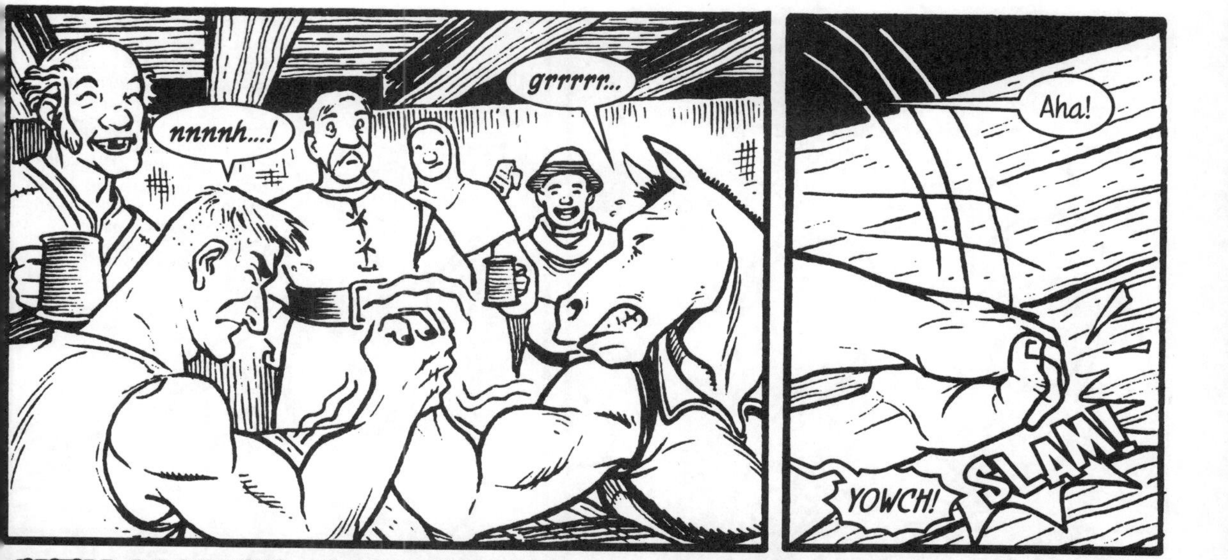
nnnnh...!
grrrrr...
Aha!
YOWCH!
SLAM!

CITY MOUSE, COUNTRY MOUSE

STORY & ART BY LINDA MEDLEY
PART TWO LETTERING BY TODD KLEIN

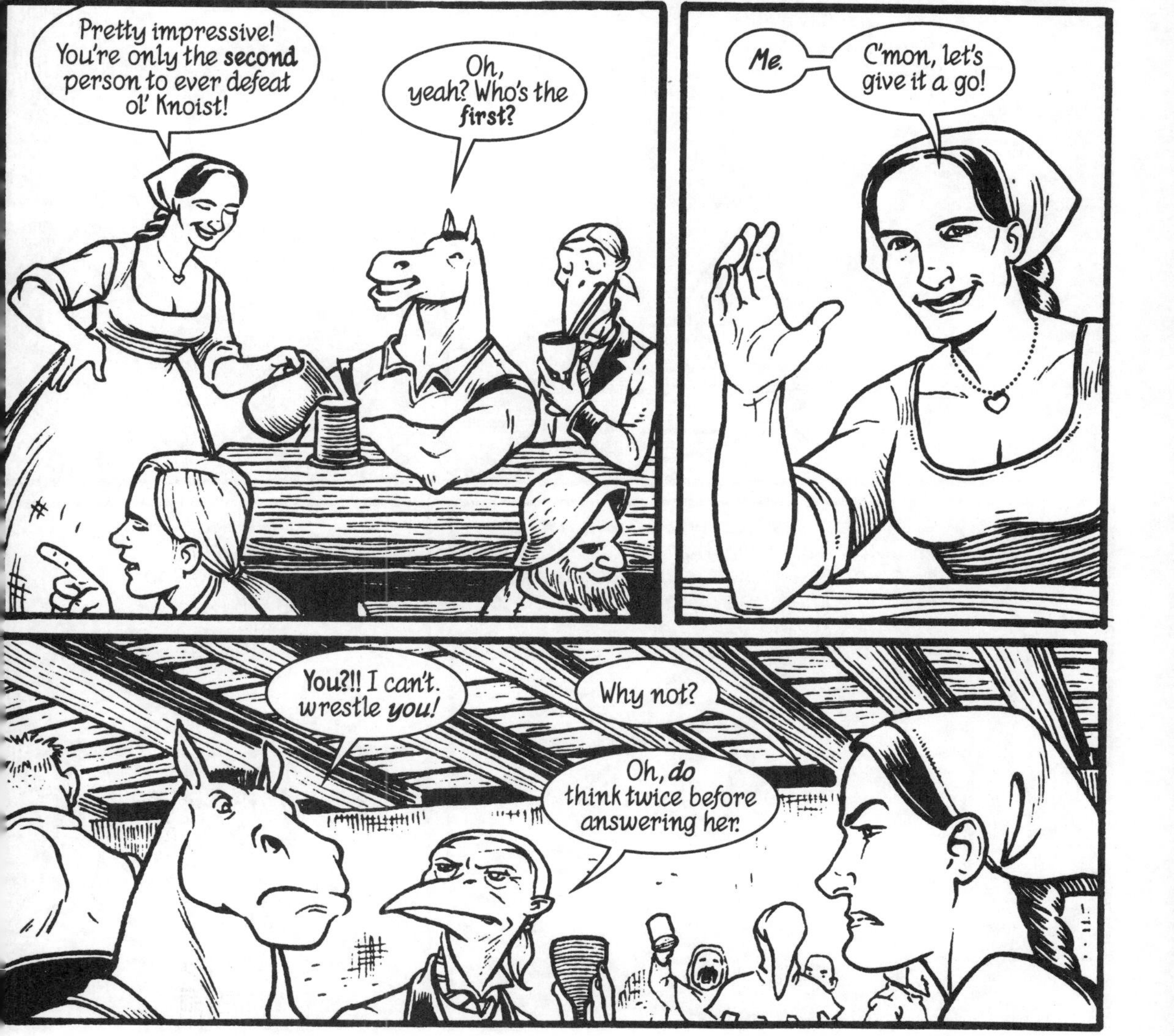
Pretty impressive! You're only the **second** person to ever defeat ol' Knoist!
Oh, yeah? Who's the **first**?
Me.
C'mon, let's give it a go!
You?!! I can't. wrestle ***you!***
Why not?
Oh, ***do*** think twice before answering her.

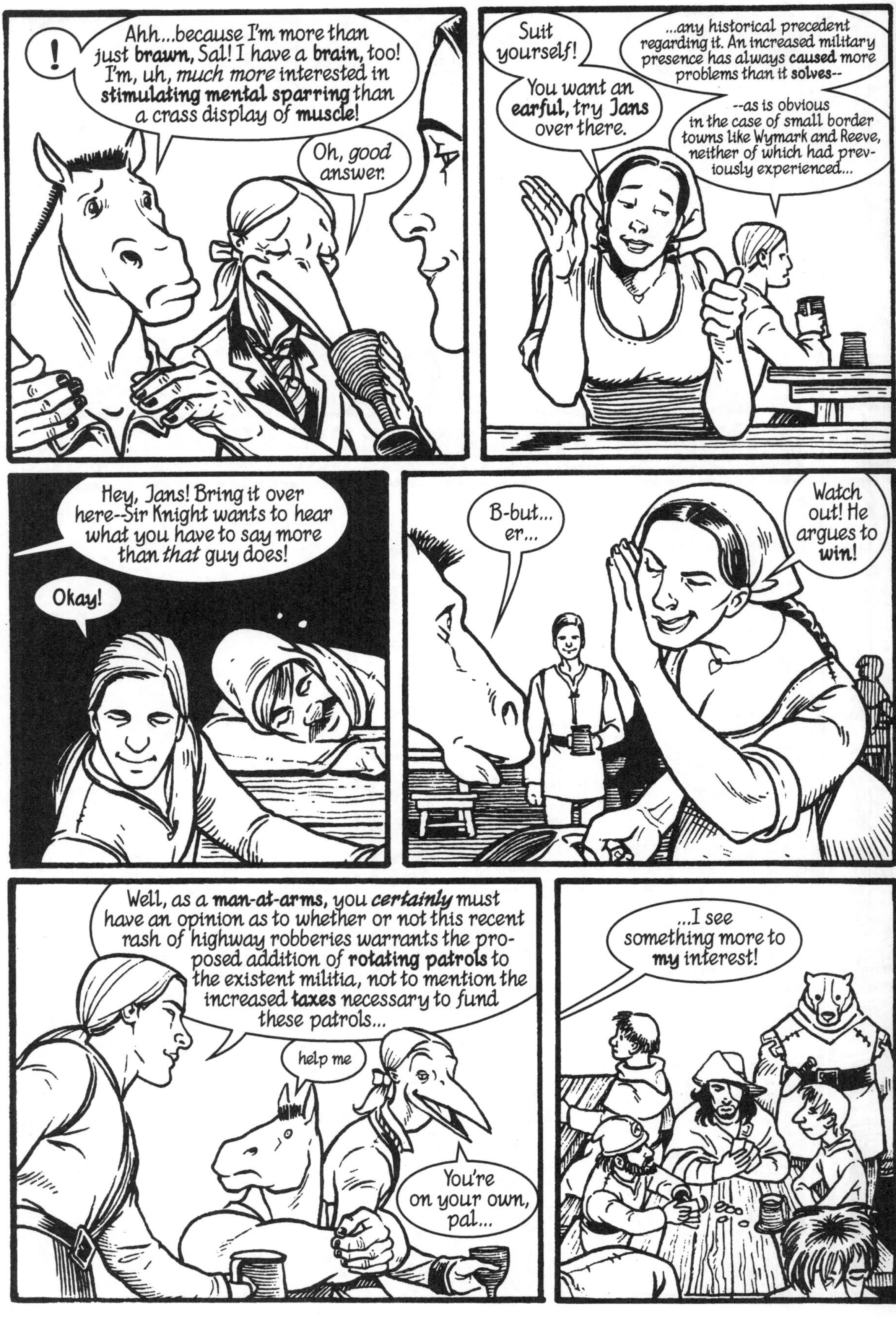
!
Ahh...because I'm more than just brawn, Sal! I have a brain, too! I'm, uh, much more interested in stimulating mental sparring than a crass display of muscle!
Oh, good answer.
Suit yourself!
You want an earful, try Jans over there.
...any historical precedent regarding it. An increased military presence has always caused more problems than it solves--
--as is obvious in the case of small border towns like Wymark and Reeve, neither of which had previously experienced...
Hey, Jans! Bring it over here--Sir Knight wants to hear what you have to say more than that guy does!
Okay!
B-but... er...
Watch out! He argues to win!
Well, as a man-at-arms, you certainly must have an opinion as to whether or not this recent rash of highway robberies warrants the proposed addition of rotating patrols to the existent militia, not to mention the increased taxes necessary to fund these patrols...
help me
You're on your own, pal...
...I see something more to my interest!

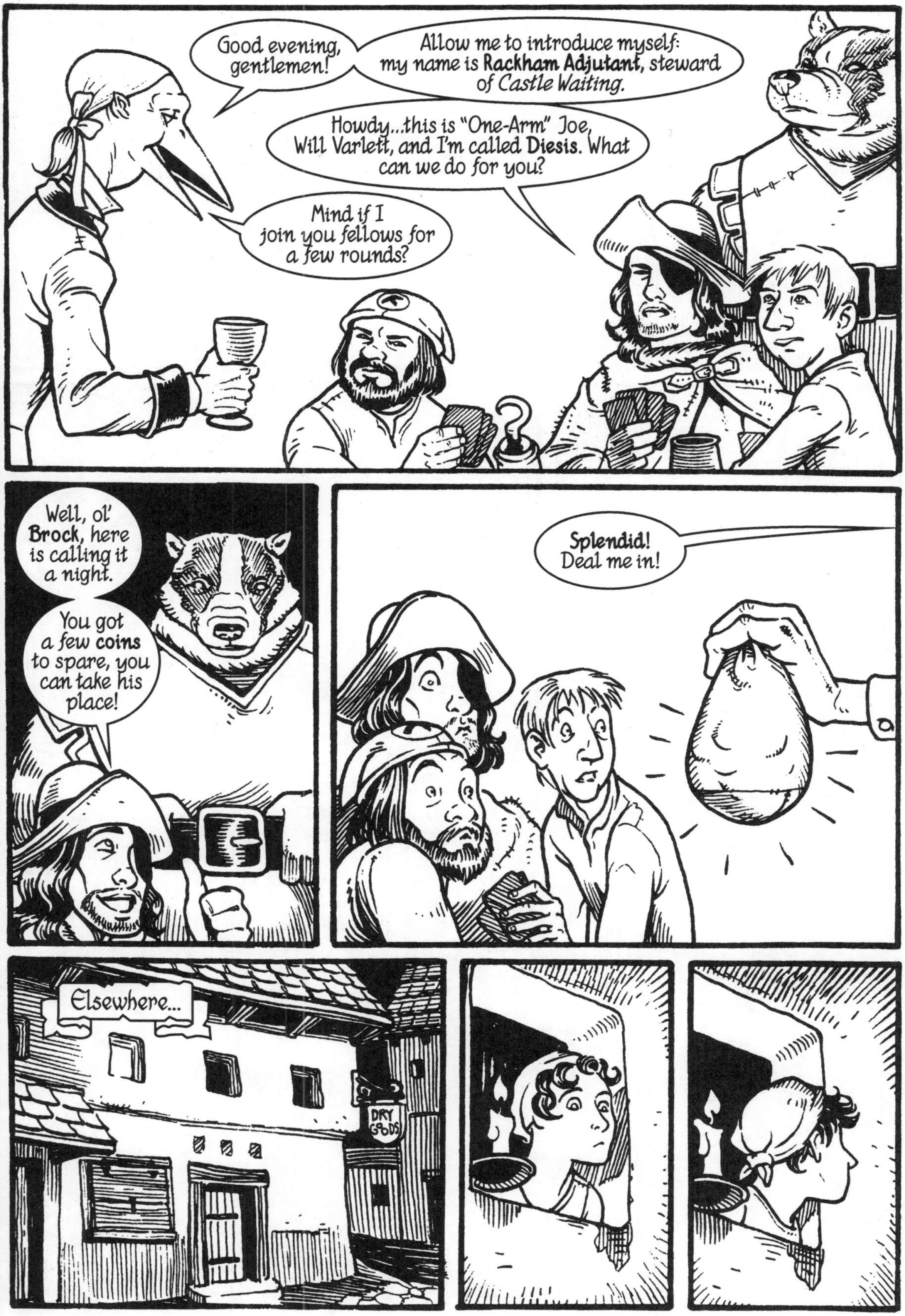
Good evening, gentlemen!
Allow me to introduce myself: my name is **Rackham Adjutant**, steward of *Castle Waiting*.
Mind if I join you fellows for a few rounds?
Howdy...this is "One-Arm" Joe, Will Varlett, and I'm called **Diesis**. What can we do for you?
Well, ol' **Brock**, here is calling it a night.
You got a few **coins** to spare, you can take his place!
Splendid! Deal me in!
Elsewhere...
DRY GOODS

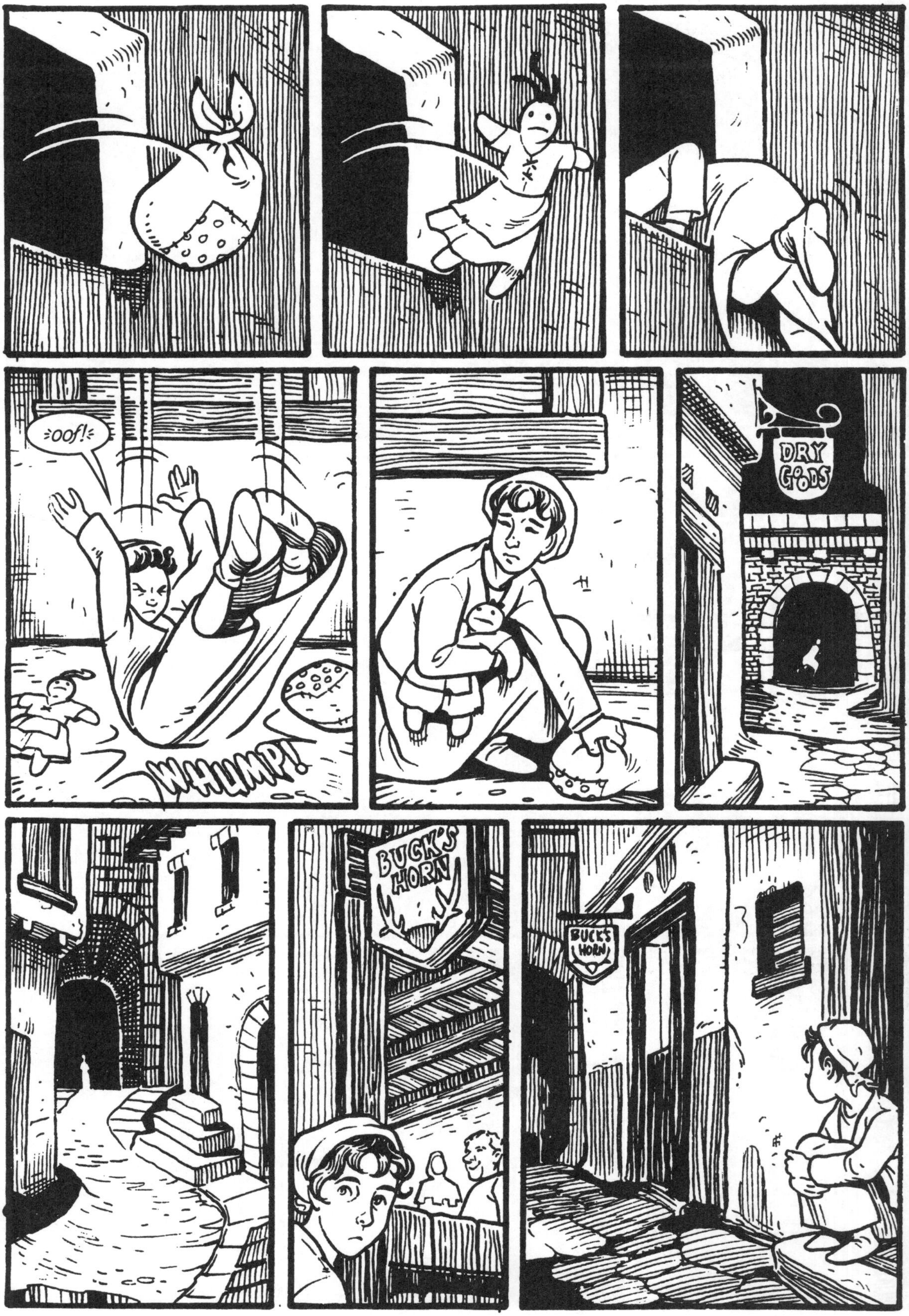

oof!
WHUMP!
DRY GOODS
BUCK'S HORN
BUCK'S HORN

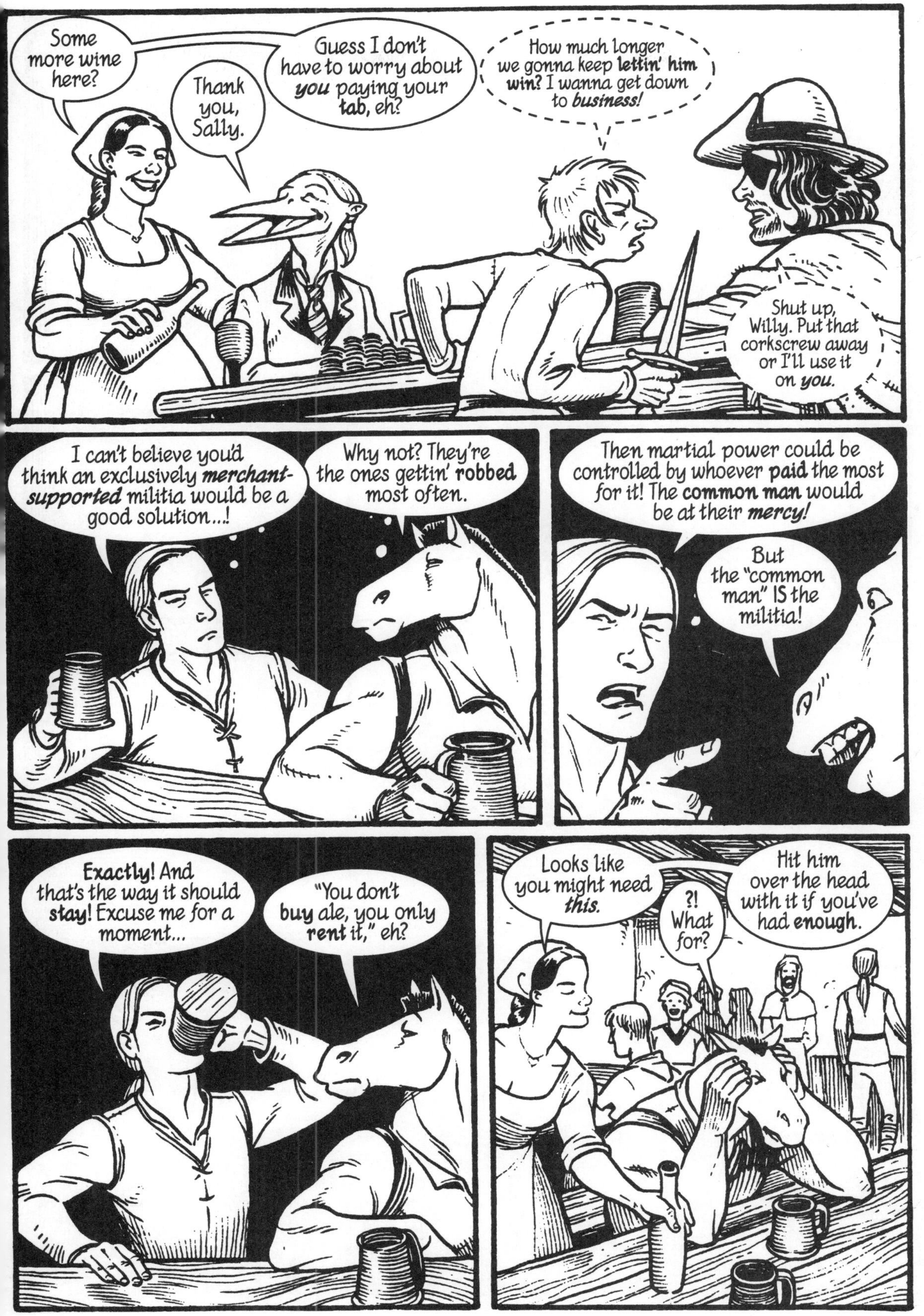

Some more wine here?
Thank you, Sally.
Guess I don't have to worry about *you* paying your **tab**, eh?
How much longer we gonna keep **lettin' him win?** I wanna get down to ***business!***
Shut up, Willy. Put that corkscrew away or I'll use it on ***you***.
I can't believe you'd think an exclusively ***merchant-supported*** militia would be a good solution...!
Why not? They're the ones gettin' **robbed** most often.
Then martial power could be controlled by whoever **paid** the most for it! The **common man** would be at their ***mercy!***
But the "common man" IS the militia!
Exactly! And that's the way it should **stay**! Excuse me for a moment...
"You don't **buy** ale, you only **rent** it," eh?
Looks like you might need ***this.***
?! What for?
Hit him over the head with it if you've had **enough**.

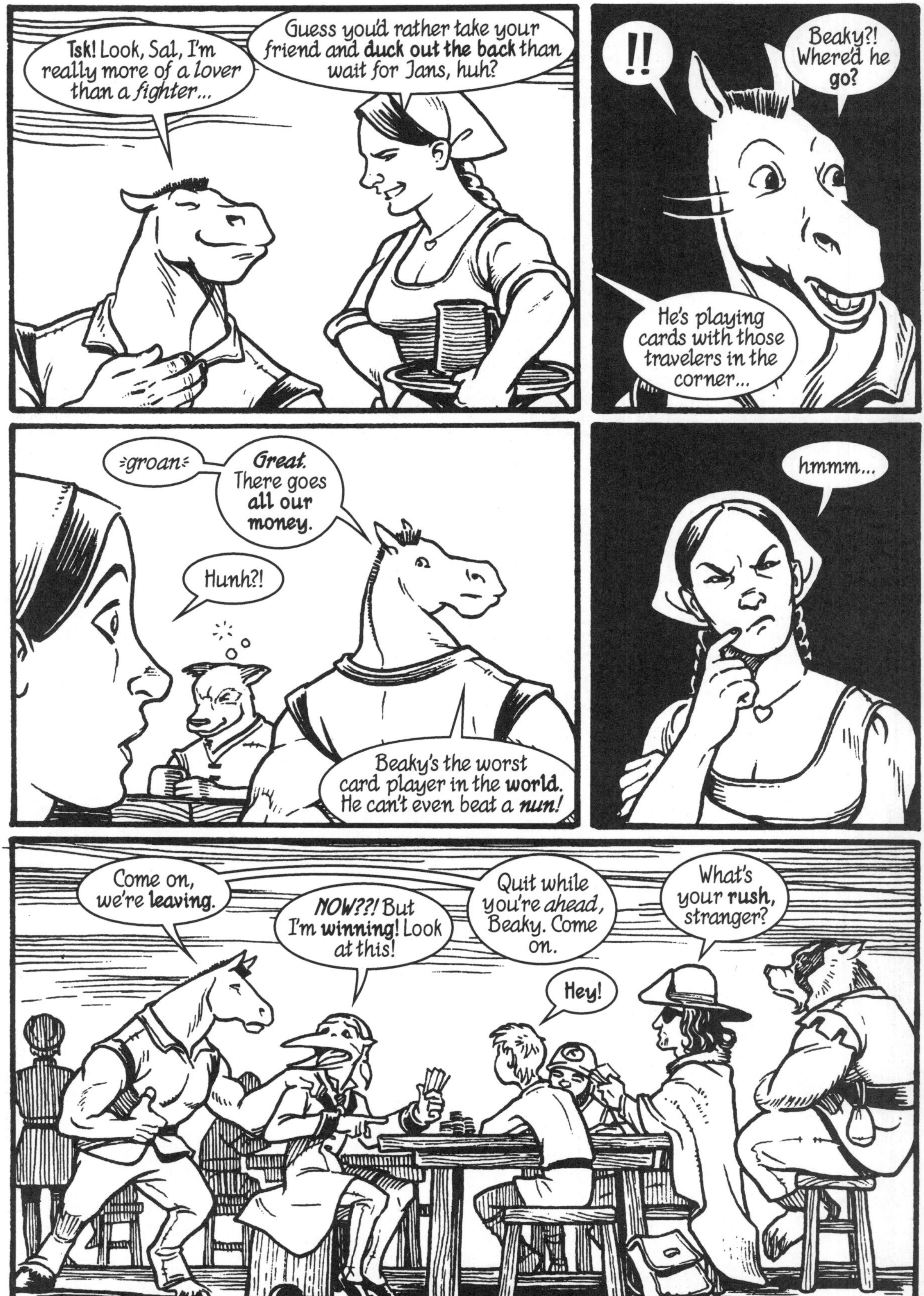
Guess you'd rather take your friend and **duck out the back** than wait for Jans, huh?
Tsk! Look, Sal, I'm really more of a *lover* than a *fighter*...
!!
Beaky?! Where'd he **go?**
He's playing cards with those travelers in the corner...
groan
Great. There goes **all our money.**
Hunh?!
Beaky's the worst card player in the **world**. He can't even beat a ***nun!***
hmmm...
Come on, we're **leaving**.
NOW??! But I'm **winning**! Look at this!
Quit while you're *ahead*, Beaky. Come on.
Hey!
What's your **rush**, stranger?

"It's late."

"Oh, that's right. We want to get an *early start* tomorrow..."

"Pleasure meeting you, gentlemen..."

"Waitaminit..."

"COME ON!"

"How d'we get our money back *now*?!"

"Patience, Willy..."

"We appreciate your hospitality, Sally. This is a *fine* establishment you have here..."

"He's back! Hide me!"

"Oh, suddenly it all becomes *clear*."

"Thank you, gentlemen. Allow me to show you to the back door."

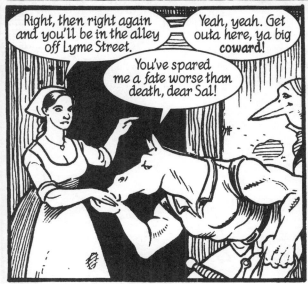

"Right, then right again and you'll be in the alley off Lyme Street."

"Yeah, yeah. Get outa here, ya big **coward**!"

"You've spared me a fate worse than death, dear Sal!"

"And you--watch your *back*, and keep your hands on your **purse-strings**!"

165

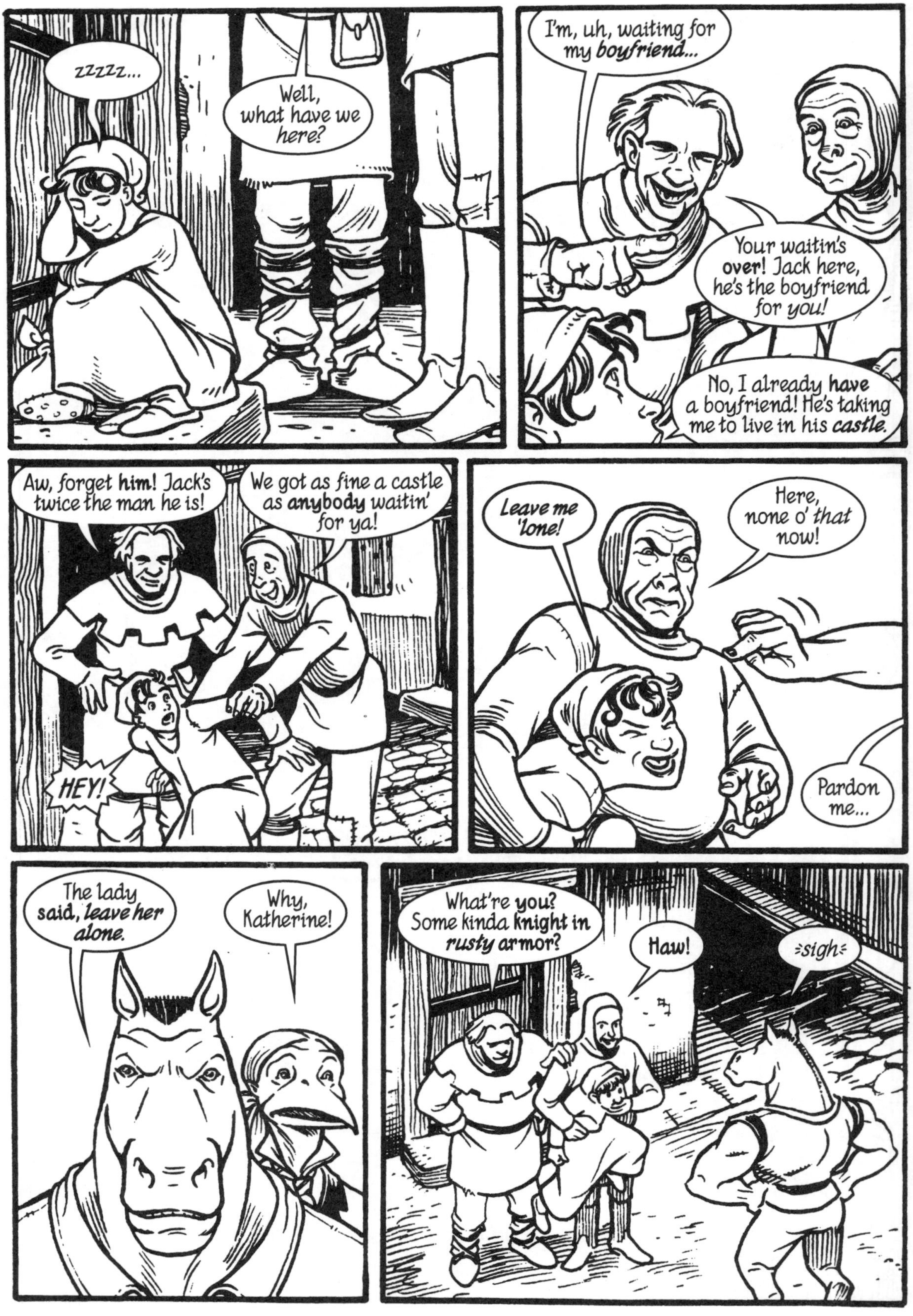

zzzzz...
Well, what have we here?
I'm, uh, waiting for my boyfriend...
Your waitin's over! Jack here, he's the boyfriend for you!
No, I already have a boyfriend! He's taking me to live in his castle.
Aw, forget him! Jack's twice the man he is!
We got as fine a castle as anybody waitin' for ya!
HEY!
Leave me 'lone!
Here, none o' that now!
Pardon me...
The lady said, leave her alone.
Why, Katherine!
What're you? Some kinda knight in rusty armor?
Haw!
sigh

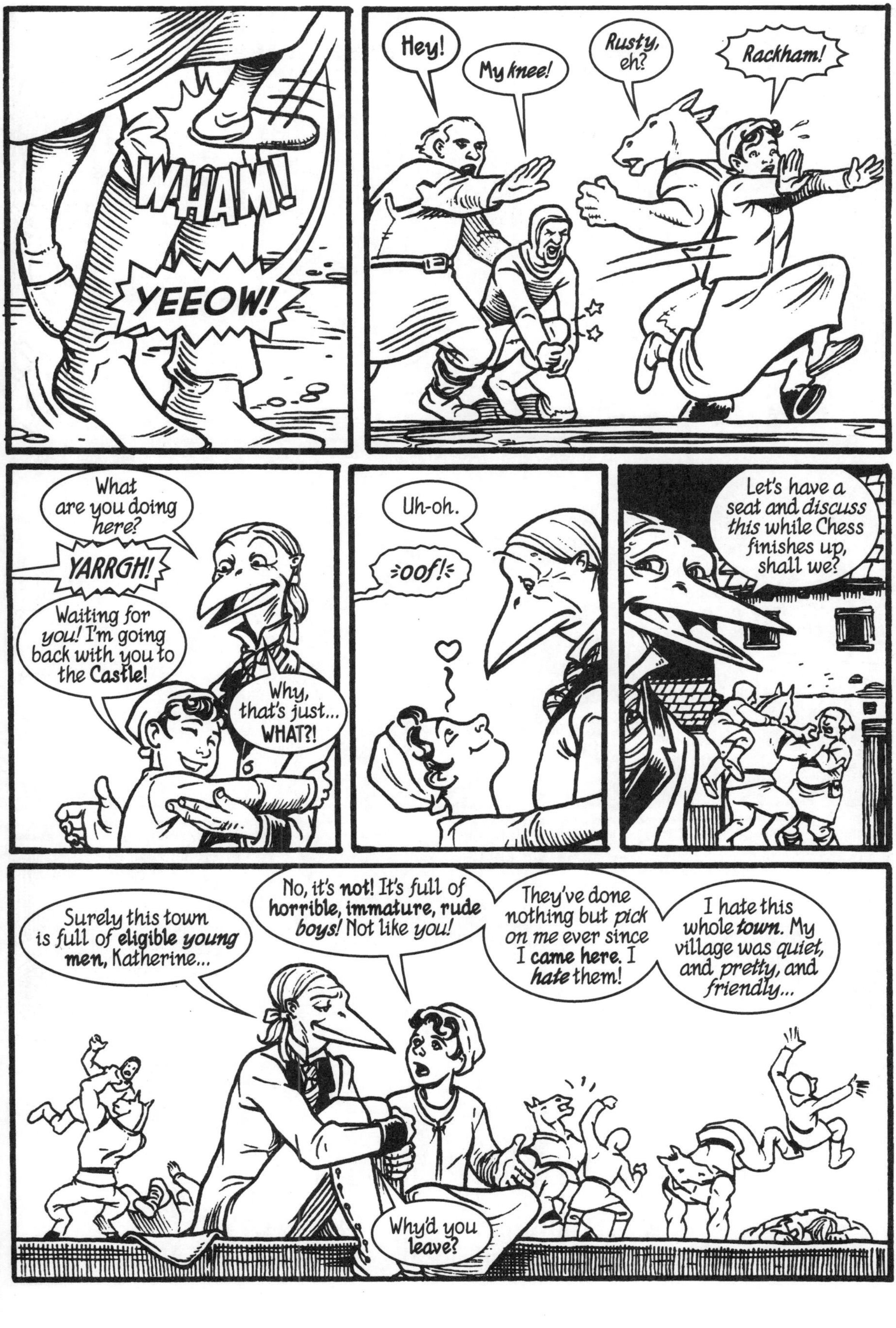
WHAM!
YEEOW!
Hey!
My knee!
Rusty, eh?
Rackham!
What are you doing here?
YARRGH!
Waiting for you! I'm going back with you to the Castle!
Why, that's just... WHAT?!
Uh-oh.
oof!
Let's have a seat and discuss this while Chess finishes up, shall we?
Surely this town is full of eligible young men, Katherine...
No, it's not! It's full of horrible, immature, rude boys! Not like you!
They've done nothing but pick on me ever since I came here. I hate them!
I hate this whole town. My village was quiet, and pretty, and friendly...
Why'd you leave?

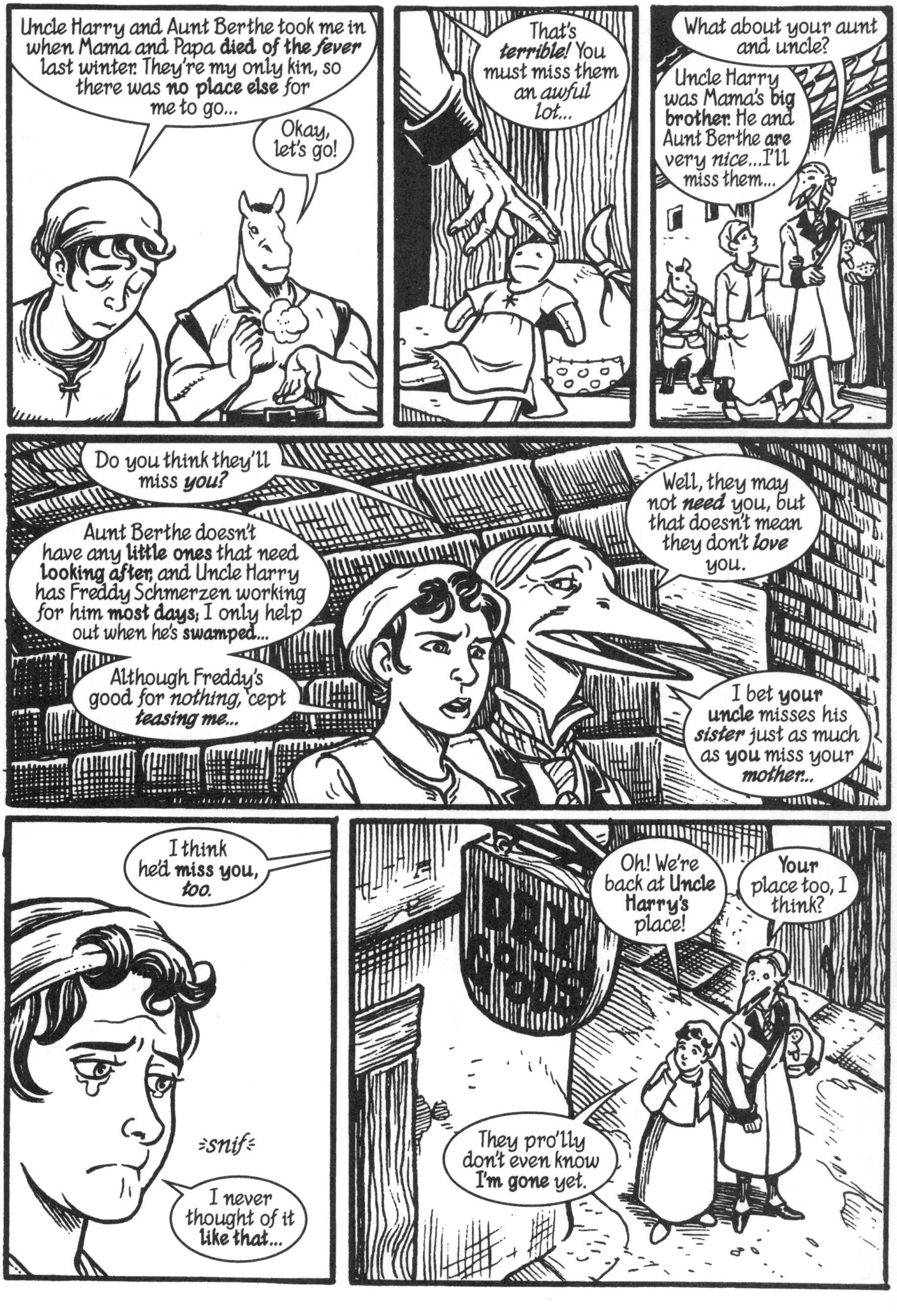

Uncle Harry and Aunt Berthe took me in when Mama and Papa died of the fever last winter. They're my only kin, so there was no place else for me to go...
Okay, let's go!
That's terrible! You must miss them an awful lot...
What about your aunt and uncle?
Uncle Harry was Mama's big brother. He and Aunt Berthe are very nice...I'll miss them...
Do you think they'll miss you?
Aunt Berthe doesn't have any little ones that need looking after, and Uncle Harry has Freddy Schmerzen working for him most days; I only help out when he's swamped...
Although Freddy's good for nothing, 'cept teasing me...
Well, they may not need you, but that doesn't mean they don't love you.
I bet your uncle misses his sister just as much as you miss your mother...
I think he'd miss you, too.
snif
I never thought of it like that...
Oh! We're back at Uncle Harry's place!
Your place too, I think?
They pro'lly don't even know I'm gone yet.

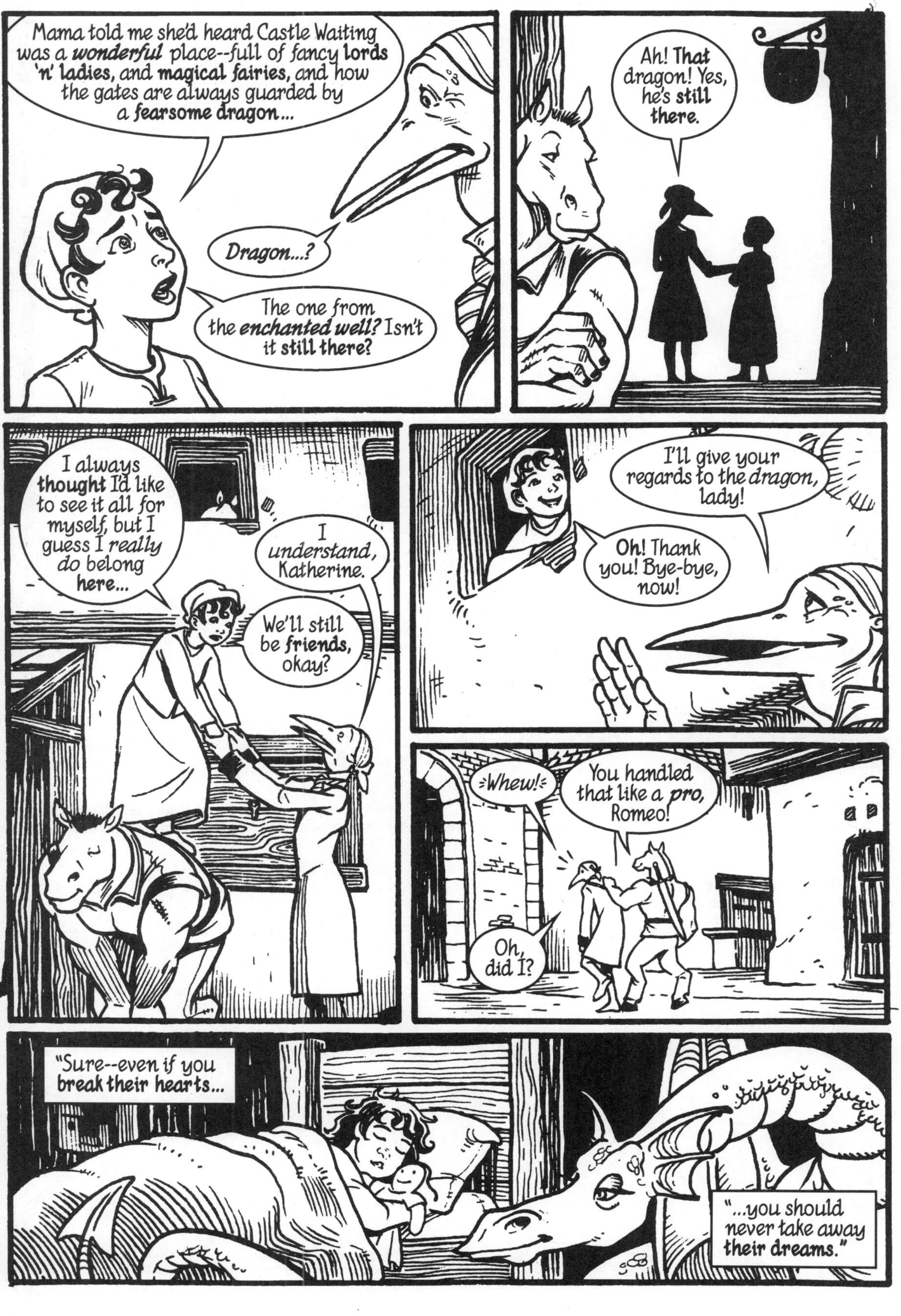

Mama told me she'd heard Castle Waiting was a **wonderful** place--full of fancy **lords 'n' ladies**, and **magical fairies**, and how the gates are always guarded by a **fearsome dragon**...
Dragon...?
The one from the **enchanted well?** Isn't it **still there?**
Ah! **That** dragon! Yes, he's **still there**.
I always **thought** I'd like to see it all for myself, but I guess I *really* do belong **here**...
I *understand*, Katherine.
We'll still be **friends**, okay?
I'll give your regards to the *dragon*, lady!
Oh! Thank you! Bye-bye, now!
Whew!
You handled that like a *pro*, Romeo!
Oh, did I?
"Sure--even if you **break their hearts**...
"...you should never take away **their dreams**."

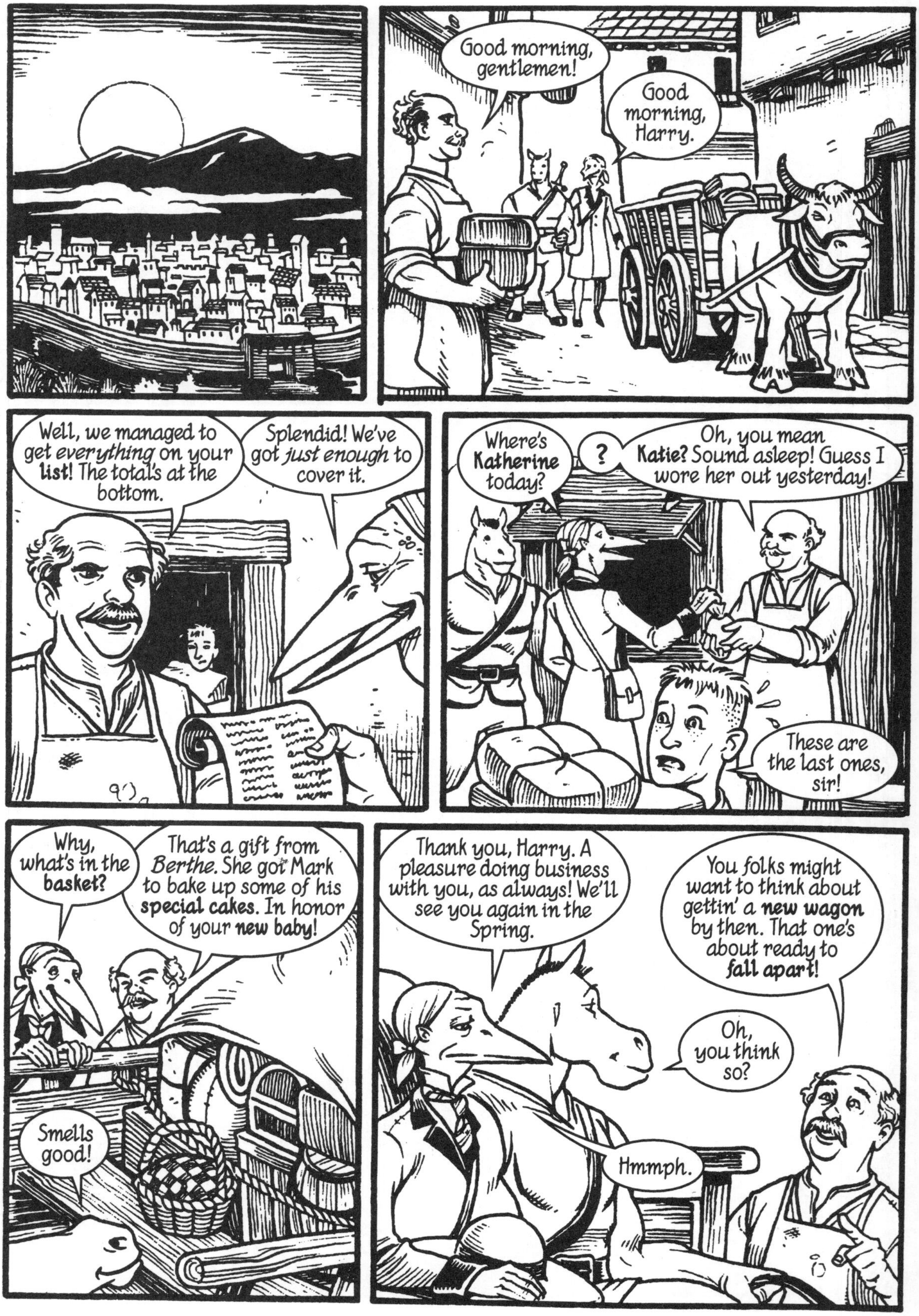
Good morning, gentlemen!
Good morning, Harry.
Well, we managed to get *everything* on your **list**! The total's at the bottom.
Splendid! We've got *just enough* to cover it.
Where's **Katherine** today?
?
Oh, you mean **Katie?** Sound asleep! Guess I wore her out yesterday!
These are the last ones, sir!
Why, what's in the **basket?**
That's a gift from *Berthe*. She got Mark to bake up some of his **special cakes**. In honor of your **new baby**!
Smells good!
Thank you, Harry. A pleasure doing business with you, as always! We'll see you again in the Spring.
You folks might want to think about gettin' a **new wagon** by then. That one's about ready to **fall apart**!
Oh, you think so?
Hmmph.

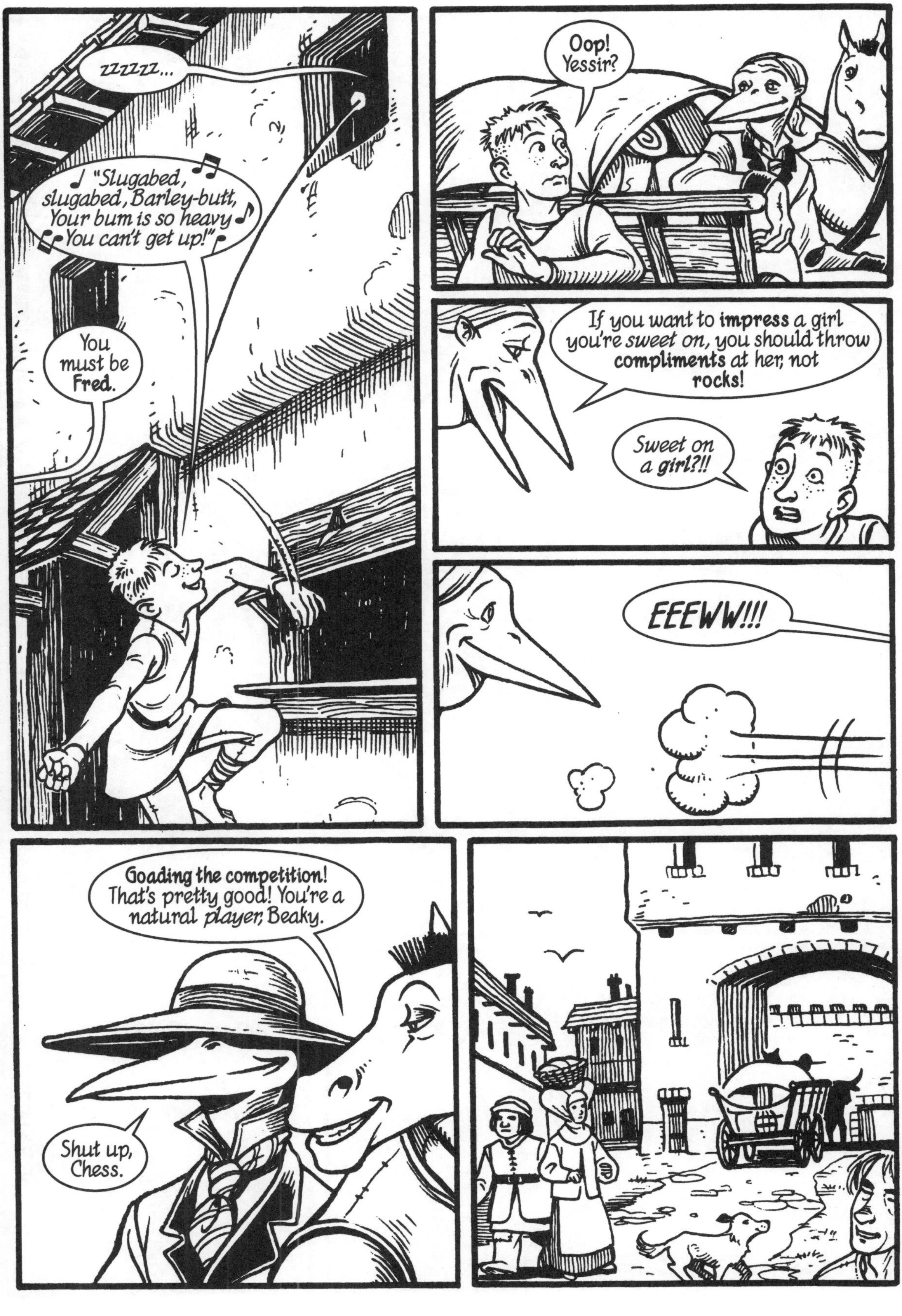

zzzzzz...
"Slugabed, slugabed, Barley-butt, Your bum is so heavy You can't get up!"
You must be **Fred**.
Oop! Yessir?
If you want to **impress** a girl you're *sweet on*, you should throw **compliments** at her, not **rocks**!
Sweet on a *girl*?!!
EEEWW!!!
Goading the competition! That's pretty good! You're a natural *player*, Beaky.
Shut up, Chess.

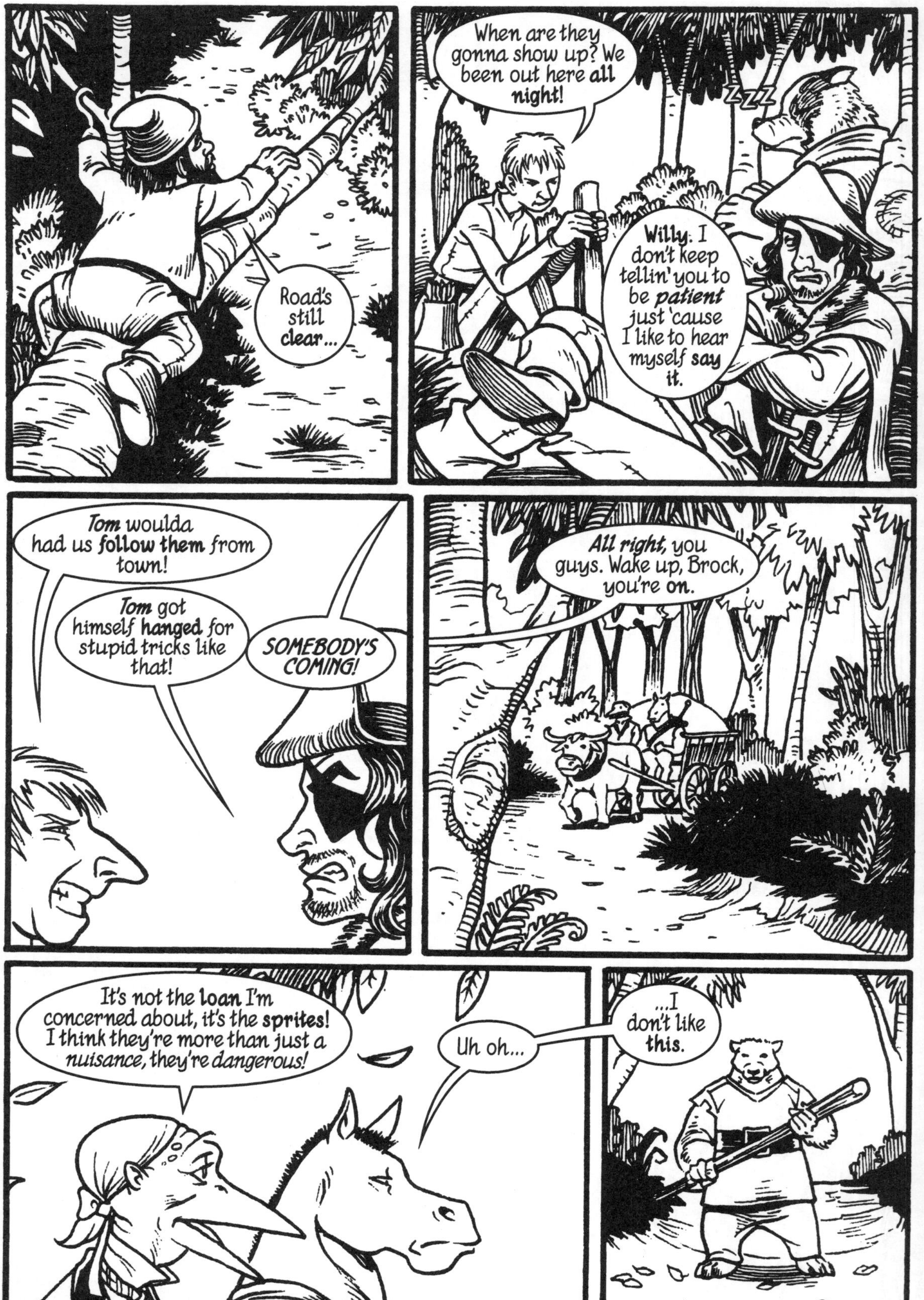
Road's still **clear**...
When are they gonna show up? We been out here **all night**!
ZZZ
Willy. I don't keep tellin' you to be ***patient*** just 'cause I like to hear myself **say it**.
Tom woulda had us **follow them** from town!
Tom got himself **hanged** for stupid tricks like that!
SOMEBODY'S COMING!
All right, you guys. Wake up, Brock, you're **on**.
It's not the **loan** I'm concerned about, it's the **sprites**! I think they're more than just a *nuisance*, they're *dangerous*!
Uh oh...
...I don't like **this**.

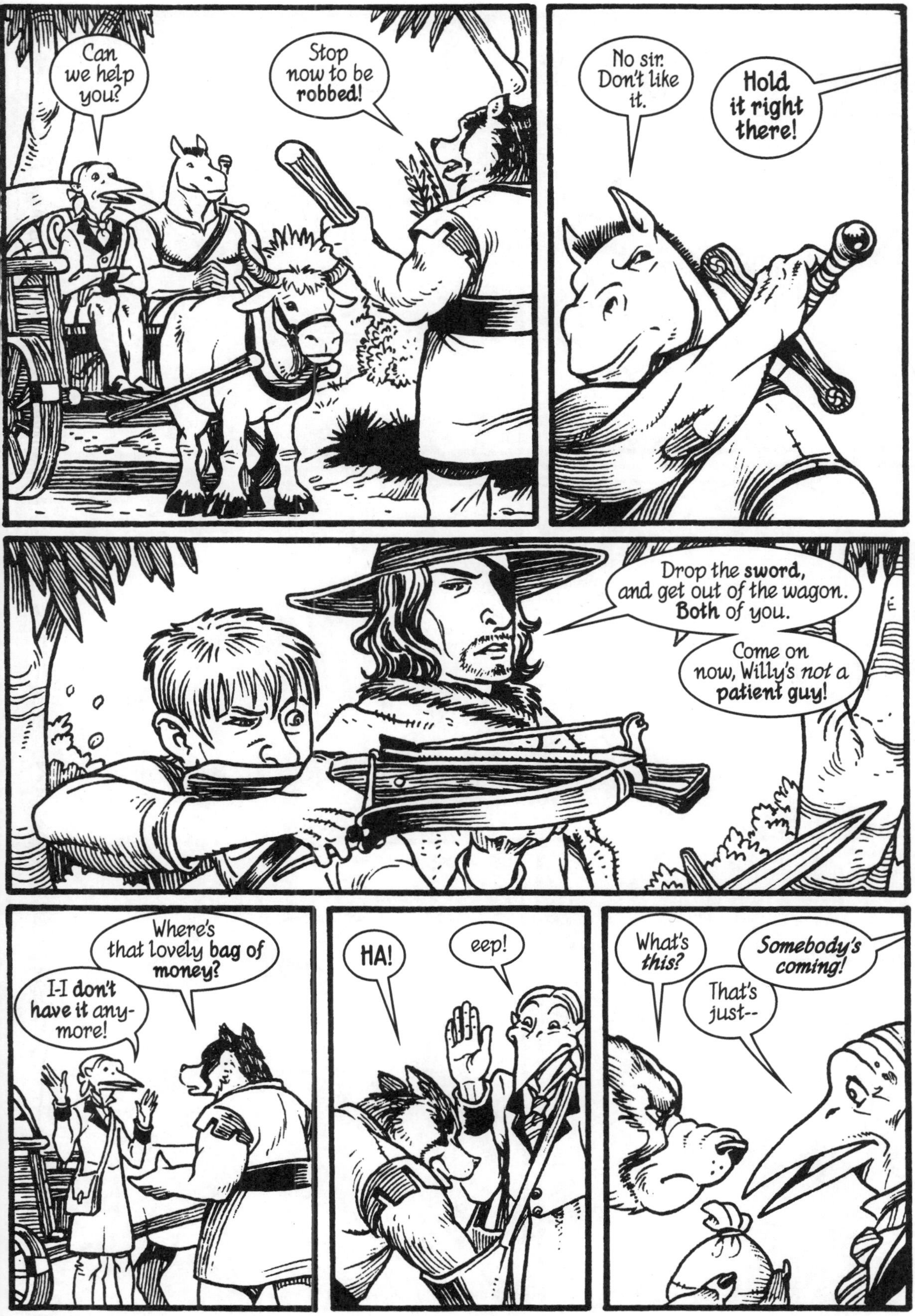

Can we help you?
Stop now to be **robbed!**
No sir. Don't like it.
Hold it right there!
Drop the **sword,** and get out of the wagon. **Both** of you.
Come on now, Willy's *not* a **patient guy!**
Where's that lovely **bag of money?**
I-I **don't have it** any-more!
HA!
eep!
What's *this?*
That's just--
Somebody's coming!

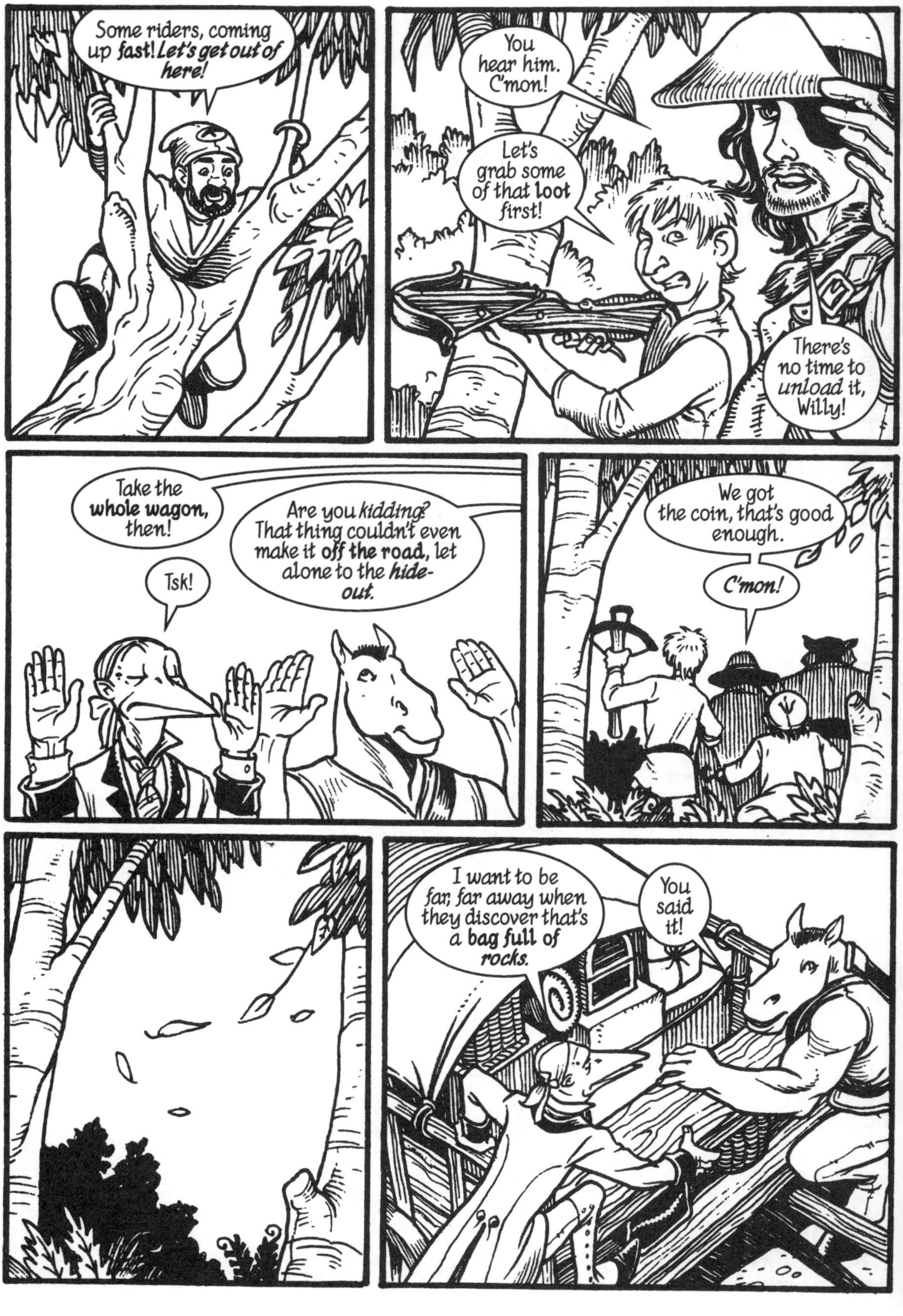

Some riders, coming up fast! Let's get out of here!
You hear him. C'mon!
Let's grab some of that loot first!
There's no time to unload it, Willy!
Take the whole wagon, then!
Tsk!
Are you kidding? That thing couldn't even make it off the road, let alone to the hide-out.
We got the coin, that's good enough.
C'mon!
I want to be far, far away when they discover that's a bag full of rocks.
You said it!

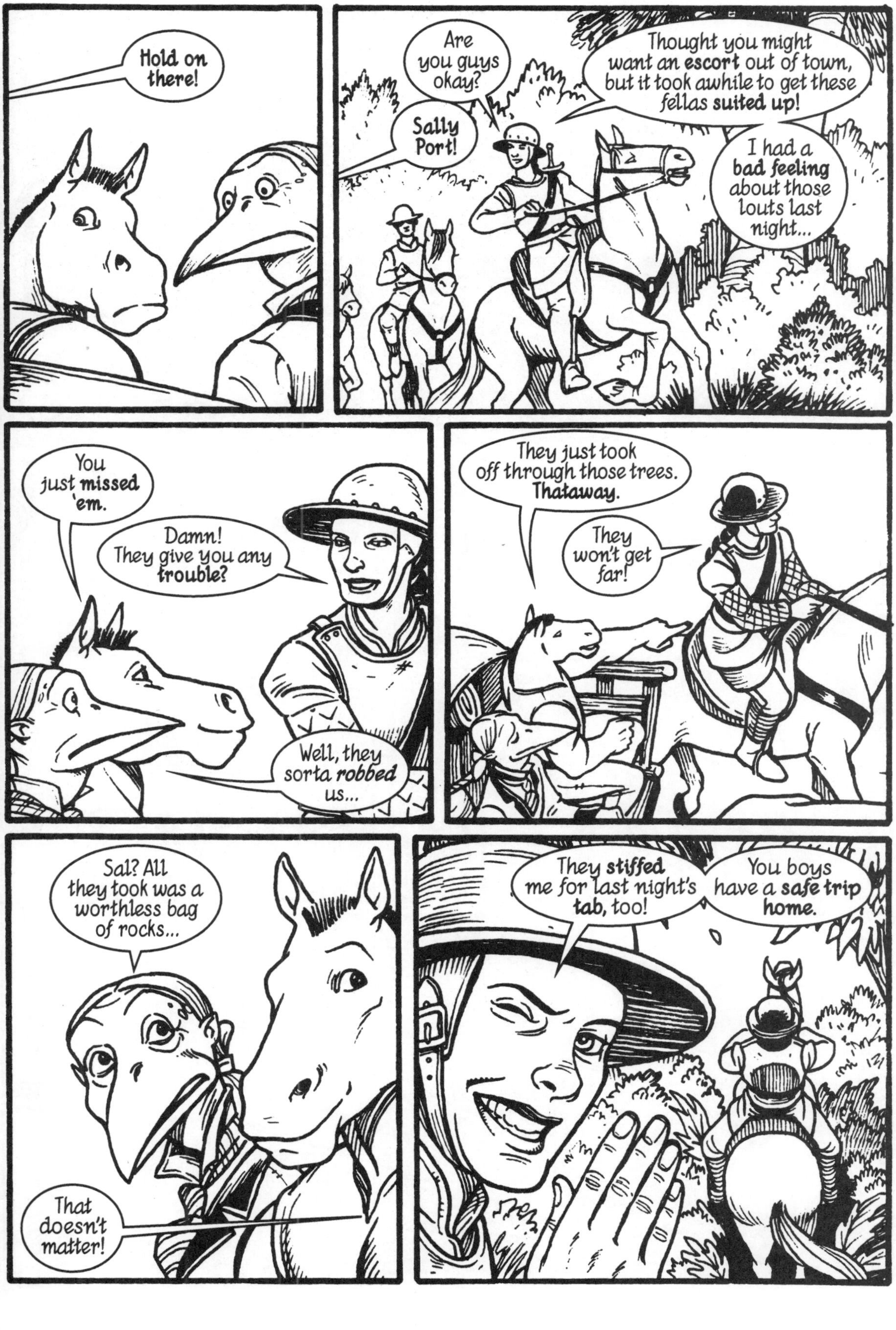
Hold on there!
Are you guys okay?
Sally Port!
Thought you might want an escort out of town, but it took awhile to get these fellas suited up!
I had a bad feeling about those louts last night...
You just missed 'em.
Damn! They give you any trouble?
Well, they sorta robbed us...
They just took off through those trees. Thataway.
They won't get far!
Sal? All they took was a worthless bag of rocks...
That doesn't matter!
They stiffed me for last night's tab, too!
You boys have a safe trip home.

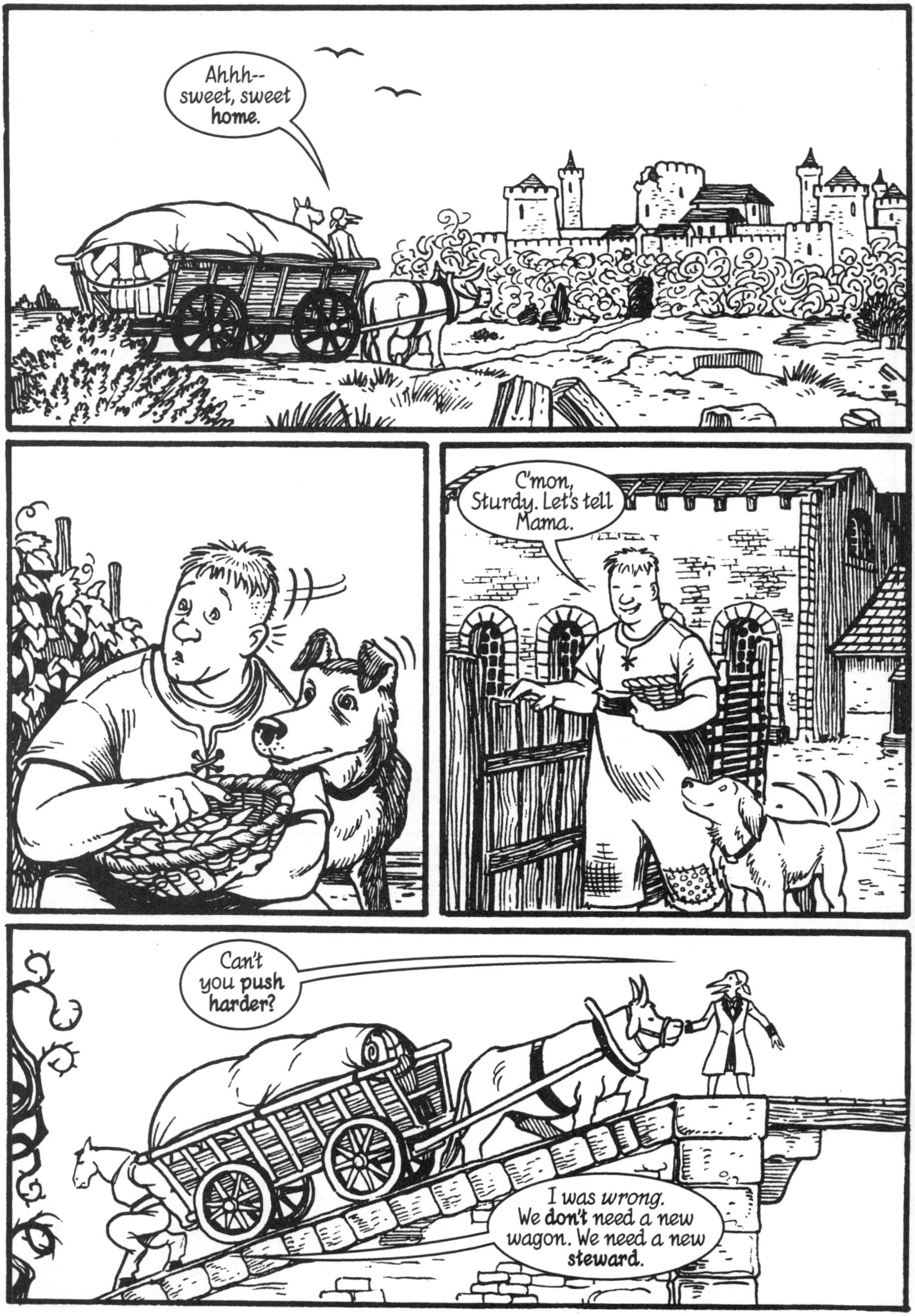
Ahhh--
sweet, sweet
home.
C'mon, Sturdy. Let's tell Mama.
Can't you **push harder?**
I was *wrong.* We **don't** need a new wagon. We need a new **steward.**

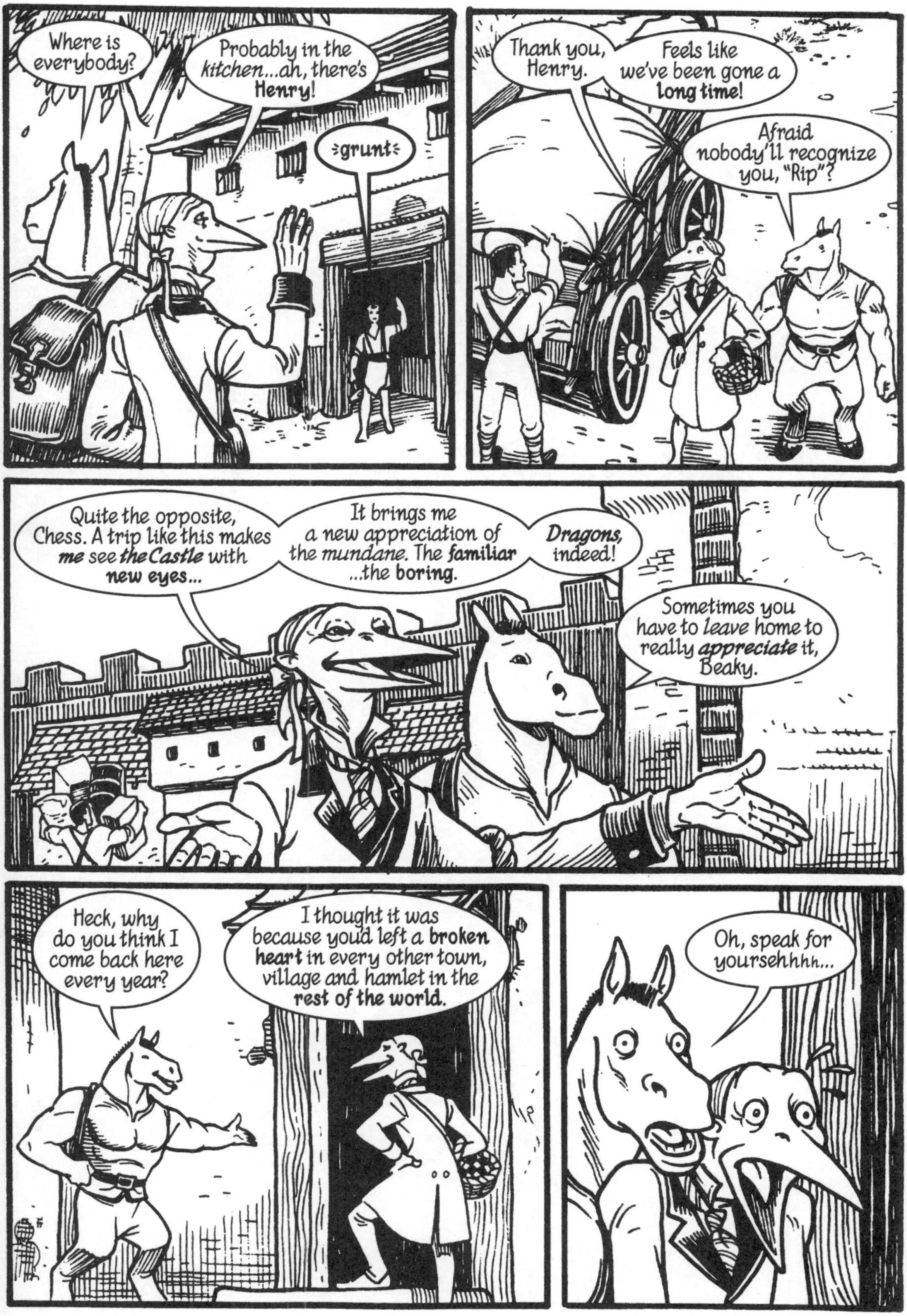

Where is everybody?
Probably in the kitchen...ah, there's Henry!
grunt
Thank you, Henry.
Feels like we've been gone a long time!
Afraid nobody'll recognize you, "Rip"?
Quite the opposite, Chess. A trip like this makes me see the Castle with new eyes...
It brings me a new appreciation of the mundane. The familiar ...the boring.
Dragons, indeed!
Sometimes you have to leave home to really appreciate it, Beaky.
Heck, why do you think I come back here every year?
I thought it was because you'd left a broken heart in every other town, village and hamlet in the rest of the world.
Oh, speak for yoursehhhh...

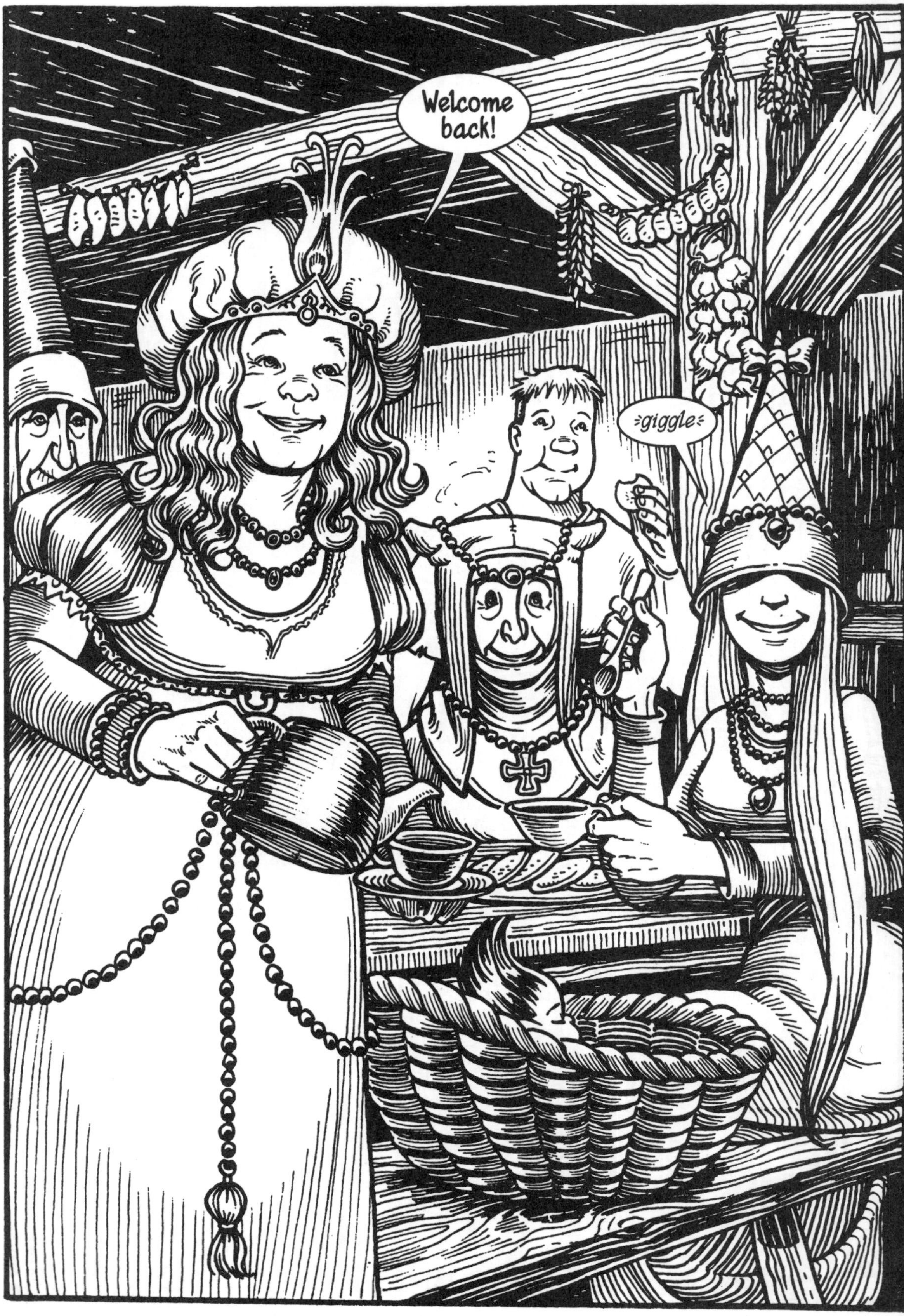
Welcome back!
giggle

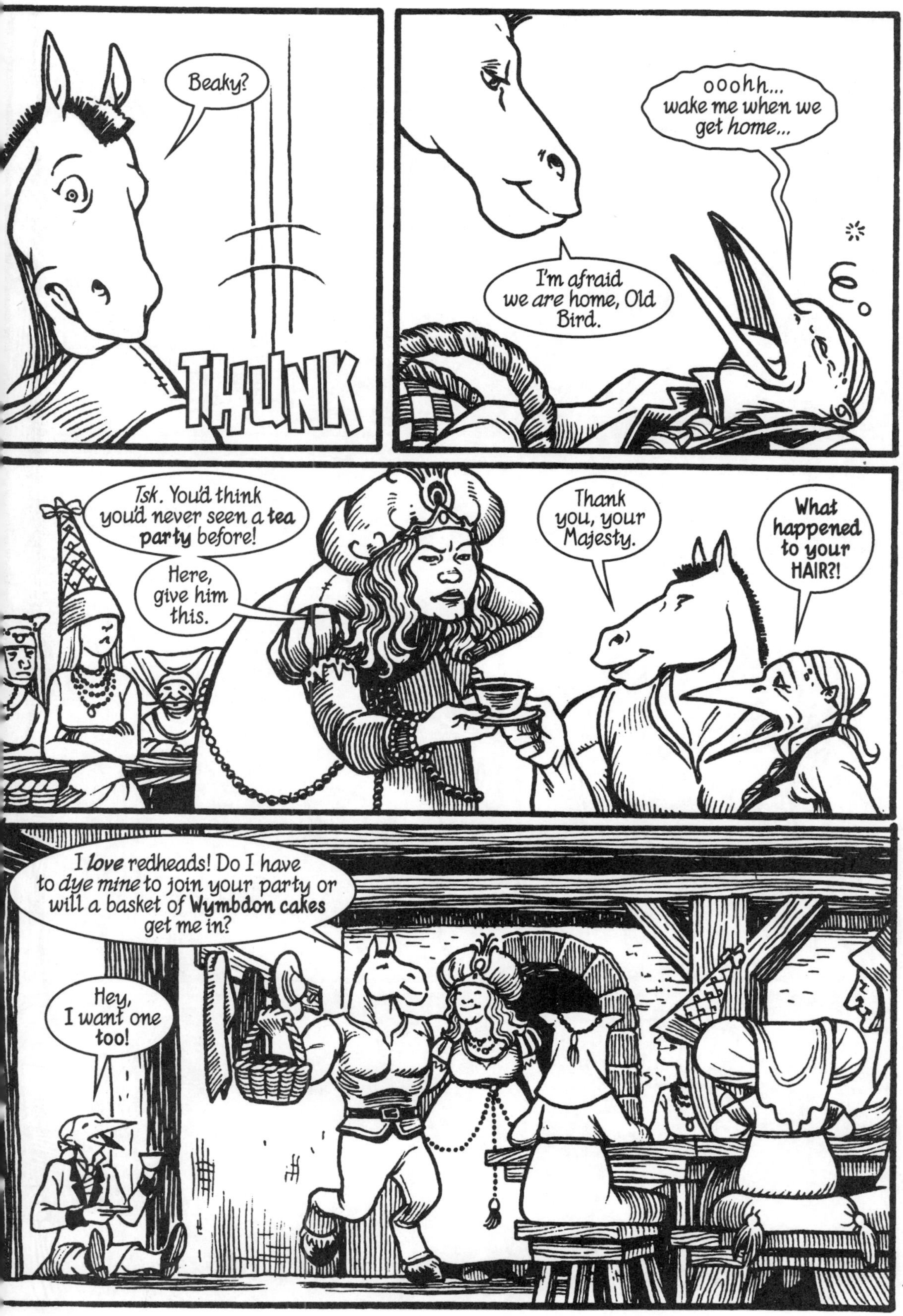
Beaky?
THUNK
oooh...
wake me when we get home...
I'm afraid we are home, Old Bird.
Tsk. You'd think you'd never seen a tea party before!
Here, give him this.
Thank you, your Majesty.
What happened to your HAIR?!
I love redheads! Do I have to dye mine to join your party or will a basket of Wymbdon cakes get me in?
Hey, I want one too!

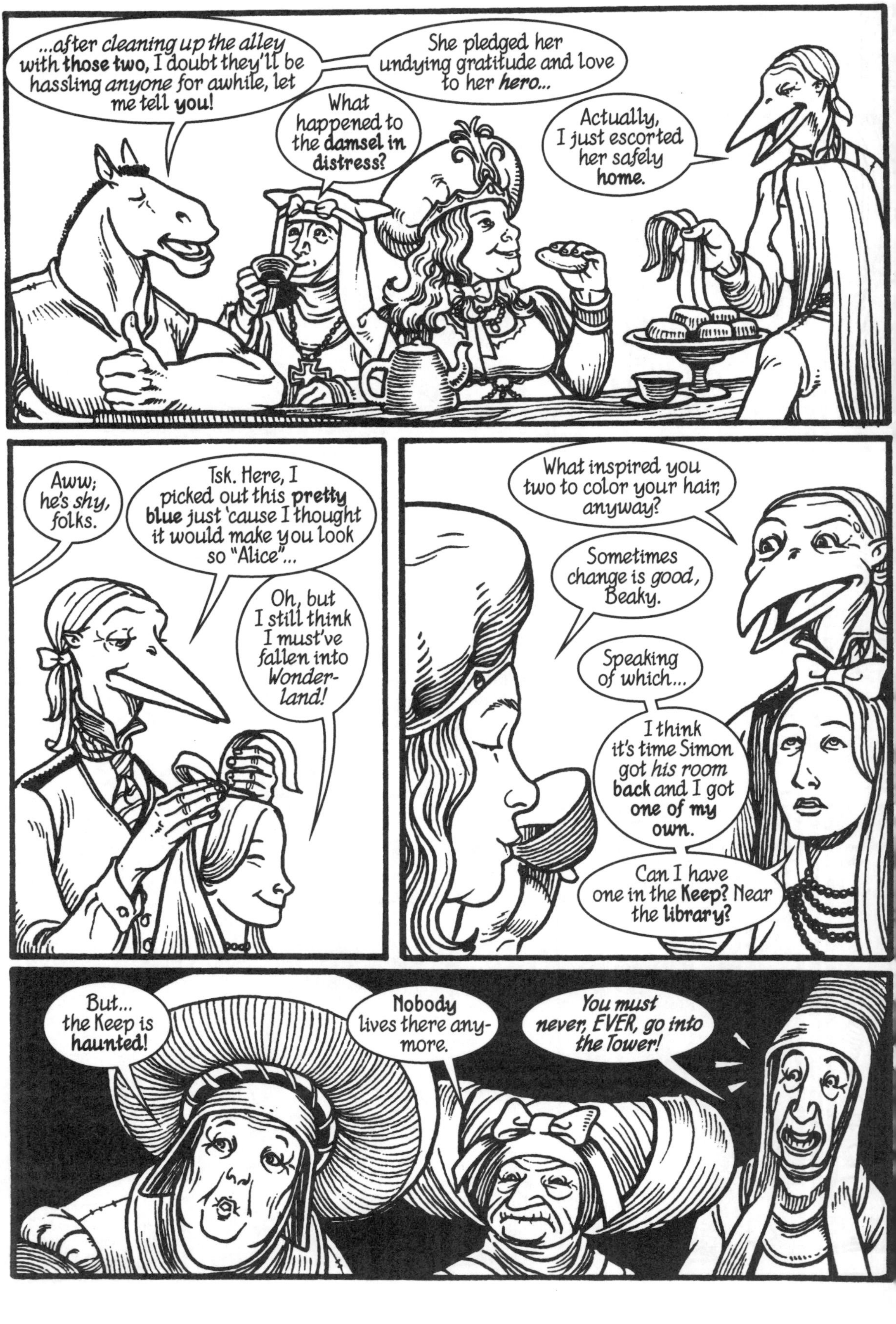
...after cleaning up the alley with those two, I doubt they'll be hassling anyone for awhile, let me tell you!
She pledged her undying gratitude and love to her hero...
What happened to the damsel in distress?
Actually, I just escorted her safely home.
Aww; he's shy, folks.
Tsk. Here, I picked out this pretty blue just 'cause I thought it would make you look so "Alice"...
Oh, but I still think I must've fallen into Wonderland!
What inspired you two to color your hair, anyway?
Sometimes change is good, Beaky.
Speaking of which...
I think it's time Simon got his room back and I got one of my own.
Can I have one in the Keep? Near the library?
But... the Keep is haunted!
Nobody lives there anymore.
You must never, EVER, go into the Tower!

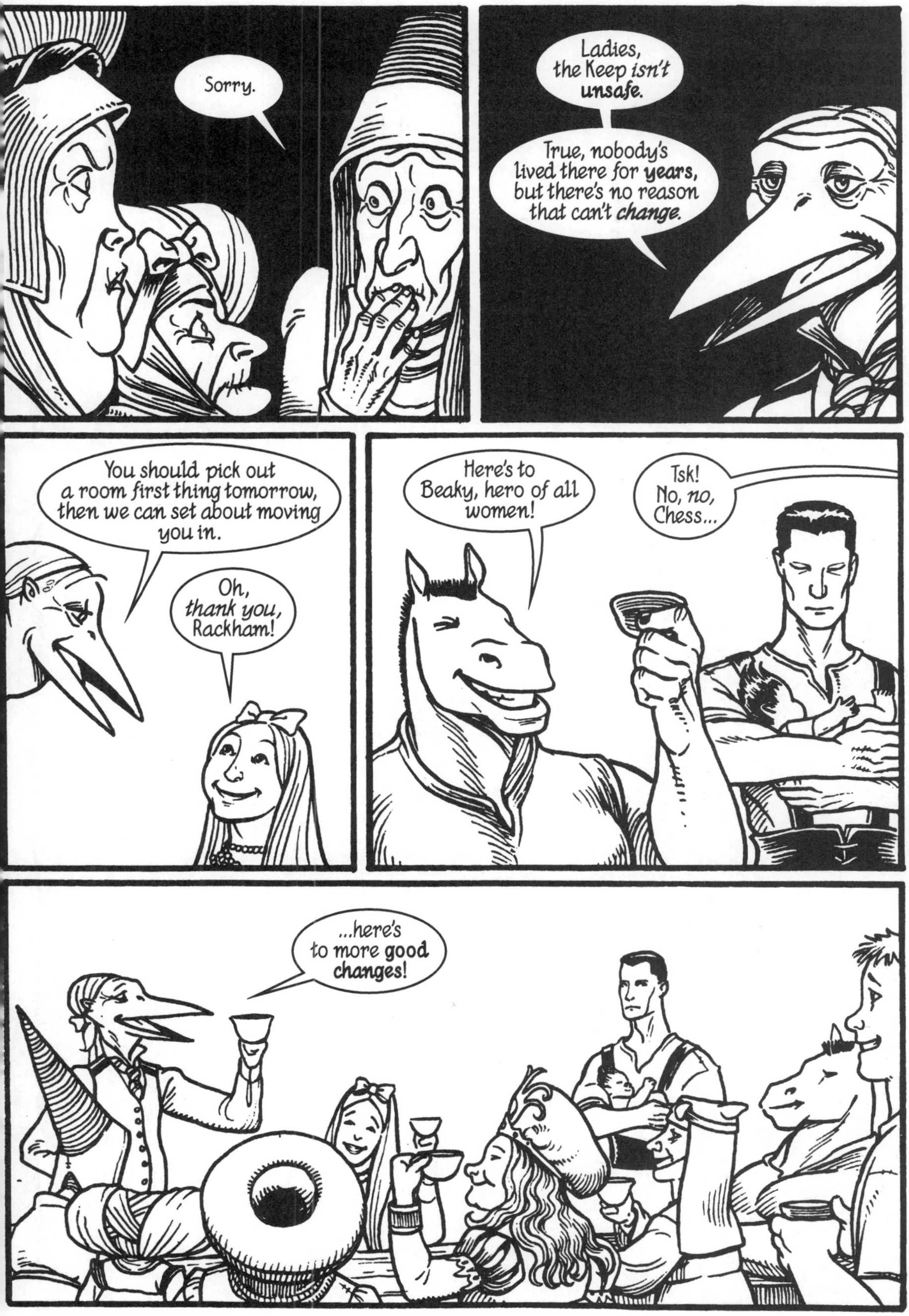
Sorry.
Ladies, the Keep isn't unsafe.
True, nobody's lived there for years, but there's no reason that can't change.
You should pick out a room first thing tomorrow, then we can set about moving you in.
Oh, thank you, Rackham!
Here's to Beaky, hero of all women!
Tsk! No, no, Chess...
...here's to more good changes!

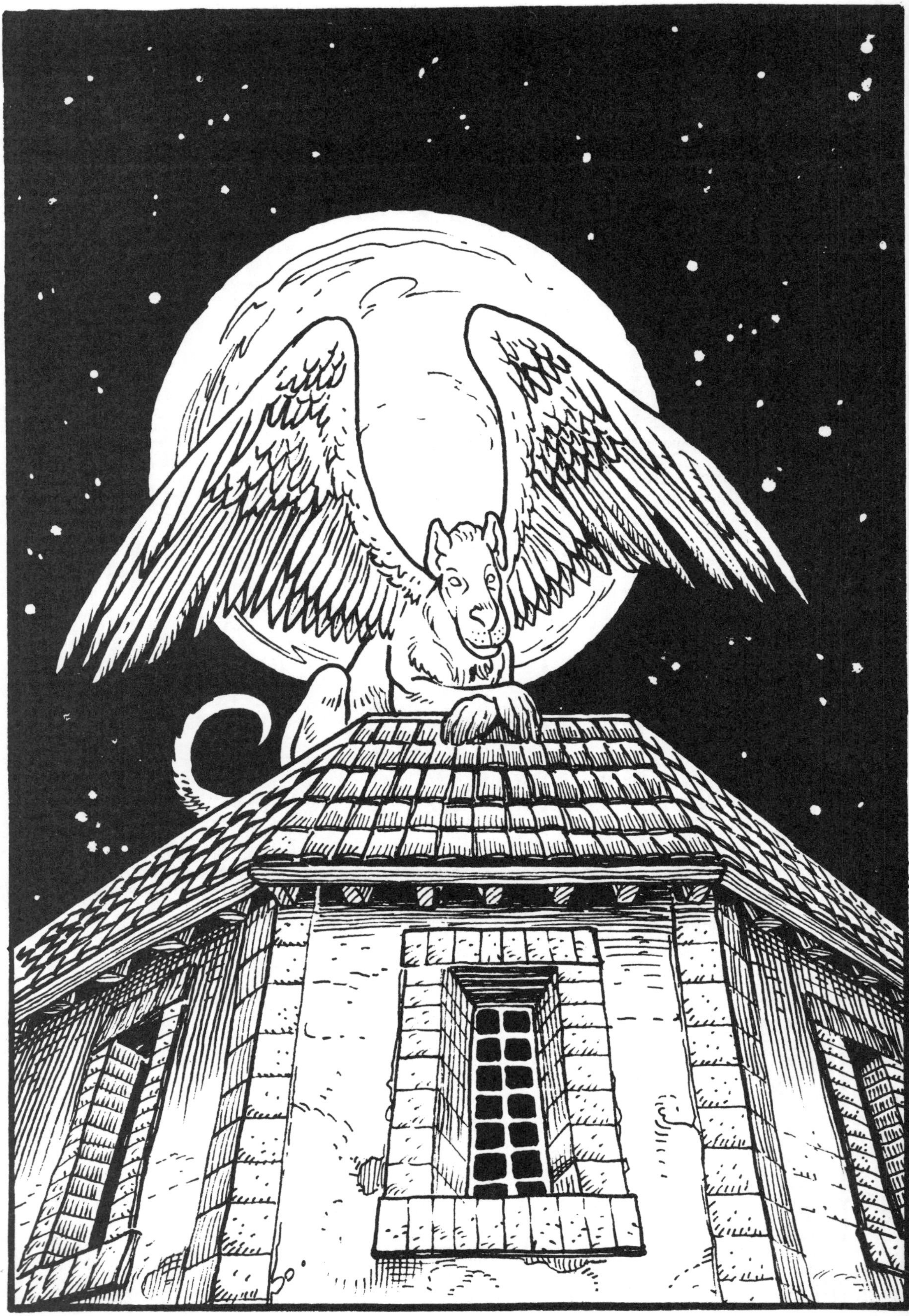

Bahtalo Drom!

You **just**
finished the
first
adventure in
the **award winning**
Castle Waiting
story!

The adventure continues in *Castle Waiting Volume Two*

Coming Summer 2001

A storyteller with over ten years experience in comics and Children's books, creator Linda Medley illustrates *CASTLE WAITING* in a classic style reminiscent of Arthur Rackham and William Heath Robinson. If you enjoy the humorous fantasy of *Time Bandits* or *The Princess Bride*, you will love *CASTLE WAITING*.